FRUIT AND VEGETABLE JUICE PROCESSING

FRUIT AND VEGETABLE JUICE PROCESSING

J.K. Paul

NOYES DATA CORPORATION

Park Ridge, New Jersey   London, England

1975

Published in the United States of America by
Noyes Data Corporation
Noyes Building, Park Ridge, New Jersey 07656

FOREWORD

The detailed, descriptive information in this book is based on U.S. patents issued mostly since 1964 and relating to fruit and vegetable juice processing.

This book serves a double purpose in that it supplies detailed technical information and can be used as a guide to the U.S. patent literature in this field. By indicating all the information that is significant, and eliminating legal jargon and juristic phraseology, this book presents an advanced, technically oriented review of the processing of fruit and vegetable juices.

The U.S. patent literature is the largest and most comprehensive collection of technical information in the world. There is more practical, commercial, timely process information assembled here than is available from any other source. The technical information obtained from a patent is extremely reliable and comprehensive; sufficient information must be included to avoid rejection for "insufficient disclosure." These patents include practically all of those issued on the subject in the United States during the period under review; there has been no bias in the selection of patents for inclusion.

The patent literature covers a substantial amount of information not available in the journal literature. The patent literature is a prime source of basic commercially useful information. This information is overlooked by those who rely primarily on the periodical journal literature. It is realized that there is a lag between a patent application on a new process development and the granting of a patent, but it is felt that this may roughly parallel or even anticipate the lag in putting that development into commercial practice.

Many of these patents are being utilized commercially. Whether used or not, they offer opportunities for technological transfer. Also, a major purpose of this book is to describe the number of technical possibilities available, which may open up profitable areas to research and development. The information contained in this book will allow you to establish a sound background before launching into research in this field.

Advanced composition and production methods developed by Noyes Data are employed to bring our new durably bound books to you in a minimum of time. Special techniques are used to close the gap between "manuscript" and "completed book." Industrial technology is progressing so rapidly that time-honored, conventional typesetting, binding and shipping methods are no longer suitable. We have bypassed the delays in the conventional book publishing cycle and provide the user with an effective and convenient means of reviewing up-to-date information in depth.

The Table of Contents is organized in such a way as to serve as a subject index. Other indexes by company, inventor and patent number help in providing easy access to the information contained in this book.

15 Reasons Why the U.S. Patent Office Literature Is Important to You —

1. The U.S. patent literature is the largest and most comprehensive collection of technical information in the world. There is more practical commercial process information assembled here than is available from any other source.

2. The technical information obtained from the patent literature is extremely comprehensive; sufficient information must be included to avoid rejection for "insufficient disclosure."

3. The patent literature is a prime source of basic commercially utilizable information. This information is overlooked by those who rely primarily on the periodical journal literature.

4. An important feature of the patent literature is that it can serve to avoid duplication of research and development.

5. Patents, unlike periodical literature, are bound by definition to contain new information, data and ideas.

6. It can serve as a source of new ideas in a different but related field, and may be outside the patent protection offered the original invention.

7. Since claims are narrowly defined, much valuable information is included that may be outside the legal protection afforded by the claims.

8. Patents discuss the difficulties associated with previous research, development or production techniques, and offer a specific method of overcoming problems. This gives clues to current process information that has not been published in periodicals or books.

9. Can aid in process design by providing a selection of alternate techniques. A powerful research and engineering tool.

10. Obtain licenses — many U.S. chemical patents have not been developed commercially.

11. Patents provide an excellent starting point for the next investigator.

12. Frequently, innovations derived from research are first disclosed in the patent literature, prior to coverage in the periodical literature.

13. Patents offer a most valuable method of keeping abreast of latest technologies, serving an individual's own "current awareness" program.

14. Copies of U.S. patents are easily obtained from the U.S. Patent Office at 50¢ a copy.

15. It is a creative source of ideas for those with imagination.

CONTENTS AND SUBJECT INDEX

INTRODUCTION

The large market for fruit and vegetable juices, because of their relatively low cost and high nutritional value coupled with modern diet appeal, accounts for the sustained interest in these products and the continued development of improved methods of technology.

It is a primary object of this technology to prepare fruit and vegetable juices in such a way that they are able to maintain their natural flavor and aroma characteristics under ordinary storage conditions over prolonged periods of time.

Considerable progress has been made in this direction. Practically every process in this book is oriented toward the ultimate goal of every juice manufacturer—the retention of natural flavors and aromas and the retardation of unnatural flavors, aromas, or colors.

Various preservatives of the past which, while stabilizing a beverage, also introduced undesirable off-flavors have been replaced by approved modern additives which not only maximize stability, but also enhance natural flavors. The use of these additives in connection with advanced extraction and concentration techniques, which were especially designed for juice manufacture, constitutes the technology of this book.

MANUFACTURING TECHNIQUES

APPLE JUICE

Two Stage Process

The commercial production of apple juice conventionally involves the following procedure. Fresh apples are washed and ground in a hammer mill to produce a pulp. This pulp is then pressed in a rack and cloth press to separate the juice from the residual solid material, termed pomace. In operating the press, a series of cloths are each loaded with a quantity of pulp and the corners of the cloths folded over to form a package called a cheese. These cheeses, each separated by a wooden rack, are placed in a hydraulic press and subjected to high pressure to express the juice through the cloths into a reservoir. The resulting juice is then pumped through a conventional device such as a filter press to remove suspended solid material. Usually, the juice, prior to filtration, is treated with pectic enzymes whereby pectin in the juice is hydrolyzed.

In this way the suspending power of the pectin is vitiated and the finely divided, insoluble particles (cloud) settle out, leaving a clear juice. After the juice has been clarified by such techniques, it is pasteurized and bottled or canned. As in any other process, the yield of juice is important and it is an obvious goal to get as much juice as possible from each pound of apples. Also critical in commercial operations is the amount of suspended material in the juice. The trade demands a clear juice and to get such it is essential that the juice extracted from ground apples contain a minimum of suspended material so that it can be clarified without undue expense. If the proportion of suspended material increases above a minimum level, the costs of clarification and the loss of juice during such clarification will render the whole operation unprofitable.

Although the procedure outlined above is widely used, it is subject to serious problems. A major item is that the rack and cloth press entails excessive labor costs because of the manual work required in loading the cloths with pulp, introducing the cheeses into the press, removing the pressed cheeses, and unloading the pomace from the cloths. Also, the pressing is not efficient in that the pomace retains a considerable portion of juice which cannot be separated therefrom. Moreover, serious problems of microbial contamination and flavor damage are involved with the rack and cloth systems.

The press cloths are primarily responsible in this connection as in continued operation the interstices of the cloths become impregnated with juice and fine particles of apple tissue. These materials act as media for growth of adventitious microorganisms and also are subject to various chemical and biochemical reactions such as oxidation, fermentation, hydrolysis,

2

enzymatic browning, etc., whereby as fresh material is processed with the cloths, the juice entrains some of this material, resulting in microbial contamination of the juice and development of off-flavors and off-odors therein.

E. Lowe, E.L. Durkee and W.E. Hamilton; U.S. Patent 3,346,392; October 10, 1967; assigned to the U.S. Secretary of Agriculture describe a two stage process for extracting juices from fruit pulps which provides not only a juice low in suspended solids but also a high yield of juice. In a first stage of the process, fruit pulp is introduced into a centrifuge. The device is rotated at a slow speed to form a compacted thick cake of pulp, then the speed is increased and maintained at extraction level until about ⅗ to ¾ of the available juice is expelled from the pulp. In a second stage, the centrifuged pulp is subjected to pressing action, using, for example, a conventional screw press, to extract the remainder of the available juice. The two fractions of juice are then combined.

A juice of especially low content of suspended matter is produced by filtering the press juice through the centrifuge cake remaining from the first stage of the process (the centrifugation of the pulp) and then combining this juice with that obtained in the centrifugation stage.

FIGURE 1.1: TWO STAGE PROCESS

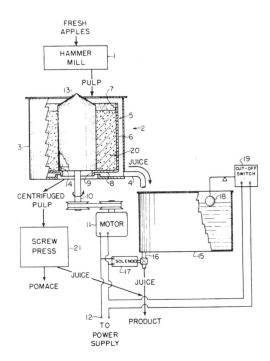

Source: E. Lowe, E.L. Durkee and W.E. Hamilton; U.S. Patent 3,346,392; October 10, 1967

Example: (a) Red Delicious apples (early season) together with 0.5% of their weight of cellulose fiber were ground in a hammer mill provided with a screen having perforations ⅜" in diameter. The resulting pulp was fed into a centrifuge as shown in Figure 1.1, where basket **5** was 3 feet in diameter and 15 inches deep. In each cycle the basket, while rotating at about 100 rpm, was loaded with 250 pounds of pulp, forming a cake 4 to 4½ inches thick. About 30 seconds after filling, the speed of rotation of the basket was gradually increased to 1,200 rpm and held at this point until the weight of juice extracted was 58% of the weight of the pulp. This took about 2 minutes. The centrifuged pulp was then run through a conventional screw press provided with a slotted cylindrical shell and a tapered screw which fed the pulp in the direction of increasing diameter of the screw to exert progressively higher pressure on the pulp against the walls of the shell. In this operation there was produced a yield of 24% of juice (based on weight of original pulp). The two fractions of juice were composited and the proportion of suspended matter determined.

(B) As a control, a batch of the same apples (plus ½% of cellulose fiber) was ground and the juice extracted in a conventional rack and cloth press. The results obtained in the two runs are summarized below.

Run	Ratio of 1st-stage to 2d-stage juice	Suspended matter in juice, percent by volume			Overall yield of juice	
		1st-stage juice	2d-stage juice	Composite	Percent	Gallons per ton of apples
A (In accordance with invention)	2.5:1	6.5	11.0	8.0	82	192
B (Conventional rack and cloth pressing)				9.1	74	168

Pome Fruit Juice Containing Pulp

The juice of pome fruits, particularly apple juice, has enjoyed relatively little commercial success as compared with citrus juices. One reason for this is that the packaged juice product does not closely resemble the appearance of the freshly cut fruit, whereas citrus juices generally appear and taste much like the freshly cut natural fruit. Apple juice, for example, is usually filtered to provide a clear product of light amber color.

The flesh of a freshly cut apple has a milky-white appearance. The juice from the cells of the flesh has the same appearance as well as a pronounced apple odor and flavor. Exposure to air for even short periods causes oxidation-reduction reactions and the formation of an unattractive brown color in the flesh and juice. The oxidation of the substrate is caused primarily by enzymes in the apple which react in the presence of oxygen to form a brown product. To combat the oxidation, such juices are usually clarified and filtered to give a clear product which lacks the appearance, odor, and flavor of fresh apple.

An improvement upon clear apple juice and filtered pome fruit juices generally available has been opalescent juice. This juice, slightly milky in color and cloudy in clarity, is opalescent in appearance and is made by retaining fine pulp particles suspended in the juice. Opalescent juices, while a significant improvement over clear, filtered pome fruit juices tend to vary widely according to the characteristics of the fruit which is crushed to form the juice. The viscosity of the juice varies considerably according to the characteristics of the source apples. Moreover, opalescent juices are low in viscosity, similar to clarified juices.

In addition, opalescent juices do not fully resemble the natural fresh fruit in body and texture. The opalescent juice alone may appear thin and watery. Accordingly, it is an object of the process of *A.R. Asti; U.S. Patent 3,518,093; June 30, 1970; assigned to Redwood Food Packing Company* to provide a pome fruit juice suspension which closely resembles the pome fruit in its natural state, an apple juice suspension having body, viscosity, and texture of fresh natural apples in liquid form.

It is essential to prevent or reverse the oxidation-reduction reactions which take place with exposed fresh pome fruit. The fruit is either subjected to cooking which serves to arrest the enzymatic action which discolors the fruit through oxidation, or the fruit is not cooked. Instead, an antioxidant is introduced into crushed fruit at a point where the natural oxidation has not proceeded beyond return. That is, if antioxidant is added to the fruit before the oxidation process has resulted in the formation of a precipitate, the process may be reversed and browning of the juice will not occur. The amount of antioxidant required is simply the amount needed to prevent the formation of a precipitate in the juice. This amount, though small, varies with the type of fruit being crushed since the rate of oxidation varies with the type of fruit.

Example: Fresh Gravenstein apples in two batches were washed in warm water, rinsed in cold water, and inspected. The sound fruits of the first batch were peeled, cored, and sliced before cooking in a continuous steam cooker. The cooked apples were strained through a pulper having openings of 20 mils and passed into a storage tank. The second batch of sound apples was crushed in a hammer mill to a coarse pulp in the presence of a fine spray of ascorbic acid introduced through a metering pump as a standard solution of 5% ascorbic acid in filtered apple juice. The disintegrated pulp was pressed in a hydraulic press with a wood rack and cloth. The juice was then passed through a vibrating screen having a mesh size of 0.015 inch and deaerated at 25" vacuum. The juice and pulp were blended in the ratio of 8 parts juice to 2 parts apple pulp. The mixture was then pasteurized, homogenized and canned in glass jars.

The product thus produced was a stable suspension of pulp fiber in apple juice which did not separate and settle on standing. The blended product has relatively high viscosity, although it was readily pourable. The body and texture gave the appearance of natural apples in a liquefied state. The color and odor also closely resembled the milky white appearance of freshly cut apples. The flavor of the resulting product was substantially closer to the flavor of fresh apples than the clarified and filtered apple juice currently marketed.

CITRUS JUICE

Pulp Treatment to Remove Off-Flavors

In the processing of citrus products, particularly oranges, it is customary to remove the juice from the fruit through the use of specially built juice extractors which operate to squeeze or ream the juice from the fruit in such a manner that the peel and albedo are discarded or conveyed to a drier where they are dried for use as animal feed. The juice from the extractors contains what is normally called pulp and consists of the juice and juice sacs and a portion of the segment membranes. The peel, core and seeds are not included within the definition of pulp.

In the usual process, the pulp-containing juice from the extractors is then passed through finishers wherein the majority of the pulp is screened out of the juice, which pulp is then usually either discarded or dried into animal feed. It is well known that the pulp separated out by the finishers contains substantial amounts of orange juice solids, pectin, and other valuable constituents of the orange. The juice solids are particularly important inasmuch as the value of the juice upon which payment to the farmer is based, is determined by the quantity of fruit solids in the juice.

The loss of fruit solids in the discarded pulp has, as indicated before, been previously recognized and attempts have been made in the past to recover the solids such as by washing the pulp with water, but even in such processes most of the solids were lost and there was of course the added expense of evaporating the wash water to obtain a usable concentration.

In accordance with the process of *H.W. Harrell; U.S. Patent 3,118,770; January 21, 1964*, however, the pulp is treated in a manner to conserve all of the valuable ingredients thereof including the solids, in such form that it can be utilized in conjunction with orange juice and orange juice products in a most beneficial manner. It should be pointed out that pulp removed from juice by the finishers contains relatively high concentrations of enzymes which, if allowed to remain active, are very detrimental to orange juice and orange juice products. If pulp containing active enzymes is added to concentrated orange juice, the enzymes produce gelation of the concentrate, probably because of a change in the pectin caused by the enzyme activity. While it is known that enzymes in orange juice may be destroyed by heating, to destroy the enzymes in the pulp by heating does not produce a pulp usable in any significant quantities with orange juice inasmuch as more than a minor amount of pulp gives an unsatisfactory appearance to the product and the pulp itself, even if treated to inactivate the enzymes, still carries into the juice much undesired flavor. The process treats pulp in a manner which not only inhibits the enzyme activity, it also removes the undesired flavors therefrom and can also be used to reduce the size of the particles forming the pulp so as not to detract from the appearance of the fruit juice if relatively large quantities of the pulp are added thereto.

The pulp is comminuted from the finisher to completely release the enzymes and other components contained within the pulp particles. The comminuted mass is then heated to a sufficient temperature to destroy the enzymes, or at least inhibit their activity, and then desirably, homogenized so as to yield a smooth paste which may be easily handled and further heated in a uniform manner. Further heating is accomplished in either an open vessel or an enclosed heater, and is carried out to the point where there is a perceptible color change from the normal lemon yellow toward a light tan. If this heating is accomplished in an open kettle at the boiling point of the comminuted homogenized mixture, undesirable flavors which are volatile are removed, while if an enclosed heating system is employed, the homogenized pulp, after being heated, is passed into a vacuum chamber to remove the volatile flavors.

After this heat treatment and volatile flavor removal, the product may again be homogenized to obtain an especially smooth mixture since the previous heating processes render the pulp more susceptible to homogenization. The pulp, after the foregoing treatment, is free from any active form of enzymes which would produce undesirable flavor and physical changes when mixed with orange juice, orange juice concentrate, or other citrus products. The pulp can also be utilized in substantial quantities to produce improved body, flavor and appearance in such products. The process as described not only removes undesirable flavors from the pulp but also, through the heating process, apparently converts a major portion of the pulp into a soluble form of orange solids.

Another advantage which may be pointed out is that the pulp treated in accordance with this process has a higher ratio than the orange juice from which it was separated. Ratio is defined as the percent citric acid divided into the percent soluble solids. Therefore, the higher the ratio the sweeter the product. Since pulp prepared in accordance with this process has a relatively high ratio, it may be utilized to increase the sweetness of low ratio juices. For example, the pulp may be added to the separated juice at a ratio of approximately one part by solids content of the pulp to ten parts by solids content of the juice.

For the heating step, the time and temperature may vary through relatively wide limits. At the outset, the pulp is of a lemon yellow color but after the heating step has commenced, the color will begin to change. Thirty minutes heating at 160°F down to 1 or 2 minutes at 210°F will initiate the color change. The preferred ratio of time and temperature is anywhere from 30 minutes at 187°F to 11 minutes at 220°F. If the time and temperature of the heating step is continued beyond that indicated, the color becomes quite dark and a cooked flavor may be imparted to the pulp.

Recovery of Residual Juice from Fruit Pulp

Since the price of oranges delivered into the processing plant is a considerable part of the cost of production of orange juice, there has been an effort to extract more and more juice from the orange. This has led to second finishing and has resulted in obtaining an additional 3 to 5% of juice. This additional juice is lighter in color, thicker in body and more astringent in taste, and therefore, lower in quality than the first finisher juice. As efforts were made to apply more and more pressure to the second finisher to obtain a larger yield of juice, the quality became so poor that the product was unsalable. The juice held in the orange pulp amounted to 85% of the mass, and it was known that the juice was chemically no different than the juice obtained by the extractor, and that the poor quality resulted from the extraction methods.

Efforts to obtain greater quantities of juice from the pulp were continued, and took the form of adding water and extracting the water and juice dissolved from the pulp. In this case the watered juice from one rotary or vibrating screen was used as the wash from subsequent screens in a counter-flow process. While additional juice was recovered, it contained increased amounts of pectin, flavinoids, pectinesterase and astringents, and finely comminuted solids. When the resulting product was processed by the frozen juice processors, it gelled to a solid mass in their evaporators, and jack hammers had to be used to clean the equipment.

J.B. Redd; U.S. Patent 3,150,981; September 29, 1964 describes a process and apparatus by which 75 to substantially 88% of the residual juice in the pulp from the first finisher may be recovered in acceptable condition, without releasing substantial quantities of pectin, pectinesterase, flavinoids and other astringents. The process is based, in general, on the discovery that when certain definite limitations of temperature, time, and abrasion of pulp are observed in a counter-flow process, a product which is equivalent to first finisher juice is obtained when it is brought to the same Brix as the first finisher juice.

Referring to Figure 1.2, there is shown at **10** a mixing tank to receive the pulp from the first finisher **F** through the conduit **11**. The pulp flows from the mixing tank to the first of a series of screening centrifuges **12**. The juice extracted from the pulp by the centrifuge is piped to the evaporator, not shown, through pipe **13**. The pulp from the centrifuge is delivered to the mixing tank **14**, from whence it is delivered to the centrifuge **15** through conduit **16**.

FIGURE 1.2: PROCESS FOR RECOVERY OF RESIDUAL JUICE FROM PULP

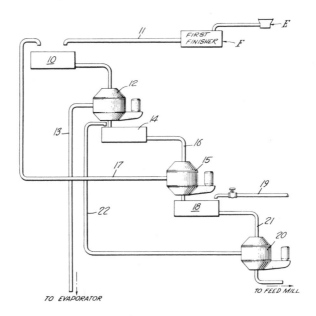

Source: J.B. Redd; U.S. Patent 3,150,981; September 29, 1964

The juice from the centrifuge **15** is piped to the mixing tank **10** by way of the pipe **17** where the juice is mixed with the pulp flowing from the first finisher, and the pulp from the centrifuge **15** is delivered to the mixing tank **18** where it is mixed with water introduced from a controlled source through the pipe **19**. Since all the water added at this point in the process must be evaporated, economics indicate that the amount of water that is added should be a ratio of 1:1 with the pulp. The water and pulp flow to the last of the screening centrifuges **20** by way of the pipe **21**. The diluent juice extracted flows to the mixing tank **14** through the pipe **22**, where it is mixed with the pulp from the centrifuge **12**. The pulp from the centrifuge **20** which contains less than 15% of the juice originally held by it is sent to a feed mill for incorporation in cattle feed.

As stated, the process is based on a temperature, time and abrasion relationship within certain definite limits. The juice at no time should exceed a temperature of 70°F, regardless of other factors in the relationship. If the temperature rises to as much as 75°F regardless of how fast the processing takes place or the degree of abrasion, gelation will take place in the evaporators when the juice is concentrated for concentrated frozen orange juice. The optimum temperature at which the process of the present invention may be carried out is 45°F with the lower temperature limit being not substantially lower than 40°F.

Pectin, pectinesterase, the flavinoids and bitter glucosides are substantially insoluble at a temperature of 45°F within the time limits of the present invention. The rate of solubility rises slowly to a temperature of 70°F, but rises very sharply above this temperature; and at 75°F within the time limits of presently known processing equipment, the resulting juice is rendered unacceptable. The maximum time limit for processing the pulp from the reaming extractor E to the juice outlet **13** of the centrifuge **12** should not exceed 30 minutes, with an optimum time of less than 20 minutes.

Known counter-flow processes using rotary or vibrating screen separators have failed when put into commercial production due largely to the fact they abrade the pulp to such an extent that the resulting fines pass through the screens. These fines contain pectin and the other undesirable elements which eventually dissolve into the juice and cause it to gell in the evaporator. It has been found that the present invention may be successfully practiced when screening centrifuges are used for separating the pulp from the juice. The screen of the centrifuge should be 0.015 and the helical wiper should be set at 0.020" clearance from the screen.

Due to the high speed of separation and the minimal amount of abrasion of the pulp by the screening centrifuge two of the requirements of the present invention may be successfully met when practicing the invention on a commercial basis.

Example: Ten 90-pound boxes of oranges were reamed, and juice extracted in a reamer-extractor. The juice and pulp were pumped to a first finisher where the juice was extracted and the pulp was processed using three Mercone screening centrifuges, as shown in Figure 1.2. The temperature of the pulp and juice was maintained throughout at 40°F. The extraction time in mixing tank **18** was five minutes, and the ratio of pulp to added water was 1:1. The screens of the Mercone centrifuges were 0.015, and the helical wiper was set for 0.020" clearance between the helix and the screen. The overall time was less than twenty minutes.

Countercurrent Extraction

The first step of extracting citrus juice from fruit consists in subjecting the fruit to the action of an extractor. In the extractor the peel is separated from the pulp which consists of the seeds, the membrane which separates the segments of the fruit and the juice cells, many of which are ruptured during this procedure or in the later handling of the pulp. Thereafter the juice which contains water soluble solids is separated from the pulp. However, this last separation is not necessarily complete since some of the cells may be found in the final product.

For economic reasons, it is encumbent upon the extractor to extract substantially all of the juice from the pulp and this is customarily achieved with finishers which are basically high pressure screw presses which squeeze the pulp rather drastically, and many times tear and abrade it so as to produce finely divided pulp which finds its way into the finished product.

The result of this is that although substantially all of the liquid carrying the water soluble solids is extracted leaving a very dry pulp which is macerated and squeezed to such an extent that undesirable quantities of pectin, enzymes and bitter principles found in the pulp and the very finely divided pulp above referred to, find their way into the juice.

When the finishing operation is carried to the point where economic quantities of juice are extracted, the quantities of the undesirable constituents often run high enough to give the juice undesirable characteristics and a relatively high viscosity so that it can only be concentrated to from 28° to 30°Brix.

In contrast to the aforesaid method, when juice is extracted according to the method of *C.B. Clark, J.L. Froscher, C.W. Du Bois, D.H. Kimball and W.R. Roy; U. S. Patent 3,169,873; February 16, 1965,* it is possible to extract the desirable water soluble constituents from the pulp substantially quantitatively. This may be done without drastically squeezing or macerating the pulp and without producing significant quantities of finely divided pulp and without extracting undesirable quantities of pectins, enzymes and bitter principles, and without increasing the viscosity so as to create serious problems when the juice is concentrated to make frozen concentrated juice, which is the form in which much of the juice is marketed.

The process consists essentially in first separating the peel from the pulp, then separating the juice and the soluble solids from the pulp without drastically squeezing or macerating the pulp. This may be done by gravity separation or by centrifugal separation and may be either a step-by-step or a continuous process. The first step is generally that of separating free juice from the pulp as it comes from the extractor. Such juice is generally at about 12° Brix. The pulp from which the juice has been separated without pressing is then washed either in a plurality of successive washings after each of which the washing liquid is separated from the pulp without pressing or macerating, or as will be described in detail later, through a continuous countercurrent flow type of extraction.

When the process is carried out in a series of steps the pulp is first drained of the juice which can be easily separated. Thereafter, the pulp is washed in a plurality of successive washings and the washing liquid is separated without excessively pressing or macerating the pulp. In the preferred form the washing water from the last step is utilized successively for the next preceding steps, so that the final liquid from the washings contains substantially all of the water soluble solids left in the pulp after the first free juice is eliminated. This washing liquid is then either processed or added to the juice taken from the pulp in the first step.

In some forms of the process the washing liquid is centrifuged to remove any fine pulp which might be entrained in it before it goes to the final product. When a continuous countercurrent flow process is employed, the pulp is introduced at one end of the process, so to speak, and the washing liquid at the other end. They flow counter to one another so that at one end the pulp is discharged while at the other end the liquid containing the extracted solids is collected for processing or addition to the initially extracted juice.

Generally, the washing process is carried out with a quantity of aqueous liquid, equal in weight to the weight of the pulp and in the preferred form the liquid employed is liquid condensate recovered from the concentration of juice because this liquid has in it many of the volatile constituents of the juice which are thus returned to the juice. In carrying out the step-by-step process the liquid is mixed with the pulp which has already been washed in several separate successive stages. It is then drained from this pulp after which it is mixed with the pulp from the next succeeding washing and draining step.

After this mixing it is drained or separated from the pulp and carried to the next preceding step repeating essentially the same steps. Throughout, in the preferred form both the juice and the extracting liquid are separated from the pulp without materially pressing or macerating the pulp. This permits the liquid to dissolve the water soluble constituents from the pulp without picking up undesirable quantities of the above mentioned undesirable elements present in the pulp. The liquid is relatively free from the undesirable pectins and other constituents which are normally extracted when the pulp is subjected to the customary finishing operations. Its viscosity is such that it can be concentrated by vacuum without the difficulties attendant upon the concentration of more viscous citrus juice from the customary finishing operation.

The extraction of the liquid from the pulp may be performed on devices which are normally used to finish the pulp. However, when this is done care is taken to see that the pulp is not subjected to the pressing and maceration which accompanies the ordinary finishing operation heretofore carried out and it is preferred that when this is done the washing liquid be centrifuged to remove any entrained pulp fines before returning the washings to the final product.

Dialysis Apparatus Comprising Endless Membrane

The process of *J.H. Brown and D.G. Conning; U.S. Patent 3,318,796; May 9, 1967; assigned to American Machine & Foundry Company* provides a fluid treatment apparatus in which fluid treatment cells are formed from a single length of a membrane material wound in a serpentine fashion about support members to form the fluid treatment cells, the membrane passing freely about the support members so that the membrane may be positioned by subjecting it to a tension drawing it about the support members.

Referring to Figures 1.3a, 1.3b and 1.3c which show an example of this process, a suitable tank 25 is open at the top and has two electrodes 26 and 27 positioned vertically along its side walls. Leads 28 and 29 extend from the electrodes to a suitable current source (not shown). Disposed within the tank are two lower rod support members 30 which are near each end of the tank. Disposed above each lower rod support member is an upper rod support member 31. Between the lower rod support members 30 there extend the lower rods 32 which are spaced apart parallel to each other and between the upper rod support members there extend the upper rods 33.

As is further shown in Figure 1.3a, an elongated sheet of membrane material 34 is drawn from roll 35 over the first rod 33, below and about a first rod 32, over a second rod 33, until the sheet 34 describes a serpentine path across the tank. If it is desired, a sheet of sponge plastic 36 may extend across the bottom of the tank between the lower rod support members to contact the membrane 34 as it passes beneath each rod 32. If the tank is filled with a suitable fluid to a level 37, fluid treatment compartments will be formed between the vertical runs 38 of the sheet 34.

Referring to Figures 1.3b and 1.3c, manifolds 40 may have a lateral portion 41 and the longitudinally projecting portions 42. The lateral portions of each manifold may extend laterally to lead through a side of the tank. Each lateral portion contains a passageway 43 which communicates with the passageways 44 in each longitudinal projection 42.

Further reference is made to Figure 1.3b, it may be seen that each longitudinal projection extends between adjacent pairs of the vertical runs of the membranes 34 directly above the rods 32. Beyond the manifolds, the tank contains an inlet tube 45 at one end and an outlet tube 46 at the other end. The first embodiment of the process may be used in the following manner.

The tank is filled with a dilute solution of sodium hydroxide to the level 37 as shown in Figure 1.3a. The solution of sodium hydroxide enters the inlet tube as shown in Figure 1.3b and flows from the outlet tube. At the same time, a citrus juice or the like, is passed through one manifold 40 to be drawn through it out of the tank. If the membrane is an anion selective membrane, hydroxyl ions will migrate through the membrane into the juice and citrate ions will pass from the juice to the caustic soda stream. The net effect will be to reduce excess acidity in the citrus or other juice to render it more palatable and generally improved as a product for human consumption.

As the membrane becomes contaminated, the end 48 of the membrane may be drawn out of the tank to pull additional portions of the membrane from the roll 35 into the tank.

This may be done while the apparatus is assembled for use. To facilitate the passage of the membrane **34** through the tank **25**, the rods **32** and **33** may be rotatably mounted in the rod support members **30** and **31**.

FIGURE 1.3: APPARATUS COMPRISING AN ENDLESS MEMBRANE

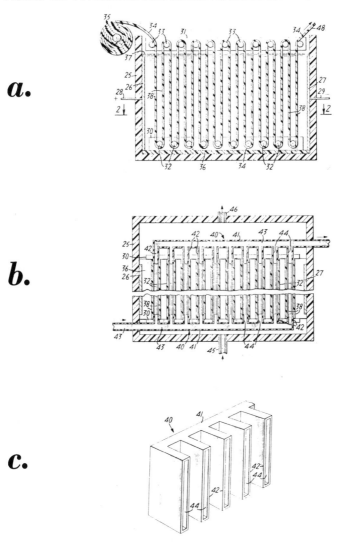

(a) Transverse Section
(b) Horizontal Section on Line **2–2**
(c) Perspective of Manifold End Fragment

Source: J.H. Brown and D.G. Conning; U.S. Patent 3,318,796; May 9, 1967

Enzyme Action to Increase Juice Yield

The process of *K.J.S. Villadsen and K.J. Moller; U.S. Patent 3,347,678; October 17, 1967; assigned to Aktieselskabet Grindstedvaerket, Denmark* comprises the step of subjecting the pulp remaining after pressing a first batch of juice from the flesh of citrus fruits and, if desired, the shells from which the flesh or albedo has to be removed, to a treatment with pectolytic enzymes. The enzymatic treatment can be carried out at room temperature for a prolonged period, preferably for a period of 1 to 48 hours, or for a shortened period at an increased temperature, preferably not exceeding 55°C. For treating the pulp, the applied amount of pectolytic enzymes is preferably 0.02 to 0.5% by weight as calculated upon the weight of the pulp.

The pectolytic enzyme is commercially available in various degrees of enzymatic strength. The said proportions of pectolytic enzyme to pulp refer to a commercial single strength enzymatic preparation which is marketed as Pectolase DE 10. The pectolytic strength of the said preparation is such that during 3 hours at 25°C and at pH 3.7, the viscosity of a 1.8% aqueous solution of citrus pectin (20 H medium rapid set) is reduced from 55 to 60 seconds to about 10 seconds, as determined in a viscosimeter, having a water value of about 7 seconds.

Stronger enzymatic preparations can also be used in the method in suitably reduced proportions. In admixing the enzymatic agent with the pulp, a thorough stirring should be applied to ensure a homogenous distribution of the enzyme throughout the pulp. A renewed stirring a couple of hours later, when the enzymatic action has set in, will often be advantageous. In dealing with unpreserved pulp, it is important that the enzymatic treatment is started at once in order to reduce the risk of fermentation of the pulp, and that pressing of the enzymatically treated pulp is carried out 2 to 6 hours after addition of the enzyme.

If the pulp cannot at once be subjected to enzymatic treatment, a preservation agent should be added, such as sulfur dioxide. In the case of thus preserved pulps, the enzymatic treatment is advantageously extended over a longer period of, for example, about 24 hours. Before pressing off the juice, which has been liberated by the enzymatic treatment, a filter aid is advantageously admixed, such as kieselguhr or diatomite in an amount of 1 to 2% by weight of the pulp. The recovered juice is screened, if necessary, and sterilized to destroy any remaining enzymes. If a reduction of viscosity of the juice is desired, additional pectolytic enzyme can be added, and the juice left standing before screening and sterilization, until the desired reduction of the viscosity is obtained.

Example 1: To 1,000 grams of orange pulp, from which the juice had been screened, and which contained 19.5% dry matter, was added 1 gram Pectolase DE 10. After standing at room temperature for 20 hours, a further yield of 254 grams of juice was obtained by pressing.

Example 2: A mixture of orange pulp and pectolytic enzyme as in Example 1 was left standing for 6 hours at 45°C. On pressing, a further yield of 349 grams of juice was obtained.

Example 3: The procedure of Example 1 was repeated, except that 10 grams of diatomaceous earth were added to the mixture of orange pulp and pectolytic enzyme. After 20 hours at room temperature, 478 grams of juice were obtained, as compared with a yield of only 32 grams, when pectolytic enzyme was omitted in the mixture of orange pulp and diatomaceous earth.

Example 4: Thirty over-ripe Israeli oranges were pressed and strained to yield 950 ml of juice and 1,050 grams of strained-off pulp. The pulp was divided into three equal portions, to each of which were added 0.1% of Pectolase DE 10 and 2% of diatomite. The first portion was pressed after 2 hours at room temperature, yielding 162 grams of juice, the second after 4 hours, yielding 215 grams of juice, and the third after 24 hours, yielding 200 grams of juice of reduced viscosity. This experiment shows that the enzymatic treatment results in an increase of the yield of juice of about 68%, and that it is possible to obtain this increased yield by only 4 hours' treatment of the pulp. The viscosity of the juice recovered after the enzymatic treatment is much higher than that of the juice of the first pressing, but can be reduced to normal by adding 0.05% pectolytic enzyme and letting the juice stand overnight before sterilizing.

Example 5: Forty Italian lemons were pressed and strained to yield 975 ml of juice and 866 grams of fruit pulp. The pulp was subjected to enzymatic treatment at 45°C after addition of filter aid as in Example 4, and the three portions were left standing for 2, 4, and 6 hours, respectively, yielding 53%, 63.5%, and 68.5% additional juice, respectively.

Example 6: Fifty grams of fresh orange pulp resulting from a treatment with 0.1% by weight of Pectolase DE 10 for 22 hours were filtered on a paper filter. Twenty-five grams of juice passed through the filter during 7 minutes. In a similar experiment, using 0.3% of the enzyme, 25 grams of juice passed during 6 minutes. In a control experiment without the enzymatic treatment, the passage of 25 grams of juice took more than 26 minutes. This experiment illustrates the time saving in using the enzymatic treatment.

Example 7: The pectolytic enzyme treatment can also be applied to the clarification of citrus juices. A freshly pressed lemon juice, which had been preserved with sulfur dioxide, but not pasteurized, was centrifuged, whereby the pulp content of about 20% was reduced to about 5%. Three portions of equal size were set up in cylinder glasses, one with an addition of 0.1% by weight of single strength pectolytic enzyme, the second with 0.3% of the enzyme, and the third as a control without addition of enzyme.

After 22 hours, the sediments measured 140 ml, 210 ml, and 70 ml, respectively. Then 200 ml of juice were decanted from each glass, equal portions of diatomite were added, and the three portions were filtered through paper filters. The filtration time for 100 ml was noted in each case, amounting to 7 minutes, 2 minutes, and 65 minutes, respectively, indicating the substantial clarification obtained by the enzymatic treatment.

Removal of Bitterness Precursors from Pulp

The juice of certain oranges, although palatable at the outset, soon develops a pronounced bitterness even when stored at deep freeze temperatures. The Florida navel orange is an example. The Italian blonde orange is another. The juices of both of these fruits are palatable when first extracted, but they both develop bitterness within a very short time.

It is not known precisely what change of a chemical nature occurs in the juice products of certain oranges to produce the bitterness; but it has been ascertained that in some cases at least the change itself is associated with the pulp (obviously this is the juice pulp), not with the liquid components of the juice. Thus the juices of the named fruits remain palatable and have satisfactory storage life if they are freed from the pulp component as by centrifuging. An orange juice or concentrate consisting of the liquid component alone is not generally desirable because the public has come to expect a certain quantity of relatively finely divided pulp in the product at the time it is consumed. It has further been ascertained that the pulp itself after separation from the liquid component, can be so treated as to be freed of the tendency to develop bitterness.

G.S. Sperti; U.S. Patent 3,385,711; May 28, 1968; assigned to Institutum Divi Thomae Foundation found that a suitable treatment is a washing of the pulp solely with either warm or cold water. Pulp so treated may be added back to the liquid component either as a whole or in such quantity as may be desired; and the combined product will have a good storage life. In one embodiment of the process which may be taken as exemplary herein, orange juice as it is expressed from fruits known to develop the bitterness characteristic is centrifuged, filtered, or decanted for the separation of the pulp.

The term expressed as used herein is intended to refer to the extraction of the juice from the fruits by ordinary juicing operations either by hand or by machine. The juicing operation is not of a kind, however, to include in the product constituents of the rind, the skin, or the more fibrous portions of the fruits. Since, as above indicated, a certain quantity of pulp is expected and desired both in orange juice as such and in concentrates, it has been found entirely possible to treat the liquid component of the expressed juice with pulp derived from types of citrus fruits which do not develop the bitterness characteristic. There is always an excess quantity of pulp from oranges which do not develop the bitterness characteristic available on the market at a very reasonable price, because it is not the general practice to add back to the liquid component all of the pulp normally contained in the expressed juice.

Instead of the practice outlined above, the separated pulp from oranges which develop the bitterness characteristic may be treated for the removal of factors producing bitterness by a washing operation. This operation is accomplished by agitating the pulp successively in several volumes of water. Agitation may be accomplished mechanically as by the use of stirring or shaking; or it may be achieved by boiling the pulp in water. Agitation which would tend to crush or comminute the particles of the pulp is to be avoided, since it is believed that a crushed or bruised pulp has a greater tendency to become bitter upon aging.

A treatment in water at an elevated temperature appears to be helpful. While washing with water at ordinary or room temperatures is in most instances effective, it may be that the bitterness characteristic is in part destroyed or decomposed by elevated temperatures. Instead of boiling, the mixture of pulp in water may be treated in an autoclave or washed by passing live steam through it. In either of the latter instances the temperature of the pulp may be raised to the boiling point of water or thereabove; but good effects are attained by temperatures higher than room temperature and below 212°F.

The use of elevated temperatures as in boiling, or treatment with steam or hot water, appears to assist in the removal of the bitterness developing factors. Boiling may be combined with mechanical agitation. An effective treatment is to boil the pulp in one or two volumes of water, separate the water from the pulp by centrifuging, then reboil the pulp in another similar quantity of water, and again separate the water from the pulp. The bitterness producing factors are, surprisingly, responsive to a washing treatment, after which the pulp will not develop further bitterness when mixed with the orange juice, unless the pulp be bruised or crushed. The washing liquid, i.e., water, will be discarded after removal from the pulp.

Example 1: Florida navel oranges were squeezed, and the juice, which contained suspended pulp, was centrifuged to remove the pulp. The pulp after such removal was suspended in water and boiled therein for 30 minutes. After cooling the pulp was separated from the water by centrifuging for 20 minutes. At this time neither the water separated from the pulp nor the pulp itself was characterized by any very great bitterness. However, to insure complete removal of the bitter material, the same pulp was resuspended in water at room temperature; and the pulp water mixture was agitated for 30 minutes on a mechanical shaker. The retreated pulp was then separated from the water by centrifuging for 20 minutes. Neither the second increment of water nor the pulp itself was bitter as this stage. The pulp retained its natural color.

The initial orange juice from which the pulp had been separated, and the pulp itself (treated as above set forth) were each separately stored in suitable containers in frozen condition. Neither substance developed bitterness during this storage. On the other hand, control samples of juice expressed at the same time but stored without removal of the pulp became extremely bitter. The juice from which the pulp was separated for treatment and the treated pulp also keep well in combination. Results similar to those set forth above have been achieved with the juice and pulp of Italian blond oranges.

Experience with the practice of the process indicates that best results are obtained when the separation of the pulp from the liquid juice occurs as promptly as possible after the juice is expressed; and experience has also indicated that for best results the separated pulp should be treated as promptly as possible. Extreme bitterness will develop in a juice from which the pulp has not been extracted as well as in the extracted pulp itself. In general, extreme bitterness in the juice and pulp of the named fruits will develop within as little as twelve hours despite refrigeration.

Coring and Extracting Rinded Fruits

R.J. Breton and D.F. Beck; U.S. Patent 3,682,092; August 8, 1972; assigned to Roto Manufacturing Company, Inc. describe an apparatus for juicing fruit having a rind and varying in hardness and size, and performing, generally the steps of supporting a fruit, cutting an opening through the rind at one side thereof, then confining the fruit and applying external pressure thereto thereby extruding a core through the opening cut through the rind and delivering the juice from the fruit via the opening and through the extruded core.

The apparatus includes a hydraulically operated and hydraulically responsive mechanism involving a ram that moves the supported whole fruit onto a tubular coring knife that is perforated, thereby cutting an opening through the rind, a pressing head for receiving the whole fruit which is moved thereinto by the ram which seals in the head, a rind ejector which closes the cylinder so as to oppose the ram, a pressure responsive hydraulic means operating the ram to press the fruit and thereby extrude a core of fruit through said opening cut through the rind and deliver juice from the core, and a core ejector within the coring knife and which is unique in its adaptability to accelerate the rind with the core attached for ejection from the pressing head. The apparatus also includes means responsive to reciprocal motions and timing the functional fruit processing elements.

The method employed involves the pressing of juice from whole fruit having a rind, and especially from citrus fruits. Such fruits are of a kind but vary widely in size and hardness, and the rind thickness thereof varies as well. For example, oranges of the same crop vary in diameter, size and character, that is, as to hardness, internal structure, and consistency of the fibers and pulp. Furthermore, the range of size between grapefruits and limes is quite substantial, it being an object herein to accommodate all such citrus fruits for juicing by one and the same process and in one and the same apparatus or machine; and with or without alteration or adaption.

For example, the pressing head and ram head can be replaceably employed in varied size ranges depending upon the particular fruit to be juiced, a feature of the method and apparatus being that a wide range of fruit sizes can be accommodated within one head-ram size. Accordingly, the method comprises the separate and distinct steps of: first, supporting a fruit; second, cutting an opening in the fruit; third, confining the fruit; fourth, applying external pressure to the fruit and thereby extruding a core and displacing juice from the fruit via said opening and through said core; and fifth, to sense a predetermined build-up of said external pressure and thereafter release the same.

This process is unique in the extrusion of a core from the interior of the whole fruit and in the utilization of said core to conduct juice from said interior, whereby the juice is extracted from the whole fruit at the exterior of its rind. The first step of supporting the fruit is performed without force applied thereto and without deformation solely for the location of and for holding the whole fruit positioned preparatory to the second step of the juicing process. This is a loose support for positioning purposes and is to be distinguished from complete embracement which characterizes so many of the prior art processes. Rotational orientation of the fruit is unimportant.

The second step of cutting an opening in the fruit is performed by the application of forces applied to one side of the supported whole fruit, incising a portion of the rind so as to separate it from the surrounding rind area but without separating it from its fibrous connection with the interior of the whole fruit. Thus, the incised area of the rind remains connected with the whole fruit. In practice, the incised area is round, substantially smaller in diameter than the whole fruit diameter, and it is necessarily coaxial with a radial axis extending through the center of the fruit.

The third step of confining the fruit is performed by the transfer of the whole fruit from the first mentioned support and into surrounding confinement of the intact rind, excluding confinement of the incised area of the rind. Thus, the area of the rind which is excluded from confinement is aligned with the axis of and is complementary with the said incised area of the rind.

The fourth step of applying external pressure is performed so as to compress the rind and interior fibers into a compaction of fibrous solids as a result of extruding a core of cross section determined by the incised area configuration, accompanied by displacement of juice from the fruit interior and which flows through the core via the opening made by the incision. In practice, the compacting force or pressure application is made in opposition to an area of the rind encompassing the said incised area. The compaction of fibers forming the said core establishes a filter body through which the juices are delivered at the exterior of the intact rind surrounding the incised portion thereof.

The fifth step of sensing a predetermined build-up of the applied external pressure is operative without regard to fruit size or hardness, and is an inevitable condition that is used advantageously to release the external pressure; thereby completing the juicing process. The said inevitable condition is evidenced by the substantially complete deliverance of juice from the whole fruit, whereupon the remaining rind and internal fibers and pulp are compacted to a degree where further compression is practically impossible, and at which point a sharp pressure increase or build-up is sensed and employed to cause a release of said applied pressure. The completed juicing process extracts substantially all liquid from the whole fruit, leaving the rind and fibers and pulp substantially dry. The patent contains detailed descriptions and diagrams of apparatus for the process.

Low Viscosity Juice or Concentrate

According to the process of *C.D. Atkins, J.A. Attaway and M.D. Maraulja; U.S. Patent 3,711,294; January 16, 1973; assigned to State of Florida, Department of Citrus* freshly extracted orange juice or reconstituted bulk orange juice concentrate is first heated to a temperature of about 155° to 210°F, preferably about 165°F, in order to inactivate the naturally present pectic enzymes in the orange juice such as pectinesterase. Subsequent to this heating, the juice is cooled to a temperature of about 70° to 120°F, preferably about 80°F, and sufficient pectic enzyme added to hydrolyze a substantial portion of the pectins present in the juice.

The pectic enzyme employed (which may contain traces of adulterating nonspecific enzymes) should, however, not be permitted to remain in contact with the citrus juice substrate for sufficient time to affect the substances responsible for maintaining the cloud, color and body of the juice. The amount of enzyme actually employed will depend on a number of factors such as time of treatment until the enzyme is deactivated, enzyme concentration and temperature. Generally, these parameters can be varied as convenient by one skilled in the art to effect a reduction of the pectic fraction to about 0.01 to 0.15 weight percent pectins and about 0.002 to 0.01 weight percent H_2O insoluble solids.

Typically, for example, about 4 to 8 volume percent based on the volume of single-strength juice of enzyme is sufficient when the juice containing the enzyme is allowed to stand for about 18 to 30 hours at about 70° to 120°F before raising the temperature to deactivate the enzyme. Following addition of the pectic enzyme to the juice, the juice is allowed to stand at a temperature of about 70° to 120°F, preferably about 80°F, in order to destroy substantially all the low pectins present in the juice which lack gelling strength and are the result of maceration of the more solid fruit parts.

Generally, it is not necessary to remove substantial amounts of high grade pectins such as protopectin which are present in insoluble solids. The juice is then heated to a temperature of about 155° to 210°F, preferably about 200°F, to inactivate the enzymes present and also destroy any microorganisms. Insoluble solids are then removed, for example, by decanting, and the remaining juice treated by centrifuging or filtering, for example, to yield a colored single-strength juice similar to that present in the cell sac of the fruit prior to normal juice extraction, but absent the insoluble solids and low grade soluble pectins which hold them in suspension. The juice, however, which has a viscosity of less than 100 centipoises at 65°Brix and 77°F, retains the desirable cloud and body naturally present in fresh juice and in addition, has good shelf life due to the removal of oxidizable fatty materials.

If desired, the juice prepared can be concentrated, for example, under vacuum, in order to preclude the use of high temperatures which result in a burned taste, to yield a sparkling colored syrup of any desired concentration (e.g., about 64° to 80°Brix) for any juice product. It may also be desirable to refilter this base prior to bottling in order to remove traces of insoluble cloud materials that may have developed on storage of the base. Suitable pectic enzymes for use can be prepared from sprouted oats, for example, or obtained commercially, for example, Spark-L.

The orange base of the process, either as a concentrate or at its original strength, prior to concentration can also have incorporated therein effective amounts of isotonic salts, such as sodium and calcium chloride, as are described in U.S. Patent 3,657,424. The purpose of these additional salts is to replace those lost from the body during strenuous physical exercise.

Example: Freshly extracted single-strength orange juice was heated to 165°F and cooled to approximately 80°F. One half pint of a suitable specific pectic enzyme (Spark-L) was added to each 100 gallons of single-strength juice. The juice was allowed to stand for 25 hours. The treated juice was then heated to about 200°F to completely inactivate the enzymes and destroy any microorganisms present. The excess insoluble solids of the juice were decanted and the remaining juice centrifuged to yield a colored single-strength juice that represented that present in the cell sac of the fruit prior to normal juice extraction.

Following this preparation, the juice was then concentrated under vacuum to yield a sparkling colored syrup of 65°Brix concentration. The analyses of the base and a control concentrate was as follows.

	Concentration	Viscosity (apparent), cp.	Insoluble solids, percent by volume	Hunter citrus colorimeter
New base	65° Brix (34.8 Bé)	70	Trace	38
Standard (Control) concentrate.	65° Brix (34.8 Bé)	3,000	9	38

GRAPE JUICE

Low Sediment Grape Juice

In the manufacture of grape juice, the grapes are usually crushed and stemmed, with the stems being separated from the crushed grapes which comprise juice and pomace, the pomace including the seeds and skins of the grapes. The crushed grapes are introduced into a preheater and cellulose pulp or paper is added to the fruit. This is followed by the addition of pectinase in order to effect improved recovery of juice from the grapes.

The mixture is substantially beaten with the pulp in it. In this step of conventional processing, the juice is depectinized and, after such step, the mixture of crushed depectinized grapes and paper is introduced into a separation device, such as a rotary screen or press. However, such devices usually have provided a juice which, in normal operation, has a high amount of sediment. This high sediment juice is then further treated for use as grape juice or in the manufacture of jelly. The pomace which is separated from the juice may be further treated by introducing it into a press which further separates juice from the pomace.

The process of G. Bosy; U.S. Patent 3,301,684; January 31, 1967; assigned to National

Dairy Products Corporation is designed to efficiently recover from grapes a juice with a low amount of sediment. Referring to Figure 1.4, the grapes of commerce are introduced into a wash tank **5** wherein the grapes are cleaned and residual dirt and other matter are washed from the grapes.

FIGURE 1.4: LOW SEDIMENT GRAPE JUICE

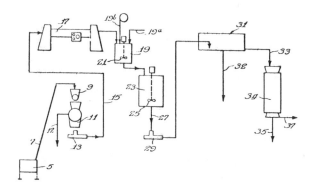

Source: G. Bosy; U.S. Patent 3,301,684; January 31, 1967

The grapes leave the wash tank on a conveyor **7**, which may be continuously operated, and are introduced into a crusher **9**. From the crusher, the grapes drop into a stemmer **11** which operates to separate the stems from grape mash which is a mixture of juice and pomace. The stems are removed through the discharge **12**. The wash tank, conveyor, crusher and stemmer are standard units which have been used in the manufacture of grape juice. The grape mash is pumped from the stemmer by means of a pump **13** through a line **15** to a heat exchanger **17**.

The grape mash enters the heat exchanger at a temperature of 70°F, though this temperature will fluctuate somewhat, depending upon the seasonal temperature. The temperature at which the mash, including the juice and pomace, enters the heat exchanger is not particularly important as the heat exchanger is adjusted to raise the temperature of the juice and pomace to 140°F, at which temperature most effective depectinization occurs. The heated grape mash is introduced into a mixing tank **19** and, in this tank, the juice and pomace are mixed with paper or cellulose pulp which is conventionally added to the mash in grape juice recovery operations. The line **19a** indicates the point of addition of pulp. Pectinase may also be added in this tank to effect the desired depectinization of the grape juice and pomace mixture, the pectinase being added through the line **19b**.

In the mixing tank there is provided an agitator **21** which is used to disperse the pulp and pectinase throughout the juice and pomace. It is important that over agitation or beating of the pulp be avoided. Accordingly, the agitator is primarily agitated to the extent necessary to mix the pectinase and disperse the pulp in the grape mash. From the mixing tank the mixture of pulp, pectinase and grape mash is introduced into a holding tank **23**. The mixture is held in this tank for a desired time to effect the desired degree of depectinization for the operation. In this connection, it is conventional to hold the mixture for one half hour before subsequent separation of the juice from the other material.

It will be understood that the mixing and holding can be accomplished in a single tank. The hold tank is provided with a mixer **25**. This mixer is operated at the end of the holding period to uniformly disperse the paper and pomace throughout the mixture so as to provide a homogeneous mixture, while, at the same time, not providing undue beating of the mixture. This is an important feature to provide most efficient operation of the process and apparatus. It has been found that excessive beating of the mixture, including the pulp, results in lower recovery of juice and inefficiency in operation.

The homogeneous mixture leaves the holding tank 23, through line 27 and is pumped by means of pump 29 to a trommel 31 which is of new construction and design. The trommel is adapted to provide (a) a moving bed of filtering material and (b) a sufficient head on the bed to cause juice to move through the bed and provide a juice which is low in sediment. In this connection, the bed should be agitated and a head of at least 5 inches established. The material introduced into the bed should be retained for a time sufficient to permit adequate drainage of the grape juice from the bed. The juice from the trommel is removed through line 32 and is then treated to remove any fibers which are present, and pasteurized. The juice may then be stored, bottled or made into jelly.

The pomace exits from the trommel through the discharge line 33 and contains absorbed juice which may be pressed out. Accordingly, the pomace is introduced into a press 34 which may be any one of several types of presses which are commercially available. In this connection, such standard presses are hydraulic presses, Zenith presses, Garolla presses, or Willmes presses. The press discharges a dried pomace material through line 35 and a low sediment juice through line 37. This juice may be pasteurized, stored or bottled, or it may be concentrated for manufacture into jelly. The pomace which leaves the press through line 35 may be leached to effect further recovery of juice.

The pomace may then be treated to recover grape seeds and the skins for further treatment. The trommel provides an important feature of this process in providing a moving bed of material through which the grape juice is filtered, the movement of the bed providing the desired efficiency of operation. The trommel is shown in detail in the patent. The trommel comprises a supporting frame on which is carried a rotating screen arrangement, the screen being driven by a suitable drive arrangement. The trommel further includes screen cleaning means which provides highly efficient operation.

In actual design of the trommel the rotating screen arrangement is 36 inches in diameter and the screen is of 12 mesh. The screen is rotated at a speed of 4 rpm. Grape mash is introduced into the trommel at the rate of 15 tons per hour and juice is recovered at the rate of 7.5 tons per hour, pomace and unseparated juice being discharged from the trommel at 32. The discharged juice has 3% sediment. The bed of grape mash in the trommel was 7" in depth.

The method and apparatus of this process provide a rapid means for dejuicing grape mash to provide a juice having a low amount of sediment. A particular feature is the moving bed of grape mash and fiber which is not hydrated to a high degree. If the fiber is overbeaten, hydration occurs causing the cellulosic pulp or paper to become ineffective in the operation of the moving bed. The repeated cleaning of the rotating screen arrangement is an additional feature which provides for highly effective operation and assures a proper bottom for the moving bed. It is important to maintain a hydraulic head, upon the bed in order to assure a most effective dejuicing of the grape mash.

Continuous Separation of Juice from Pulp

The process of *M.S. Nury; U.S. Patent 3,401,040; September 10, 1968* comprises the separation of insoluble fruit pulp from the juice of fruit by crushing the fruit, charging the crushed fruit so formed to a separator tank and permitting the crushed fruit to separate into a lighter pulp solids layer and a heavier liquid layer. Thereafter, additional crushed fruit is introduced into the separator tank at a point intermediate to the pulp solids accumulated at the surface and the lowermost portions of the liquid while withdrawing solids from the surface of the separator tank and liquid from a point near the bottom of the separator tank. This process has a large cylindrical tank with a sloping bottom to facilitate drainage of fluid, and with a double auger conveyor suspended from the center of the top with the opposite sides of the conveyor trough removed to expose one side of each screw. The individual screws are driven to convey material scooped up by the conveyor troughs toward the center; the screws are mounted to rotate slowly with their leading surfaces exposed. A vertical conduit is positioned at the center of the tank beneath the discharge ends of the screws which leads down to another screw conveyor in communication therewith capable of conveying solid materials through a discharge port in the side of the tank. Figure 1.5 shows a cylindrical tank **10** formed of cylindrical segments secured one to the next having a trough shaped bottom **12**.

FIGURE 1.5: CONTINUOUS SEPARATION OF JUICE FROM GRAPE PULP

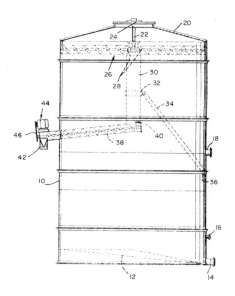

Source: M.S. Nury; U.S. Patent 3,401,040; September 10, 1968

As shown in phantom view in Figure 1.5, the bottom is sloped toward a liquid discharge port **14**. Another smaller discharge port **16** appears immediately thereabove, together with an inlet stub **18** through which a crushed pulpy mass of fruit may be introduced into the tank. Suspended from the top **20** by means of shaft **22** journaled in the generally horizontal collar **24** is the double auger or screw conveyor, generally **26**.

Immediately beneath each discharge end **28** of the halves of the double auger conveyor is the vertical pipe **30** supported by means of steel hoop **32** and brace **34**, in turn secured at **36** to one side of the tank. At the lowermost end of the vertical pipe is an additional screw conveyor **38** consisting of a conventional screw entirely enclosed by the conduit excepting at the uppermost end **40** where it is in communication with the discharge end of pipe **30** and at the lowermost end where it discharges into a conveyor or hopper **42**. The screw of conveyor **38** is operated by motor and gear reducer system, generally **44**, and by chain drive **46**.

The process is dependent on the fact that conventional crushing adds a significant amount of air, finely dispersed, to grape pulp. Because of the fibrous, fluffy nature of the pulp, the air remains incorporated therein and may be used in a system to buoy up the pulp. Furthermore, after crushing, when the pulp is passed into the separator tank of this process, the natural enzymes continue to work and some of these break down the cell walls of the juice sacs so as to allow the juice to drain. Over generally longer periods of time, other enzymes affect the colloidal material present so as to allow coagulation of this colloidal matter and clarification of the juice. The pulp is pumped into the inlet 18 at a rate such that the surface solids, when ready for removal, contain less than 85% liquid. The pulp in the tank continues to undergo changes, throughout its residence in the tank, allowing the juice to drain out and a change in the colloidal structure so as to permit the juice to break or clarify through the action of the second group of enzymes mentioned above. Simultaneously, the conveyor assembly 26 is rotated and solids containing less than 85% liquid are advanced to the vertical conduit 30 and are discharged by means of the conveyor 38.

As a practical matter, the enzymatic step permitting separation of the pulp and especially the skins from the liquid requires two to four hours for proper drainage, with faster enzyme activity in the early part of the harvest season and a slower enzyme activity and hence slower drainage in the latter part of the season. The second enzyme induced change to which reference has been made, wherein the colloidal material is acted upon by enzymes so as to permit coagulation and clarification of the juice, requires from 3 to 10 hours and generally from 4 to 6 hours, depending upon the condition of the grapes.

Conveniently, this step may take place in a tank separate from that of this process. It may be that an adequate time has been permitted for the break or clarification step when hourly removal of the juice from the collecting tank followed by heating to a temperature of at least 165°F reveals that the juice, either during or shortly after heating, forms floccular masses with clear juice between the floc islands. This control procedure will indicate the time at which the juice is ready for further processing, which generally consists of heating the entire quantity of juice to at least 160°F to kill yeasts and inhibit further enzyme activity.

Therefore, two alternative procedures are possible. After a relatively short period of time when enzymes have simply opened the juice cells sufficiently to permit the juice to drain out and the surface solids have reached a level of something less than 85% liquid, the unclarified juice may be removed from the bottom of the tank through outlet 16 and solids skimmed from the surface. This juice may be placed in a different tank and permitted to remain there for a sufficient period of time for the second stage of enzyme activity, resulting in the break or clarification.

In the alternative, the juice and solids may be retained in the tank 10 for a sufficient period of time to permit both the drainage of a relatively large percentage of the liquid from the solids and also to permit the second stage of enzyme activity wherein the juice clarifies, as determined by the sampling and testing procedure.

Generally, if the tank of this process is to be used at greatest efficiency, however, the clarification step will be permitted to take place in a separate tank, in which case crushed grapes will be fed into the settling tank at a rate equal to the time required to drain the solids to something less than 85% liquid. If this takes two hours at 70° to 90°F, thereby producing a well drained, low liquid content solids layer at the surface and a low solids juice near the bottom of the tank, crushed grapes would be fed to a 30,000 gallon tank at a rate of 15,000 gallons per hour. Generally, the rate of feed will be equal to $\frac{1}{8}$ to $\frac{1}{3}$ of the volume of the vessel.

Example: Processing of White Grapes for Juice Production — 188 tons of Emperor grapes were crushed and pumped into a square concrete tank of 19,000 gallon capacity. When the tank which had a total capacity suitable for 86 tons of grapes was 80% filled, juice draw was started at a rate slightly slower than the addition rate of 30 tons per hour of the crushed grapes. When the tank was full the surface solids were found to be well drained and were then continuously removed with a single auger conveyor with half the auger trough removed. This auger unit slowly swept across the tank surface and removed the surface solids. The juice removed during this run contained 0.5% solids by volume, as determined by centrifuging, and the surface solids contained 82% moisture by weight. The withdrawn juice two hours later was heated to a temperature of 165°F to stop the enzymatic action.

Sulfite Treatment of Pomace

The method of *R.G. Peterson and E.B. Jaffe; U.S. Patent 3,484,254; December 16, 1969; assigned to E & J Gallo Winery* involves the treatment of grape pomace with a sulfite, specifically sulfur dioxide carried in a suitable solvent, in a simple extraction procedure which is readily included as part of a grape treating process commonly employed in commercial juice and wine production operations.

The pomace, after the grapes have been crushed and the pomace has been separated from the natural juices thereof, is treated with a solvent which contains sufficient sulfur dioxide to positively arrest or preclude fermentation of the pomace while simultaneously counteracting the characteristics of the undesirable constituents of the pomace, so that the desirable constituents of the pomace may be dissolved into solution by the solvent.

The exact nature of the chemical reaction which takes place is not fully known but the sulfite treatment is known to result in a reversible altering of the chemical structure of the desirable constituents, as for example anthocyanin pigment, making them adhere less strongly to the pomace solids and therefore more readily soluble in the solvent. After the reversibly altered constituents, such as the pigment, have been extracted from the pomace, such constituents in solution are changed to convert the same back to their original form in a suitable concentration processing step.

The reaction of the anthocyanin pigments, which are chemically defined as polyhydroxy flavylium salts, is a reversible bleaching reaction attributable directly to the inclusion of sulfur dioxide in the treating solvent. This reversible reaction effected on the pigment constituents transforms the pigment molecules, which normally are positively charged, into a colorless form which is uncharged and which is readily removed from the grape pomace solids by the solvent carrying the sulfur dioxide therein. That is, the sulfur dioxide, or the bisulfite ion thereof, contacts the pomace pigment and produces the color changing reaction noted.

After the solvent has performed its intended function, the resulting solution is separated from the depleted and essentially colorless pomace. The sulfur dioxide is then removed from the solution and the pigment carried in the solution reverts back to its original colored form as the solution is condensed and the sulfur dioxide is removed. The remaining juice concentrate possesses true varietal color characteristics and varietal flavor characteristics but without accompanying bitter and astringent characteristics attributable to the presence of tannin.

The improved flavor characteristics of the resulting concentrate become evident from tasting thereof but the presence of these flavor characteristics is not as readily determinable as is the presence of the desirable color constituents which are readily apparent upon visual inspection and comparison with the juice concentrate of similar grapes which have been treated with a conventional solvent extraction process. In this regard, the desirable sugars, acids and pigment constituents are removed from the pomace to an extent heretofore not possible.

Example: A sufficient quantity of fresh ripe Ruby Cabernet grapes were crushed and pressed to obtain 1.3 gallons of fresh juice and two pounds of sweet (unfermented) pomace. The juice thus separated was pink in color and contained only a small portion of the natural Ruby Cabernet color and flavor. The pomace, however, was dark red in color and had a strong Ruby Cabernet aroma and flavor.

The separated pomace was then thoroughly mixed with one liter of fresh water containing 1,000 ppm sulfur dioxide. The color of the pomace bleached out within a few minutes and the resulting solvent solution maintained its nearly water white color. After forty-five minutes the solvent solution was filtered off from the pomace, placed in a suitable flask, and evaporated in vacuo at approximately 28 inches mercury and 110°F to a concentrated volume of 50 ml. This concentrated volume was dark red in color, had a strong natural Ruby Cabernet flavor and aroma, and no undesirable tannin characteristics.

The 50 ml of concentrate thereafter was then added to the 1.3 gallons of fresh grape juice separated immediately after crushing. The resulting product was a dark red juice which possessed strong Ruby Cabernet character and excellent overall flavor and aroma qualities. The juice thereafter was further concentrated in a vacuum concentrator to a Ruby Cabernet concentrate of 65°Balling which had excellent color, varietal character and overall quality.

By way of contrast, a similar quantity of Ruby Cabernet grapes was crushed but the free juice was allowed to stand in contact with the pomace for six hours at room temperature before being separated therefrom. The separated juice was red in color and contained desirable Ruby Cabernet characteristics but was considerably inferior in both color and flavor to the concentrate and resulting juice product to which the concentrate was added as described.

Apparatus to Minimize Mechanical Treatment

It is well known that the flavor of fruit juices, particularly those intended for the production of wine, is sensitive to the mechanical treatment to which the fruit is subjected. This is why the best vintage wines are produced by the ancient method of treading on the grapes. Present day costs, as well as present day standards of sanitation, prohibit the use of this probably optimum treatment.

It is an object of the method of *W.L. Cooley; U.S. Patent 3,592,127; July 13, 1971* therefore, to provide an apparatus for extracting juices from fruit and the like in which the severity of mechanical treatment and compression is minimized. It is a further object of this method to provide a means as aforesaid in which the total output is divided into two parts, one of which undergoes a minimum of mechanical treatment and the second stage of which extracts a maximum possible amount of juice from the material originally supplied.

FIGURE 1.6: APPARATUS TO MINIMIZE MECHANICAL TREATMENT

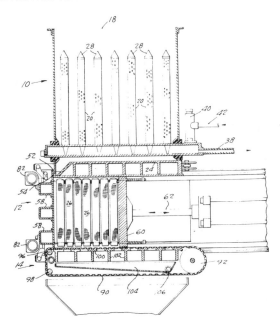

Source: W.L. Cooley; U.S. Patent 3,592,127; July 13, 1971

This enables the first output which has received the most gentle treatment to be reserved for high-quality products and the output of the second stage to be put into a product of less demanding quality. For example, in pressing grapes, the best output can go into quality wine with the second output going to wine of lesser quality or into jellies. At the same time, this method and apparatus, considered as a whole, performs the job of absolute maximum extraction of juice from the particular material.

Apparatus for extracting the juice from fruit and the like is presented in the patent. Said apparatus comprises a vat to receive material to be treated; a plurality of laterally spaced vertical perforated drainage tubes; manifolds receiving juice from said vertical tubes; an outlet connected to said manifolds; a gate forming a bottom for said vat; means for moving said gate into and out of position whereby to dump at least the lower portion of said vat when said gate is out of its vat-bottoming position; a press receiving material from said vat; a plurality of vertical drainage tubes in laterally spaced rows in said press, drainage means below said tubes and means for separating said drainage means from said tubes whereby to permit dumping of the residue from said tubes and means to compress material inside said press and to bring said tubes into mutual close juxtaposition.

Figure 1.6 is a diagram of the apparatus showing the parts in the position occupied at the conclusion of the pressing cycle. Several additional drawings and a detailed description of the process are included in the patent.

TOMATO JUICE

High Viscosity Juice by Acidification During Maceration of Whole Fruit

It is recognized in the industry that consistency is an important attribute of tomato juice. In particular, higher consistency represents better quality. It is to be especially noted that consistency has no fixed relationship with solids contents so that whereas two lots of tomato juice prepared by different procedures and/or different raw materials may have identical solids contents, their consistencies may be radically different.

Consistency of tomato juice may be controlled to some extent by the method of manufacturing the juice, particularly by choice of the cold break method or the hot break method. In the cold break method, raw tomatoes are macerated at ambient temperatures and the resulting pulp is pressed through perforated sheet metal or wire mesh screens to separate the juice from the seeds, skins, cores, etc. This process yields a juice of relatively low consistency due, it is believed, to degradation of pectin-containing colloids by enzymes such as pectinesterase and polygalacturonase which naturally occur in the fruit.

In the hot break method, the same mechanical steps are used but in addition heat is applied, i.e., the tomatoes, during maceration or immediately after they are broken up, are quickly heated to a temperature of 185°F or higher so as to inactivate the enzymes responsible for the loss of consistency. The juice obtained in this technique has a higher consistency than that produced by the cold break system and thus the hot break procedure is generally preferred in industry.

In accordance with the process of *J.R. Wagner, J.C. Miers and H.K. Burr; U.S. Patent 3,366,490; January 30, 1968; assigned to U.S. Secretary of Agriculture* the basic step to achieve a juice of increased consistency involves macerating raw tomatoes in the presence of added acid. For use as the added acid, hydrochloric acid is preferred because it is effective, inexpensive, and particularly because eventual neutralization of the produce (with sodium hydroxide) yields sodium chloride, a common additive in tomato products.

The hydrochloric acid may be added as such or in the form of hydrogen chloride gas. Moreover, acids other than hydrochloric can be employed as the primary consideration in the establishment of a low pH. Thus, for example, one may employ such strongly ionized acids as sulfuric, orthophosphoric, metaphosphoric, and pyrophosphoric. Weaker acids such as tartaric or citric may also be used. However, though effective, these weaker acids are not preferred because large proportions are required to attain the necessary reduction in pH.

In general, it has been observed that addition of enough acid to establish a pH in the macerate of less than 3.5 will provide an increase in consistency over that attained in the absence of added acid. Moreover, as the pH is reduced below the aforesaid level, greater increases in consistency are achieved. It has also been observed that as the pH is reduced below about 2, little if any further increase in consistency is attained. Thus, whereas the pH may be decreased to very low levels, there is no practical purpose gained by going below a pH of 1.

Usually, it is preferable to operate at a pH range of 2.5 to 3.0, particularly in a system where maceration is conducted hot, whereby a large increase in consistency is achieved without requiring excessive amounts of added acid. As noted above, the primary consideration of the added acid is to establish a reduced pH. However, there is some variation in effect between different acids applied at the same pH and this is particularly noticeable with metaphosphoric acid which provides a virtually maximum increase in consistency at a pH of 2.97.

Addition of the acid will produce a juice of excessively sour taste. Accordingly, the product is neutralized to its normal pH (usually in the range 3.8 to 4.2) by incorporation of sodium hydroxide. Other alkaline materials such as sodium carbonate or bicarbonate may be used but are not preferred because of their foaming effect (caused by release of CO_2). The neutralization can be applied to the juice, or preferably, to the macerate prior to passing it to the juice extractor. In the event that a cold break system is used, the juice (or macerate) should be heated to an enzyme inactivating temperature (185° to 212°F) before application of the neutralization step.

Such heating will prevent loss of consistency when the effect of the added acid is cancelled by the neutralization. The process is further demonstrated by the following illustrative example. The macerating and blending operations referred to in the example were carried out in a large Waring Blendor equipped with a 1 gallon bowl and a rotating blade assembly in the base of the bowl to cut and blend the material contained therein. Where the material was to be concomitantly heated, a steam heated coil was inserted in the bowl in contact with the material undergoing treatment.

In the example, the following procedure was applied. After maceration and blending, with or without application of heat, the juice was extracted from the macerate by passing the latter through a tapered screw-type extractor provided with a perforated metal screen (0.033 inch perforations). Consistency of the juice products was determined at 25°C (77°F) by measuring the time required for 96 ml of the liquid to pass through the 3.3 mm (i.d.) orifice of a 100 ml pipette. With this test, a longer flow time reflects a higher consistency.

Example: Effect of Added HCl in Preparing Cold Break and Hot Break — Four kg of ripe T-2 variety tomatoes were subdivided into four comparable 1 kg lots by quartering each fruit and distributing the quarters to the four lots. Each lot was then treated as shown below.

Lot 1: Macerated and blended at room temperature for 1.5 minutes.

Lot 2: Eighteen ml of concentrated hydrochloric acid were added to the tomatoes; maceration and blending at room temperature was then applied for 1.5 minutes.

Lot 3: Macerated and blended, initially at room temperature for 10 seconds then with a steam coil in the system for an additional 102 seconds to bring the macerate to 203°F.

Lot 4: Same treatment as with Lot 3 except that 18 ml of concentrated hydrochloric acid was added to the tomatoes before initiating the process.

Immediately following the above treatments, each lot was separately passed through the extractor. The juice from each lot was brought to 25°C (77°F) and tested for consistency, density, and pH. The results are tabulated below.

Treatment	Lot 1	Lot 2	Lot 3	Lot 4
	Cold-break	Cold-break	Hot-break	Hot-break
Acid added (ml. conc. HCl per kg.)..	None	18	None	18
Consistency, sec	24.4	57.2	22.4	97.6
Density, deg. Brix	5.5	6.5	5.9	6.6
pH	4.22	1.08	4.10	1.04

It is evident from the above data that the acidification improved the consistency of both the cold break juice (Lot 2 vs. Lot 1) and the hot break juice (Lot 4 vs. Lot 3) and that the combination of acidification plus hot break (Lot 4) provided the highest consistency. The acidified hot break juice (Lot 4) was restored to the natural pH level (4.2) by addition of sodium hydroxide. Consistency of the neutralized juice was 117 sec, proving that the high consistency of the acidified hot break product was a stable property. In the case of the acidified cold break juice (Lot 2) direct neutralization (to pH 4.2 with NaOH) caused a sharp drop in consistency to 19 sec. This loss in consistency could, however, be prevented by heating the juice to an enzyme inactivating temperature (185° to 212°F) prior to its neutralization.

High Viscosity Juice After Acidification of Liberated Juice

J.R. Wagner, J.C. Miers and H.K. Burr; U.S. Patent 3,366,488; January 30, 1968; assigned to U.S. Secretary of Agriculture have found that production of juice of increased consistency is achieved when the added acid is applied, not to raw tomatoes, but to tomato material which previously has been subjected to heating to inactivate enzymes.

The application of the principles of the process to the production of tomato juice of increased consistency is illustrated by the following detailed description. Raw tomatoes, at their natural pH, are subjected to heating to inactivate the enzymes. This heating can be accomplished in various ways. One technique involves exposing whole tomatoes or pieces of tomatoes to steam or to a source of radiant energy such as infrared lamps or a microwave irradiation device. Preferably, the tomatoes are heated while concomitantly subjected to maceration.

To achieve such an end, one may utilize the usual heating and macerating procedure in producing tomato juice by the hot break system. Thus, raw tomatoes are fed into a vessel provided with steam coils (or steam jackets) and a rotating blade assembly for comminuting the tomatoes and agitating the material in the vessel so that good heat transfer will be obtained. By use of such equipment the raw tomatoes can be efficiently formed into a hot macerate which is ready for the next step.

In cases where it is desired to achieve an especially rapid heating, one may employ a drop-in technique. This involves establishing a pool of tomato juice or tomato macerate (from a previous batch) in a vessel equipped with heating means and a rotor for comminuting and mixing the contents of the vessel. The pool of juice is maintained at 200°F and the tomatoes are fed into it at a predetermined rate. Because of the intimate contact with the hot juice, the entering tomato material is very rapidly brought up to an enzyme inactivating temperature.

The hot macerate produced in the vessel is withdrawn at a rate commensurate with the feed rate and this hot material is forwarded to the next step in the procedure. The temperature and time of heating applied to the tomatoes should be sufficient to inactivate the enzymes, but not so drastic as to damage the tomato material. After the tomatoes have been heated to inactivate the enzymes, the resulting tomato material, preferably in the form of a macerate, is mixed with an acid.

After the tomato material has been intimately mixed with the added acid, the acidified macerate is treated by any of several optional routes to produce a juice. In one alternative system, the acidified macerate without any delay is passed through conventional equipment to separate the juice from the skins, seeds, cores, etc. The juice is then neutralized to its normal pH (usually in the range 3.8 to 4.5) by incorporation of sodium hydroxide. Other alkaline materials such as sodium carbonate or bicarbonate may be used but are not preferred because of their foaming effect (caused by release of CO_2). A more preferable alternative involves first neutralizing the acidified pulp to restore it to the natural pH, as described above, and then passing the pulp to the juice extractor.

Example: In these runs, the starting material was heated by a drop-in technique to attain rapid inactivation of enzyme. Thus, a heated (200°F) pool of tomato juice was provided to serve as a direct contact heating medium. Tomatoes were fed into this pool in portions, while applying macerating action and heating to maintain the system at 200°F. Because of the intimate contact with the hot juice, the entering tomato material was very rapidly brought up to the desired temperature.

More particulars of the procedure used are given. The runs were carried out employing a large Waring Blendor equipped with a 1 gallon bowl and a rotating blade assembly in the base of the bowl to cut and blend the material contained therein. A steam coil was also provided for heating the material in the bowl.

At the beginning of each run, 500 grams of previously prepared tomato juice was placed in the blender and heated to 200°F and maintained in the range of 190° to 200°F throughout the run while rotating the blade continuously. A 1 kg lot of fresh tomatoes (cut into quarters) was divided into four portions and these portions were fed into the hot juice at 15 second intervals. At 2 minutes from the start of the run, heating was discontinued (by removing the stream coil from the bowl) but operation of the blade was continued to complete breakdown of any fragments of intact tissue.

At this point, hydrochloric acid was added to the macerate in an amount to provide a particular pH (as specified below). After the acid was blended into the macerate (approximately 4 minutes from the start of the run), the macerate was put through a pulper to separate the juice from the skins, seeds, etc. and the juice was cooled. It was then tested for pH and consistency. (In one run, no acid was used, thus to provide a control.) The juice used as the heated liquid for the runs was a conventional juice. It was prepared by macerating raw tomatoes at their natural pH without any additives, heating to destroy enzymes, and extraction of the juice from the macerate with a conventional pulper. The results are tabulated below.

Run	Acid Added	pH	Consistency of Juice,* seconds
1 (control)	None	4.48	30.3
2	HCl	3.10	43.3
3	HCl	2.52	58.5
4	HCl	1.47	63.7

*Consistency was determined at 25°C by measuring the time required for 200 ml of the juice to pass through the 0.125 inch (i.d.) orifice of a 250-ml pipette.

High Viscosity Juice from Acid-Alkaline Treatment

J.R. Wagner and J.C. Miers; U.S. Patent 3,366,489; January 30, 1968; assigned to U.S. Secretary of Agriculture found that an increase in pH is also effective to obtain juices of increased consistency. Thus, in accordance with the preferred embodiment of this process, the basic step involves macerating raw tomatoes in the presence of added alkali.

Usually, sodium hydroxide is preferred for use as the added alkali because it is effective, relatively inexpensive and because eventual neutralization of the produce (with hydrochloric acid) yields sodium chloride, a common additive in tomato products. However, other nontoxic alkalis can be employed as the primary consideration is an increase in pH. Thus, such alkalis as potassium hydroxide, sodium or potassium carbonate, or the like may be employed.

In general, it has been observed that addition of enough alkali to establish a pH in the macerate of 5 will provide a substantial increase in consistency over that attained in the absence of added alkali. Usually, it is preferred to use sufficient alkali to provide a pH of from 5.5 to 8.5, whereby to yield a large increase in consistency. Generally, as the pH is increased above 8.5 the degree of consistency improvement tends to taper off. For this reason, pH's above 8.5, particularly above 9, are preferably avoided. In conducting particular runs, the pH may be varied within the above ranges depending on such factors as the consistency desired and the nature of the tomatoes being processed, i.e., the consistency they would yield in absence of added alkali.

A preferred embodiment of the process involves a combination procedure utilizing both an acid treatment similar to that described in the previous patent and the alkali treatment of this process. A typical system involves the following.

(1) A lot of tomatoes is divided into two batches.

(2) One batch of tomatoes is macerated and heated, for example, to 200°F, to inactivate enzymes. A nontoxic acid is added to the macerate in an amount required to establish a pH less then 3.5. (Hydrochloric acid is usually used but other acids stronger than acetic, as above exemplified, can also be used.) After mixing in the acid, the macerate is passed through a screw press or other conventional device to separate the juice from the skins, seeds, etc.

(3) The other batch of tomatoes is macerated with added alkali to produce a macerate of pH above 5. This macerate is then heated to 200°F, and then put through a screw press or other conventional device to separate the juice from the skins, seeds, etc.

(4) The juices from steps 2 and 3 are then blended to produce a juice product which is not only of increased consistency but of natural pH.

It is evident from the above that the combination procedure results in utilizing the added acid and the added alkali for both their consistency increasing action and their neutralizing action. A further modification of the process is concerned with a procedure for increasing the consistency of previously prepared tomato juices. The starting material for this procedure is a tomato juice, preferably of high pectin content, prepared by standard techniques. To such juice alkali is added to increase the pH above 5. Preferably, alkali is added to give a pH of 6 or 7. Into this mixture is stirred a minor proportion, 5 to 25%, of raw juice.

The mixture is held for a short period, heated to inactivate enzymes, and then restored to the natural pH of the tomato material by addition of a nontoxic acid. The product will be found to be of high consistency, and in most cases to form a gel particularly useful in aspic products. The process is further demonstrated by the following example.

The macerating and blending operation referred to in the example was carried out in a large Waring Blendor, equipped with a 1 gallon bowl and a rotating blade assembly in the base of the bowl to cut and blend the material contained therein. Where the material was to be concomitantly heated, a steam heated coil was inserted in the bowl in contact with the material undergoing treatment.

After maceration and blending, with or without application of heat, the juice was extracted from the macerate by passing the latter through a tapered screw-type extractor provided with a perforated metal screen (0.033 inch perforations). Consistency of the juice product was determined at 25°C (77°F) by measuring the time required for 96 ml of the liquid to pass through the 3.3 mm (i.d.) orifice of a 100 ml pipette.

Example: A batch of raw tomatoes was quartered and divided into a series of 1 kg lots. Each of these lots was then treated as follows.

Lot 1 (blank):   Macerated and blended, initially for 10 seconds at room temperature, then with a steam coil in the system for an additional 2.5 minutes to
bring the macerate to 200°F.

Lot 2: Same as Lot 1 except 12 ml of 12N HCl was added to the tomatoes before
initiating the maceration.

Lots 3, 4, 5:   Same as Lot 1 except that 16, 20, and 24 ml, respectively of 3N
NaOH solution was added to the tomatoes prior to starting the maceration.

Following these treatments, each lot of hot macerate was separately passed through the
extractor. The resulting juices were collected for evaluation. The results are tabulated below.

Lot	Additive	pH of Juice	Consistency of Juice, sec
1	None	4.09	27
2	HCl	1.43	213
3	NaOH	5.52	98
4	NaOH	5.63	88
5	NaOH	6.19	109

Juice No. 2 (derived from the acid treatment) was then formed into blends with the juices
prepared by the alkali treatment. In each case, the proportions of juices were designed to
yield a composite juice having a pH approximately the same as that of the control (Lot 1,
pH 4.09). The results are tabulated below.

Blend	Composition	pH	Consistency
A	1 part #2, 3 parts #3	4.09	Gelled
B	5 parts #2, 12 parts #4	4.28	Gelled
C	3 parts #2, 5 parts #5	3.73	Fluid, but too thick for consistency determination

Apparatus for Minimizing Enzyme Action

It is known that by cutting or chopping a fruit such as a tomato, enzymic action will immediately occur with the result of a 20 to 25% loss in the pectin content of the tomato.
*W.L. Prosser; U.S. Patent 3,835,763; September 17, 1974; assigned to F.H. Langsenkamp
Company* describes a method and apparatus for obtaining juices from tomatoes by heating
the tomatoes to minimize enzymic action. The method includes the steps of heating the
tomatoes to a minimum temperature of 190°F or higher and then chopping the tomatoes
so as to allow the juices to flow into a vat.

The apparatus has a rotatable heating element mounted within a vat receiving the tomatoes
through a chute. A rotating cutter is mounted to the vat immediately adjacent the bottom
open end of the chute and immediately above the heating element. A conveyor drops the
tomatoes into the chute where they are then heated by the heated juices circulated within
the vat prior to cutting.

Referring now to Figures 1.7a and 1.7b, there is shown an apparatus **10** for obtaining juices
from tomatoes while reducing enzymic action. The apparatus includes a vat **11** having a
bottom end **12** and an open top end **13**. Flange **14** is attached to the vat and extends
therearound receiving the top ends of poles **15** for the mounting of the vat. Chute **16** is
mounted to the top end **13** of the vat. The chute includes an open top end **17** through
which the tomatoes fall from conveyor **18**. Side wall **19** of the chute extends vertically
downward and then curves around cutter **20** at location **21**.

Side wall **19** terminates at a location **36**. Side wall **22** of the chute extends vertically downward and then converges toward wall **19** terminating at location **23** immediately above cutter

20 and above the axis of rotation 24 of the cutter. Cutter 24 includes a rod 25 which is rotatably mounted by bushings 26 to vat 11. Rod 25 extends sealingly through the side wall of the vat having a sprocket 27 mounted thereon which is drivingly coupled to motor 28. A plurality of blades 29 are fixedly mounted to the rod with each blade having an equal length so as to just clear the bottom edge 23 of wall 22 and the inside surface of the curved portion of wall 19 with the cutter rotating. Blades 29 extend radially outward from rod 25 with the blades being positioned under chute 16.

A heating element is rotatably mounted to the side walls of the vat. The heating element includes a pair of hollow coils 30a and 30b which are helically wound about shaft 31 mounted to and between coupling 31a and 31b. Steam enters a flexible stationary hose 50 which is connected to rotary coupling 51 which is attached to sprocket 52 in driving engagement with chain 34 rotated by motor 35. Coupling 31a is connected by various fastening devices to sprocket 52 so that one revolution of the sprocket will cause one revolution of shaft 31.

The opposite end of shaft 31 connected to coupling 31b is in turn coupled to various couplings and fastening devices to the outlet flexible hose 53. Thus, steam enters heating element 30 via hose 50 whereas condensate exits the heating element and returns back to the central heating system via hose 53. Suitable bearings are provided for the rotatable mounting of heating element 30. In addition, suitable packing is provided adjacent to the side walls of the vat through which the hollow rods extend which are coupled to heating element 30 and hoses 50 and 53.

FIGURE 1.7: APPARATUS FOR MINIMIZING ENZYME ACTION

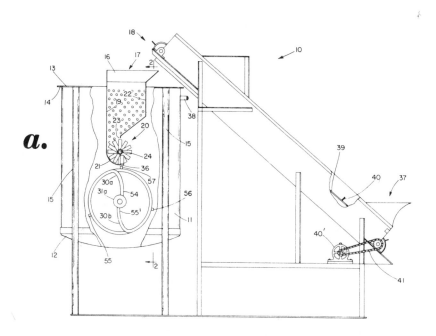

Fragmentary View of Apparatus

(continued)

FIGURE 1.7: (continued)

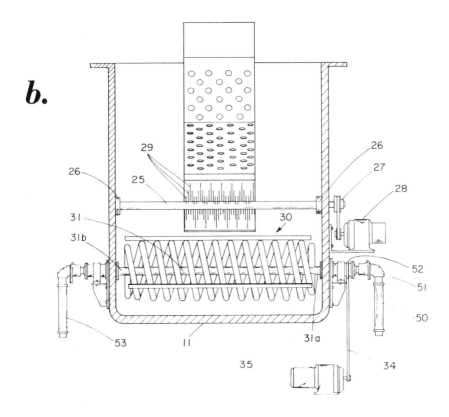

b.

Cross Section Along Line 2–2 of Figure 1.7a

Source: W.L. Prosser; U.S. Patent 3,835,763; September 17, 1974

Coupling **31a** is hollow and is connected to a hollow rod projecting through the vat side wall and fixedly connected to sprocket **52**. End **54** of coil **30a** is connected to coupling **31a** for receiving the steam. Likewise, end **55'** of coil **30b** is connected to coupling **31a** for receiving the steam. Likewise, the opposite ends of coils **30a** and **30b** are connected to coupling **31b** which in turn is connected to a hollow rod extending through the vat side wall for directing the condensate into flexible hose **53**.

Three agitator bars **55, 56** and **57** are mounted to heating element **30**, 120° apart around the axis of rotation of the heating element. The agitator bars are fixedly mounted to spokes which project inwardly being fixedly mounted to the heating element. Thus, as the heating element is rotated, the agitator bars will increase the agitation of the juices within the vat. All of the side walls of chute **16** are perforated to allow the heated juices within the vat to flow through the chute thereby heating the tomatoes within the chute. After the tomatoes are picked from the vine and cleaned, the tomatoes are positioned in hopper **37** and conveyed upwardly by conveyor **18** so as to be dropped into chute **16**. In certain cases, the elevation of chute **16** will be such that conveyor **18** will not be required. Heating element **30** is connected to a source of steam. In one embodiment, the steam pressure was approximately 150 psi. The heating element is rotated to provide for uniform heating throughout the vat. The juices within the vat are thereby heated and circulated through the vat as the heating element is rotated so as to pass through chute 16 to heat the tomatoes within the chute to a minimum temperature of 190°F or higher.

The perforated walls of chute 16 allow the juices to pass therethrough so as to be in direct contact with the tomatoes. The method includes the step of allowing the tomatoes to sink through chute 16 to cutter 20 which breaks the skins of each tomato by a cutting, chopping and mashing operation.

OTHER JUICES

Carrot, Celery, and Cabbage Juices

F.G. Keitel; U.S. Patent 3,420,676; January 7, 1969 describes a method for the production of durably preserved vegetable juices with simultaneous recovery of lactic-acidic residues by lactic acid fermentation and subsequent pasteurization, comprising the steps of producing a vegetable mash, exposing said vegetable mash to lactic fermentation until the pH value has dropped to below 4.5, admixing the fermented acid vegetable mash with an unfermented mash, then squeezing the juice out of the vegetable mash, and pasteurizing the squeezed-out juice.

By performing the lactic acid fermentation on the mash rather than on the juices themselves, the taste of the juices recovered from the fermented mash is less pronouncedly sour. Examples of juices obtained in this manner are carrot juice, celery juice, and cabbage juice.

Pretreatment of Carrots with Acid

T.S. Stephens, G. Saldana and H.E. Brown; U.S. Patent 3,787,589; January 22, 1974; assigned to the U.S. Secretary of Agriculture describe a process for preparing carrot juice which incorporates a step of cooking in an acidic aqueous solution the whole carrots immediately prior to juice extraction.

Several different process modifications of vegetable juice extraction and of preservation are practiced in the manufacture of carrot juice. Some start with washed raw (peeled or unpeeled), blanched (water or steam), or cooked carrots. Some extract juice from whole carrots by means of an hydraulic press; others pass the carrots through a hammer mill, other type comminutor, or an homogenizer, prior to separation of the juice and fiber by means of presses, finishers, screens, centrifuges or other items of liquid-solid separation equipment to give maximum yield of a juice with body (density), smooth creamy mouthfeel, and characteristic carrot flavor.

Heretofore in the case of all the prior art processes, a problem arises if juice extracted from fresh raw carrots is heated to about 180°F before or during conventional canning practices. An unsightly, unappetizing coagulum forms. Canning practices typically involve heating the separated juice in a heat-exchanger, or exhausting the juice in the container, followed by retorting for periods of from 22 to 30 minutes at temperatures of from 240° to 250°F.

Time and temperature combinations are determined by such variables as the initial temperature of the preheated juice, can size, and juice acidity. Acidification of carrot juice allows some reduction in sterilization time and temperature or both. Regardless of whether the freshly extracted juice is acidified within palatability ranges, neutralized, or homogenized, a coagulum forms in the processed product after it has been exposed to conventional canning temperatures. This coagulum limits the market acceptance of canned carrot juice and deprives the vegetable processing industry of a profitable outlet for utilizing surplus and edible cull carrots. In general, the process for the preparation of carrot juice having improved properties involves the following.

(1) Submerging washed whole carrots in an 0.05N to 0.1N solution of a food grade acid

such as acetic, citric, fumaric, malic, lactic, succinic, phosphoric or hydrochloric at boiling temperature. The normality required of any selected acid will be that normality required to yield an extracted juice with a pH within the range 5.5 to 5.3. It is recognized that a lower pH may be used but results with acidities above pH 5.6 tend to be erratic.

It is important that the whole carrots be treated in this step and not cut, chopped, or ground carrots since as will be shown later on, the acid treatment of chopped or ground material causes the carotene or color constituents to remain in the exhausted pulp and not pass on into the extracted carrot juice. Chopping or grinding prior to the recommended acid treatment adversely affects both juice color and juice yield.

(2) Cooking the carrots in the acidified boiling cover medium (i.e., the carrots were submerged in one medium) for approximately 5 minutes. Time intervals can vary slightly depending on the size of the carrots. However, optimum time intervals for yield and for prevention of the formation of a coagulum can easily be determined by preliminary tests.

Other steps in the overall process involve washing, grading selection, extraction and canning treatments and follow those practiced in the industry. The acidified extracted carrot juice may be neutralized before further processing depending upon contemplated end use and taste preferences.

Example: Whole Imperator carrots were covered with (submerged in) approximately 8 gallons of a 0.05N acetic acid solution and different batches were cooked at 212°F for 5 minutes. The acid solution was drained from the carrots. Juice yields ranged in 9 tests from 69.3 to 75.8%. The results of the analysis of the canned juice are presented in the following table.

Sample number	Percent					Color		
	Juice yield	Light trans.	Brix	pH	Acid, percent	Rd	a	b
1	69.8	33	8.0	5.4	.11	25.5	36.2	34.9
2	66.9	31	10.4	5.3	.13	25.1	33.7	35.2
3	72.2	33	9.0	5.4	.16	23.3	27.8	34.9
4	72.1	35	8.6	5.4	.16	23.4	27.3	35.0
5	74.2	39	8.6	5.4	.16	23.2	25.3	34.7
6	75.8	43	8.4	5.5	.15	23.1	29.3	34.6
7	69.3	33	9.6	5.5	.16	22.7	31.7	34.7
8	71.9	31	9.7	5.3	.16	24.0	31.8	34.6
9	72.9	38	9.4	5.4	.15	23.3	30.9	34.5

A coagulum did not form in any of the juice samples extracted from carrots which had been heated in an acidified medium. The percentage light which could be transmitted through the juice varied from 31 to 43%. The color of the juice was brighter orange than the color of the juice extracted from carrots cooked 5 minutes in water. The pH of the juice varied from 5.3 to 5.5. The flavor of the juice was rated excellent and was in no way damaged by the acid cooking treatment.

By way of comparison, carrot juice prepared without any pretreatment exhibited 95 to 100% light transmission. Juice prepared by pretreatment in boiling water containing no acid showed 42 to 59% transmission.

Pineapple Processing

A pineapple is a multiple fruit composed of a large number of fruitlets growing from a central stem commonly called the core. Each fruitlet is a portion of a small flower which forms off the stem before the fruit matures. The flowers mature from the lower end of the fruit upward just as subsequently the fruitlets mature progressively upward. As a result the pineapple at the lower end of the fruit is usually more flavorful and contains less fiber and more sugar than the upward portions.

The part of the pineapple in the core is fibrous and woody but is clean and suitable for use in juice though its fruit quality is somewhat lower than some outer portions. Outward from the core is the fruit cylinder portion of prime pineapple meat used in cutting the familiar pineapple rings. As the outside of the fruitlet and its skin covering are approached from the central cylinder, the fruit becomes less porous and contains a greater amount of fiber which is attached to the skin. The fruit in this area is marred by the presence of the deep blossom cups or eye cavities and embedded insect carcasses but the fruit quality is excellent: it has good flavor, good color and fine texture. It also contains a high percentage of aromatics and vitamins and makes an excellent juice product.

It has been customary in pineapple processing to feed the whole fruit into an automatic machine which cuts off both ends, cores the cylinder and trims the cylinder from the shell. An early example of such a machine is shown in U.S. Patent 1,060,250 to Ginaca. The thus treated fruit comprising the hollow fruit cylinder is appropriately sliced, canned and sold. The core has been used in the past for crushed pineapple or juice and the fruit adjacent the shell similarly has been processed into crushed pineapple or juice, usually both.

The shell has been flattened out skin side down against a corrugated table or a cleated moving belt and a knife called an eradicator has shaved the juicy meat portion from the top of the shell for use in the crush pack. Lest the crush pack be contaminated care has been taken to avoid making this cut so deep as to include the eyes and embedded specks adjacent the skin. A thin second eradicator cut has been made for use in the juice pack and has included a portion of this contaminated zone and been carefully disintegrated.

As a result the rich meat adjacent the skin which contains a high amount of valuable aromatics has not been used in quality juice. Alternatively, processors have made their second cut deeply to garner this rich meat at the expense of also including contaminants and have later very finely disintegrated the entire cut so that the objectionable specks become so small as to be not visible in the juice. This latter processing is subject to criticism in the trade as well as by governmental inspectors.

F.J. Cygan and J. Farmer; U.S. Patent 3,318,709; May 9, 1967; assigned to Pennsalt Chemicals Corporation provide a pineapple juice process in which the rich outer portions of the pineapple adjacent the skin and rich in quality juice may be used to the greatest advantage and still avoid undue contamination of the juice pack with eyes, insect specks, etc.

For the preparation of juice two successive cuts are made by the eradicator into the fruit. The first eradicator cut may be set to come within $1/32$" of the top of the eyes and hence includes little or no portions of the eyes, insect specks, etc. The fruit of this cut is the best flavored in the pineapple. It is less fibrous than material near the core or the skin and contains a high proportion of soft celled fruit. It contains a portion of the carpel and septum and is composed of fully developed mature fruit parts and its structure is soft and porous and its solids after disintegration are preferred for a high quality juice.

The second cut which may be set for about $3/16$" from the outside of the skin does not contain substantial amounts of eyes, insect specks, etc. This setting is well toward the skin from the second eradicator cuts of the prior art and this greater depth into an area extremely rich in juice represents one of the advantages of the process. The second eradicator cut is made at least $1/16$" deeper than formerly and utilization of this additional material in the juice means higher yields of juice.

It is possible to use this outer material which formerly has been eschewed because of its eye and speck contaminants. It has been found that the product of this second eradicator cut which has high fruit quality contains short radial fibers that lend little support to the fruit structure and that this fragile material may be easily broken into small pieces. Such gentle breaking leaves the eyes and insect specks intact for later simple separation from the fruit, preferably by centrifuging.

FIGURE 1.8: PINEAPPLE PROCESSING

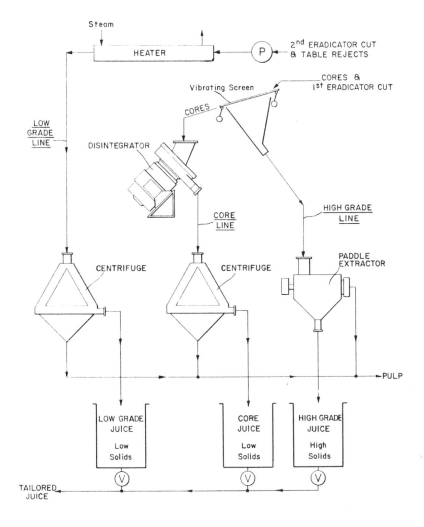

Source: F.J. Cygan and J. Farmer; U.S. Patent 3,318,709; May 9, 1967

Under a process embodying the method as diagrammed in Figure 1.8, the material from the first eradicator cut along with the cylindrical cores from the Ginaca machine is delivered to a vibrating screen which may be comprised of ½" diameter rods spaced on 1¼" centers. The soft meat portions of the first eradicator meat will fall through the openings in the screen while the cores will remain on the top of the sloping screen and move to a disintegrating device. The disintegrating device may be a Reitz disintegrator. Such a machine will comprise a rotating shaft with fixed or pivoted disintegrating arms to which the fruit is introduced axially.

The arms are surrounded by a screen through which the material may pass after it has been appropriately reduced in size. In a form of the process the openings in the disintegrator screen are ¼". The material emerges from the disintegrator as a free-flowing clean sweet juice containing small sharp free-draining fibers. This material is passed directly to a centrifuge in the preferred form of the process. The machine preferred is of the rotary perforate frusto-conical basket type in which feed is delivered to the smaller end and the separated solids discharge from the wider end. A screw conveyor controls movement of the solids through the machine. The particular machine may have screen openings of 0.030", 0.020" to 0.040" being the preferred range.

The solids from the centrifuge are led to the pulp line as shown and may later be pressed to recover some juice values. The liquid discharge of the centrifuge, being sweet and having low solids content is collected and conducted to a container for subsequent blending. The soft eradicated material which passed through the vibrating screen is funneled into a paddle extractor in which a rotary paddle rotating at high speed, for instance, 400 to 500 rpm tumbles the fruit inside a perforate cylinder breaking it up to small sizes and forces them through the perforations. This is a disintegrating action. The high solids material passing through the screen is collected and stored in a high grade juice container for subsequent use as in a blended product, while the solid discharge passes to the pulp line for pressing.

The second eradicator cut which is juicy but contains contaminants as noted is led to a low grade processing line along with table rejects. Table rejects comprise the customary pineapple ring slices which because of being slightly over or under ripe or badly formed are unacceptable for the solid pack. It may include bits of skin, especially if it comes from the small end of the fruit and some coarse fiber. For this reason it is processed by the gentle low grade line.

In the preferred form of the process the material for the low grade line is received by a pump, preferably one of the well-known Moyno type which gently breaks the pieces of fruit, reducing their size and fluidizing them. The action of the pump, however, is not so violent or thorough as to disintegrate the eyes or inspect parts, but is gentle breaking action. It should be noted that this action may be achieved by other means as, for instance, a pair of cooperating rollers or a mangle set to break the fruit but not disintegrate the eyes, insects, etc. However, a pump is selected since it not only breaks the fruit but also conveys it through the line.

From the pump or equivalent device the broken fruit with contaminants progresses to a heat exchanger. This may be in the form of a steam jacketed pipe. The exchange walls are heated by the steam to raise the temperature of the fruit to about 170°F, at least 160°F, to break the cell walls and release the juice from the fruit. It will be understood that the material in the line is a slurry so that it is easily moved on.

Subsequent to the heater the solids are separated from the liquid. This is preferably accomplished by a centrifuge of the same type as is used in the line for disintegrated fruit. Because they have not been disintegrated the eyes and insect specks are easily removed. In the low grade line, however, to assure that the eyes and insect carcasses are not part of the liquid discharge, the openings of the centrifuge basket are preferably smaller than in the core line.

The openings may be in the range 0.015" to 0.030", 0.020" being most preferred. The liquid discharge from the machine is largely liquid with low solids. This liquid discharge is led to a container as shown for subsequent blending or other use. The solids discharge or pulp may be joined with the other solids discharges for additional extraction as in a press.

It will be noted that the liquid discharges from the various separating devices are collected separately. Each is characterized by individual and separate characteristics of taste, solids content, Brix-acid content, etc. From the respective containers the liquid discharges may be blended as desired to constitute a juice product of characteristics best for the selected end use. This is one of the major advantages of the process, as it has long been known that to mix all juice materials together to produce a single grade of standard juice drastically limits the sales possibilities of the product.

In the process juice products are tailored with the particular end use in mind. For instance, a single strength juice can be prepared by blending the products of the three juice lines and the blending can be carefully controlled to achieve the desired 17 to 24% solids content and the desired flavor, for instance, drawing more from the high grade juice or low grade juice line to increase or decrease solids content.

For frozen concentrate, juice can be tailored from the products of the high grade juice line and the core line to give the most satisfactory combination of solids and Brix-acid content. For blending with other fruit juices the low grade line juice with strong flavor is selected as the heavy proportion of the blend. For fancy syrups the product of the core line (low in solids and high in sugar) after passing through an evaporator to increase the sugar concentration is found highly desirable as the predominate part.

The high grade line comprising the first eradicator cut material of highest quality and purity is ideally suitable for baby foods. On the other hand, for a pineapple nectar material the low grade line with some eradicator meat containing some amounts of skin for flavor is ideally suitable.

CLARIFIED JUICE

Single Step Process for Polished Juices

Several methods have been devised, and numerous methods have been proposed, for the production of polished juices. In commercial methods, the whole fruit or vegetable is first comminuted into discrete pieces and pressed in a press or centrifuged, separating the juice from solid portions of the fruit. Several types of presses have been employed for this purpose, primarily of the hydraulic or screw types. When using a hydraulic type of press, the fruit or vegetable, usually already comminuted, is placed between filter cloths in a filter rack and subjected to high pressures.

The juice escapes through the cloth, leaving the pulp behind. For economic reasons most of the industry in recent years has turned to the continuously operating and more sanitary screw type presses, or to Willmes-type air-actuated squeeze-type presses, or the like. Although these latter type presses are economically advantageous, they still require considerable labor to operate and clean. Moreover, regardless of the type of press employed, the juice obtained from the pressing step still contains excessive insoluble solids, at least about 1 and often as high as 10%, and therefore requires at least one further filtration step before it can be considered a polished juice.

In an alternate procedure, a substantial part of the juice may be extracted from the comminuted fruit or vegetable by centrifugation, and the wet residual pulp then pressed to recover the considerable remaining juice and render the process economic. The combined juices then require a further filtration to produce a polished juice. In many cases, when a polished juice. e.g., grape juice, is to be produced commercially, a long period of standing in huge settling tanks, e.g., for up to about three months, is required to allow insoluble solids to settle prior to the filtration.

Although many variations and improvements have been made in these general methods, all require at least two separate steps in which the juice is separated from insoluble solids, whether by pressing, centrifugation, filtration, or some other technique. Moreover, all previous commercial methods require pressing and/or centrifugation, followed by a further filtration or equivalent step for separation of insoluble solids.

A.F. Murch and J.A. Murch; U.S. Patent 3,236,655; February 22, 1966 provide a method for the production of polished juices wherein the juice is separated from insoluble solids in a single step. The whole fruit or vegetable is pulverized into a fine pulverulent fluid mass comprising both solids and juice, treated with a depectinizing enzyme to depectinize the mass, the depectinizing enzyme inactivated, a filter aid added to the pulverulent mass, and the fluid mass then filtered to yield the final polished juice in a single solids separation step, without the use of a press and without the need of further filtration. Because the method is continuous, gives increased yields of polished juice or juice concentrate, and obviates the use of labor and time-consuming presses, centrifuges, and two separate separations of insoluble solids, it is considerably more economical than conventional methods which do not have these advantages. It is moreover a cleaner, more efficient process.

Example 1: Apples — A quantity of apples weighing 2,538 tons total weight was washed and pulverized to a fine slurry by running through a hammer mill and then pulping the resulting pomace on a Food Machinery pulper. The finely pulverulent fluid mass was heated to 220°F and 30% of the volume vaporized into steam and fractionated to isolate and collect the volatile flavor.

The fluid mass, partially concentrated by this process, was cooled by vacuum to 140°F and pumped into holding tanks where it was treated for a period of 45 minutes with a depectinizing enzyme (Klearzyme 200 or 50). At the end of this period the fluid mass was pasteurized at 180°F for three minutes, and then recooled to 140°F.

A 500-square foot rotary vacuum precoat filter (Eimco) equipped with a leaching bar at the top of the drum for continuously washing the surface of the drum while in operation was used to filter the fluid mass. The filter was prepared for filtering by building up, by means of a vacuum, a precoat of diatomaceous earth filter aid powder (Dicalite) mixed with water to a suitable level, e.g., an approximately three-inch thickness. When a perlite filter aid powder is employed as filter aid, the precoat may be built up to an approximately five-inch thickness.

After completion of the precoating operation the water was emptied from the sump surrounding the filter drum and the finely pulverulent fluid apple mass to be filtered then fed into the sump. In order to obtain a faster rate of flow, approximately fifty pounds of filter aid powder per ton of fruit processed was added to the fluid mass in the filter sump. An original vacuum of 23 inches of mercury was applied on the inner surface of the drum and the drum slowly rotated in the sump.

The juice was forced through the filter cake by the difference in pressure on the two surfaces of the precoat layer, and collected from inside the drum. A knife on an advance mechanism was used to shave the full length of the surface of the rotating drum as it returned to the juice sump, thus continually exposing new filtering surfaces. The knife advanced at the rate of about 0.002 inch per revolution.

The filtered juice, already partially concentrated by the stripping, was then fed into an evaporator where it was concentrated to 70°Brix (i.e., 70% dissolved solids, mainly sugar). It was then cooled to 60°F and the volatile flavor collected prior to filtration was returned and thoroughly blended. The filtration process was run continuously for 48-hour periods, during each of which periods approximately 175,000 gallons of polished juice were produced. At the end of each period, remaining filter aid was stripped from the decking of the rotary drum and replaced with a new layer of filter aid of approximately three- to five-inch thickness, depending upon the exact filter aid employed, and the operation continued until the entire pack of apples had been processed.

The final yield of polished apple juice was 484,186 gallons of single strength juice of 13°Brix, for a yield of 190.8 gallons of 13°Brix juice per ton of fruit processed, almost a 20% increase over the usual yield of approximately 160 gallons of 11.5°Brix (weaker) apple juice per ton of apples processed according to conventional procedure. The product was a clear sparkling liquid which contained less than 0.001% insoluble solids, which could not be measured with standard measuring equipment. The product moreover had an enhanced flavor of freshly produced apple juice.

This yield represented an approximately 22.8 gallons per ton increase (as well as an approximately 1.5% increase in soluble solids) over the yield realized from the previous year's pack, using what was then considered the best process available.

Example 2: Grapes — In the manner of Example 1, a pack of 452.2 tons of Concord grapes was processed after removal of stems to give 89,581 gallons of polished single strength grape juice of 17°Brix, for a yield of 198.1 gallons per ton at 17°Brix. The pectic enzyme used was Pectinase-LM. This yield represented an approximately 8.5 gallons per ton increase over the yield realized from an earlier pack of the same year, and an approximately 6.1 gallons per ton increase over the yield realized from the previous year's pack, in each case using what was then considered the best process available.

In the same manner as Example 1 polished juices were prepared from crabapples, cherries, strawberries, onions, celery, and carrots. Leaching of the filter cake was omitted for onions, celery, and carrots. In every case yields of juice per ton were substantially higher than those obtained by methods previously employed.

DIALYSIS

Changing pH of Fruit Juice by Dialysis

In accordance with the process of *R.W. Kilburn and H.P. Gregor; U.S. Patent 3,165,415; January 12, 1965 and U.S. Patent 3,265,607; August 9, 1966; both assigned to American Machine & Foundry Company* there is provided a method for improving the taste of fruit juice without modification of the vitamin content or imparting a salt taste to the juice and without the use of additives. The pH of the juice can be raised from its natural or normal value to a desired value by lowering the concentration of free acid by ion exchange to reduce the anion concentration.

This process does not change the saltiness and a more natural tasting juice results. The ion exchange process substitutes the anion of a more weakly ionized acid for a portion of the organic acid normally present in the juice. The type of organic acid present is determined by the type of juice. For example, in citrus fruits and pineapple, the predominant organic acid is citric acid; in grapes, it is tartaric acid; in apples, it is malic acid; and all fruits have a small amount of succinic acid. The most effective anions for the purpose of substitution are hydroxyl, carbonate and bicarbonate.

Vitamin C, the main vitamin in fruit, is a weak acid and its ionization is greatly repressed in juice. Carotene or provitamin A, the second most abundant vitamin in fruit, is not water-soluble and hence nonionic. Thus, there is substantially no modification of the vitamin content by the process. The process is not only applicable to fruit juices of the foregoing type, and particularly citrus fruit juices, such as grapefruit and orange juice, but it is also applicable to vegetable juices, such as tomato juice. In certain parts of the United States, for example, California, tomato juice has a high normal pH value as the result of a high potassium citrate-citric acid ratio. The juice is too low in acid to be pasteurized easily and no citric acid can be added because of the FDA.

Therefore, it is necessary to utilize pressure cookers in the pasteurization of California tomato juice. If the normal pH of about 4.2 were lowered by 0.2 to 0.3 unit, pressure would not be required for pasteurization. Thus is it a further object of the process to lower the normal pH of the juice through ion exchange by substituting hydrogen ions for salt cations normally present. The natural or normal pH values for most fruits and vegetables to which the process is particularly applicable fall within the range of 2.5 to 5.5 pH and the range of adjustment of pH by the method is ±0.5 pH change from the natural value.

For example, grapefruit juice having a natural pH of 3.1 may be raised to a desired value of 3.6. Orange juice having a natural pH of 3.3 may be raised to a desired value of 3.8 and tomato juice having a natural pH of 4.2 may be lowered to a desired value of 3.7.

The method comprises the steps of passing a flow of natural juice of normal pH through chambers of a multichamber dialysis apparatus having a plurality of alternating juice and electrolyte chambers which are separated from each other by ion perm-selective membranes.

A flow of electrolyte is passed through the electrolyte chambers to create an ion exchange through the membranes to alter the relative concentration of acids and salts in the juice and the concurrent flow of the juice and the electrolyte continues until the ion exchange between the adjacent chambers has altered the pH of the natural juice to the desired value affording the improved taste.

Referring to Figure 1.9a, there is diagrammatically illustrated a sample cell **10** for raising the pH of fruit juices.

FIGURE 1.9: CHANGING pH BY MEANS OF ION EXCHANGE

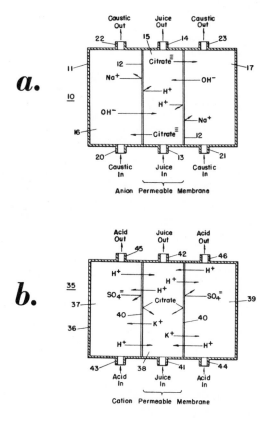

Source: R.W. Kilburn and H.P. Gregor; U.S. Patent 3,165,415; January 12, 1965

The cell or device **10** comprises a container **11** which is divided into three separate compartments or chambers **15** to **17** by a pair of anion permeable membranes **12**. The anion permeable membranes **12** may be of various suitable types, such as, for example, the type known as Nalfilm 2 or the type disclosed in Belgian Patents 537,438 and 568,266 (TNO), the latter type being preferred.

The TNO membranes are made of styrenized polythene to which the appropriate ion exchange groups are attached. As will be seen from Figure 1.9a, the fruit juice, which in its normal state has a pH below the desired value affording improved taste, is introduced into the chamber 15 of the container 11 by way of an inlet 13 at the bottom of container 11. In the line to the inlet 13 there normally is a proportioning means such as a valve or pump, not shown (for controlling the flow rate of the juice).

The flow of juice through container 11 is in an upward direction, passing through an outlet 14 at the top of container 11. The juice compartment or chamber 15 is located between compartments 16 and 17 through each of which passes a flow of caustic. The flows of caustic are also in an upward direction, the same as the juice, the caustic entering the respective chambers 16 and 17 through inlets 20 and 21 at the bottom of container 11 and leaving the respective chambers 16 and 17 by way of outlets 22 and 23 at the top of container 11.

In the lines to the inlets 20 and 21 there normally are proportioning means such as valves, or pumps, not shown, for controlling the flow rate of the caustic relative to that of the juice. The normal pH of the juice as it passes through the chamber 15 is raised to the desired value without imparting a salt taste to it by lowering the concentration of free acid by ion exchange to reduce the anion concentration. This process does not change the saltiness or materially modify the vitamin content and an improved or more natural tasting juice results.

The ion exchange process substitutes the anion of a more weakly ionized acid for a portion of the organic acids, such as citric or malic acid, normally present in the juice. The most effective anions for the purpose are hydroxyl (OH^-), carbonate ($CO_3^=$) and bicarbonate (HCO_3^-). The speed with which the process of ion exchange takes place, can be increased by the application of direct electric current to cause migration of the ions at speeds in excess of the diffusion rate.

A sample cell for lowering the pH of buffered solutions such as tomato juice or the like by the use of cation selective membranes is illustrated in Figure 1.9b. The cell 35 includes a container 36 which is separated into compartments 37 to 39 by a pair of cation permeable membranes 40 which may be of the type disclosed in the aforementioned Belgian patents. The membranes or films 40 provide the opposite walls of the central juice chamber 38. Juice is introduced through an inlet 41 at the lower end of container 36 and flows upwardly through chamber 38 where it passes outwardly through an outlet 42.

The acid cells 37 and 39 which are disposed on opposite sides of the juice cell 38 are each provided with inlets 43, 44 and outlets 45 and 46 respectively. In Figure 1.9b the acid illustrated is H_2SO_4. It will be noted that the hydrogen (H^+) cations pass freely through the cation permeable membranes 40 while the sulfate ($SO_4^=$) anions do not pass through the membranes 40 but instead are confined within their respective compartments 37 and 39.

The citrate anions likewise are confined within the central juice compartment 38 while the potassium cations are free to move from the juice chamber 38 through the opposite walls 40 into the adjacent acid chambers 37 and 39. While no cations can be substituted for hydrogen, (H^+), many anions may be substituted for sulfate ($SO_4^=$) such as, for example Cl^-, NO_3^-, PO_3^-, $PO_4^\equiv$, acetate, citrate and lactate.

For example, in one electrodialysis device, constructed in accordance with the process, which was adapted to deliver at least 250 gallons per hour of juice, there were employed two electrode compartments, 13 solution compartments and 12 juice compartments. The compartments were substantially rectangular in cross-section and were separated by rectangular frames. The power supply was derived from a unit capable of delivering 240 volts DC and a current density in the order of 20 amperes per square foot, with the membranes having an approximate area of 3 feet square. The frames were made from ¼ inch stock and were provided with ⅛ inch feed holes drilled edgewise through the stock on one pair of opposite sides.

The frames were assembled in the stack in alternate positions displaced 90° from each other with a membrane between adjacent frames so that the flow of juice through the device was in one direction, while the flow of solution was through the device at 90° from the juice flow. The electrodes were made from stainless steel sheet approximately ³/₁₆" thick and the anolyte and catolyte streams were predominantly sodium hydroxide or sodium sulfate.

For raising the pH of the juice, anion permeable membranes were employed and for lowering the pH of the juice, cation permeable membranes were employed. The power consumption for treating 1,000 gallons of juice was approximately 80 kwh. However, by decreasing the thickness of each frame from ¼" to ⅛", the voltage requirements may be approximately cut in half.

ULTRASONIC TREATMENT

Use of Orbital-Mass Type Generator

The process of *A.G. Bodine; U.S. Patent 3,320,992; May 23, 1967* involves the application to a vegetable substance of sonic waves of relatively low frequency as compared with the audible spectrum, typically of from 20 cycles per second to an order of hundreds of cycles per second, but at relatively great amplitude or intensity. A mechanical orbital-mass type of sound wave generator is especially applicable, because such generators readily produce relatively high amplitude in the comparatively low frequency range mentioned, and have other unique features of advantage. In the process sugarcane, or other vegetable substance, is first chopped up, preferably into fairly small pieces or chunks, though the size is not critical.

The chopped material is then placed in a treatment chamber, and preferably, unless the chopping has released sufficient juice to serve the purpose, covered with a small quantity of liquid such as water to serve as an acoustic coupling medium. As the process proceeds, sufficient juice is generally extracted to act or substitute thereafter as the coupling medium. Within the treatment chamber, or forming a portion of one wall thereof, is a sound wave radiating surface which is vibrated by the aforementioned mechanical oscillator. The sound wave radiating surface radiates sound waves which are transmitted via the liquid coupling medium to and through the pieces of sugarcane.

The sonic wave energy has an action on the vegetable substance which results in a differential vibration of the fibers and the juice. To begin with, the acoustic impedances of the fiber and of the juice, while within a range which matches sufficiently well with the output impedance of the oscillator and radiator, do inherently differ somewhat from one another, both in magnitude and phase angle. These differences come about because of differences in density, in elasticity, and in frictional resistance when caused to vibrate by reason of transmission of sonic waves therethrough.

With differences in impedance, the fiber and juice substances must vibrate at different amplitudes and in different time phase in response to transmission therethrough of a sonic wave. Involved in this process is the fact that sound wave transmission results in the juice and fiber ingredients vibrating with different accelerations, and to different maximum velocities. The differential movements and displacements thus brought about will be seen to periodically move the liquid relative to the fibers.

Further, the velocity of sound in fiber differs from that in the juice. Thus the sound wave transmitted through the sugarcane will travel at a different velocity when or where it encounters a fibrous transmission path than when or where it finds continuous paths through the juice between and around the fibers. By reason of reflections at the interfaces between the fibers and juice, the waves tend to remain within whichever medium they are already in.

One consequence of these conditions is that the waves travel at different speeds through the juice and the fiber, and thus soon fall out of phase with one another in adjacent portions of fiber and juice. The fiber and juice thus, for this additional reason, have movement relative to one another.

Thus the juice periodically moves relative to the fibers, and so washes back and forth over, around and between the fibers, and over the surfaces thereof. The overall result is that the juices are extracted from within, around and between the fibers. The physical result, insofar as removal of juices is concerned, is to some extent like heating though produced without significant temperature rise. Avoidance of substantial heating is of course important, particularly in vegetable juice extraction, where heating may in many cases be undesirable.

Use of Sonic Whistle

M.L. Coltart and D. Paton; U.S. Patent 3,667,967; June 6, 1972; assigned to Sun-Rype Products Ltd., Canada describe a process and apparatus for improving the yield of juice which may be extracted from a vegetable or fruit pulp. The process subjects the pulp to ultrasonic vibrations in the frequency range between 20 and 300 kc/sec at a sound intensity of up to about 20 w/cm². It has also been found advantageous to treat expressed juice, which has been produced by ultrasonic means or otherwise, with ultrasonic vibrations, in order to improve the quality and filterability of the juice. Although ultrasonic vibrations may be generated in many ways it has been found particularly suitable to employ a sonic whistle which may be placed in line in continuous production equipment.

Commercial apple juice extraction methods are well-known and generally involve comminuting the fruit in a hammer mill to a coarse pulp, and subsequently expressing the juice from the pulp by a hydraulic ram, screw press or centrifugal separator. The pulp is normally obtained by passing the raw material through a ¾" screen as fine pulping tends to cause slippage in the presses and the formation of excess fines in the expressed juice. The coarse pulp has a deleterious effect on juice yield and many attempts have been made to increase the overall yield with little or no success. These attempts have generally concentrated on modifications to existing presses or the development of new continuous presses.

The prior art processes normally prepare a coarse pulp which will pass a ¾" screen in order to avoid excessive press slippage and fines in the juices, however, it has been found that in order to provide a pulp which may be advantageously treated with ultrasonic vibrations that it is preferable, although not essential, to prepare a finer pulp of the order that will pass a ⅜" screen. As shown in Figure 1.10, apples, for example, are washed, conveyed to a Reitz mill 1 where they are pulped to pass a ⅜" screen 2. The pulp falls, under gravity, to a storage hopper 3, and is pumped, as required, by a pump 4 into the first ultrasonic vibration chamber 5.

The ultrasonic vibrations may be generated by any of a number of known techniques. In one form the ultrasonic treatment chamber may be a tank into which transducers are inserted, and which generate frequencies of the order of 20 kc/sec and up to 300 kc/sec with an acoustic power of up to 20 w/cm². Usually the acoustic power is in the region of 2.0 to 2.8 w/cm², and therefore treatment times are relatively long, in the order to 10 to 30 minutes. It may be necessary when employing this technique to incorporate cooling coils in the tank to minimize temperature rises due to the energy dissipation. An operating temperature of 32° to 75°F is preferred. Alternatively, and more preferred, the ultrasonic treatment chamber may be a sonic whistle, such as the Sonolator (Sonic Engineering Corporation).

A sonic whistle does not employ transducers but rather the pulp is pumped at moderate pressures, between about 50 and 350 psi, through a special orifice forming a flat, high pressure jet stream. This jet is directed toward the edge of a flat, flexible steel blade, so that impingement of the jet on the blade causes the blade to vibrate and thus cause intense ultrasonic vibrations within the liquid itself. The orifice/blade distance may be varied at will to obtain maximum intensity as measured on an arbitrary scale indicative of maximum cavitation for the particular system or pulp being treated.

Cavitation takes place continuously producing violent local pressure changes in the liquid. The process is completed in microseconds so there is a very high throughput of material through the equipment. The feed is uniformly treated and there is virtually no heating effect. It is believed that there are about eight exciting frequencies, and although one frequency may be emphasized, a sonic whistle cannot be limited to a single frequency. Frequency is not believed to be critical in the present case provided the cavitational intensity is high.

Consequently a white noise spectrum is employed having frequencies which vary between about 20 and 300 kc/sec. It is believed that the acoustic power is between about 10 and 20 watts per square centimeter at the point of generation. The size and precise shape of the orifice depends upon the type of pulp being treated. Generally the orifice is circular on the upstream side changing to an ellipse on the downstream side. The orifice may be referred to as a cat's eye type orifice. When treating an apple pulp it is desirable to use an orifice having a cross-sectional area in excess of 0.075 square inch in order to avoid excessive plugging by seeds, stems and cellular debris.

FIGURE 1.10: ULTRASONIC TREATMENT

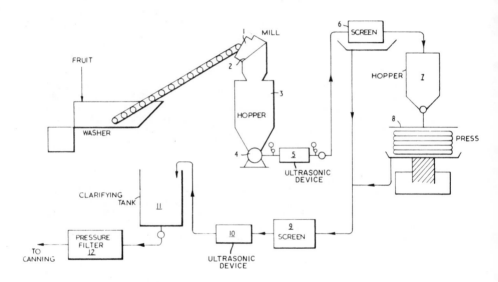

Source: M.L. Coltart and D. Paton; U.S. Patent 3,667,967; June 6, 1972

Good results have been achieved with an orifice having a cross-sectional area of about 0.100 square inch and for high throughput it is preferred that the cross-sectional area of the orifice is about 0.166 square inch. It must be stressed, however that the exact shape and size of the orifice is a function of the particular equipment and type of pulp, and should be adjusted to achieve the maximum intensity of cavitation, which, as previously mentioned, may be measured directly on an arbitrary dimensionless scale.

Subsequent to the ultrasonic treatment which improves the juice yield, apparently by breaking down the cellular structure and solubilizing more of the pectic substances which cement the cells together, the pulp is passed over a rotary screen 6, from which the free run juice is continuously withdrawn under the influence of gravity. The free run juice accounts for about 20% of the total juice in the pulp, as compared with about 15% free run juice from pulp not treated by ultrasonics. The term free run in this specification means that portion of the juice which flows out under gravity immediately following the pulping or pulping and ultrasonic treatment.

No settling time is permitted. The percentage of free run juice would rise somewhat if the pulp were allowed to settle for a short period of time, say one hour. The cake from the screen falls into a hopper 7 from which it is transferred to a continuous belt press, pneumatic, hydraulic or screw press 8 as required. Alternatively the cake may be centrifuged. The press is of conventional design and operation and will not be described in detail herein. Depending upon the quality of the particular vegetable pulp treated at different times of the year it may be necessary to employ lighter and more closely woven press blankets in the press filter. Ultrasonically treated pulp requires less wood fiber press aid such as Silvacel than nontreated pulp in order to prevent slippage.

The expressed juice and the free run juice are combined and passed over a second rotary screen 9 to remove as much suspended solids as possible. The screened juice may then be subjected to a second ultrasonic treatment 10 by either a transducer system, or preferably a sonic whistle system as described hereinabove. The product of the secondary ultrasonic treatment is then passed through a clarifying tank 11 containing a standard gelatin suspension known in the art.

The clarified juice is then passed through a pressure filter 12. The secondary ultrasonic treatment reduces the viscosity of the juice by approximately 25%, apparently by causing degradation of the suspended solids and pectin molecules and other naturally occurring hydrocolloids. Tannin is normally added to commercial apple juice to control the astringency of the final product but more natural tannin is apparently released by the ultrasonic treatment so that it is usually unnecessary to add additional tannin to the juice.

The reduced viscosity is advantageous inasmuch as the filtration temperature can be reduced from about 75° to 50°F and furthermore the amount of filter powder such as a diatomaceous earth (Celite), can be reduced from about 175 pounds per 1,000 Imperial gallons to about 100 pounds per 1,000 Imperial gallons. The secondary ultrasonic treatment does not result in an appreciably faster filtration rate, but it has been found that even the first few gallons through the filter are clear and are of acceptable quality. Previously the first few gallons were commonly cloudy and it was necessary that they be recycled.

Example: A laboratory scale quantity of Winesap apples, of suitable quality for juice processing were pulped in a Waring Blendor Mill. Approximately 30 grams of the pulp were pumped into a laboratory ultrasonic disintegrator tank approximately 1.625" wide by 1.5" deep by 7" long equipped with transducers which were located in the base and cooling coils in the lid to minimize temperature change. The transducers were activated to provide an ultrasonic vibration having a frequency of 20 kc/sec, at a power input of 200 watts, which power input provided a sound intensity of about 2.8 w/cm². The pulp was treated for 15 minutes and the temperature was maintained between 68° and 75°F.

The pulp was then withdrawn and squeezed through several layers of cheese cloth. A control sample was pulped in the same way and squeezed omitting the ultrasonic step. The quantities of juice extracted are shown in the following table.

	Control			Ultrasonic treatment		
Run number	1	2	3	1	2	3
Wt. of pulp (gm.)	305	215	295	294	205	291
Juice recovered (ccs.)	200	160	194	220	202	216
Percent recovery (V./W.)	65.5	65.5	64.5	75.5	75.0	74.5
Imp. gal./ton fruit equivalent (calculated)	131.0	131.0	129.0	152.0	151.0	150.0

This example indicates that the primary ultrasonic treatment results in an increase in juice yield as compared with normal processing.

CONCENTRATION PROCESSES

CITRUS JUICE

A Basic Process

A basic commercial practice for preparing fruit juice concentrate was developed by *L.G. MacDowell, E.L. Moore and C.D. Atkins; U.S. Patent 2,453,109; November 9, 1948; assigned to the U.S. Secretary of Agriculture.* It was found that a concentrated fruit juice containing a substantial portion of the original aroma, flavor, and palatability could be made by adding a portion of fresh, single-strength juice to a relatively strong concentrate (however prepared) and thereby obtaining a concentrate of medium strength. The fresh juice returns much of the natural aroma, flavor, and palatability to the concentrate. When concentrates prepared in this manner were diluted to original concentration with water, the resulting product was hardly distinguishable from fresh juice. An example will illustrate the process.

Example: Valencia oranges were washed, allowed to dry, and halved. The juice was extracted on a revolving burr and screened of suspended pulp. Four gallons of this juice (12°Brix) were concentrated under vacuum at a temperature of 40° to 65°Brix (about 7-fold). Fresh deaerated single-strength juice was added to the concentrate until a Brix of 42° (about 4-fold) was obtained. The product was then sealed under vacuum and placed in cold storage and frozen storage.

Evaporation Using Dielectric Heating

Citrus juices are commonly packaged at a density of 42°Brix, thereby yielding a 4-fold concentrate. A density of 72°Brix would yield an 8-fold concentrate and would be desirable for such things as export to foreign countries, since it would result in a big saving in freight costs. Moreover, while the 42°Brix concentrate has to be stored at a temperature close to zero, the 65°Brix concentrate will stand storage temperatures as high as 20° to 30°F without deterioration.

A process and apparatus is described by *R.G. Sargeant; U.S. Patent 3,072,490; January 8, 1963* in which there is shown apparatus for and a method of producing high density, low viscosity citrus juice concentrate, involving subjecting the juice to the action of radio frequency electrical energy. The juice is circulated by means of a pump from the bottom of a vertical evaporating chamber through a conduit and a high frequency electrical device, and thence through a spray head into the top of the evaporating chamber again.

One of the problems encountered in the concentrated fruit juice industry is caused by the well-known fact that, when a pectin containing juice is heated and then cooled, jellification occurs. This is particularly noticeable where the juice is concentrated by conventional steam evaporators, in which the juice is subjected to relatively high temperatures. In many cases, where an attempt has been made to run the density of orange juice concentrate, for example, up to 65° to 70°Brix with steam evaporators, the concentrate becomes very viscous, and tends to gel, and when placed in the cans and cooled, was found to be practically solid jelly. As a result of such jellification, the product, when reconstituted by the addition of water to produce a juice suitable for drinking, tended to separate, upon standing, into different strata or layers, instead of remaining a uniform mixture, and this separating tendency seriously detracts from the commercial acceptability of the product.

The process described by *R.G. Sargeant; U.S. Patent 3,366,497; January 30, 1968; assigned to Pet Incorporated* is directed particularly to the problem of producing acceptable high density concentrates from fruit juices containing substantial amounts of pectin or pectin compounds, such, for example, as apple juice, grape juice, and citrus fruit juices. Some of the citrus fruits, as for example, the popular variety of oranges, known as pineapple oranges, contain particularly large amounts of pectin.

The problem of jellification and high viscosity can be partially solved by the following method. The whole juice, before being introduced into the evaporator, is first run through a suitable centrifuge to separate it into two parts. One of these parts is a heavier portion containing most of the water, acids, sugars, etc., and containing about 80% of the entire juice. The other part is a lighter portion containing the pectin compounds and complexes, as well as other ingredients such as cellulose fibers, lipids, etc., and constituting about 20% of the entire juice. This pectin containing portion is then stored in a tank or the like, while the watery portion only is evaporated to the desired concentration. By thus first removing the pectin complexes, they are not subjected to the heat of the evaporator.

Separation of the pectin containing portion from the other portion is not absolutely complete. Thus, the pectin containing portion will contain small amounts of water, sugars, etc., and the watery portion will necessarily contain a certain amount of pectin complexes, cellulose, etc. But the centrifuge effects the separation of the major amounts of the several ingredients. Because of the fact that the watery portion of the juice necessarily contains a certain amount of pectin, it is highly desirable, when evaporating this watery portion, to maintain the temperature very low, preferably not over 85°F, the same as when evaporating whole juice, in order to hold down the viscosity. Moreover, much of the pectin complexes are contained in the cellulose or fibrous material. After having substantially separated the juice into the two portions described, and evaporated the watery portion to the desired concentration, several alternate procedures may be followed:

(a)   The pectin containing portion, in its natural state, may be at once recombined with the concentrated portion to produce the final product.

(b)   The pectin containing portion may be heated or flash-pasteurized to inactivate the pectin complexes and any enzymes present before being recombined with the concentrated portion.

(c)   A small amount of water may be added to the fibrous mass containing the pectin complexes to thin it, and then the fibrous material may be strained out and discarded, thus getting rid of the pectin complexes which the fibrous material contained. The liquid passing through the strainer may be added directly back to the concentrated portion, or it may be first heat-treated or flash-pasteurized.

In any event, the separating out of the major part of the pectin complexes, concentrating only the remaining, watery portion of the juice, and thereafter recombining the two portions, results in a product of lower viscosity and less tendency to separate, whatever the method of evaporating employed. Fruit juices may be evaporated by means of high frequency electrical energy.

R.G. Sargeant; U.S. Patent 3,428,463; February 18, 1969 gives improvements made for the process of preparing orange or other fruit juice concentrates by means of radio or other high frequency electrical energy. Referring to Figure 2.1, a centrifuge is shown at **1**. The juice to be treated is delivered from the finisher through pipe **2**, and is separated by the centrifuge into two portions, one of which is designated as the water-containing portion, and the other the ester-carrying portion. This latter contains the major portion of the pulp and pectin complexes, while the watery portion contains most of the sugars and acids

FIGURE 2.1: METHOD OF PRODUCING HIGH DENSITY, LOW VISCOSITY FRUIT JUICE CONCENTRATE

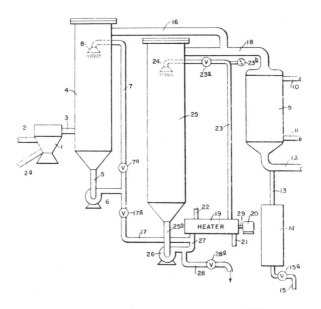

Source: R.G. Sargeant; U.S. Patent 3,428,463; February 18, 1969

The water-containing portion is delivered through a pipe **3** to a vertically disposed, elongated deaerating chamber **4**. From the bottom of this chamber extends a pipe **5** to a centrifugal pump **6**, from the discharge side of which extends a pipe **7** which enters the chamber at a point near the top, where it terminates in a spray head **8**. Thus, the watery juice is recycled by the pump through the pipe and spray head from which it falls to the bottom of the chamber. Meanwhile, the deaerating chamber is maintained under a partial vacuum by means of a conduit **16**, which, through a conduit **18** and a condenser **9**, communicates with a pipe **12** connected with any suitable type of vacuum pump (not shown). Thus, any air contained in the juice is effectively removed.

From the discharge side of the pump extends another pipe **17**, which, through a third pipe **27**, connects with a heating device **19**, the construction of which will be hereinafter described in detail. A heating medium, such as steam or hot water, is supplied through pipes **21** and **22**, and the heater includes a shaft **29**, driven by a motor **20**. From the heater extends a pipe **23** into the upper end of a vertical, elongated evaporating chamber **25**, where it terminates in a spray head **24**. This chamber is preferably jacketed. From the bottom of this evaporating chamber extends a pipe **25a** to a centrifugal pump **26**, which delivers into a pipe **28**, connected with the pipe **27**. Valves **7a, 17a, 23a** and **28a** are interposed in the pipes **7, 17, 23** and **28**, respectively, to control the flow of liquid therethrough, and a pressure gauge **23b** is preferably mounted on the pipe **23**.

From the top of the evaporating chamber extends a conduit **18** to a condenser **9**, a cooling medium being supplied through pipes **10** and **11**. From the vacuum pump pipe **12** at the bottom of the condenser extends a pipe **13** to a condensate receptacle **14**, from which the condensate may be drawn off through a discharge pipe **15**, controlled by a valve **15a**.

With valve **7a** open and valve **17a** closed, the pump **6** continues to recycle the juice through the deaerating chamber until all of the contained air is completely removed. Then, when valve **17a** is opened, the pump forces the juice from the deaerating chamber through pipe **17** to pipe **27**, where it joins the juice being concentrated and recycled by the pump **26** through the evaporating chamber **25**. This latter pump forces the juice through the heater **19** and pipe **23** to the spray head **24**, when the valve **23a** is open. The concentrated juice may be withdrawn from the pipe **28**. It will be noted that the juice is forced through the heater under substantial hydraulic pressure. By way of example, pressure of from 10 to 40 or more psi has been successfully used.

The heater **19** is of a very special kind known as the swept surface type. In comprises a cylindrical casing or housing through the center of which extends a cylindrical drum supported on a shaft. Surrounding this drum and separated therefrom by an annular space is a cylinder. Mounted on the surface of the drum are a pair of diametrically disposed scraper blades extending the length of the cylinder and having free edges adapted to engage and sweep over the inner surface of this cylinder as the shaft is driven by the motor.

Surrounding the cylinder and separated from it by a space is another cylindrical casing, this second cylinder being covered by suitable insulating material, the latter being enclosed by a metal shell. The juice being treated circulates through the annular space and flows from end to end in contact with the outside of the metal cylinder and is thus heated. Either steam or hot water may be used. The temperature of the water may be as high as 140° to 150°F, or more. By the use of a swept surface heater, such as described, the density can be carried to more than 72°Brix, without any difficulty.

In operation, the juice from the finisher comes in through pipe **2** to the centrifuge. From this, the esters and the major portion of the pulp and pectin complexes are discharged from the pipe **2a**, while the part designated as the watery portion is delivered through pipe **3**. This watery portion, which includes most of the sugars and acids, contains sufficient pulp so that the completed 72°Brix concentrate, drawn off from the pipe **28**, will have, when reconstituted, a pulp content of 5 to 13%. It is best to use an 0.020 screen on the finisher, set loosely. This usually would allow too much pulp to pass through, so, to meet some specifications, a centrifuge is used to reduce the amount of pulp in the juice portion going to the evaporator.

Another figure included in the patent shows apparatus for subjecting the juice to radio or other high frequency electrical energy before it enters the evaporating chamber. With the above described equipment and method, juice concentrates of a density of 72°Brix, and higher, and of a viscosity of 4,000 to 10,000 cp at 75°F have been produced. These concentrates, having a pulp content of around 7%, can be stored indefinitely without deterioration at up to 30°F, and when stored at 0°F do not gel. Moreover, when reconstituted by mixing with water, they show no tendency to separate. It will be understood that satisfactory products of this character can be made either with or without the high frequency electrical treatment. The use of the electrical energy, however, produces a concentrate of better flavor and stability, and of lower viscosity, as well as a lower bacteria count.

Osmotic Transfer of Orange Essence from Single Strength Juice to Concentrate

In carrying out the process of *J.A. Brent and W.A. Bucek; U.S. Patent 3,127,276; Mar. 31, 1964; assigned to The Coca-Cola Company* single strength fresh citrus juice is concentrated by vacuum concentration. During this procedure, the essence which imparts the fresh juice flavoring is removed from the concentrate and may be lost. It consists of various water soluble alcohols, esters, aldehydes and the like, which are quite volatile and generally go off to a large extent with the first 15 to 20% of the liquid removed in concentrating the juice by vacuum concentration.

Such essence is then transferred to the concentrate by osmosis from fresh juice. This is accomplished by placing the concentrate on one side of a permeable membrane and fresh single strength juice on the other side thereof. The difference in osmotic pressure brings about the transfer.

Thereafter, the fresh juice from which the essence has been transferred is subjected to vacuum concentration and this concentrate in turn has an essence fraction transferred by osmosis from another quantity of single strength juice. The method may be carried out either by a batch or continuous process.

In Figure 2.2a there is shown diagrammatically suitable apparatus for carrying out a batch process. A container 1 is divided by a partition 2 which is the porous membrane. This may be regenerated cellulose, cellophane, nitrated cellulose, polyethylene or other suitable materials. The concentrated juice indicated at 3 is placed on one side of the membrane and fresh juice indicated at 4 is placed on the other side of the membrane. The concentrated juice may be at any suitable Brix, such as 55° or 60° and may be the result of vacuum concentration. Other forms of concentration may be employed if desired.

The concentration by vacuum is effected in the usual vacuum concentration equipment in which the water is removed by applying a vacuum to juice in a suitable closed container. The concentrated juice is generally quite free from the essence or flavor liquor which generally consists of water soluble alcohol, aldehyde or the like. The fresh juice, just as it comes from the fruit is placed at 4 and since it has a lower content of dissolved sugar solids, osmotic pressure will cause water containing the flavor liquor or essence or the alcoholic esters and aldehydes to pass through the permeable membrane into the concentrated juice.

FIGURE 2.2: OSMOTIC TRANSFER OF ORANGE ESSENCE

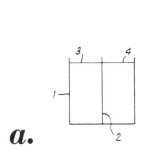

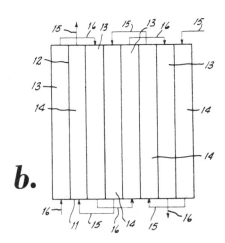

Container with Porous Membrane

Countercurrent Apparatus with
Plurality of Cells

Source: J.A. Brent and W.A. Bucek; U.S. Patent 3,127,276; March 31, 1964

Thereafter, the single strength juice from **4** is subjected to vacuum concentration and since much of the essence has been removed by osmosis, the losses of essence through the vacuum concentration are greatly minimized and the flavor essence is conserved.

In Figure 2.2b there is shown diagrammatically a countercurrent apparatus consisting of a plurality of cells **13** and **14** formed in a container **11** provided with a plurality of partitions **12** comprising porous membranes suitable for osmotic transfer, such as regenerated cellulose, cellophane, nitrated cellulose or polyethylenes.

In the apparatus shown in Figure 2.2b the cells **14**, for instance, receive the concentrated juice, concentrated as indicated above and the cells **13** contain the single strength fresh juice from which the essence has not been removed. The flow through the cells **14** is indicated by the arrows **15** and the flow through the cells **13** is indicated by arrows **16**.

With such an arrangement there is a countercurrent flow and the osmotic transfer takes place as indicated above. The single strength juice from which the essence has been extracted by the apparatus is then passed to the vacuum concentrating equipment.

When, for example, 100 gallons of 55°Brix concentrate and 551 gallons of 12°Brix fresh single strength juice are employed, after the process has been carried out 7.1% or more by volume of the flavor liquor from the single strength juice will be added to the concentrated juice, thus producing a concentrate with materially more essence than before the interchange. In fact, considerably more essence or flavor then contained in the same volume of single strength juice will be transferred, thus conserving the essence and preventing its loss during the vacuum concentration.

In carrying out this method the essence from the fresh juice is transferred to the concentrated juice before vacuum concentration. The essence is thus protected from the rigors and loss due to vacuum concentration.

Addition of Frozen Essence to Concentrated Juice

It is common practice to concentrate orange juice under vacuum and freeze the concentrate for merchandising. However, in the course of concentrating the juice, much of the essence which gives the characteristic flavor to fresh orange juice is removed during evaporation.

Essence may be recovered from the juice in various ways. It can be taken off during juice concentration and the accompanying water vapors may be eliminated by appropriate condensation procedures, after which the essence may be condensed at low temperatures. Essence may also be recovered in reduced volume by appropriate stripping columns or the like from the vapors given off during juice concentration. The essence thus recovered may be returned to the concentrated juice. However, if the essence is added back to the concentrate and the concentrate is stored under conditions familiar to the art, the flavor imparted by the essence is gradually lost.

This may be due to hydrolysis aided by the natural acidity of the juice or may be the result of enzyme activity. If the essence, however, is separated and stored separately at 40°F or below, it is very stable toward flavor deterioration for months and even for more than a year.

J.A. Brent; U.S. Patent 3,140,187; July 7, 1964; assigned to The Coca-Cola Company describes a process for recovering the essence of orange juice and adding it back to the orange concentrate in such a way that the concentrate and essence do not mix. This preserves against flavor deterioration.

Since the essence freezes at approximately 30° to 32°F and the orange concentrate of normal Brix, such as 42° to 50°Brix, will not freeze until the temperature is reduced to approximately 20°F, in carrying out this process, the essence is frozen and is then added to the orange concentrate when it is at a temperature below the freezing point of the essence. The essence is thus maintained in discrete frozen form and does not become intimately mixed with the orange concentrate as is the case when the essence is returned to the concentrate without maintaining its discrete nature by the freezing manipulation here employed.

In carrying out the process fresh juice is stripped of the essence. This may be done in a Mojonnier evaporator or in any suitable flash equipment. The fresh juice is heated to a temperature of approximately 195°F. It is then sprayed into an enclosed space where it is subjected to vacuum evaporation. The fresh juice which may be at 12°Brix is stripped of approximately 15 to 20% of the liquid.

In the flash evaporator substantially all of the essence and approximately 15 to 20% of the water of the original juice are vaporized. The essence is recovered from these vapors by separating it from the majority of the water vapor. This may be done by selectively condensing the water vapors and the essence in suitable condensers. It is usually accomplished by passing the condensate through appropriate strippers or scrubbers to reduce the volume to approximately one-twentieth of the original volume of the condensate.

The juice which has been stripped in the Mojonnier evaporator or in the flash equipment is taken to the regular evaporators where it is concentrated to any desired concentration. It is quite common to concentrate it to 42° to 50°Brix, after which it is cooled to the desired temperature. In general, the orange concentrate is taken down to a temperature of from 20° to 25°F where it is still fluid and unfrozen. In this respect, the procedure is similar to that involved in normal concentration of orange juice.

The frozen essence, which is at a temperature of 30°F, or just under the freezing point, is added to the orange concentrate which is at a temperature below the freezing point of the essence. The frozen essence which may be in snow form or in frozen pellet form, may be added to the colder orange concentrate. Since the concentrate is at a temperature below the freezing point of the essence, the essence will remain in discrete form. Thereafter, the mixture of concentrate and frozen essence are placed in containers for sealing and freezing as is customary in handling frozen orange juice concentrate.

The product thus produced consists of concentrated orange juice having therein discrete pieces or a portion of frozen essence of the fresh juice, the product being at a temperature below the melting point of the frozen essence so that the frozen essence will remain discrete from the concentrate.

This product has many advantages over other concentrated citrus or other fruit juices in that it does not tend to lose the flavor characteristics imparted by the essence on storage as would be the case if the concentrate and the essence were not maintained in discrete form. The product may be stored for long periods of time during merchandising and since the deterioration of the flavor does not take place when the juice is reconstituted by adding water, the reconstituted juice will have a flavor substantially the same as fresh juice.

Low Brix to Acid Ratio Concentrate Stable at Ambient Temperature

In the fruit juice concentrate industry, the relative sweetness-to-tartness relationship is known as the Brix-acid ratio. The Brix unit is a commonly used unit of measurement to express the concentration of dissolved solids in an aqueous solution and has been specified as the unit to be used in all Food and Drug Administration, U.S. Department of Agriculture and the Florida Citrus Code for fruit products and particularly for concentrated fruit juices. The acid unit is the citric acid concentration in the citrus juice. A Brix-acid ratio is obtained by dividing the Brix value by the acid value of a given product, and this gives a ratio compared with unity which forms a comparative scale for acceptability of such juice concentrates.

As examples of Brix-acid ratios of concentrated citrus fruit juices, high-grade fresh-frozen orange juice or grapefruit juice concentrate will usually have a Brix-acid ratio of 14:1. A range of Brix-acid ratios for many well known commercial fruit juice drinks of citrus base ranges from 17:1 all the way to 54:1.

Normally, Brix-acid ratios below 14:1 yield a drink which is excessively tart and are commercially unacceptable to the consumer. Even the addition of large quantities of sugar to offset the sour taste fail to make these low ratio drinks palatable since the result is a syrupy or cloying taste which is objectionable to the average consumer.

C.I. Houghtaling, F.S. Houghtaling, N.E. Houghtaling and R.W. Kilburn; U.S. Patent 3,227,562; January 4, 1966 describe a citrus fruit concentrate, preferably made up of several species of citrus fruit with or without the juices of other fruit, which is formed in combination with an additive or additives which allow a low Brix-acid ratio to be attained, such as 11:1, and prevent the need of refrigeration of the finished concentrate or its original freezing, the juice or drink formed from the concentrate of the process being of a natural, tart, pleasing taste, flavor and appearance and, moreover, being capable of a variation of dilution, even dilutions of as much as 15:1, and more, without becoming thin, watery or otherwise unacceptable.

The fruit juice concentrate of the process can be stored on open shelves, i.e., without refrigeration, is not a frozen product and therefore does not have to be defrosted but is available for instant use, yet takes up little shelf room in store or home due to its concentrated condition. The concentrate possesses an unusually tart taste with a Brix-acid ratio of 11:1. Having such a low ratio, its pleasant flavor is a distinct surprise to workers in blending and concentrating fresh citrus juices.

The product comprises a mixture of sugar and concentrated fruit juices, some of which are from citrus fruits blended together in proportion to yield a concentration of soluble solids between 68° and 75°Brix and with a citric acid concentration between 6.2 and 6.8% by weight to which may be added essential oils from natural citrus fruits, together with an additive comprising an intimate mixture of the salts containing the cations sodium, magnesium, calcium, iron, potassium, manganese and aluminum and the anions chloride, oxide, silicate, iodide, bromide and sulfate. The concentration thus obtained will have a Brix-acid ratio which is very low and which will be below 14:1 and which will normally be nearer a value of 10:1 or 11:1.

A general procedure for carrying out the process is the following: A blend is formulated from the concentrated juices of fresh lemon, lime, orange, grapefruit and pineapple. Sugar is added in the proper amount to raise the Brix-acid ratio which balances the tartness of the mixture and imparts consistency to the product. An additive containing minerals is added not merely to enhance the flavor but because the components in the additive materially affect the blend in taste and in action so that the addition is necessary. It is believed that the presence of these additive compounds in the blend are extremely efficient from a bactericidal standpoint as well as contributing to its appealing taste.

The total amount of fruit ingredients is maintained uniform and the relative amounts of the various fruits are adjusted, to impart finally the desirable and distinctive flavor of the blend. It is to be noted that the blend contains only fresh fruit; that no preservatives are added; that it is not pasteurized. This concentrate dilutes immediately to such drinking strength as may be desired individually. Although fortified with a formulation of additives, no flavors predominate, the proper formulation of ingredients yielding an end-product with high commercial appeal without the addition of flavor synthetics. The mixture was tested at 70°Brix or more.

The addition of salt to the juice drink was tried because consumers frequently sprinkle salt on fresh fruit to improve the flavor. It was found that juice drinks do not lend themselves to the use of common household salt, i.e., sodium chloride, and the resulting product was frequently harsh and bitter. Other salts were mixed with common household salt to see if this effect could be eliminated and a zestful refreshing drink produced without the cloying effect of large amounts of sugar.

A large number of inorganic salts are available, each with taste which differs from common table salts. A balanced blend of these salts was found to be unusually effective in enhancing the flavor of fruit juice to yield a pleasant zestful drink. This mixture of minerals as an additive was found to enhance the flavor of fruit juices to a degree which was completely unexpected.

In particular, it was found that sodium chloride plus magnesium chloride, calcium chloride and sodium silicate formed an excellent base for an additive for the desired purpose. If trace elements were added including materials selected from the list of ferric oxide, ferrous iodide, amorphous sulfur, sodium bromide, manganese oxide (black), these tend to improve the additive and render the results of addition to the concentrate as better. Also, gold compound, silver compound, potassium bichromate, and organic carbon may be used in small quantities in the additive if desired.

A quantity of calcium sulfate and aluminum oxide is also used in the mixture of concentrated fruit juices. Additional details on the mixing of specific batches of juice concentrates are included in the patent.

Concentrate Containing Discrete Pulp Mass

The process of *W.W. Brown, J.W. Brown and W.G. Mitchell; U.S. Patent 3,278,315; October 11, 1966; assigned to Pasco Packing Co.* is concerned with the method and the product produced where the juice and insoluble pulp of a citrus product is separated into a juice portion and an insoluble pulp mass containing the pectin destroying enzymes, pectase and pectinesterase, etc. The insoluble pulp mass is then frozen by cooling the pulp mass to a temperature of approximately 28°F, or below, depending upon the soluble content in the pulp, and then the juice which may be concentrated is combined with the frozen pulp mass while maintaining the temperature no greater than 28°F in order that the insoluble pulp remain frozen.

The product produced will maintain the enzymes in the insoluble pulp mass separated and isolated from the pectin in the juice, thereby preventing any reaction between the enzymes such as pectinesterase, pectase, etc., and the pectin which would cause gelation, clarification and off-flavor. A specific example of the use of the process follows.

The citrus fruits are the conventional fruits such as oranges, lemons, limes, grapefruits and the like. The usual steps of inspecting the fruit for defects, washing the fruit, sterilization, rinsing and juice extraction are first performed on the citrus fruits. The extracted juice and insoluble pulp is then processed to effect a separation of an insoluble pulp mass from the juice. The method of extraction may be by screening or centrifuging by any common procedure. The two portions, one of which comprises the gross pulp particles or mass and the other the juice effects a gross separation of the enzymes from the pectin inasmuch as the enzymes, such as pectinesterase and pectase, will be contained in the insoluble pulp mass.

The juice can, of course, be further screened or centrifuged to collect the smallest particles of the insoluble pulp mass if it is desired to remove essentially all of the enzymes. However, a simple conventional screening or centrifuging will usually be adequate. A centrifuged separation would remove all but the finest particles and would produce a juice with maximum stability. The juice portion is then concentrated by any of the commonly used methods which may include freeze concentration, vacuum evaporation or distillation of the water in the juice to produce a liquid concentrate which should be in the range of approximately 20° to 70°Brix.

Upon the separation of the citrus fruit into two portions, namely, the insoluble pulp mass and juice, the unique aspects of the process become apparent. For instance, it has been determined that the insoluble pulp containing the enzymes normally has a soluble solids content of no higher than approximately 18° to 9°Brix, and will freeze at a temperature of approximately 26° to 28°F, respectively. As can be readily understood, a higher juice soluble content, such as the natural sugar present in the fruit, will lower the freezing point of the pulp.

For instance, an 18°Brix soluble content will lower the freezing point from 28°F for a 9°Brix content to 26°F. In contrast, the freezing point of the juice concentrate is considerably lower due to the significantly higher soluble solids content obtained from the juice concentration step to 20° to 70°Brix. The freezing point is, of course, dependent upon the percentage of soluble solids, i.e., a tangerine concentrate having 20% soluble solids would freeze at the same temperature as an orange concentrate of 20% soluble solids. It is on the basis of these definitive freezing aspects of the juice and the insoluble pulp mass that the process is derived.

It has been discovered that if the insoluble pulp mass is frozen by reducing its temperature from 26° to 28°F, or below, the enzymes will be tightly bound within this frozen mass of insoluble pulp and, therefore, as long as this insoluble pulp mass remains frozen, the enzymes would be essentially isolated from their surroundings, even if the surroundings were liquid juice which contained a pectin. The theory behind this discovery is that when the enzymes are maintained in a medium having a high freezing point, such as the pulp mass, rather than a low freezing medium such as the juice, the enzymes are isolated and immobilized and cannot react with the pectin unless the pulp is melted.

Consequently, it has been determined that when the insoluble pulp mass is maintained in frozen condition, the temperature of the entire citrus fruit product, which would include the juice portion and the insoluble pulp mass, can be maintained at a temperature up to approximately 26° to 28°F, since at this temperature the insoluble pulp mass remains frozen and no reaction will occur with the enzymes in this pulp. This would permit greater variations of the surrounding temperature which the juice product would normally encounter, resulting in greater flexibility in the requirements for storage.

The freezing of the insoluble pulp mass may produce a solid unitary mass in a block form or actually the frozen pulp mass may take the form of pellets or smaller unit sizes. The size of the frozen pulp mass units is not critical, but rather only the temperature at which they are maintained is important.

When the insoluble pulp mass is frozen, it can be added to a suitable container or can and then the container or can filled with the juice concentrate which, of course, cannot be higher in temperature than 28°F. The juice and the frozen pulp therefore are to remain as separate entities even though they may be commingled. The closing of the container can be done by conventional means; however, again, the contents of the can cannot be raised to a point to which the insoluble pulp mass containing the enzymes will liquefy and therefore have the opportunity of reacting with the pectin of the juice concentrate.

The juice concentrate is normally filled in the container at 17° to 20°F; however, these temperatures are not critical as long as they are not such as to melt the frozen insoluble pulp mass when the juice concentrate is combined with the frozen pulp mass. It is therefore possible to add the juice concentrate as a cold liquid or the juice concentrate may be frozen in a block and the frozen juice concentrate added to the can or container along with the frozen pulp mass. It is an important aspect of the process that when the juice is combined with the frozen pulp mass either as liquid or solid, the pectin would be isolated from the pectinesterase and pectase as long as the latter were in the frozen insoluble pulp mass. The citrus product can be rehydrated upon thawing in the conventional manner to produce a flavorful, fresh tasting citrus juice.

Concentration Without External Heat Application

A process for concentrating citrus juices without the application of external heat is described by *H.W. Harrell; U.S. Patent 3,340,071; September 5, 1967.* This method minimizes the destruction of the nascent qualities of the juice. It has been found that by vigorous agitation of confined liquids by internal mechanical means, vaporization of certain constituents, emulsifications and like combinations of liquids will occur. Vigorous agitation or turbulence generated by internal mechanical means will produce liquid vapor which may include droplets, atomized liquid and free floating aerosol particles, as well as volatilized portions of the lighter constituents of liquid combinations, dispersals, or suspensions.

While the nature and amount of vapor produced by mechanical agitation and turbulence of the body of a liquid will, of course vary with the pressure applied to the liquid within a closed receptacle, as well as the type of agitation employed, it has been found that with this process apparatus considerable vaporization, both by volatilization and mechanical atomization will occur under atmospheric pressure. In the treatment of citrus juices the vigorous internal mechanical agitation and resultant turbulence produces a water vapor which may be drawn off from the body of the liquid to leave therein a more concentrated solution of the juices, the constituents of which are heavier and less volatile than the water content of the natural juices.

In this method and by use of the described apparatus internal heat is generated through the frictional action of contact with the liquid and the turbulence produced by rotating blades preferably operating between stationary blades. The relation of the blades is somewhat in the fashion of a maze to force the fluid in a tortuous turbulent path whereby the skin friction of the liquid in contact with such mechanical means produced the elevation of temperature of the liquid.

It is to be noted that in accordance with the well-known principle of fluid motivation mechanical impellers produce a localized reduction of pressure behind the blades. Thus, as the front or leading face of a rotating impeller pushes forwardly the fluid in front of the blade, substantially reduced pressure is effected behind the blade to provide for the inflow of fluid to compensate for that which has moved forward.

In the present device this localized reduction of pressure in combination with the increased temperature produced by skin friction provides a localized continuously moving evaporation zone or zones where the heat and pressure are such as to induce distillation despite overall pressures and temperatures well below the temperatures and pressures required for conventional distillation. Thus the chamber pressure may be atmospheric and the mass temperature relatively low despite which volatilization will occur.

With respect to the concentration of citrus juices, deleterious effect upon the character of the juice such as taste, aroma and appearance, frequently ensues from evaporation by the application of external heat to elevate the mass temperature of the total liquid to the evaporation point, reduced pressure having been employed to minimize such required temperature.

It has been suggested that such destruction of the nascent qualities of the juices by evaporation in a cooking method permits the enzymes and microorganisms to affect the pectin content whereby it may be precipitated, thus contributing to the disqualification of such concentrate from wide areas of the market. It has further been suggested that by a brief subjection of at least portions of the natural juices, while in motion to vaporizing temperatures by externally applied heat and the instant commingling of such portions with the body of the juice, will be effective to immunize the enzymes and microorganisms within acceptable limits.

The method and the operation of this apparatus may produce a like inactivation, neutralization, or pacification of the enzyme and/or microorganism effect on the pectin to produce a citrus juice concentrate free of previously encountered objections. Drawings and a detailed description of the apparatus are included in the patent.

Ultrasonic High Frequency Vibration

A process for concentrating citrus juice has been developed by *Z. Berk; U.S. Patent 3,352,693; November 14, 1967; assigned to Technion Research and Development Founda-*

tion Ltd., Israel which uses ultrasonic high frequency vibration, thus minimizing the likelihood of impairment of flavor. A thixotropic composition is concentrated here by a process which comprises the steps of submitting the composition to an ultrasonic treatment and to solvent evaporation.

Where the concentration is effected in stages it is possible to precede each individual evaporation stage by an ultrasonic treatment. The process may also be carried out by continuously recycling the product withdrawn from the evaporator back through the ultrasonic treatment unit into the evaporator. In this manner the concentration is increased gradually up to the desired level.

Fruit juices of a concentration of 75° to 80°Brix can be prepared. The preparation of juices or purees of such high concentration is very desirable since at this level of concentration no special measures for preservation such as pasteurization or freezing have to be taken. All that is required with such a product is to store it under refrigeration so as to prevent nonenzymatic browning. Such a degree of concentration could hitherto not be achieved even with modern evaporators containing heat exchangers designed to cause a high turbulence of the concentrate.

The highly concentrated juices obtained with this process are considerably less viscous than would be the case if concentrates of the same degree of concentration were prepared in a conventional manner, and this state of comparatively reduced concentration appears to be permanent. Thus, for example, the viscosity of a 70°Brix orange juice concentrate prepared in accordance with this process was only 1.5 times that of the original 60°Brix concentrate. Against this, the viscosity of a 70°Brix concentrate obtained by evaporation without ultrasonic treatment was almost 8 times that of this original 60°Brix concentrate.

The process also consists in an apparatus for the concentration of a thixotropic composition comprising means for the ultrasonic treatment of the composition, an evaporator, and means for conducting the composition from the ultrasonic treatment means to the evaporator.

FIGURE 2.3: CONCENTRATION OF THIXOTROPIC COMPOSITIONS

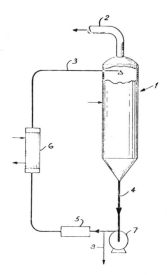

Source: Z. Berk; U.S. Patent 3,352,693; November 14, 1967

The process is illustrated by Figure 2.3 which is a diagrammatic representation of the apparatus which comprises an evaporator 1 having an adapter 2 for connection to a condenser, an inlet 3 for feeding the composition to be concentrated and outlet 4 for the discharge of the concentrated product. The apparatus further comprises an ultrasonic treatment unit 5, a heater 6, a pump 7 and an outlet 8 for the takeoff of the final product.

During operation, the treated composition is circulated continuously from the evaporator through the ultrasonic treatment unit and the heater back into the evaporator and in this manner a gradual concentration takes place. As soon as the final degree of concentration is reached the product is discharged through outlet 8.

The process is further illustrated by the following two working examples. In these examples the relative viscosity measurements were effected by comparing the time of flow in a No. 400 Ostwald Pipette. Where concentrates of different degrees of concentration were compared, correction was made for the differences in specific gravity.

Example 1: Fifty grams of commercial Shamouti orange juice concentrate with a soluble solids content of 60°Brix, was subjected to ultrasonic waves with a frequency of 20,000 cycles per second. The ultrasonic generator had a power output of 60 watts. The relative viscosity of the sample decreased as follows:

Period of Treatment, min	Relative Viscosity
0	100
2	85
4	64
7	53
12	51
15	26

This example illustrates the very pronounced lowering of the viscosity by a suitable ultrasonic treatment. The applicability of this phenomenon in the concentration of orange juice is illustrated in the following example.

Example 2: A commercial sample of Shamouti orange juice concentrate, as described in Example 1, was subjected to ultrasonic treatment for 10 minutes by means of the apparatus described in Example 1, and then concentrated, under reduced pressure to a soluble solids content of 63°Brix. The material was given another 10 minutes of ultrasonic treatment and further concentrated to 70°Brix. The viscosity of this 70°Brix concentrate was only 150% of that of the original 60°Brix concentrate. The viscosity of the 70°Brix concentrate obtained without ultrasonic treatment was 700% that of the original 60°Brix concentrate. The sample concentrated in accordance with the process was capable of further concentration without scorching and browning.

Spray Concentration

The process of *J.F. King, Jr. and M.W. Hoover; U.S. Patent 3,362,456; January 9, 1968* relates in general to methods and apparatus for concentrating fruit juices, such as orange juice and the like, and more particularly to a process and apparatus for eliminating water from fruit juice to effect concentration of the same for commercial distribution, where water is extracted from the juice by spraying the juice in very small droplet size into a moving air or gaseous stream which extracts water constituents from the juice through evaporation, the liquid and solid state juice constituents being physically separated from the air or gaseous stream for delivery along a selected recovery path.

The process and apparatus involves a system of juice concentration. Instead of relying upon direct heat exchange with the fruit juice to effect evaporation in the usual manner achieved by conventional evaporators, condensation is achieved by spraying the juice into an enclosure in minute droplet form to effect evaporation of the water constituents into a high velocity inert gas or air stream until the stream attains a saturated or near saturated state, and rotating in the inert gas or air stream a rotary eliminator wheel having radial, circumferentially spaced plates which intercept the liquid and solid constituents of the spray field and propel them centrifugally outwardly in a thin film for discharge from the periphery of the wheel to a collecting sump. The saturated air or inert gas passes through the spaces between plates of the wheel and may be discharged in the case of air or recycled through cooling condensers and heaters in the case of inert gas.

Example: Just prior to injecting fresh single strength (about 10 to 14% soluble solids) juice, the system illustrated in Figure 2.4 is vacuumized, and is filled with an inert gas such as gaseous nitrogen to a pressure slightly greater than atmospheric pressure, for example, about 1.1 atmospheres. The purpose of establishing such a pressure level is to insure that any purging or leakage that occurs will be to the exterior of the system and thus prevent infiltration of oxygen into the system.

FIGURE 2.4: SPRAY CONCENTRATION OF ORANGE JUICE

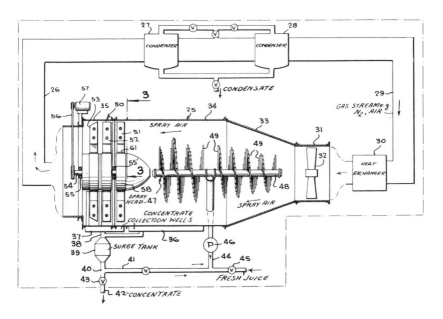

Source: J.F. King, Jr. and M.W. Hoover; U.S. Patent 3,362,456; January 9, 1968

The circulation of the gaseous nitrogen through the closed circuit system is started by turning on the fan **32** and energizing the motor **57** to drive the rotary eliminator wheels **51, 52** and **53**. The condensers **27** and **28**, which may for example have heat exchanger coils supplied with liquid nitrogen, are set to cool the moist gas to just below the dew point for drying out the gas. The circulating pressure pump **46** is then started up and fresh juice is injected into the system through the supply conduit **45** with the valve therein open and the valve in the return conduit **41** closed.

The juice is then discharged in a spray pattern through the header **48** and nozzles **49** and dewatered by evaporation of water into the gaseous nitrogen stream and centrifugal discharge of the liquid and solid constituents by the eliminator wheel blades into the sumps to gravitationally collect in the concentrate surge tank **39** until the latter is full. Then the valve in the conduit **41** is opened and the valve in the supply conduit is closed, and the concentrate is recirculated through the pressure pump and spray nozzles until the concentrate reaches the desired Brix, probably about 42°, in the case of orange juice and higher with grape or apple juice.

Upon attainment of the desired Brix, the concentrate is then withdrawn through the outlet 42 by opening of the valve 43, to pass the concentrate on to a freezer. It will be appreciated that the concentration of the orange juice may be effected in plural stages, under which circumstances the concentrate in the surge tank 39 would be withdrawn when a selected Brix level is attained for transfer to a second or additional like concentrating system for successive processing until the desired final Brix is reached.

This system may be used as a single stage concentrator for continuous operation, if desired, in which event fresh juice would be introduced in the system during recirculation of juice through the pump 46, nozzles 49 and eliminator assembly at such a rate that the juice in the surge tank is kept at the desired concentration. Continuous operation may also be effected by feeding the concentrate in the surge tank to a second like concentrating system as referred to above when the concentrate reaches a selected level of concentration.

By the system described above, rapid concentration of juice in a highly efficient manner can be achieved with minimal loss of natural oils, esters and other constituents that tend to add the distinguishing flavor to natural juice, as the concentration is effected at such low temperatures, for example at substantially room temperature or below, so that the volatile constituents which contribute the desired flavor and aroma are not lost. The highly effective evaporating and liquid and solid constituent recovering apparatus permits rapid concentration in a manner which particularly lends itself to commercial juice concentration installations.

Low Viscosity Concentrate Stabilized with Flavor Emulsion

The process of *E.R. Fehlberg, G.H. Kraft and W.A. Gorman; U.S. Patent 3,391,009; July 2, 1968; assigned to National Dairy Products Corporation* relates to a method for the manufacture of high Brix fruit juice concentrates of low viscosity which are readily reconstituted with water. More specifically, the process relates to a method for the manufacture of an orange juice concentrate, which method comprises extracting orange juice from oranges, deaerating and heating the juice, adjusting the pulp content of the juice to less than 8% pulp and usually to between about 4% and about 8%, concentrating the juice to provide an orange juice concentrate of at least about 50°Brix and stabilizing the juice concentrate by adding a minor amount of orange oil, or emulsion thereof to the concentrate.

It has been discovered that when an orange juice concentrate is manufactured in accordance with the described method, a high yield of at least about 50°Brix orange juice concentrate is obtained which has a viscosity below about 10,000 cp. The viscosity of the orange juice concentrate does not substantially increase when stored and the orange juice concentrate does not gel upon extended storage. The concentrate is easily reconstituted with water to provide a reconstituted orange juice having an acceptable color, flavor and aroma which does not require the addition of cut back juice, though cut back juice may be utilized. The described method is particularly suited for manufacturing 72°Brix orange juice, i.e., 7 plus 1 orange juice concentrate.

Orange oil is a commercially available cold pressed product which has in the past, been conventionally added to orange juice concentrates of low Brix to increase their flavor. Orange oil comprises about 98% d-limonene and about 1.65% aldehydes. The orange oil is added in an amount between 0.15% and about 0.25% by volume of the orange juice concentrate.

It has been observed that the presence of the orange oil in the orange juice concentrate acts to maintain low viscosity in the concentrate and, if the orange oil is not added to the orange juice concentrate, it has been found that the concentrate will often gel or set on storage and is not readily reconstituted with water. It is believed that the orange oil provides a surfactant effect when added to orange juice concentrates of high Brix value.

Example: A 72°Brix orange juice concentrate is manufactured in a continuous process by extracting the juice from oranges in a conventional fruit juice extractor. The extractor is operated at 90 psig to provide 33 gallons of single strength orange juice per minute. The orange juice obtained from the extractor is finished in a finisher having 0.020" finisher screens at a pressure of 95 psig. The orange juice obtained from the finisher contains 12% pulp.

The orange juice is passed into a deaerator which is maintained at 3" of mercury absolute and air is removed from the orange juice. The deaerated orange juice is passed into a plate and frame pasteurizer and is pasteurized by heating the juice to a temperature of 195°F to 200°F for 3 seconds. The juice is cooled to 110°F in the cooling section of the pasteurizer and the pasteurized juice is introduced into a continuous centrifuge which is operated at 40 psig back pressure. About 32.6 gal/min of orange juice is obtained from the centrifuge which contains 5 to 6% pulp.

The pulp sludge from the separated orange juice in the centrifuge is removed from the centrifuge and mixed with 3 volumes of water per volume of pulp sludge in a mixing tank. The water and pulp slurry is centrifuged in a centrifuge operated at a back pressure of 40 psig to provide about 1.2 gal/min of pulp-wash liquor containing 5 to 6% pulp which is mixed with the orange juice in a storage tank.

The mixed orange juice and pulp-wash liquor are passed into a deaerator which is operated at a pressure of 1" of mercury absolute. The deaerated orange juice mixture is then introduced into a double effect evaporator having a single stage in the first effect and two stages in the second effect. The flow rate of the orange juice mixture to the evaporator is about 33 gal/min.

The orange juice mixture is concentrated to 27°Brix in the first effect of the evaporator at a temperature of 76°F. The orange juice mixture is further concentrated to 50°Brix at a temperature of 75°F in the first stage of the second effect after which it is introduced into the second stage of the second effect of the evaporator where it is concentrated to 72°Brix at a temperature of 83°F. The evaporator withdraws 11,000 pounds of water vapor per hour from the orange juice mixture.

The orange juice concentrate obtained from the evaporator is introduced into a cold wall mixing tank where it is cooled to 50°F. To the concentrate is added 0.20% of orange oil with agitation in the mixing tank to stabilize orange juice against gelling and setting.

The stabilized orange juice concentrate is withdrawn from the cold wall mixing tank and is transferred to conventional canning apparatus where it is canned. The orange juice concentrate may be stored at 10°F for a period of as much as 12 months and reconstituted with 7 parts of water per part of concentrate. The orange juice concentrate is readily reconstituted with water and provides a reconstituted orange juice which has an acceptable flavor and aroma.

Washing of Ice Crystals with Liquid Butane

N. Graniaris; U.S. Patent 3,827,248; August 6, 1974; assigned to Struthers Patent Corp. describes a process whereby ice crystals formed in a solution, such as in the ice crystallization conversion of sea water to fresh water or slush freezing of citrus juice are washed in liquid butane at a temperature below 32°F. The crystals rest on an inclined screen sinking down in the butane and they are agitated mechanically by butane jets and/or by vibration of the screen. Brine, which is mechanically washed from the crystals, sinks through the screen to be collected below it. Washed ice crystals move down the screen to be collected, melted and debutanized.

As shown in Figure 2.5, a brine and ice slurry **10** enters tank **11** through duct **12** propelled by any suitable conveyor (not shown). The tank is rectangular and contains a

downward sloping screen **13** which may be a sheet of perforated metal. The screen is
mounted in a resilient frame **14** of rubber or the like so that the vibrator **15** may be connected to it by means of the push rod **16** which enters the tank **11** through a seal **17**.

FIGURE 2.5: APPARATUS FOR WASHING CRYSTALS

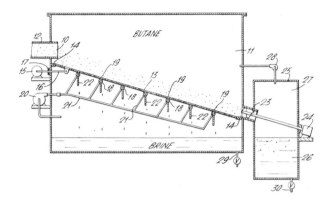

Source: N. Graniaris; U.S. Patent 3,827,248; August 6, 1974

Transverse tubes **18** containing upward facing jets **19** are fixed to the bottom of the
screen. Pump **20** draws butane from the tank and passes it through flexible tubes **21** to
each transverse tube. Transverse drip baffles **22** extend down from each tube **18** or from
the bottom of the screen. The screen, tubes **18**, and the baffles may be of metal welded
together. Tubes **21** may be of vinyl or other flexible material. A screw **23** or the like
driven by motor **24** draws washed ice crystals into the melt and butane separation tank **25**.

This apparatus is used in the following manner. The ice crystals fall on the screen which
is agitated by the vibrator in its resilient frame. The mechanical agitation of the crystals
in liquid butane removes brine from their surfaces. This removed brine and any other
brine introduced with the crystals sinks through the screen to drip from it and collect in
the bottom of the tank. The agitation of the ice crystals on the screen may alternately
be accomplished by the jets of butane pumped up through the screen by the pump
through the tubes **21** and **18**.

If desired both forms of mechanical agitation may be used together. The liquid butane
in the tank is best kept above the freezing temperature of the brine which is usually
about 26° to 27°F in the freeze crystallization of sea water and below the 32°F melting
temperature of the ice crystals. Tanks **11** and **25** are pressurized to enable the butane
to be liquid at the desired operating temperatures. During the washing of the ice crystals
on the screen, some surface ice will melt on each crystal to achieve equilibrium, but the
ice lost during butane washing will be minimal compared to the conventional water washing.

The washed crystals at the lower end of the screen are removed by the screw conveyor
into tank **25**. Any conventional means, such as heat exchanger coils (not shown) are
used to melt ice to water **26** which separates from any liquid butane **27** carried into tank
25 on the crystals. Pump **28** is automatically controlled to return separated butane to
tank **11**. Brine is drawn off through pipe **29** and fresh water as a product through pipe
30. Further debutanizing may be carried out in the brine and the fresh water product
if required.

OSMOTIC PROCESSES

Semipermeable Membrane of Hollow Fiber Bundles

There has been for many years concentrated effort to use semipermeable membranes as a separatory means. The already developed art encompasses a diversity of known membranes which have, to a greater or lesser degree, the property of being selectively permeable to different components of fluid mixtures. Thus, some membranes (of the type that are referred to as osmotic membranes) will pass water but restrain ions. Other membranes will selectively pass ions in solution. These are usually known as being ion exchange membranes.

Still other membranes possess selective permeation rates for two or more nonionic components of fluid mixtures. Yet additional types of membranes are of the so-called molecular sieve type (such as those utilized for dialysis), which can pass ions or other materials but tend to restrain passage of high molecular weight components or, similarly, which are adapted to pass only certain molecular weight fractions of given materials, depending on actual molecular size and proportions.

Despite the recognition of the inherent advantages that are achievable with permeability separatory apparatus, commercial adoption of such devices has been undertaken on only a very limited scale. The common inherent limitation that seems to militate against more widespread employment of the prior permeability separatory procedures has been the slow and relatively inefficient (at least for commercial purposes) rate of transfer of the desired component from one side of the membrane to the other.

H.I. Mahon; U.S. Patents 3,228,876; January 11, 1966; and 3,228,877; January 11, 1966; both assigned to The Dow Chemical Company describes a specific cell that incorporates a specific membrane element comprising a multiplicity of substantially unsupported, fine, continuously hollow fiber and, even more advantageously for most purposes a multiplicity of bundles of a substantially parallel plurality of such fibers in which the thin wall of each of the hollow fibers employed forms the transfer membrane area in and for the cell or element, all as hereinafter more particularly described and specified.

Prior art permeability membranes have consisted, for the most part, of thin, uniplanar plates rigidly supported on solid backing members. Obviously, in such apparatus, a plate of exceedingly large area or large pluralities of such uniplanar plates are necessary to achieve practical transfer rates. Additionally, in such installations, the backing plates take up space in considerable proportion and may be considered, at best, as mere dead weight. Besides, due to the necessary construction of such apparatus, the membranes tend to be relatively weak and susceptible to rupture in use.

Practice of this process, however, allows permeability separatory apparatus to be used for any of a wide variety of applications in which great advantage can be derived from installations characterized in having exceedingly large transfer areas for given volumes of space occupied by the apparatus.

Such an objective is readily accomplishable with the present membrane elements wherein, most beneficially, very large bundles of any desired plurality, even up to a million or more, of the hollow fibers that form the transfer area can be maintained, if desired, in spaces having cross sections no greater than an inch or so of width or diameter. The ratio of transfer area to apparatus volume achievable by this process is invariably many times (and significantly) greater than may be had by following of prior art techniques.

For example, the process permits installations to be employed that have surface areas for transfer of material to be separated that are as much as ten thousand square feet or more per cubic foot of volume actually occupied by the installation. This represents a transfer area to apparatus volume ratio that is greater by a factor of at least 30 than the same characteristic in conventional apparatus for the same purpose, wherein (depending somewhat on the type and configuration of the backing plates or other supports used for the membrane) the apparatus may provide only three hundred square feet or less per cubic foot of installation.

Furthermore, the thin-walled hollow fibers used in the membrane elements achieve much greater membrane strength than is possible in prior art membranes having different configurations. This nicely overcomes difficulties occasioned by the requisite use, for purposes of adequate strength, of relatively thicker membrane materials. At the same time, backing plates and equivalent types of membrane supports are eliminated and avoided in the hollow fiber membrane elements of the method.

Referring first to Figure 2.6a, there is shown the overall structure of one embodiment of the basic permeability cell of the process. This is generally designated, in its entirety, by reference numeral 10. The cell 10 includes an inlet 11 for untreated fluid having means such as a pump or the like, not shown, to apply a desired fluid pressure to fluid entering the inlet, and an outlet 12 for the discharge of the treated fluid. An additional outlet 13 is formed for discharge of the fluid component after it has passed through the permeable membranes of the cell.

FIGURE 2.6: PERMEABILITY SEPARATORY APPARATUS

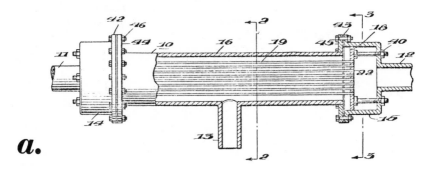

a.

Overall Structure of Permeability Cell

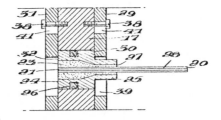

b.

End Seal for Hollow Fiber Bundle

Source: H.I. Mahon; U.S. Patent 3,228,876; January 11, 1966

At the entrance end the inlet feeds a header chamber 14. At the exit end there is positioned a second header chamber 15 which feeds the outlet 12. Situated between the headers and supporting the same is a casing 16. Advantageously, the casing is tubular, although it may have other desired configuration. The casing **16** is sealed at its end from headers **14** and **15** by means of header end plates **17** and **18**. Outlet **13** provides an exit for fluid accumulated in the casing. Positioned within the casing are a multiplicity of bundles **19** of hollow, fine fibers **20**. The nature of the hollow fibers is hereinafter described in greater detail.

As is best shown in Figures 2.6a and 2.6b, each of the bundles has its terminal portions **21, 22** sealed in openings in the end plates by means of a suitable adhesive or cement, resin or the like, indicated generally at **23**. The bundles are thus supported at their terminal portions only by the header plates. In this way, the opposite open ends of the many small hollow fibers are all in fluid communication with the header chambers. Each of the hollow fibers in each bundle has the same or about the same length.

Likewise, it is generally desirable for the other dimensioned parameters of all the hollow fibers in each bundle (i.e., outside diameter and wall thickness) to be the same in each fiber although, if desired, bundles of fibers having different individual outside diameters and wall thicknesses may be employed. Similarly, each of the bundles advantageously has the same dimensional parameters as the other bundles; i.e., the same length and outside diameters, although the latter of these can, if desired, also be varied in individual bundles. Thus it will be seen that each of the fibers has a uniform bore therethrough.

There is thus formed a permeability cell that includes a multiplicity of parallel, fine, hollow fibers each of which is supported only at its terminal portions and substantially unsupported throughout its length. Such a cell, as indicated, provides the maximum unimpaired transfer area for a given membrane material. The hollow fibers can withstand pressures of many hundreds of pounds per square inch and their wall thickness is so small that they present minimum resistance to passage of a permeable fluid component.

The choice of materials for this process is, of course, dictated by the particular separatory process in which the permeability cells are to be utilized, including a consideration of the strength which is necessary to efficient process production.

Among other factors which are determinative of the material chosen for a particular separatory process are: resistance to chemical reaction with the fluid components, specific and selective permeability constants of the material for the chosen fluid components at the chosen concentration, solubility or recrystallization of the membrane material in one or more of the fluid components, and cost of the membrane material. In addition, the membrane material chosen for use must be capable of formation into thin-walled, hollow fibers. Such materials are generally hydrophilic in character and include cellulose esters such as cellulose acetate and triacetate.

The system and separatory procedure of the process is successfully applicable to a wide range of separating operations. Two such applications actually accomplished are illustrated below. In each instance, for purposes of uniform operation and to aid in comparison, the tests were conducted using a single 350 fiber bundle of cellulose triacetate fibers, each of which had an outside diameter of about 45 microns and a wall thickness of about 10 microns. The yield of permeate obtained in each example is that obtained from the entire fiber bundle.

Example 1:

Material	Apple cider
Osmotic pressure	380 to 400 psi
Applied pressure	425 psi
Permeation rate	0.05 cc/hr
Permeate	White, negative for sugar, refractive index = distilled water

Example 2:

Material	Orange juice
Osmotic pressure	200 psi
Applied pressure	380 psi
Permeation rate	0.07 cc/hr
Permeate	Substantially only water; very slight trace of sugar

Concentration by Molecular Filtration

Ultrafiltration is widely used to isolate colloids such as proteins from aqueous solutions or suspensions. Basically, ultrafiltration is like ordinary filtration through a screen or cloth except that in this case the filter is a semipermeable membrane such as a·film of cellulose nitrate, regenerated cellulose, or the like. The solution to be treated is applied under pressure to one side of the membrane; the colloidal material remains on the upstream side of the membrane while water and crystalloids such as salts, sugars, etc. pass through the membrane.

Although the semipermeable membranes used in ultrafiltration possess quite small pores, they will only prevent passage of colloids and other macromolecules; crystalloids such as acids, salts, sugars, and the like pass through these pores very readily. Consequently, application of ultrafiltration to a liquid food such as a fruit juice would accomplish no concentration. For example, if the juice was a clear liquid free from colloids, the entire juice would pass through the semipermeable membrane.

If the juice contained colloidal material, the juice would merely be separated into a fraction containing all the original water, acids, sugars, salts, flavor components, etc. In contrast, the apparatus of the process utilizes special membranes which have the properties of (a) permitting the passage of water and (b) preventing the passage of crystalloids such as acids, salts, sugar, flavor components, etc.

As a result, a true concentration is achieved. Because the separation technique utilized herein is at such a sophisticated level as to yield a separation of water from noncolloidal substances such as electrolytes and other crystalloids, it is termed molecular filtration to distinguish it from the relatively ancient art of ultrafiltration. The technique may also be termed reverse osmosis because the flow of water is opposite to that encountered in ordinary osmosis.

It has been shown in U.S. Patents 3,133,132 and 3,133,137 that sea water can be desalinated by molecular filtration to prepare potable water, utilizing a special membrane which allows passage of water at a high flux rate while preventing passage of salt. Although the apparatus is suitable for pilot studies and for demonstrating the functions of the special membrane, it is not adapted for large-scale operations.

Contributing to this deficiency is the following. The passages through which the starting liquid (e.g., salt water) is channeled are not conductive to uniform flow because of their angular and/or tortuous construction. This leads to localized areas of high solute concentration which are conductive to inadequate demineralization and to localized areas of low solute concentration which lead to inefficient utilization of the membrane filtration capacity. Another point is that the water flowing through the membrane does not pass directly out of the system but must flow through a considerable length of the porous backing of the membrane. This is likely to lead to back-pressures which will impede proper operation of the molecular filtration system.

It might readily be visualized that for large scale industrial operations, it would be preferable if the membrane were shaped into a cylinder of relatively small diameter and long length and the liquid to be treated were pumped through the interior of this cylinder, thereby attaining a good scavenging action and avoiding any localized high or low concentrations of solute. It might further be visualized that if the cylindrical membrane were provided with a cylindrical porous backing or support, the water passing through the membrane would take a radial path through the porous backing and hence leave the system by a short path, consequently offering minimum back-pressure.

A primary object of the process of *E. Lowe and E.L. Durkee; U.S. Patent 3,341,024; September 12, 1967; assigned to the U.S. Secretary of Agriculture* lies in the fabrication of apparatus which provides the advantages mentioned above.

Example: A casting solution was prepared containing:

	Percent
Cellulose acetate	22.2
Acetone	66.7
Water	10.0
Magnesium perchlorate	1.1

A quantity of this solution was poured into a one foot section of 0.5" i.d. precision-bored glass tubing and drawn with a rod along the length of the tube to spread it uniformly in the longitudinal dimension of the tube. The tube was then capped at each end and spun about its axis at about 1,200 rpm for 20 minutes to distribute the solution uniformly in the radial sense. The tube was then uncapped and a very gentle stream of air, at room temperature, was passed through the tube for 1 minute in one direction, then for the same time in the opposite direction.

The tube was immersed in ice water and moved about in the water to promote leaching of perchlorate and residual acetone from the film. The film was then withdrawn from the glass tube. It was observed to have a wall thickness of 4 mils, it was clear with a tinge of milkiness and was self-supporting and quite rigid. It was heat cured for 10 minutes in water at 86°C, then utilized as the membrane in a structure fabricated as described below.

Wool felt strip, 1" wide, was spirally wound on a ½" diameter mandrel. Woven glass fiber tape, 1.5" wide and 15 mils thick, was spirally wound over the felt in the opposite direction. A conventional epoxy resin (settable at room temperature) was then coated onto the glass fiber winding.

Application of the glass fibers and resin was repeated, with opposite direction of winding for each layer, for a total of 10 layers of resin coated glass fibers. The entire assembly was placed in a chamber where it was held under a pressure of about 29" Hg for 10 to 15 minutes. The assembly was then removed from the vacuum chamber and allowed to stand until the resin had set. The assembly was then removed from the mandrel and the ends squared off.

The ends of the assembly were made imperforate by stopping up one end, taping the side of the structure except for the last inch, dipping the untaped, plugged end into a bath of the same epoxy liquid as used before, and applying vacuum to the hollow core of the structure, whereby to suck the resin into the end of the structure. This procedure was repeated to render imperforate the opposite end.

Tapered drift pins were then inserted into each end of the assembly to compress the felt layer to a tapered configuration and the device was allowed to stand until the resin had hardened. The drift pins were removed and a seamless tubular membrane was inserted into the hollow core and sealed in place by inserting a perforated rubber stopper in each end. The tubes were threaded, and couplings were screwed on. The completed structure was found to be useful for preparing concentrated apple juice by pumping single-strength (14°Brix) apple juice through the hollow core of the apparatus at a pressure of 1,000 psig.

Combination of Direct and Reverse Osmosis

The process of *K. Popper; U.S. Patent 3,423,310; January 21, 1969; assigned to U.S. Secretary of Agriculture* is based on the principle of utilizing osmotic pressure as a driving force to operate a reverse osmosis cycle. Thus for example, the process encompasses a system wherein osmotic pressure is generated in a first cell (one involving direct osmosis) and this pressure is then utilized to drive a second osmotic cell (one involving reverse osmosis). The process can be utilized for the concentration of all types of liquid products such as fruit juices and vegetable juices.

In desalinating sea water or other source of water containing salt, it is preferred to operate both the direct and reverse cells with brines. On the other hand, in utilization of the process in concentrating fruit juices or other material of relatively high cost, it is preferred to operate only the reverse cell with the juice or other material which is to end up in the final product. The direct osmosis cell is operated with lower cost materials such as a brine, or, if desired, with aqueous solutions of other inorganic salts.

Referring to Figure 2.7, which schematically depicts the apparatus for the process, an example is given for the concentration (dewatering) of fruit juice.

FIGURE 2.7: OSMOTIC PROCESSES AND APPARATUS

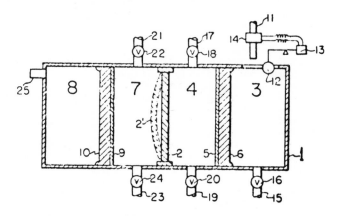

Source: K. Popper; U.S. Patent 3,423,310; January 21, 1969

Example: In starting the operation, discharge valves **16, 20,** and **24** are in closed position and kept closed during the production cycle. Plain water is filled into compartment **3** via feed pipe **11,** and during operation the compartment is kept full of water by operation of float **12.**

Compartment **4** is filled with brine or, more preferably, a concentrated aqueous solution of a salt which is highly soluble in water. Typically, one may use calcium chloride, sodium sulphate, calcium nitrate, sodium diacid phosphate, etc. Especially preferred is an about 6 N solution of calcium nitrate which, in a couple with water, provides a very high osmotic pressure. After filling compartment **4,** feed valve **18** is then closed to seal this compartment.

Compartment **7** is filled with juice, e.g., orange juice, which is to be concentrated. Feed valve **22** is then closed to seal the compartment. It may be noted that orange juice has a solids content of about 12%, or 0.75 N, calculated as glucose.

Compartment **8** is filled with water, or is full from a previous run. In the direct osmosis cell, water diffuses from compartment **3** into the concentrated solution in compartment **4**. The pressure so produced is transferred by diaphragm **2** to the juice in compartment **7** whereby water from the juice is caused to flow into compartment **8**. As a result, the juice in compartment **7** becomes concentrated.

When production slows down, due, for example, to dilution of the solution in compartment **4**, the concentrated juice is drained from compartment **7** as the product. The contents of compartment **4** are dumped. (The spent liquor may be evaporated for reuse.) To restart the production cycle, fresh juice is filled into compartment **7** and concentrated salt solution into compartment **4**, as above described. No changes are required as to either compartments **3** or **8**.

Controlling Degree of Liquid Concentration During Process

In further work *E. Lowe and E.L. Durkee; U.S. Patents 3,552,566; January 5, 1971; and 3,634,103; January 11, 1972; both assigned to U.S. Secretary of Agriculture* describe an apparatus and process for controlling the degree of concentration attained in reverse osmosis operations, and for discharging concentrated product from such operations without damage to the product.

In conducting reverse osmosis the liquid to be concentrated is applied under superatmospheric pressure against a suitable membrane. Water (from the liquid) passes through the membrane, leaving a residue of concentrated liquid on the upstream side of the membrane. The permeate (water) and concentrate are separately discharged from the system. In conducting reverse osmosis operations, various problems are encountered. One involves the matter of controlling the degree of concentration achieved.

For example, the operator may require a product of two-fold concentration or of four-fold concentration, etc., depending on particular circumstances. Because of the fact that fruit and vegetable juices are non-Newtonian liquids whose viscosity is a function of the shear rate imposed upon them, the usual techniques for controlling the degree of concentration are inoperative.

The apparatus and process are explained by having reference to Figure 2.8, where the liquid to be concentrated is held in reservoir **1**. The liquid is forced under superatmospheric pressure by pump **2** into the reverse osmosis concentrator represented by block **3**. This latter device may embody any of the known devices such as that of U.S. Patent 3,341,024 above.

Reverse osmosis unit **3** is provided with pipe **4** for discharge of water (permeate), and pipe **5** for discharge of the concentrated product. It will, of course, be understood by those skilled in the art that the concentrated product leaving the unit is under superatmospheric pressure, typically on the order of 100 to 2,000 psig. The illustrated apparatus includes an automatic syphon, generally designated as **6**.

This syphon meters the outflow of water (permeate) from the reverse osmosis unit, and also cooperates with a discharge metering unit (hereinafter described) to correlate the discharge of concentrate with the discharge of water (permeate), thereby providing means for controlling the degree of concentration attained in the reverse osmosis concentration. Details on the construction and operation of the syphon are provided below.

The syphon includes an open-topped container **7** and a discharge pipe **8**. The water leaving the unit via pipe **4** flows into the container. When the water collecting in the container rises to the level indicated, syphon action takes over and the container is quickly emptied via pipe **8**.

During operation of the system, the container is repeatedly filled and emptied by this syphon action. A liquid-level switch **9** (which may take the form of a 0 current relay, for example) is provided near the top of container **7**. Each time the water level rises to the point that syphon action takes over, the switch is actuated and it in turn actuates sequential motor **13**.

FIGURE 2.8: CONTROLLING DEGREE OF LIQUID CONCENTRATION DURING
REVERSE OSMOSIS

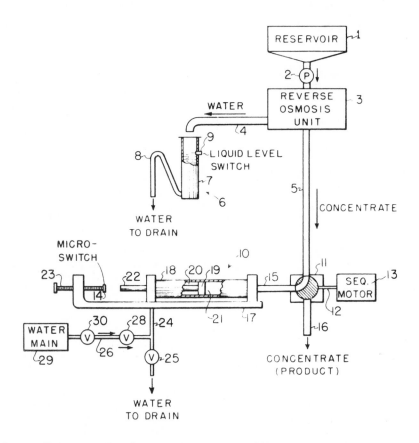

Source: E. Lowe and E.L. Durkee; U.S. Patent 3,634,103; January 11, 1972

Reference numeral **11** designates a rotary ball valve operated through shaft **12** by the motor. This motor is of the sequential type, that is, when it is energized (by liquid-level switch **9** or by microswitch **14**) it will rotate 180° and come to a dead stop. Thus, when the motor is energized by liquid-level switch it rotates the valve to the position shown in Figure 2.8, that is, with communication between pipe **5** and pipe **15**. When energized by the microswitch, the motor rotates the valve 180° so that there is communication between pipe **15** and pipe **16**.

For controlling the discharge of concentrate in cooperation with syphon **6**, there is provided a concentrate metering unit generally designated as **10**. This unit includes baseplate **17** on which is mounted cylinder **18**. A free piston **19** subdivides the cylinder into compartments **20** and **21**.

Attached to piston **19** is a piston rod **22** which passes (via a conventional gland or seal, not illustrated) to the exterior of cylinder **18**. Microswitch **14** is mounted on threaded rod **23** so that the position of the switch can be adjusted for particular conditions. In operation, the microswitch cooperates with the piston rod as hereinafter explained.

At its right end the cylinder communicates with pipe **15** and at its left end with pipe **24** equipped with needle valve (adjustable orifice) **25**. A branch pipe **26** equipped with check valve **28** is connected to main **29** which provides a supply of water under usual house pressure, e.g., 35 to 75 psig. During operation, compartment **20** is kept full of water at the pressure supplied by the main.

Needle valve **25** permits the discharge of excess water from compartment **20** as the piston traverses to the left, while maintaining the desired back pressure of water in this compartment. Check valve **28** prevents water from backing up into the house line. A valve **30** is also included in the system so that one may control the rate at which water from the main will enter pipe **26** and other units connected therewith.

During the operation, valve **30** remains in a set position. The operation of the controlled discharge system is explained as follows. As the action in reverse osmosis unit **3** takes place, water (permeate) is discharged into cylinder **7**. When the water level rises to contact switch **9**, motor **13** is triggered to rotate valve **11** to the position shown in Figure 2.8.

This allows concentrate to flow into compartment **21** where it meets the resistance offered by the water present in compartment **20**. The concentrate being at higher pressure, forces the piston to the left and this, in turn, forces excess water out of the system via the needle valve, this valve having been preset to provide a small orifice. By providing a back pressure of water in this manner the concentrate is gradually removed from the reverse osmosis unit without subjecting it to excessive stress. At the same time a metering effect is attained.

Thus, when the piston rod moves far enough to the left to contact the microswitch, the valve **11** is rotated to a second position whereby flow of concentrate into compartment **21** ceases. Instead, this compartment is now in communication with product discharge pipe **16**. Since the end of this pipe is open to the atmosphere, the concentrate in the compartment is instantly depressurized.

The concentrated product is, however, not damaged because there is no flow, i.e., the product is not subjected to shear forces. It is thus a significant advantage of the process that the concentrated product is depressurized while in a static condition, whereby the pressure reduction is achieved without damage to its properties.

After the above described depressurization takes place, the pressure on the left side of the piston is the higher and consequently the influx of water through pipe **24** forces the concentrate from compartment **21** via valve **11** and pipe **16** out of the system. The rate at which the concentrate is discharged depends on the setting of valve **30**.

In typical operations, this valve is set so that the concentrate is discharged gradually, rather than in a sudden burst, whereby to avoid subjecting it to undue stresses. Meanwhile, of course, additional water (permeate) has been flowing into container **7** and when the level of water reaches the switch the discharge cycle commences again. The following explanation illustrates how the system may be adjusted to secure a desired degree of concentration.

If, for example, it is desired to obtain a two-fold concentrate one proceeds as follows. The position of the microswitch is so set that the piston rod contacts this switch when compartment **21** takes on the same volume as the effective volume of the container. (By effective volume is meant the volume of the container considered from its base up to the level at which syphon action takes over.) In this way one obtains one volume of concentrate per volume of water removed from the starting liquid.

If, on the other hand, a more highly concentrated product is desired, one would adjust the position of microswitch 14 so that it is contacted by piston rod 20 when the volume of compartment 21 is a predetermined fraction of the effective volume of container 7. For example, if the strength of rod 23 is such that the switch is triggered when the compartment has a volume one-half of the effective volume of the container, one will achieve a 2/1 concentration, or, expressed in other terms, a three-fold concentrate.

As explained above, in the system of the process the discharge of concentrate is controlled by metering the discharge of permeate. This system not only provides the desired result that the ratio of concentration can be set and maintained at any desired level, but also provides additional advantages of simplicity and economy.

These latter advantages stem from the fact that the permeate is discharged from the reverse osmosis concentrator at essentially atmospheric pressure. Hence the metering of this liquid, the permeate, can be done with simple and inexpensive equipment, such as the syphon arrangement shown in Figure 2.7.

This process is of wide applicability and can be used for the concentration of liquid foods of all kinds. Typical liquids to which the process may be applied are juices, extracts, pulps, purees, and similar liquid products derived from fruits or vegetables such as orange, grapefruit, lemon, lime, apple, pear, apricot, strawberry, raspberry, cranberry, pineapple, grape, prune, plum, peach, cherry, tomato, celery, carrot, spinach, onion, lettuce, cabbage, potato, sweet potato, watercress, etc.

The liquid products may be prepared in customary manner by subjecting edible portions of the produce to such operations as reaming, pressing, macerating, crushing, comminuting, extracting with water, cooking, steaming, etc. These operations may be applied to the fresh produce or to processed produce, that is, produce which has been subjected to such operations as cooking, blanching, freezing, canning, sun-drying, sulfiting, or preservation by application of chemical preservatives or ionizing radiations.

Concentration Using Indirect Heat at Membrane

In accordance with the process of *H.R. Bolin; U.S. Patent 3,634,128; January 11, 1972; assigned to U.S. Secretary of Agriculture* fruit juices or other liquid foods are concentrated by a procedure which avoids direct application of heat and evaporation to the liquid. An indirect approach is employed which involves evaporation of water after it has been separated from the liquid under treatment.

Basically, the process involves the following operations: The liquid food is applied to one side of a suitable membrane. Concomitantly, a stream of warm air is applied to the opposite side of the membrane. Water (from the liquid food) diffuses through the membrane and on arriving at the opposite side is evaporated and carried away by the stream of warm air. As a net result, a residue of concentrated liquid remains on the upstream side of the membrane.

A primary advantage of the process is that evaporation is not applied directly to the liquid under treatment. As a result the original content of volatile flavoring principles is retained in the product. Moreover, since heat is not directly applied to the liquid, the original flavor, color, and nutrient values of the liquid are preserved. Another significant advantage of the process is that it does not require vacuum pumps, or any other equipment for producing or retaining subatmospheric pressures.

It is recognized that it is known to concentrate juices by reverse osmosis. In that procedure, the juice is applied under high pressure against a membrane whereby water (from the juice) passes through the membrane and is removed as liquid water. The concentrated juice is collected from the upstream side of the membrane. In order to achieve the desired reverse osmotic effect it is essential to employ very high pressures; the juice must be applied at a pressure high enough to overcome the osmotic pressure of the juice.

Moreover, as the juice becomes concentrated the osmotic pressure increases so that a progressively higher pressure must be applied to maintain the flow in the desired (reverse) direction. Because of the need for high pressures, reverse osmosis systems require heavy and elaborate equipment.

Another problem is that food products may be altered in their properties by shear forces applied thereto as they are fed into the high-pressure reverse osmosis system or as the concentrated product is discharged therefrom.

The system of the process avoids the disadvantages outlined above. High pressures are not used; instead, one uses moderate pressures, i.e., those which are below the osmotic pressure of the juice with respect to water.

Because the system involves the use of moderate pressures, i.e., those incapable of effectuating reverse osmosis, the apparatus is of simple and inexpensive construction, and no supports need be provided for the membrane; their inherent strength is capable of resisting the applied pressure. Also, in the process no significant shear stresses are applied to the material under treatment so that the original properties of the material are preserved.

The concentration in accordance with the process is carried out in apparatus which may take various forms. Basically, the apparatus will include a membrane, means for applying the liquid against the membrane, and means for applying a current of heated air to the reverse side of the membrane. As the membrane one may use any of the known films which display semipermeable properties, and particularly those which have a high water/solute diffusivity ratio, in other words, those which exhibit a high permeability to water but a low permeability to solutes.

Thereby water can flow through the membrane whereas passage of solutes, e.g., dissolved salts; sugars; citric, malic, and other fruit acids; and other nutrient, flavor, and color components as may be present in the liquid under treatment, is prevented or at least impeded to a large degree. Various membranes which exhibit these properties are known in the art, for example, U.S. Patent 3,341,024. Useful, for example, are membranes of regenerated cellulose (cellophane), cellulose nitrate, cellulose acetate, perchlorate-modified cellulose acetate, etc.

Preferably the apparatus should include some means to stir, circulate, or otherwise affect the liquid under treatment to prevent formation of localized areas of high solute concentration (which could be conducive to inadequate dewatering) or localized areas of low solute concentration (which would lead to inefficient utilization of the membrane diffusion capacity). In a preferred system, the membrane takes a tubular form with a high ratio of length to diameter.

In operation the liquid is circulated through the tubular membrane until it reaches the desired solids content. This system has the advantage that the flow of liquid through the tube causes an optimum scavenging effect whereby the permeability of creating localized high or low concentrations of solute is avoided. Moreover with this system, any undissolved material, either originally present or formed during the dewatering, is swept through the system so that the process can be run for prolonged periods without fouling.

Referring to Figure 2.9, the apparatus includes a chamber 3. In operation, a current of heated air is continuously blown through this chamber by blower 4. This blower takes in atmospheric air, forces it through heater 5 where its temperature is raised to the operating level (for example, about 90° to 165°F), and impels the heated air through duct 6, the chamber, and out of the system via vent 7.

Vertically disposed within the chamber are tubular membranes 8, fastened at their upper ends to header 9 and at their lower ends to header 10. Equipment communicating with the headers is provided for circulating the liquid to be treated through the tubular membranes. This equipment includes pipes 11 and 12, and circulating pump 13.

FIGURE 2.9: PROCESS USING INDIRECT HEATING AT MEMBRANE

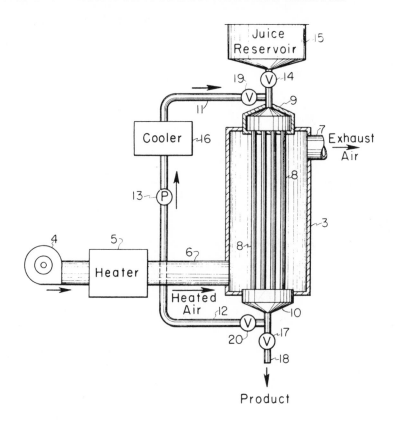

Source: H.R. Bolin; U.S. Patent 3,634,128; January 11, 1972

When the apparatus is to be started up, valve **14** is opened to allow juice from reservoir **15** to fill the liquid circulation system. The valve is then closed and pump **13** is operated continuously during the run to circulate the juice about the loop represented by pipe **11**, header **9**, tubular membranes **8**, header **10**, and pipe **12**. It may be observed that the liquid in the system is pressurized to at most a small extent as dictated by the column of liquid in the tubular membranes.

The portion of liquid at the top of the tubular membranes will be at atmospheric pressure, and the portion of the liquid at the base of the columns will be at a pressure dependent on the height of the membranes. In typical cases, the maximum pressure will be on the order of 0.5 to 10 psig.

A cooler **16** is included in the aforesaid loop, and may be operated from time to time as necessary to maintain the liquid at a temperature below that which would be detrimental to it. Thus, if the liquid becomes heated in its passage through the tubes, the cooler will reduce its temperature to a desired level.

Usually, it is preferred to maintain the liquid at ambient temperatures or below, for example, from 50° to 85°F. In many cases, little or no cooling need be applied as the liquid is maintained at the desired temperature level by the cooling effect taking place as water is evaporated on the outer surfaces of tubular membranes **8**.

During passage of the juice through the tubes, water contained in the juice will diffuse through the walls of these tubes. The water so diffusing is then evaporated and carried out of the system by the current of heated air moving through chamber **3** and contacting the outer surfaces of the tubes. Circulation of the juice is continued until it reaches a selected solids content and the concentrated juice is then drawn out of the system via valve **17** and pipe **18**.

In an alternative procedure, the juice in the system is circulated as above described while fresh juice is continuously metered into the system via valve **14** at a predetermined rate, and concentrate is continuously metered out of the system via valve **17** at a predetermined rate which provides a concentrate of desired solids content.

Example 1: Apple juice (11.5°Brix) was filled into tubular cellophane membranes having a diameter of 1⅛" and a length of 10". The tubes were sealed and suspended vertically in a conventional dehydrator where they were exposed to a draft of air heated to 100°F.

After 10 hours, the run was discontinued and the concentrate remaining in the tubes was collected. It was found to have a density of 42°Brix. A sample of the concentrate was reconstituted by addition of water and submitted to a panel of skilled food tasters, along with a sample of the original juice. The panel found that the reconstituted concentrate has an excellent taste, and no flavor difference from the control could be detected.

Example 2: In this experiment, there was used an apparatus as shown in Figure 2.9, except that it did not have the circulation loop. Tubular membranes **8** were of cellophane, three-fourths inch in diameter and 40 inches long.

The process was conducted on a continuous basis by first filling the tubes with apple juice (12°Brix) and then continuously adding this juice at the rate of 180 ml/hr. Temperature of the hot air entering chamber **3** was 150°F. The concentrated product was continuously withdrawn from the base of the system at the rate of 60 ml/hr. Density of the concentrated product was 38°Brix.

Blend of Vacuum and Reverse Osmosis Concentrates

In the usual process of concentrating fruit juices by evaporation, most of their volatile flavoring compounds, generally referred to as volatile esters or essence are lost. The volatile flavoring compounds comprise various water-soluble alcohols, esters, aldehydes and the like, which are quite volatile and generally go off to a large extent with the first 15 to 20% of the liquid removed in concentrating the juice by vacuum concentration.

Another prior art technique involves first preparing an initial concentrate from fresh juice by evaporation under vacuum to produce a concentrate of 55° to 60°Brix, referred to as Hibrix juice. To impart flavoring to the juice, this concentrate is then passed along one side of a permeable membrane, while fresh juice is passed on the other side of the membrane so that the difference in osmotic pressure transfers the essence of the fresh juice to the concentrated juice, thus restoring some of its flavor qualities while maintaining its concentration.

The fresh juice is then passed to the concentrator and cycled back along the other side of the membrane to produce a continuous process. Still other processes have relied solely on reverse osmosis to concentrate fresh juice to produce a fresh juice concentrate. Reverse osmosis in principle can be used to concentrate juice beyond 43% solids, however, it is a more expensive process than evaporation and as the concentration increases, the cost of further concentration by reverse osmosis increases very rapidly. The cost of reverse osmosis therefore has effectively limited it to the production of concentrates of no more than 45°Brix.

M.P. Tulin; U.S. Patent 3,743,513; July 3, 1973; assigned to Hydronautics, Incorporated has developed a process for providing a fruit juice concentrate capable of speedy reconstitution by addition of water to make a cold drink having a substantial portion of the original aroma, flavor and palatability of the fruit comprising concentrating whole fruit juice under vacuum and blending the vacuum concentrated juice with a concentrated fruit juice prepared by reverse osmosis to form a full flavored concentrate.

The fruit juice is preferably a citrus juice and more preferably is orange juice. The vacuum concentrated juice is preferably concentrated to between 60° to 72°Brix, and blended with a reverse osmosis concentrate of 20° to 45°Brix. The vacuum concentrated juice is blended with from 30 to 60% by volume of reverse osmosis concentrate based on the volume of the final concentrate to yield a final concentration of 55° to 60°Brix.

The first step of the process for preparing a Hibrix concentrated juice comprises concentrating whole juice of fruit under vacuum. The concentration by vacuum is effected in the usual vacuum concentration equipment in which the water is removed by applying vacuum to fresh juice in a suitable closed container.

The concentrated juice thus obtained is generally quite free from the essence of flavoring compounds which, as pointed out above, generally comprise water-soluble alcohols, aldehydes and the like. At present most vacuum concentrations of juices are designed to produce a product having a concentration of from 65° to 75°Brix.

Juices that can be concentrated by the process include apple juice, grape juice, orange juice, tomato juice, tangerine juice, and other citrus juices. The concentrated fruit juice produced by vacuum concentration is blended with a concentrated juice prepared by reverse osmosis to produce a full flavored concentrate. The reverse osmosis concentrated juice can be prepared by any of the commonly used reverse osmosis techniques for juice concentrations.

Single strength fresh juice is concentrated by a reverse osmosis technique to a concentration of from 20° to 45°Brix. The fresh fruit juice for preparing the reverse osmosis concentrate can be from the same batch of juice used to prepare the vacuum concentrate, or can be from a different batch. Fruit juice concentrates prepared by reverse osmosis retain their volatile flavor compounds.

The concentrated fruit juice prepared by reverse osmosis is then blended with the concentrated juice prepared by vacuum evaporation and from which all of the flavor essences essentially have been removed.

The blending of the vacuum concentrated juice with the reverse osmosis produced juice is accomplished in any suitable blending apparatus such as a Waring blendor. The reverse osmosis concentrate imparts its volatile flavoring compounds to the final blended concentrate.

About 30 to 60% by volume of reverse osmosis produced concentrated juice is blended with from 70 to 40% by volume of the vacuum concentrated juice, based on the volume of the final concentrate. Preferably, the concentrates are mixed to provide a final concentrate having a density of between 55° to 60°Brix.

For example, when mixing a juice evaporated to a concentration of 72°Brix with an equal volume proportion of a juice concentrated to 45°Brix by reverse osmosis, a blend is produced having a concentration of 58°Brix.

The concentrates of the process have a density higher than those obtained by the prior art processes of mixing single strength fresh juice with a vacuum concentrated juice, yet retain all of the flavor properties of such concentrates. Thus, the blends upon reconstituting with water, produce a product having a taste quality substantially similar to fresh juice. The following examples are given by way of illustration. All percentages referred to are by volume unless otherwise specifically indicated.

Example 1: Valencia oranges are washed, allowed to dry and halved. The juice is then extracted and screened of suspended pulp. A portion of the fresh juice having a concentration of 12°Brix is concentrated under vacuum and at a temperature of 40°F to 72°Brix.

The remaining portion of juice is concentrated by reverse osmosis to 45°Brix. The reverse osmosis produced concentrate is blended with the vacuum concentrated juice in equal proportions to obtain a final concentrate of 58°Brix. The product is then sealed under vacuum, and placed in cold or frozen storage.

Example 2: The process of Example 1 is repeated except that 60% of the reverse osmosis concentrate is blended with 40% of the vacuum concentrated juice to produce a final concentrate of 56°Brix.

Example 3: The process of Example 1 is repeated except that the juice concentrated by reverse osmosis is concentrated to 20°Brix. About 30% of the 20°Brix reverse osmosis concentrate is then blended with 70% of vacuum concentrated juice to produce a final concentrate of 56°Brix.

Fruit Juice Concentrate Prepared in Its Container by Dialysis

R.D. Scott; U.S. Patent 3,758,313; September 11, 1973 has developed a process to provide liquid foodstuff concentrates through the use of dialysis, in a rapid, commercial manner, which concentrates and packages the product in a single operation. The wall of the package comprises a dialysis membrane. These advantages accrue from the process:

(a) there is reduced handling of the food product;

(b) bacteria are destroyed by the osmotic pressure across the dialysis membrane, so the concentrate is sealed in a sanitary state;

(c) production costs are minimized;

(d) the consumer receives an easily handled package, ready for use;

(e) heat exposure is minimal, so that delicate organoleptic factors are not lost or destroyed;

(f) automated handling is facilitated; and

(g) a great variety of different foodstuffs can be packaged on the same equipment with only minimal changes, if any.

The food product package comprises a sealed container having a dialytically responsive wall, such as a bag formed of semipermeable membranous film, and the food product concentrate therein consists of the nondialyzable portion of the food product. The bag typically has a sealable filler opening and means adjacent the opening for supporting the bag during filling operations.

Method is provided for preparing packaged food concentrates which includes sealing a liquid food portion to be concentrated in a container having a wall comprising a semipermeable membrane, and dialyzing the food product through the membrane against a dialyzing solution to remove water from the food product sealed within the container.

A bath of dialyzing aqueous salt solution is maintained, e.g., at a temperature between 40° and 200°F and preferably to 120°F, and the sealed container is immersed in it for food product dialysis.

The container preferably takes the form of a bag comprising a flexible, semipermeable film having a sealable filler opening. The bag is then filled through its filler opening with the food portion to be concentrated, the bag opening sealed and the bag immersed in a dialyzing aqueous salt solution to concentrate the food portion contents of the bag.

In a specific embodiment of the process particularly adapted for high speed automated production, the method includes advancing a series of individual food containers having a wall portion comprising a semipermeable membrane to a fill station, filling the food product to be concentrated, e.g., orange juice into the containers in sequence at the fill station, sealing each food product portion in its individual container, immersing the containers in a bath comprising a dialyzing aqueous salt solution, e.g., a solution of sodium chloride in water at a temperature between 40° and 120°F and a concentration between 1 and 10% by weight in a manner and for a time to dehydrate the food product through the dialysis membrane wall portion of the container, e.g., to remove from 50 to 90% of the product water and thereafter withdrawing the containers from the bath.

The containers may be bags formed of flexible semipermeable film, e.g., cellulosic, proteinaceous or synthetic organic polymeric film which is differentially permeable to food product components. Apparatus for carrying out the process is illustrated and described in the patent.

PINEAPPLE JUICE CONCENTRATE

Distillation and Crystallization

E.A. Malick and G.H. Dale; U.S. Patent 3,358,464; December 19, 1967; assigned to Phillips Petroleum Company have discovered a process for the concentration of aqueous solutions which comprises passing an aqueous solution to a distillation zone, withdrawing a concentrated phase from the distillation zone, passing at least a portion of a dilute phase withdrawn from the distillation zone to a crystallization zone, withdrawing a concentrated phase from the crystallization zone, and combining the concentrated phases withdrawn from the distillation and crystallization zones.

Referring to Figure 2.10a, an aqueous solution is passed via conduit means 11 to distillation zone 10. The distillation zone is maintained at a temperature and pressure so as to form a concentrated phase and a dilute phase.

The concentrated phase comprises a recoverable product in concentrated form whereas the dilute phase comprises a recoverable product and water, the dilute phase recoverable product in dilute form. The concentrated and dilute phases can be either vaporous or liquid, depending upon the aqueous solution passed to distillation zone 10 via the conduit means.

The concentrated phase is withdrawn from the distillation zone via conduit means 12. In one embodiment of the process, the dilute phase is withdrawn from the distillation zone via conduit means 13 and passed via valve means 14 to a separation zone 16. Within the separation zone, the feed mixture is separated into a fraction containing substantially all of the recoverable product passed to the separation zone via conduit means 13, and into a fraction comprising water.

If the feed to the distillation zone comprises, for example, a fruit juice, the separation zone can comprise a conventional means for fractionally condensing the dilute vaporous phase passed to the separation zone via conduit means 13.

If the feed to the distillation zone comprises, for example, beer, the separation zone can comprise a means for fractionally distilling an ethyl alcohol and water feed mixture passed to the separation zone via conduit means 13. In the latter case, the vaporous stream withdrawn from the distillation zone via conduit 13 would be condensed by a means not herein illustrated.

FIGURE 2.10: DISTILLATION AND CRYSTALLIZATION

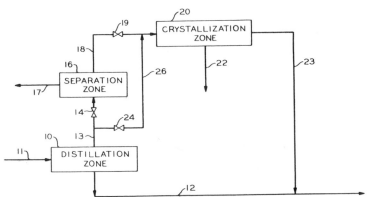

a.

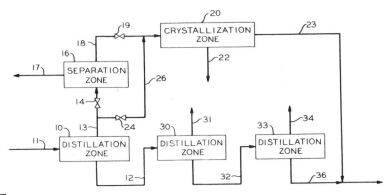

b.

(a) Single Distillation Zone
(b) Multiple Distillation Zones

Source: E.A. Malick and G.H. Dale; U.S. Patent 3,358,464; December 19, 1967

Water is withdrawn from separation zone **16** via conduit means **17**. The fraction containing the recoverable product in a more concentrated form is withdrawn from the separation zone via conduit means **18** and passed via valve means **19** to a crystallization zone **20**.

It is also within the scope of this process to pass a dilute phase withdrawn from distillation zone **10** via conduit means **13** directly to the crystallization zone via conduit means **26** and valve means **24**. In those cases where the dilute phase is vaporous, the dilute phase is condensed prior to passage of the condensed dilute phase to the crystallization zone.

The crystallization zone comprises a conventional process and apparatus for chilling a liquid feed mixture to form crystals of at least a higher melting component and separating the crystals of the higher melting component from a mother liquor.

Ice crystals are formed within the crystallization zone and are separated from the mother liquor comprising a recoverable product in concentrated form and withdrawn from the crystallization via conduit means **22**. A mother liquor comprising the recoverable product in concentrated form is withdrawn from the crystallization zone via conduit means **23** and combined with the concentrated phase withdrawn from the distillation zone.

It is within the scope of this process to employ multiple distillation zones as shown in Figure 2.10b. In this case, the distillation zone can comprise a means for evaporation. The vaporous dilute phase withdrawn from the distillation zone via conduit means **13** comprises water and a relatively volatile portion of the recoverable concentrated product. A liquid is withdrawn from the distillation zone via conduit means **12** and passed to distillation zone **30**, the distillation zone **30** comprising a second means for evaporation.

Water is withdrawn from distillation zone **30** via conduit means **31**. A more concentrated liquid phase is withdrawn from distillation zone **30** via conduit means **32** and passed to distillation zone **33**, the distillation zone **33** comprising a third means for evaporation. A vaporous water phase is withdrawn from distillation zone **33** via conduit means **34** and a concentrated liquid phase is withdrawn from distillation zone **33** via conduit means **35** and combined in heretofore described manner with the concentrated phase withdrawn from the crystallization zone via conduit means **23**.

The following example is presented as illustrative of the process. All percentages are by volume.

Example: Pineapple juice having the following composition

Sugars	14.0%
Acid (citric)	0.8%
Pineapple esters (ethyl and methyl esters of acetic, butyric, caproic and caprylic acids)	2.5%
Ethyl alcohol	1.3%

is passed to distillation zone **10**, distillation zone **10** comprising an evaporator maintained at a temperature of 70°F and a pressure of 0.5 psia. A vaporous stream comprising

Esters	0.6%
Ethyl alcohol	1.8%
Water	97.6%

is withdrawn from distillation zone **10** via conduit means **13**, condensed and passed to the crystallization zone via conduit means **26**. A liquid stream having a sugar concentration of 20.0 volume percent is withdrawn from distillation zone **10** and passed via conduit means **12** to distillation zone **30**.

Distillation zone **30** comprises an evaporator maintained at a temperature of 70°F and a pressure of 0.5 psia. A vaporous stream comprising water is withdrawn from distillation zone **30** via conduit means **31**. A liquid stream having a sugar concentration of 32.0 volume percent is withdrawn from distillation zone **30** via conduit means **32** and passed to distillation zone **33**.

Distillation zone **33** comprises an evaporator maintained at a temperature of 70°F and a pressure of 0.5 psia. A vaporous stream comprising water is withdrawn from distillation zone **33** via conduit means **34**. A liquid concentrate having a sugar concentration of 55.0 volume percent is withdrawn from distillation zone **33** via conduit means **36**.

Within the crystallization zone, the feed mixture is cooled to a temperature of 26°F in a chilling zone, forming a slurry comprising 35 volume percent ice crystals. The slurry is passed to a purification column, the temperature in the melt zone within the purification column maintained at 75°F. Mother liquor comprising

Esters	9.0%
Ethyl alcohol	27.0%
Water	64.0%

is withdrawn from the filter section of the purification column and from the crystallization zone via conduit means **23**. A portion of the mother liquor withdrawn from the purification column is recycled to the chilling zone, thereby bringing the concentration of esters within the chilling zone to 6 to 7 volume percent. Melt comprising less than 0.2 volume percent esters and water is withdrawn from crystallization zone **20** via conduit means **22**.

The mother liquor withdrawn from the crystallization zone and the liquid concentrate withdrawn from distillation zone **33** are combined to yield a concentrated product.

TOMATO JUICE CONCENTRATE

Direct Heat Exchange with Combustion Gases

In accordance with the method of *A. Williams; U.S. Patent 3,247,890; April 26, 1966; assigned to Selas Corporation of America* a liquid containing a heat sensitive substance is evaporated by introducing it into a stream of hot combustion gases concurrently with recirculated cooler combustion gases and thereafter passing the intimate mixture of gases and liquid into a separating zone.

Briefly, the apparatus comprises a refractory lined combustion zone having an inlet at one end and an outlet at an opposing end, the outlet in the combustion zone being joined with a tubular member which projects outwardly from the combustion zone, the tubular member being surrounded by an annular chamber having an annular opening therein adjacent the outer wall of the tubular member, and means for introducing recirculated combustion gases to the annular chamber so that they can pass axially adjacent the outer wall of the tubular member.

Further, the apparatus comprises a second annular chamber around the tubular member, slanted outlets in the second annular chamber, the center lines of which converge in the path of hot gases passing out of the tubular member, means to introduce a liquid to be evaporated into the second annular chamber, thereby causing converging streams of the liquid to be mixed concurrently with the heated gases and the recirculated gases, and separating means where vaporizable liquids and incondensible gases of the resultant intimate mixture are separated from the residual concentrate.

Briefly, the process comprises feeding a central stream of hot combustion gases into an upstream part of a mixing zone converging toward a narrow throat in the downstream direction, simultaneously feeding into the mixing zone cooler gases in the form of an annular, concurrent stream about the central stream, of which cooler gases cooled, recycled combustion gases are an example, and simultaneously feeding a liquid composition to be concentrated into the mixing zone in the form of streams emanating outside the streams of gases and directed angularly thereinto in the downstream direction. The liquid streams preferably converge toward a common point in the vicinity of the throat.

As an illustrative example, tomato juice is concentrated in the apparatus of Figure 2.11. Air and natural gas are burned at a volume ratio of about 10:1, respectively, in combustion chamber **15**. The temperature of the combustion gases in tube **20** is about 1410°F. The temperature of the gas and liquid stream at opening **26** of separator **27** is about 170°F by virtue of the vaporization of some of the water of the tomato juice fed through tubes **51** to the heat exchange zone **21** and the introduction as an annular stream of recycle gases at about 150°F via chamber **44**.

The recycle gases, after separation from the liquid and solid components in the separator, are cooled by water sprayed at about 70°F onto packing **35**. The recycle gas at tap-off **40** has an incondensible gas to water vapor volume ratio of about 20:1.5. The process and apparatus are especially useful in evaporating heat sensitive liquids, such as, tomato juice, orange juice, pineapple juice, grape juice, apple juice, milk, corn syrup, and other liquids containing sugars or other carbohydrates or proteins which are sensitive to heat.

FIGURE 2.11: DIRECT HEAT EXCHANGE WITH COMBUSTION GASES

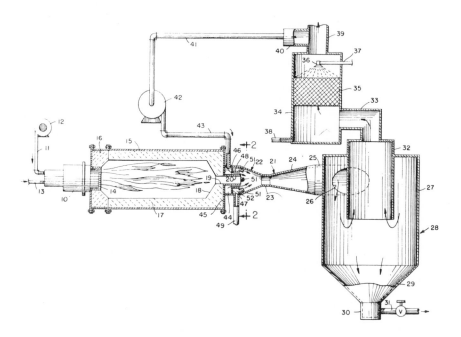

Source: A. Williams; U.S. Patent 3,247,890; April 26, 1966

FREEZE CONCENTRATION

Continuous Concentration by Freezing

U.S. Patent 2,588,337 described a process for concentrating orange juice which preserved the advantages of freezing concentrate with respect to retention of volatile flavor and elimination of cooked taste, and at the same time eliminated losses of solids in the ice. In general, the process involved first concentrating fresh juice by freezing and separating the resulting concentrate, preferably by centrifuging the frozen juice mass. This concentrate contained a substantial part of the solids of the fresh juice and also practically all of its volatile flavor constituents.

The residue ice was then thawed to release occluded pulp, sugars, and other soluble constituents in a liquid solution suspension which was practically free of volatile flavor constituents. Since the pulp, sugars and other soluble constituents are not heat labile, this liquor was concentrated by evaporation, preferably under vacuum, without objectionable deterioration of taste and flavor. After most of the water had been removed, the concentrated liquor was returned to and mixed with the concentrated juice so that the resulting mixture contained practically all of the valuable constituents of the crushed juice without material loss or deterioration of volatile flavor.

C.S. Walker; U.S. Patent 3,156,571; November 10, 1964; assigned to Institutum Divi Thomae Foundation has devised an improved method of carrying out the process of the abovementioned patent in a continuous manner. This is accomplished by circulating the beverage between a cooler and a holding tank so that the formation of ice crystals takes place in the beverage being processed. The cooling is not carried out to such an extent, however, that the mass of beverage is not in a flowable condition so that it cannot be pumped. While the beverage undergoing cooling is being circulated between the cooler and the holding tank, fresh beverage is introduced into the circulating stream and partially frozen beverage including unfrozen liquid and ice crystals are withdrawn from the circulating stream.

The material withdrawn can then be centrifuged conveniently to separate concentrated liquid from solids including ice crystals. The solids can then be thawed, the resulting liquid concentrated by evaporation, and the liquid thus formed admixed with the concentrated liquid from the centrifuge in accordance with the procedure of U.S. Patent 2,588,337. The circulating procedure of this process possessed the advantage that when it is employed it is possible to control accurately the formation of ice crystals in the beverage undergoing freezing, so that the separation of solids from concentrated beverage in a centrifuge can be conveniently and effectively accomplished with high productivity.

In Figure 2.12 which diagrams the process **1** indicates a conventional paddle type pulp cooler into which orange juice from conventional juice extractors is fed by means of line **2**. From the cooler **1** the juice passes to a conventional screw type fine juice finisher **3** by means of lines **4** and **5** and pulp of desirable characteristics passes by means of line **6** to pulp tank **7** to be used as hereinafter described. From finisher **3** fine juice containing some finely divided insoluble solids passes by means of line **8** to holding tank **9** for further processing and the remainder of the material fed to finisher **3** is passed to a second screw type juice finisher **10** in which there is produced a relatively low grade of juice. This low grade juice passes by means of line **11** to evaporator feed tank **12**, the purpose here being to improve slightly the over-all yield of the final product.

From holding tank **9** the juice is pumped by means of pump **13** to prechiller **14**, from which the juice flows by means of line **15** to an exit line **16** of holding tank **17** or back to holding tank **9** by means of line **18**. The purpose of line **18** is to provide a means whereby the juice can be maintained in a cold condition when the holding tank **17** is filled to capacity and partially frozen juice is not being fed to the centrifuge **19** herafter described. From tank **17** the juice is withdrawn by means of lines **16** and **20** and is pumped by means of pump **21** through line **22** to a three tunnel Votator **23**, which is a conventional rapid slush freezer. From Votator **23** the juice passes by means of line **24** back to holding tank **17**.

FIGURE 2.12: CONTINUOUS PROCESS FOR MAKING CONCENTRATED LIQUIDS

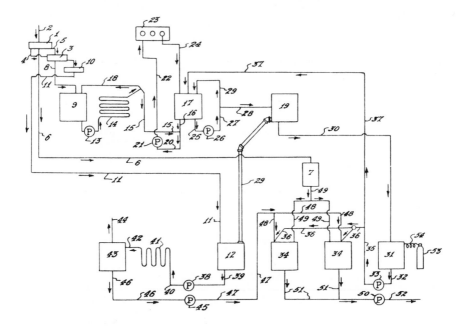

Source: C.S. Walker; U.S. Patent 3,156,571; November 10, 1964

From holding tank **17** partially frozen juice is withdrawn by means of line **25** and is pumped by pump **26** into line **27**. This line connects with line **28**, which is the feed line to a centrifuge **19**, and also with line **29**, which is used for recirculating when the centrifuge is not being charged. In the centrifuge **19** solids are separated from concentrated liquid as hereinafter explained.

The initial concentrate derived from the continuous centrifuge must be carefully controlled both as to flavor and as to Brix value, since it is not possible to compensate for wide variation in these matters by a second or vacuum evaporated concentrate. As a consequence, the material reaching the continuous centrifuge must be quite accurately predetermined as to crystal size and crystal condition, so that a first concentrate of suitable characteristics may be obtained.

A material suitable for centrifuging must, of course, be sufficiently mobile to be handled, as by pumping. It should be frozen to such an extent that when the removable ice has been separated out, a concentrate containing the desired percentage of solids will remain. At the same time, however, the nature of the removable ice crystals must be such as to minimize entrapment, since otherwise an efficient separation will not be had, and some of the flavor imparting constituents of the original liquid may be lost from the initial concentrate. Undue entrapment can result not only from over-freezing, but also from the nature of the ice crystals produced.

The centrifuge may be a basket type dehydrator in which an intermittent operation is performed. The operation is broken down into a feed cycle, a spin cycle and an unload cycle. The speed of the centrifuge and the length of time of feed, spin and unload cycles are set as accurately as possible to obtain a high Brix product on the liquid discharge and as much ice as possible at a relatively low Brix. While the screen size for the basket of the centrifuge is initially important, the actual separation in the centrifuge when used batchwise is secured through the porosity of the filter cake rather than through the perforations of the screens during the greater part of the batch operation. Therefore, the size and condition of ice crystals is important because the ice crystal size, in conjunction with the fine solids which are in admixture with them, regulates the porosity of the filter cake. During most effective operation, ice forming a part of the filter cake continually is melting and passing through the screen.

The separated ice from the centrifuge passes by means of line 29 to evaporator 12, while the liquid concentrate passes by means of line 30 to tank 31, from which liquid is withdrawn by means of line 32 and pumped by pump 33 to blend tanks 34 by means of lines 35 and 36, or back to the holding tank 17 by means of lines 35 and 37. Line 37 is provided to enable further concentration of liquid by recirculation through the system. This is advantageously done intermittently since, in addition to effecting further concentration, recycling removes the majority of the finely divided pump solids in this portion of the juice.

This reduction in finely divided solids is advantageous since it has been found that some pectin esterase activity of the juice is directly related to the finely divided solids. Moreover, the increase in Brix caused by recirculating through line 37 decreases the size of the ice particles formed in tank 17, thereby providing a finer crystal to form the filter cake in the centrifuge and increasing the ability of the centrifuge to keep the finely divided solids in the ice phase of the process.

The relatively low grade juice passing through line 11 and the ice passing through line 29 are admixed in evaporator feed tank 12, and thence are pumped by means of pump 38 through lines 39 and 40 to pasteurizer 41, from which liquid passes by means of line 42 into evaporator 43. Water vapor removed in this evaporator passes from the system by line 44 and the concentrated liquid produced in the evaporator is pumped by pump 45 through lines 46, 47 and 48 into blend tanks 34.

Pulp from tank 7 is also introduced into these blend tanks by means of lines 49. From these blend tanks the final concentrated product is pumped by means of pump 50 through lines 51 and 52 to the canning operation. A tank of nitrogen 53 may be connected by means of line 54 to tank 31 to provide an atmosphere of nitrogen over the liquid contained therein.

In a typical operation, the orange juice in holding tank 9 has a Brix value of about 13° and is maintained at a temperature of about 31°F. Under these conditions the juice passes through line 15 at a rate of about 25 gallons per minute. Pump 21 operates at a flow of about 50 gallons per minute, and upon leaving Votator 23 the juice is at a temperature of about 27°F. Holding tank 17 has a capacity of about 300 gallons. The centrifuge 19 may be operated batchwise with a filter cake about three-eighth inch thick to provide an ice phase having a Brix value of about 10.2° when melted and a liquid phase having a Brix value of about 28°.

In the pasteurizer 41 the ice phase in admixture with low grade juice is heated to a temperature of about 170° to 175°F and the evaporation in evaporator 43 is carried out at a temperature of about 70°F. Evaporation in this evaporator is preferably carried out to such an extent that when the product produced therein, the pulp from pulp tank 7 and the liquid from tank 31, are admixed in blending tanks 34 the final product passing through line 52 has a Brix value of about 42°. When operating in the manner just described, for each 100 gallons of fresh orange juice having a Brix value of 13° and containing 113.9 pounds of total sugars, 97.63 gallons of juice having a Brix value of 13° and containing 111.2 pounds of sugars pass through line 8 into holding tank 9 and 2.37 gallons of juice having a Brix value of 13° and containing 2.6 pounds of sugars pass through line 11 into evaporator feed tank 12.

When melted, the ice passing through line 16 will amount to 82.98 gallons having a Brix value of 10.2° and containing 73.0 pounds of sugars and the liquid passing through line 30 will amount to 14.65 gallons having a Brix value of 28° and containing 38.2 pounds of sugars. The material contained in evaporator feed tank 12 will amount to 85.35 gallons having a Brix value of 10.8° and containing 75.6 pounds of sugars. Upon evaporation in evaporator 43, the material passing through line 46 will amount to 12.75 gallons having a Brix value of 56.2° and containing 75.6 pounds of sugars. The final concentrate passing through line 51 amounts to 27.4 gallons having a Brix value of 43° and containing 113.9 pounds of sugars.

Immiscible Liquid Phase Coolant

L.B. Torobin and D.L. Baeder; U.S. Patent 3,178,899; April 20, 1965; assigned to Esso Research and Engineering Company describe a process of separating water from an aqueous solution in which the water is soluble at certain temperatures and insoluble at lower temperatures in which the water is crystallized from its solution by countercurrently contacting it with a liquid immiscible coolant of different density than the aqueous solution containing the water to be separated, wherein the aqueous solution is introduced in the form of a dense dispersion of uniform size droplets and the coolant as a continuous phase.

Further, there is described a process of obtaining controlled rates of heat transfer between an aqueous solution and an immiscible liquid coolant of different density wherein ice crystals are grown in the aqueous solution, which comprises countercurrently contacting the liquids by introducing the aqueous solution into the top or bottom of the column in the form of a bed of a dense dispersion of uniform size droplets and introducing the coolant liquid into the other end of the column as a continuous phase.

In accordance with this process, an aqueous solution containing a crystallizable water is fed to a treating column which has no internals, at a temperature above the freezing point of the water solution, which enters the top or bottom of the treating column in the form of a dense dispersion. This dense dispersion is produced by a modified spray head and is made up of very closely packed uniform diameter droplets which rise or descend in the column as a bed of spheres, depending on the density of the coolant and at which end of the column it is fed.

A continuous liquid coolant phase is fed at the opposite end of the column as the feed and moves countercurrently to the dense bed of spheres. Because of the uniformity of size of the droplets making up the dense bed of spheres, the droplets move uniformly as a bed in the column and because of the uniformity of the size of the droplets, they have about the same volume density throughout the column and are chilled at a controlled rate. Within the dense bed the individual droplets exhibit a localized random motion which enhances heat transfer and crystal growth.

The coolant should be immiscible or at most only partially miscible with the aqueous solution. Where it is undesirable to have the coolant contaminate the decrystallized feed, the coolant should be substantially immiscible with the feed. The only other requirements for the coolant are that it be of a different density than the feed and that it be liquid at the temperature to which the feed is to be cooled.

The suitable coolants for crystallizing water from an aqueous solution are oil fractions, pure chemicals, liquid metals, and the like. However, certain coolants may be selected to simultaneously effect chemical reactions or extractions. In concentrating beverages, suitable coolants are oil fractions, edible vegetable oils, cottonseed oil, normally gaseous liquid hydrocarbons, halogenated hydrocarbons, Freons, etc.

The coolant is charged to the column at a temperature below the freezing point of the aqueous solution. By the time the dense bed of droplets reach the opposite end of the column, part or substantially all of the crystallizable water in the droplets is crystallized out as ice. At the opposite end of the tower, the ice crystals and mother liquor form a slurry. This ice crystal and mother liquor slurry is withdrawn from the tower and can be either filtered or centrifuged to separate the crystals from the mother liquor. The warm coolant is withdrawn from the tower at the end opposite to which feed is withdrawn and then cooled to its inlet temperature for reuse.

In order to obtain uniform size droplets from the spray head, an annular baffle at the periphery of the spray head was constructed, i.e., at the outer edge of the orifice plate, which serves to deflect the standing continuous phase vortex away from the orifice holes at the outer edge of the orifice plate. The orifices are made to protrude to discourage the wetting of the spray head surface. In doing this, it was unexpectedly found that the critical throughput for a specific rate, above which nonuniform drops occurred, could be increased by about 80 to 100% with the annular baffle, over that without the annular baffle. It is known that at low throughput rates uniform drops can be obtained; however, at throughput rates required to form the dense bed, nonuniform distribution normally occurs.

In one example of this method, aqueous solutions are dehydrated to obtain more concentrated solutions by countercurrently contacting the aqueous solution with a cold immiscible coolant. In this application, the aqueous solution is sprayed into the treating column in the form of a dense dispersion of uniform size droplets which are countercurrently contacted with an immiscible coolant continuous phase. The coolant is charged to the tower as the continuous phase at a temperature below the freezing point of the water solution and crystallizes a portion of the water present in the solution which is removed as a slurry of ice crystals and mother liquor from the bottom of the column. The ice crystals can be separated from the more concentrated aqueous solution or mother liquor by using a basket centrifuge, by filtration, or other conventional means.

This example has specific applications to temperature sensitive solutions, for example, beverages, wherein the flavor or the vitamins present may be altered or detrimentally affected by heat, if heat were used to concentrate the solutions by evaporation. This process can be advantageously used to preserve in the concentrated solution volatile constituents which would normally be entrained or vaporized and removed during concentration at low temperatures employing vacuum evaporation or in crystallizing by vaporizing a direct contact refrigerant. Also, economic concentration of aqueous industrial waste streams can be carried out in accordance with the process and the concentrated waste materials more easily disposed.

Example: Fresh orange juice containing about 0.005% oil and a sugar to acid ratio of about 13 to 1 is countercurrently contacted with a light edible oil coolant. The orange juice is introduced as a dense dispersion of uniform diameter droplets and is contacted with the continuous coolant phase. The orange juice is fed to a first tower at a temperature of about 68°F and is rapidly cooled to a temperature of about 30°F in the tower which is used solely as a heat exchange means. The orange juice is then fed into the top of the second tower at a temperature of about 30°F in which it is countercurrently contacted in a similar manner with the coolant fed into the bottom of the tower at a temperature of about 10° to 20°F.

The ice crystals initially form within the orange juice droplets in the top of the tower and grow as they descend countercurrently to the ascending continuous phase of coolant. The orange juice droplets are cooled at a rate of 1 to 4 degrees per minute, facilitating the formation of large ice crystals and concentrating the orange juice with a minimum loss of dissolved solids to the ice crystals. Cooling of the orange juice droplets and the growing of the crystals is controlled so that the crystals have sufficient time as they grow to reject otherwise occluded dissolved solids.

The water crystals are removed from the bottom of the column with the concentrated orange juice solution and are found to have a size between 200 and 500 microns. Very few small crystals are present. The crystals and concentrated orange juice solution is fed to a basket centrifuge wherein the crystals are separated. About 50% by volume of the orange juice feed is removed as relatively pure ice crystals.

The cold orange juice concentrate is then countercurrently contacted in a second crystallization tower at a lower temperature to remove 50% by volume of the remaining concentrate as ice crystals. The final concentrate is about one-fourth the original volume and is canned and frozen for shipment.

Atomized Particle Mist

G.C.W. van Olphen; U.S. Patent 3,188,825; June 15, 1965 describes a freeze concentration process which involves atomizing a liquid solution or suspension to a fine mist, and thereafter passing a coolant through such mist in a manner to achieve a thorough intermixture thereof. The coolant is at a sufficiently low temperature that one constituent, normally the solvent, of the solution will freeze wherefore a mixture of solid and liquid particles are formed. Thereafter, the mixture of solid and liquid particles are separated, and the liquid effluent normally constitutes the concentrate product.

The details of a practical application of the apparatus will more readily be understood by reference to a particular concentration process, that of the continuous dehydration of orange juice. Initially, the orange juice is preferably precooled to a temperature slightly above the freezing point of water, that is, 32°F, to thus enable the actual freezing of the subsequently formed particles to occur rapidly and enable application of the apparatus to large scale commercial production.

The precooled juice is thereafter atomized into a fine mist form, preferably by spraying it into a substantially enclosed chamber in a manner to achieve even distribution of the liquid particles in the upper portion thereof. The particles are delivered into the chamber with a substantial horizontal or transverse component of motion and preferably with a median particle size of approximately 50 microns.

Gaseous coolant in the form of air is continuously blown downwardly from the top of the chamber so as to engage the liquid particles and urge the same downwardly toward the bottom of the chamber where they are subsequently collected as will be described hereinafter. The air temperature is preferably between 0° and 16°F dependent upon the initial concentration and sugar content of the raw juice. Since, as will be apparent from the described small size of the particles, a large surface area is exposed to the air, excellent heat transfer is afforded and rapid freezing of the solvent water particles occurs. Since the juice has been precooled to substantially freezing temperature, little more than the heat of fusion is necessary to convert the water to ice.

The air flow is turbulent so that continuous agitation of the particles is achieved to maintain their small size and preclude agglomeration. Since the particles are thus maintained at their size, substantially no occlusion of the juice (solute) within the freezing water (solvent) particles occurs. As a consequence, the downwardly moving air selectively freezes the water into small microcrystals of clear ice and delivers the same together with the droplets of juice concentrate to the bottom portion of the chamber. The mixture of ice particles and juice concentrate is collected as a slurry which is then separated by filtration. Preferably, such filtration is performed continuously and rapidly with the utilization of centrifugal force.

The amount of concentration achieved by the described steps will depend upon several factors and can most easily be changed through varying the amount and temperature of the air. It has been determined as a practical matter that optimum effectiveness of the method is obtained if the concentration of the orange juice is approximately doubled. Under such conditions a negligible amount of the juice concentrate is removed with the ice particles wherefore substantially 100% recovery of the juice results. In view of the fact that frozen orange juice is commercially distributed with a quadruple concentration, two stages of operation of the apparatus are requisite to obtain such desired degree of concentration.

However, in accordance with an additional aspect of the method, a recycling step can be utilized optionally to avoid the necessity of two separate stages of concentration. Generally, such additional step entails the removal of a portion of the liquid concentrate and the subsequent mixing of such concentrate with the incoming supply of raw juice in predetermined proportion and recycling this mixture through the described steps so that the withdrawn product is concentrated to the desired amount, in the case of orange juice, four times that of the raw juice. If it is assumed that the initial concentration of the raw juice is 10% and a final concentration of 40% is thus desired, one quart of the 40% concentrate is mixed with each 2 quarts of the raw juice of 10% concentration to result in a mixture having a concentration of 20% which then undergoes the recited steps of the apparatus.

In undergoing such steps, the concentration is doubled, as is desired for optimum operation of the apparatus; wherefore, approximately one half of the mixture is removed as ice, and the other half, being one and one-half quarts, is removed as juice concentrate. In turn, one quart of this concentrate is mixed and recycled with two quarts of the raw juice for recycling therewith, while one-half quart is withdrawn as the concentrate product. In this manner, the optimum concentration conditions of the apparatus are maintained, but the withdrawn product has a concentration quadruple that of the raw juice, as is desired.

Increased Crystal Size

Freeze concentration processes for fruit juices have been developed to overcome the problems of flavor and aroma loss which result from the use of heat in evaporation processes. Unfortunately, freeze concentration processes also suffer from difficulties including (a) loss of concentrate when the liquid adheres to the ice crystals by capillary action; (b) extremely small ice crystals which make separation from the liquid fraction difficult when continuous concentration is practiced; and (c) expense caused by poor heat balance in the process.

Attempts to solve these difficulties have been made in a process developed by *A.F. Lund; U.S. Patent 3,205,078; September 7, 1965; assigned to Cherry-Burrell Corporation* which is explained with reference to Figure 2.13. After being extracted from the fruit and processed through a finisher 8 to remove the seeds and rag, the whole juice is passed through line 9 into a separator 10 of suitable design and type. The separator separates the whole juice into a pulp fraction and a liquid fraction, reducing the pulp fraction remaining in the liquid to less than 6% insoluble solids. The liquid fraction, which has a concentration of 9° to 15°Brix, is discharged through line 12 into a heat exchanger 14 and the pulp fraction is drawn off from the separator for heat treatment or other processing.

The heat exchanger serves to precool the liquid fraction before it is passed through line 16 and mixed with a concentrated, cold liquid that is drawn off a separating vessel 18 through line 20. This liquid from vessel 18 is at a temperature of 24° to 29°F and has been concentrated to 18° to 30°Brix. Since it is at a temperature below the freezing point of the water phase of the incoming liquid in line 16, seed crystals of ice will be formed instantaneously in the mixture. The mixture is then pumped by pump 22 into one or more chillers 24 preferably of the swept surface type. The minute seed crystals of ice are rapidly increased in size by the fast cooling in the chillers resulting in a larger, more durable ice crystal than can be produced by other known continuous methods. Also, the addition of the higher concentrated liquid from vessel 18 minimizes the formation of ice on the heat transfer surfaces of the chillers because of the increased soluble solids content of the mixture.

After discharge from the chillers the ice crystals and liquid are separated by passing the mixture into separating vessel 18 where the ice crystals are allowed to rise naturally to the top level of the liquid. As already mentioned, liquid of a concentration of 18° to 30°Brix is drawn off the vessel at a level below line 26, through line 20, and mixed with the incoming liquid in line 16. A strainer 28 preferably is provided at the connection of line 20 with vessel 18 to prevent ice crystals from being carried out at this point. The ice mass formed at the top of the vessel is then removed either mechanically or by gravity. With some products, such as citrus juice, the ice crystals withdrawn from the top of the vessel carry with them some of the concentrated liquid. This is because capillary action holds the liquid on the surfaces of the ice crystals, and as these ice crystals become joined together in a soft mass, they will entrain the liquid. Therefore, the mixture is passed through a vacuum strainer 30 or into a basket-type centrifuge (not shown) for separation into ice and concentrated liquid, the ice fraction being discharged into a tank 32.

FIGURE 2.13: METHOD OF FREEZE CONCENTRATING CITRUS JUICE

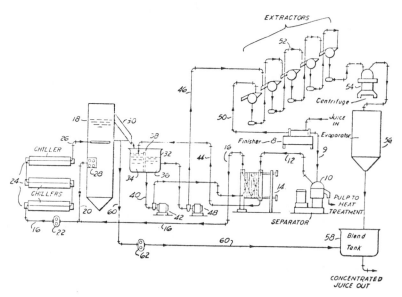

Source: A.F. Lund; U.S. Patent 3,205,078; September 7, 1965

The tank is divided into two compartments 34 and 36 by a screen 38. The ice crystals from vessel 18 are discharged into compartment 34 where those that do not melt will remain. The ice water formed from the melting ice will pass through the screen into compartment 36 from where it is withdrawn through a line 40 and circulated through the heat exchanger 14. A pump 42 circulates the ice water through the heat exchanger to precool the juice fraction from separator 10 and returns the water to compartment 34 of tank 32 through line 44. Here the water is used to melt the ice in compartment 34, the cold ice water then passing through the screen into the compartment 36. This arrangement utilizes available refrigeration to lessen the load on the chillers. Generally, there is refrigeration in excess of that required to precool the incoming juice in the heat exchanger and this excess can be utilized for other purposes in the processing plant.

The ice separated from the liquid juice fraction is also utilized for a second important purpose. The ice water in compartment 36, in addition to being used to precool the incoming juice, is withdrawn through line 46 by pump 48 and used for water extraction of the pulp originally separated from the juice by finisher 8. This pulp is withdrawn from the finisher through line 50 and passed into suitable extraction apparatus 52, the ice water being pumped into this apparatus through line 46. This is a highly desirable arrangement for at least two reasons. First, since the ice water from compartment 36 contains some juice, even though a very small amount, loss of soluble solids is thereby reduced to almost zero. Also, some of the disadvantages of water extraction of the pulp with tap water are avoided since this arrangement makes the system a completely closed one, nothing being introduced into the system except the product to be processed.

The liquid extracted from the pulp is withdrawn from the apparatus 52 and insoluble solids are removed by centrifuge 54. The liquid fraction discharged from the centrifuge is at a concentration of 3° to 7°Brix and therefore is passed into a suitable evaporator 56 where it is concentrated. The heat utilized in the evaporation process unfortunately destroys much of the flavor and, therefore, the concentrate is passed into a blend tank 58 where it is mixed with the liquid juice fraction that has been concentrated by the freeze method and pumped through line 60 from the vacuum strainer 30 by pump 62. These two fractions are blended in suitable amounts to obtain the desired concentration, which for commercial frozen orange juice concentrate is above 42°Brix.

Controlled Rate of Product Formation

F.L. Stoller; U.S. Patent 3,212,282; October 19, 1965; assigned to Phillips Petroleum Company has noted that in order to obtain and maintain optimum production of purified product it has become desirable to withdraw the purified product at a substantially constant rate. Difficulties have been encountered in maintaining the desired constant withdrawal rate of purified product due to various fluctuations within the system such as channeling of melt liquid through a void in the crystal bed.

These difficulties can be substantially reduced, if not eliminated, and the desired constant rate of withdrawal of purified product can be maintained by controlling the addition of heat to the contents of the melting section responsive to the temperature of the melt.

Referring now to Figure 2.14 in detail, a feed mixture comprising two or more components, one of which is separable from the mixture by crystallization, is passed through conduit 11 and is forced by means of pump 12 through conduit 13 into chilling section 14. This chilling section comprises an inner cylindrical shell 15, one end of which is closed by means of an end member 16, and a cooling jacket 17 having an inlet 18 and an outlet 19. Agitating means or scraping means 21 are positioned within cylindrical shell 15 and are designed to prevent the accumulation of solid material on the inner surface of this cylindrical shell.

The scraping means can be constructed of strips of metal or other suitable material known in the art and can be fabricated in the form of a helix, as shown in the drawing, or can be straight. Any suitable form of scraping means can be provided. The scraping means are mounted on a rotatable shaft 22 by means of members 23. This shaft is axially positioned within cylindrical shell 15 and is connected to any suitable source of power which rotates the scraping means, such power source not being shown in the drawing. Shaft 22 is suitably sealed in end member 16 by means of a packing gland of any desired type known in the art.

Cooling of the feed which enters the chilling section can be provided by passing a suitable coolant through inlet 18 and withdrawing the coolant through outlet 19. Sufficient cooling in the chilling section is provided so that a predetermined amount of solid crystals is produced from the feed passing therethrough. The resulting slurry of crystals in mother liquor is passed into purification column 24 which comprises filtration section 25, reflux section 26 and melting section. This filtration section comprises a suitable filter screen or medium 28 and an external shell 29, the latter being provided with an outlet pipe 31 through which the filtrate, that is, the mother liquor is passed.

Filter medium 28 can be of any desired type known in the art. For example, it can comprise a metallic screen, a sintered perforate metal member or a perforate metal member supporting a filter cloth. It is desirable that the filter member be positioned integrally with respect to adjacent walls of reflux section 26. Although filtration section 25 has been illustrated in the drawing as being an external filter, it is within the scope of the process to utilize an internal filter, in which event, external shell 29 could be positioned integrally with respect to the wall of reflux section 26, and the filter medium would be disposed within shell 29 and preferably positioned axially with respect to purification column 24. The filtrate produced in filtration section 25 is removed from the purification column through conduit 31. This conduit can contain a suitable means, such as pressure reducing valve 32, to maintain a predetermined back pressure.

FIGURE 2.14: FRACTIONAL CRYSTALLIZATION CONTROL SYSTEM

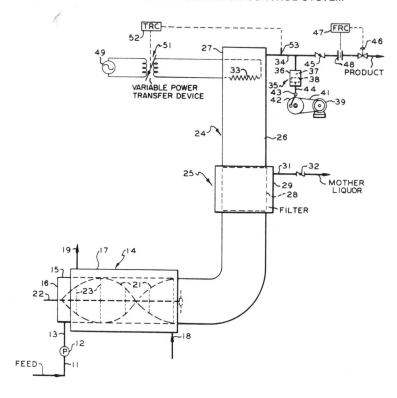

Source: F.L. Stoller; U.S. Patent 3,212,282; October 19, 1965

The remaining crystal mass is passed into reflux section **26** wherein it is countercurrently contacted with liquid reflux as subsequently described. As the crystal mass approaches heating element **33** in melting section **27**, the crystals are melted. A portion of the melt produced by the heat from heating element **33** is withdrawn through product withdrawal conduit **34** as a purified product of the process. The remainder of the melt is forced back through reflux section **26** to form reflux which effects crystal purification.

The pulsation-producing means **35** comprises a cylinder **36**, one end of which is in fluid communication with the purified product withdrawal line **34**, and reciprocable piston **37** mounted within cylinder **36**. The piston is suitably sealed in cylinder **36**, for example, by means of rings **38**, to prevent leakage of the purified product. Reciprocation of the piston is produced by any suitable means, for example, by an electrical motor **39**, a belt **41**, a crank means **42**, and connecting rods **43** and **44**. While the crystal mass is being advanced from chilling section **14** through filtration section **25** and reflux section **26** into melting section **27**, the piston is reciprocated at a suitable rate, such as in the range of about 50 to 400 pulsations per minute, so that a pulsating pressure is exerted on the melt reflux which is intermittently forced back, countercurrently with respect to the crystal mass through reflux section **26**.

A check valve **45** can be provided in product withdrawal line **34** to prevent the backflow of withdrawn product into the crystal purification column **24**. If desired, the check valve can be replaced or augmented by a suitable valve, such as a solenoid valve, which is cyclically opened and closed in synchronism with the movement of the piston. The rate of withdrawal of purified product in conduit 34 is set for a substantially constant rate by means of valve 46 which is actuated by flow rate controller 47 responsive to the pressure drop across an orifice 48 in conduit 34.

Electrical power is transmitted to electrical heating element 33 from electrical power source 49 by means of a suitable variable power transferring device, such as a servo motor rotated Powerstat 51. The position of Powerstat 51 is controlled by temperature recorder-controller 52 responsive to the temperature of the melt passing through conduit 34 as determined by temperature sensing device 53 which can suitably be a thermocouple.

A crystallization purification system which utilizes the control system of the process can operate with the purified product withdrawal rate being substantially constant at the optimum value through the utilization of the means for varying the heat input to the melting section of the purification column responsive to the temperature of the melt. The theory for this phenomenon is not understood. The temperature of the melt can be measured either in the melting section itself or in the product withdrawal line.

Concentration Using Crystal Purification Columns

D.L. McKay and E.W. Mellow; U.S. Patent 3,216,833; November 9, 1965; assigned to Phillips Petroleum Company provide a process for concentrating an aqueous solution such as a beverage or food product, which comprises cooling the aqueous solution to form a slurry of ice crystals in a mother liquor and passing the slurry into a crystal purification column. The crystals in the mother liquor are introduced to a confined zone where the ice crystals are passed in a compact mass into a body of crystal melt and the ice crystals are heated to form the melt in the downstream portion of the confined zone. The process further comprises withdrawing the mother liquor as a concentrated aqueous solution from an upstream portion of the confined zone and withdrawing melt containing water and non-aqueous components of the mother liquor from the downstream portion of the zone.

Thereafter, the withdrawn crystal melt containing mother liquor components is distilled to effect a separation between the components and the water, and the recovered components are then recombined with the mother liquor in the process. These recovered components can be recombined with the mother liquor by returning them to the cooling step in which the ice crystals are formed in the mother liquor, or the recovered components can be added directly to the concentrated solution removed as a product from the purification column. The essential advantages of the concentration by crystallization are realized in the process since a very small fraction of the over-all recovered product is subjected to heat in the distillation step.

By relying upon distillation for recovery of the final fractions of product, however, the crystal purification columns can be operated at substantially greater throughputs. That is to say, by operating the crystal purification columns at lower efficiencies so that a small portion of the mother liquor components are passed out of the column with the crystal melt, the over-all capacity of the operation can be greatly increased and the mother liquor components can be recovered from the crystal melt by distillation without seriously detracting from the quality of the final product. The patent contains a flow diagram of the apparatus used along with a detailed description of its use.

Concentration Using Hydrate Formers

S.B. Tuwiner; U.S. Patent 3,217,505; November 16, 1965; assigned to The Lummus Company describes a method utilizing both freezing and hydrate methods. Generally, (as described with reference to the demineralization of saline water), precooled saline water is contacted with a hydrate forming substance which forms a hydrate at a temperature above the melting point of ice in water. During the contact a minor portion of the hydrate forming substance may be vaporized and provides a portion of the cooling requirements necessary to form the hydrate, but the remaining portion of the cooling requirements being provided by indirect heat exchange. The hydrate and enriched brine is thereafter passed to another zone where the temperature of the hydrate enriched brine mixture is reduced to the fusion temperature of water in brine whereby ice crystals are formed.

The ice crystals in slurry form are passed to the hydrate forming step and are melted by indirect heat exchange relation to provide a portion of the cooling requirements for such step. Thus, an important feature of the process is the thermodynamic cycle where the hydrate is decomposed while simultaneously forming ice crystals and using the ice crystals after separation from the enriched brine to abstract the heat given off by the hydrate forming reaction.

Example: The process may also be utilized in concentrating aqueous solutions such as fruit juices, waste sulfite liquors and the like. Of course, a hydrate forming substance must be chosen which will not impart a foreign taste to the orange juice when reconstituted nor be harmful to the user should a minor portion thereof remain in the concentrated juice. While the basic concept is employed to make large ice crystals, the processing steps are performed batchwise. To illustrate this embodiment, 1,000 gallons of 12°Brix fresh orange juice was added to 500 gallons of previously concentrated 42°Brix orange juice. The vessel is provided with twin opposed Centricone agitators mounted on a cover plate having a vapor tight seal against the side walls of the reactor and a vapor tight gland for the propeller shaft.

Cooling water at a temperature of 32°F is circulated through the jacket of the vessel while continuously agitating the orange juice. 1,743 pounds of Freon 21 is gradually introduced over a period of an hour at a rate whereby the pressure in the vessel does not exceed 14.7 psia. At the completion of the hydrate reaction, the pressure in the vessel falls below 9 psia. At this point, the circulating cooling water is stopped, the pressure in the vessel is reduced by applying a suction of 70 millimeters absolute. Gaseous Freon 21 is withdrawn at a rate of 100 pounds per hour. During vapor withdrawal, the hydrate of Freon 21 decomposes producing ice crystals and Freon 21 vapor which is compressed at 15.33 psia and condensed for recycle. The magma of ice crystals in the juice concentrate is then passed to a 36 inch basket centrifuge where the crystals are separated from 750 gallons of 42°Brix juice, 500 of which is recycled thereby providing for 250 gallons of net product.

The ice crystals withdrawn from the centrifuge are added to ice water and the ice slurry is circulated through the jacket vessel during the hydrate formation step. Approximately 750 gallons of ice water is discharged per batch of treated orange juice.

Improved Method for Separation of Components

J.F. Tooke; U.S. Patent 3,218,817; November 23, 1965; assigned to Phillips Petroleum Company provides an improved method and apparatus for separating the components of a fluid mixture. A refrigerant is injected into a body of the fluid mixture. The mixture is chilled by the evaporation of the refrigerant thus forming a slurry of crystals of a first component of the mixture in the remaining fluid. The slurry is passed to a purification operation where the remaining fluid is separated out as a concentrate and the crystals are melted by contact with a heated liquid stream of the first component.

This produces a purified liquid product stream of the first component. The refrigerant vapors from the chilling operation are compressed in a first compression zone and then passed in direct heat exchanging relationship with the liquid product stream. A portion of the thus heated liquid product stream is passed to the purification operation as the heated liquid stream of the first component while the cooled refrigerant is compressed in a second compression zone and is then passed in indirect heat exchange relationship with the remainder of the heated liquid product stream and the concentrate. While the process, which is described and illustrated in the patent, is particularly applicable to the production of fresh water from seawater, it is useful for the concentration of fruit juices.

Combination of Crystal Slurries from Separate Chillings

Crystallization processes conventionally comprise a chilling step followed by the separation of the formed crystals from the mother liquor. The chilling step comprises lowering the temperature of the feed in a chilling zone until the crystals are formed. While it would be desirable to concentrate as much as possible of the crystallizable component in the chilling zone by the formation of crystal solids, if the solids content is too high, the resulting slurry becomes quite stiff and difficult to transmit from the chilling zone. It has been found desirable that the slurry passed from the chilling zone comprises from about 20 to 60 and preferably about 35 to 55 weight percent solids.

Control of the chilling zone conventionally comprises controlling the temperature of the slurry passed from the chilling zone as the temperature of the slurry is representative of the concentration of solids present therein. It is highly desirable that the concentration of solids in the slurry passed from the chilling zone to the purification or separation step be substantially constant so as to provide a proper basis for control of the separation or purification step. The effect of varying the concentration of the solids to the purification step will hereinafter be discussed.

In fruit juices and other aqueous systems, the concentration of crystallizable component (water) is high and the concentration of recoverable product to be separated as mother liquor is relatively low. A slight change in the temperature of the slurry passed from the chilling zone represents a substantial change in the solids content of the slurry. Therefore, a control system based upon measuring a temperature representative of the percent solids in the slurry and manipulating the flow of coolant to the chilling zone, or otherwise adjusting the temperature of the chilling zone, in a conventional feedback method of control is highly unsatisfactory. With an aqueous feed to the chilling zone, the concentration of solids in the slurry passed from the chilling zone varies widely.

J.E. Cottle; U.S. Patent 3,255,598; June 14, 1966; assigned to Phillips Petroleum Company found that the concentration of solids in the slurry feed to the separation step can be controlled by chilling a portion of the mother liquor recovered from the separation or purification step in a second chilling zone and combining the slurry passed from the second chilling zone with the slurry from a first chilling zone wherein the feed to the crystallization process is chilled, and passing the combined slurries to the separation step.

Figure 2.15 illustrates the process as applied to the concentration of beer by crystallization. Beer comprising, for example, about 3.6 weight percent alcohol, 5.5 weight percent sugars and 90.9 weight percent water is passed via conduit means 10 to chiller 11 wherein the temperature of the beer feed is lowered so as to produce a slurry containing ice crystals. The chiller can comprise any conventional apparatus wherein the temperature of the feed can be lowered so as to produce a slurry of crystals and a means for passing the slurry of crystals therefrom.

Conventional chilling apparatus comprises a jacketed vessel equipped with a rotary scraper with a cooling medium passed through the jacket in indirect heat exchange with the feed to the chiller. Within the chiller water is crystallized to form a crystal slurry which contains from about 10 to 55, and preferably about 15 to 45 weight percent solids. As previously noted, while it is desirable to concentrate to as high a degree as possible the formation of crystal solids, if the solids content is too high, the slurry becomes quite stiff and becomes too difficult to pass from the chiller.

The slurry of ice crystals passed from the chiller via conduit means 12 is combined with a slurry of ice crystals from a source hereinafter described to provide a slurry wherein the concentration of solids is in the previously stated desired range of from about 20 to 60 and preferably about 35 to 55 weight percent and passed to the conduit means 12 via conduit means 13. A combined slurry feed having a substantially constant percent solids concentration is passed to purification column 16.

FIGURE 2.15: CRYSTAL FORMING PROCESS

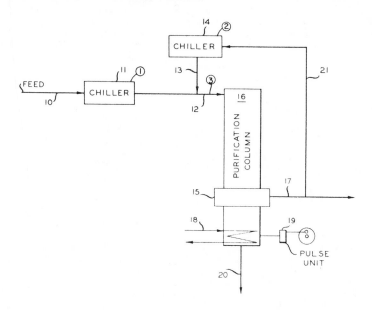

Source: J.E. Cottle; U.S. Patent 3,255,598; June 14, 1966

The purification column can be a piston type column or a pulse type column as described
in U.S. Patent 2,854,494. As illustrated, the crystal purification column is a pulse type
column having a pulse unit **19**. In either type of column, a compacted mass of crystals is
forced through the column and into a body of melt at the downstream end thereof. The
body of melt is formed by melting the crystals through the introduction of heat via heating
means **18**, such as heating coils. The passage of the melt from the purification column is
restricted so that some of the melt is passed into the crystal mass as the crystals are passed
through the column into the body of melt.

A filter section **15** is provided in an intermediate region in the purification column so that
mother liquor containing about 18 weight percent alcohol can be withdrawn from the column via conduit means **17** and thereby separated from the crystals. The melt comprising
water is withdrawn from the purification column via conduit means **20**.

At least a portion of the mother liquor (beer concentrate) withdrawn from the purification
column via conduit means **17** is recycled or passed to chiller **14** via conduit means **21**.
Chiller **14** can comprise apparatus such as described in connection with chiller **11**.

The slurry passed from chiller **14** via conduit means **13** has a solids content ranging from
40 to 60 weight percent, preferably about 45 to 55 weight percent. The slurry passed
from chiller **14** is combined with the slurry passed from chiller **11** in the heretofore
described manner with the ratio of the slurry from chiller **14** to the slurry from chiller
11 preferably ranging from 0.5:1 to 5:1 on a weight basis.

By, for example, combining the slurry from chiller **14** and the slurry from chiller **11** in
the weight ratio of 1:1, the weight percent solids concentration deviation from the desired
control level of the slurry from chiller **11** passed to the purification column is reduced by
nearly one half. This is to say that should the temperature of the slurry passed from chiller

11 deviate one-half degree from the desired control level, producing a deviation of 4.5 weight percent solids concentration, the combined slurries will deviate less than 2.55 weight percent solids concentration from the desired control level by controlling the temperature of the slurry passed from chiller **14** within one degree of the desired control temperature.

Multistage Crystallization

When the components of a mixture form solid solutions, it is not possible either theoretically or actually to obtain a pure material by one stage of crystallization, i.e., by a single freezing step followed by a crystal-liquor separation step. In such cases pure crystals of a single component do not separate from the feed. The material so crystallized is a mixture of the components present, the ratio depending on the composition of the starting material and on the equilibrium characteristics for the particular system. The crystals will be richer with respect to the higher melting component of the mixture than the liquid from which those crystals were solidified.

If equilibrium between the crystals separated from a mixture of solid solution forming components in the remaining liquid could be easily obtained, then separation of the components could be obtained by moving the crystals countercurrently to a liquid which becomes increasingly richer with respect to that component tending to be preferentially removed by freezing. The crystals reaching the end would be substantially pure. At least a portion of the crystals would be melted and the melt returned countercurrently to the moving crystals where the remaining crystals would be removed as product. At the opposite end of such a crystallizer, cooling could be applied to generate the crystals, the unfrozen liquid would be removed as a pure, less easily frozen fraction of the original mixtures. The crystals formed would always be moved toward the warmer end of the crystallizer.

While such a process is theoretically possible, its efficiency is disappointingly low. This is due to the length of time required for the solid and remaining liquid to reach equilibrium. Resort to alternate partial or complete melting and freezing is usually the result of attempts to obtain purer products by countercurrent continuous crystallization. In such a process, the energy requirements and amount of heat transfer required are inordinately large because the heat of crystallization must be added and removed many times throughout the process.

W.C. McCarthy and G.H. Dale; U.S. Patent 3,261,170; July 19, 1966; assigned to Phillips Petroleum Company describe a process for separating a mixture of compounds into high-purity higher melting and lower melting fractions by maintaining an elongated, confined body of the mixture to be separated, maintaining a temperature differential between the ends of the body, maintaining within the body a temperature such that a portion of the mixture can be made to solidify by the application of pressure to said body.

The body is subjected to a first pulsating pressure to cause portions of the mixture to solidify and portions of the solid to melt. The solids formed are moved towards the warmer end of the body which is then subjected to a second pulsating pressure which forces the liquid countercurrent to the solids and toward the colder end of the body. Thus a higher melting fraction can be withdrawn from the warmer end and a lower melting fraction from the colder end.

The process is illustrated by Figure 2.15 which is an elevational view of a preferred modification of the chiller and purification column. A feed mixture comprising two or more components, one of which is separable from a mixture by crystallization, enters the system through feed inlet **2**. A pump, not shown, may be provided to force the mixture into the chilling section. The chiller may be cooled by any suitable means such as a jacket **10** through which a heat exchange medium is passed through conduits **12** and **14**. Conditions are maintained in the chiller to form a slurry of crystals and mother liquor, said slurry then being passed through conduit **16** into the purification column **18**.

FIGURE 2.16: MULTISTAGE CRYSTALLIZATION PROCESS

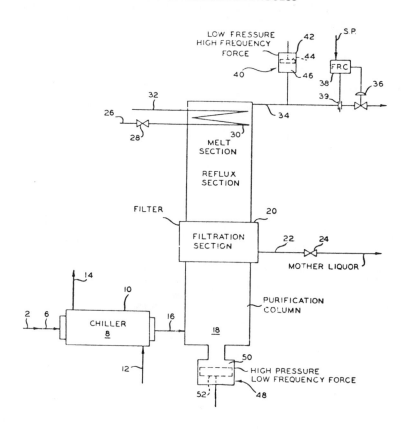

Source: W.C. McCarthy and G.H. Dale; U.S. Patent 3,261,170; July 19, 1966

The chiller also generally contains (not shown) an agitating or scraping means which is designed to prevent the accumulation of solid material on the heat exchange surface. These are frequently fabricated in the form of a helix and any suitable number of scrapers can be provided.

The purification apparatus is preferably composed of a cylindrical shell closed at both ends and comprising in series an inlet section, a filtration section, a reflux section, a melt section, and a withdrawal section. The slurry upon leaving the inlet section of the purification column passes first through a filtration section comprising a suitable filter medium 20, the latter being provided with an outlet pipe 22 for the filtrate. The filter medium can be of any type known in the art. For example, it can comprise a metallic screen, a sintered perforate metal member, or a perforate metal member, supporting a filter cloth.

Generally, it is desirable that the filter member 20 be positioned integrally with respect to the shell. The filtrate produced in the filter zone is removed through conduits 20 and 24 and comprises essentially all of the mother liquor. In some systems of the eutectic type, it may be desirable to recycle at least a portion of the mother liquor through conduit 2 back to the feed to the chiller. This is especially true when concentrating dilute aqueous systems such as beer. The remaining crystal mass passes through the reflux section wherein it is countercurrently contacted with the liquid reflux produced as subsequently described. As the crystal mass approaches heater 30 in the melt section, the crystals are melted. The heater can be in the form of an electrical heater or a heat transfer coil through which a suitably heated fluid is pumped through conduits 26, valve 28 and heat exchange surface 30 and conduit 32. Part of the melt produced by heater 30 is withdrawn through the outlet pipe 34 as a purified product of the process. The remainder of the melt is forced back through the reflux zone to form reflux which affects crystal purification, the resulting liquid being drawn out through outlet 22.

Although an internal heater 30 is shown, an external heater can be used, for example, a heating jacket encompassing the melt section and provided with means for circulating heating fluid therethrough. In addition, it is also possible to remove a portion of the crystals and melt them externally of the purification column and then return the melt back to the purification column for reflux.

In order to provide back pressure in the purification column so as to restrain flow therethrough and produce a constant product rate, a flow sensing means 39 determines the flow in the conduit 34 and transmits a signal to a pressure recorder controller 38 which, in turn, actuates valve 36 so as to control the flow of product therethrough.

A low pressure, high frequency force is maintained on the melt by any suitable means such as a pulsating producing member 40 comprising a cylinder 42, a chamber 46 and a piston 44, the piston being reciprocated by any suitable means such as by connection to an electrical motor through suitable valve, crank means, connecting rods, etc. While the crystal mass is being advanced from the chilling section 8 through the filtration section, reflux section and melting section, the piston is reciprocated at a suitable rate so that a pulsating pressure is exerted on the melt reflux so that it is intermittently forced back countercurrently with respect to the crystal mass through the reflux zone. Any suitable means may be provided for producing an intermittent pressure at a relatively high frequency on the melt.

Crystallization with Sonic Defoaming

L.W. Pollock; U.S. Patent 3,266,263; August 16, 1966; assigned to Phillips Petroleum Company provides an improved method of and apparatus for concentrating an aqueous solution by crystallization whereby the aqueous solution is contacted with carbon dioxide to form a slurry of ice crystals in mother liquor, the slurry is passed to a crystal growth zone, and the ice crystals separated from the mother liquor in a crystal purification zone.

Figure 2.17 illustrates the process using beer as the representative aqueous solution. Beer is passed through conduit means 10 to a freezer 11 (contact zone). Liquid carbon dioxide at a relatively high pressure and from a source hereinafter described is passed via conduit means 31 to the freezer. The liquid carbon dioxide is vaporized in passing through a conventional pressure reducing valve 32 positioned immediately adjacent to the freezer and through means 14 for dispersing the carbon dioxide upwardly throughout the cross section of the freezer. Upon the vaporization of the carbon dioxide in the freezer, the temperature of the beer feed is lowered to form a slurry of ice crystals.

The temperature within the freezer can range from about 0° to 32°F and the pressure can range from about 150 to 500 psig. The weight ratio of liquid carbon dioxide to beer passed to the freezer can range from about 1:2 to 2:1. The freezer is provided with a means for mixing 12 the carbon dioxide and beer feed streams. In order to prevent foaming, conventional sonic defoamers 13 are employed.

Vaporous carbon dioxide is withdrawn from the freezer via conduit means 16 and passed to a conventional means for separating 17 the vaporous carbon dioxide from entrained liquid such as a cyclone separator. A slurry comprising beer concentrate and ice crystals is withdrawn from the freezer via conduit means 33 and passed to a crystal growth vessel

34. The solids content of the slurry withdrawn from the freezer should not exceed 50 weight percent so that the slurry can be handled properly. Preferably, the slurry withdrawn from the freezer will contain 30 to 40 weight percent solids. The process conditions thus maintained within the freezer are such as to provide a slurry having the desired solids content.

Dissolved carbon dioxide in the slurry feed to crystal growth vessel **34** is flashed within crystal growth vessel **34**, resulting in further freezing and a slight drop in temperature of the beer concentrate-ice slurry. The pressure within the crystal growth vessel is less than the pressure within the freezer so as to permit flashing of the dissolved carbon dioxide but above atmospheric pressure so as to prevent oxygen from entering the system. Preferably, the pressure within the crystal growth vessel will range from about 5 to 25 psig, as higher pressures would require a higher pressure in the subsequent purification step. The carbon dioxide flashing step within the crystal growth vessel will only slightly reduce the temperature of the slurry feed, the temperature within the crystal growth vessel will range from 1° to 2°F below the temperature within the freezer.

The crystal growth vessel contains low pressure sonic defoamers **37** to inhibit foaming within the vessel. The growth of ice crystals within the vessel is aided by a conventional agitation means **36** maintaining continuous and intimate contact between the beer concentrate and the ice crystals. It is desired that the slurry passed to the crystal growth vessel have as long a residence time within the vessel as possible. The residence time within the vessel is limited by the maximum economical capacity of the vessel. Residence time within the crystal growth vessel for the slurry feed is in the range of 0.5 to 10 hours, preferably 0.5 to 4 hours.

FIGURE 2.17: CRYSTALLIZATION WITH SONIC DEFOAMING

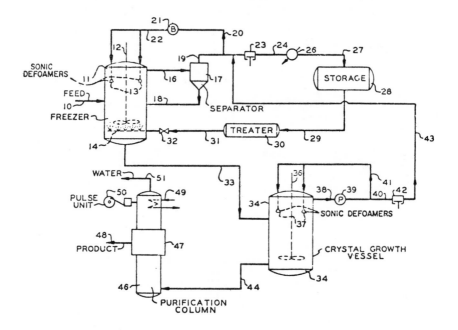

Source: L.W. Pollock; U.S. Patent 3,266,263; August 16, 1966

Vaporous carbon dioxide is withdrawn from the crystal growth vessel via conduit means **38** and a conventional vacuum pump **39**. A portion of the vaporous carbon dioxide withdrawn from the crystal growth vessel is recycled via conduit means **40** and **41** to the sonic defoamers **37**. In the operation of the sonic defoamers, the carbon dioxide is jetted through a nozzle of the sonic defoamer into a chamber causing the chamber to resonate. The reflector of each of the sonic defoamers directs the sound toward the foam causing the formed bubbles to burst when the pressure outside the bubble becomes less than the inside pressure of the bubble during a part of the sonic wave cycle. The remainder of the withdrawn vaporous carbon dioxide is passed via conduit means **40** to a compression means **42**, and recycled via conduit means **43** from compression means **42** to the carbon dioxide recovery system hereinafter described.

The slurry is withdrawn from the crystal growth vessel via conduit means **44** and passed to a conventional purification column **46**. This crystal purification column can be a piston-type column or a pulse-type column. As illustrated, the crystal purification column is a pulse-type column having a pulse unit **50**. The compacted mass of ice crystals is forced through the column by a pumping means not illustrated and into a body of melt at the downstream end of the purification column. The body of melt is formed by melting the crystals through the introduction of heat via heating means **49**. The passage of the melt from the purification column is restricted by a means not illustrated so that some of the melt is passed into the crystal mass as the crystals are forced through the column into the body of melt. A filter section **47** is provided at an intermediate point in the purification column so that mother liquor can be withdrawn from the column and separated from the crystals. The melt comprising water is withdrawn from the purification column via conduit means **51**.

Tubular Crystallizer for Larger Crystals

In the freeze concentration of comestibles, such as orange juice, apple juice and the like, the ice crystals must be filtered or centrifuged from the solution being concentrated in the freeze concentration process. Irregular and small crystals are difficult and may even be impossible to efficiently separate from solution. Thus it is desirable to provide an apparatus which will produce larger and more uniform crystals.

It has been found that properly designed agitator blades may be used to remove the stagnant supercooled layer of fluid adjacent to the crystallizer walls before it freezes and forms ice crystals on the walls. The supercooled liquid removed from the walls must be adequately mixed with the solution passing through the crystallizer so that the supercooled fluid will cause growth of existing crystals. Without adequate mixing, the supercooled liquid will nucleate to produce additional crystals. This reduces the size of the crystals grown. Proper mixing of more viscous solutions is difficult to obtain within a crystallizer while agitating the solution to prevent the formation of ice crystals on the walls.

R.H. Hedrick; U.S. Patent 3,277,667; October 11, 1966; assigned to Struthers Scientific and International Corporation provides a tubular crystallizer for growing larger and more uniform crystals in relatively concentrated solutions, having an internal agitator which does not scrape the wall of the crystallizer while preventing crystals from forming on the wall.

Figure 2.18a is a side view of a crystallizer. Figure 2.18b is a vertical section taken on line 2–2 of Figure 2.18a. Figure 2.18c is a front elevation of the agitator shaft bearing support frame. Figure 2.18d is a longitudinal vertical section through a fragment of the discharge end of the crystallizer of Figure 2.18a with a crystallizer tube broken away in section. Figure 2.18e is a longitudinal vertical section through a fragment of the inlet end of the crystallizer with a crystallizer tube broken away in section. Figure 2.18f is a vertical section taken on line 6–6 of Figure 2.18d. Figure 2.18g is a vertical section taken on line 7–7 of Figure 2.18d. Figure 2.18h is a side view of a fragment of an agitator shaft with a spider arm broken away in section and with a fragment of a planetary shaft and attached blades shown in position.

FIGURE 2.18: TUBULAR CRYSTALLIZER FOR LARGER CRYSTALS

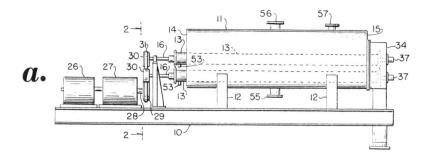

a.

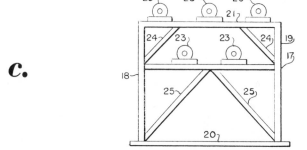

b.

c.

(continued)

FIGURE 2.18: (continued)

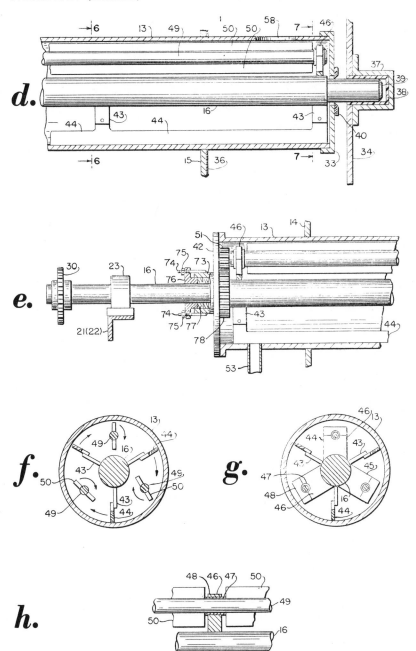

Source: R.H. Hedrick; U.S. Patent 3,277,667; October 11, 1966

Figures 2.18a and 2.18b show the generally rectangular base 10 above which the crystallizer body 11 is supported by the four legs 12. Five crystallizer tubes 13 extend through the crystallizer body and project beyond its end walls 14 and 15. Agitator shafts 16 extend from the inlet ends of the crystallizer tubes.

As shown in Figure 2.18c, an agitator shaft bearing support frame 17 has two vertical upright members 18 and 19 extending upward from a base plate 20. Disposed between the upright members are the upper and lower bearing support members 21 and 22. Three bearings or pillow blocks 23 containing ball bearings are mounted on the upper bearing support member 21 and two bearings or pillow blocks are mounted on the lower bearing support member 22. Pairs of braces 24 and 25 stiffen and strengthen the agitator shaft bearing support frame 17.

Referring again to Figures 2.18a and 2.18b, a motor 26 is mounted on the base 10 to drive the speed reducing unit 27 from which the shaft 28 extends carrying the sprocket 29. Each of the agitator shafts 16 has a sprocket 30 mounted on it. A chain 31 extends about sprocket 29 and winds about the sprockets 30 so that sprocket 29 may drive all the sprockets 30. Any suitable drive means may be used in place of the sprockets 29 and 30 and the chain 31.

Referring to Figures 2.18a and 2.18d, each crystallizer tube 13 extends through the wall 15 of the crystallizer body 11. The end of the crystallizer tube may be threaded to have a correspondingly threaded cover plate 33 screwed in place over it. The agitator shaft 16 extends through the cover plate. A discharge housing 34 having a rear wall 35 is placed over the ends of the crystallizer tubes with its front wall 36 disposed against wall 15 of the crystallizer body. Bearing caps 37 are bolted to the rear wall 35. The bearing caps contain the Teflon bearings 38 which receive the ends 39 of the shafts 16. A Teflon seal 40 prevents liquid from flowing past the cover plate.

Referring now to Figure 2.18e, each crystallizer tube 13 has its inlet end extend through wall 14 of the crystallizer body 11. A cover plate 42 extends over the end of each tube and has an agitator shaft 16 pass through it. An annular flange 73 extends about the center of cover 42 and about the shaft. Bolts 74 are welded to the flange so that nuts 75 may be tightened to urge a compression member 76 against the ring type seals 77 which provide for the fluid tight passage of the shaft through cover plate 42. A spur gear 78 extends about the shaft and is welded or otherwise fixed to the cover plate.

Referring now to Figures 2.18d through 2.18h, tabs 43 are welded to shaft 16 in rows along its length disposed equidistant from each other. Agitator blades 44 are bolted or otherwise fixed to the tabs 43 to extend with a slight clearance from the inner surface of the crystallizer tube 13. A number of spiders 45 having three arms 46 are welded or otherwise fixed to shaft 16. Each arm has a bearing 47 secured to it by means of a bearing cap 48 which may be bolted in place. Planetary shafts 49 are rotatably journalled in the bearings and have a pair of planetary blades 50 fixed to extend from them. On the inlet end of each planetary shaft there is mounted a spur gear 51 which engages the fixed gear 78. Thus it may be seen that rotation of shaft 16 causes the planetary rotation of shafts 49 and blades 50 between the blades 44.

As shown in Figures 2.18a, 2.18d and 2.18e, a viscous fluid to be concentrated is introduced through the inlet tubes 53. A cooling medium or refrigerant is passed through the fittings 55, 56 and 57 and the crystallizer body 11 to cool the crystallizer tubes 13. A relatively large upwardly facing discharge aperture 58 is formed in each crystallizer tube within the discharge housing 34. Thus a slurry of liquid and ice crystals passes through the crystallizer tubes to fall downward within the discharge housing to be collected and have the ice crystals removed from it.

Nuclei Formed in Indirect Heat Exchange with Refrigerant

H. Svanoe; U.S. Patent 3,285,021; November 15, 1966; assigned to Struthers Scientific and International Corporation reports a process for the concentration of citrus liquids and other potable extracts by a controlled crystallization process which produces dense ice crystals from the fruit or vegetable juice extracts. The process maintains a uniform refrigeration environment which provides for the nucleation of ice crystals from the extract, the growth of crystals resulting therefrom, and subsequent separation of concentrate.

The steps in the process are:

(a) cooling an aqueous product in the presence of ice forming nuclei in indirect heat exchange with a volatile refrigerant by passing the aqueous product through tubular parallel flow paths, in a folded zig-zag pattern, submerged in a pool of the refrigerant, to form an ice slurry, each flow path comprising at least three connected horizontal legs;

(b) maintaining each leg in a pool of liquid refrigerant, supplied thereto in parallel paths;

(c) withdrawing refrigerant vapor from each pool of refrigerant in parallel paths to cool the refrigerant pool;

(d) withdrawing the ice slurry from the heat exchanger;

(e) passing a portion of the slurry to a retention zone for growth of crystals;

(f) returning the remaining portion of the ice slurry containing nuclei to the cooling step (a); and

(g) separating ice slurry into ice and concentrated aqueous product by centrifuging.

The process is operable on such fruit juices as orange, lemon, pear, grape and apple and on vegetable juices such as tomato, carrot, cabbage, onion and beet.

Sub-Cooling in Boundary Film Area

Related work of *H. Svanoe; U.S. Patent 3,328,972; July 4, 1967; assigned to Struthers Scientific and International Corporation* is directed to a process for the concentration of a solute in a solvent by the removal of the solvent by freezing. A slurry containing a solute, solvent, and crystals of the solute is circulated in a closed cycle or alternatively may be passed through a single crystallizer without recycling or through a plurality of crystallizers in series depending on the amount of concentration desired. A feed of a dilute solution of the solute is fed into the circulating slurry. The augmented and diluted slurry is passed through a sub-cooling zone and, if desired, a separate crystallization zone of the cycle.

The sub-cooling of the dilute solution is effected in a confined area, hereinafter referred to as a boundary film, an area that is formed between an agitator periphery, and a metal cooling surface, the sub-cooling being effected in such a way that the boundary film is maintained at a temperature below the freezing point of the solution placed therein and importantly subjected to sufficient intensity of turbulence that on the one hand the film of solution is sub-cooled to a temperature below its freezing point and on the other hand the sub-cooling of the solution is not released in the boundary film as heat of crystallization. The sub-cooling on the contrary is released as the heat of crystallization outside the boundary film, as crystals of the solvent and as crystal growth. The dilute solvent feed is continuously introduced into the crystallization zone, the solvent concentrated by crystal growth and the concentrated extract removed.

An embodiment of the process constitutes passing the dilute solution into an apparatus, such as that illustrated in Figure 2.19 through inlet **1** and into the circulating slurry of the solution and crystals, thereof flowing in conduit **9**. The slurry contains a solution (of the extract to be concentrated), the solute and crystals of the solvent. The slurry passes into zone **2**, then into the heat exchanger (referred to more specifically below) and crystallizer **3** and pump **4**, the latter forcing the slurry continuously through the crystallizer at a desired velocity. A propeller shaft **5** is centered in the crystallizer to which are fixed agitators **6**. As the slurry with its load of feed passes into the crystallizer, it meets the slurry therein which is in a state of turbulence. Agitators **6** are so constructed and arranged and are so rotated and also so propelled in vertical directions by propeller shaft **5** that the boundary film, i.e., the layer of liquid proximate to the inside wall of the crystallizer, is in a state of turbulence which will be more fully particularized hereinafter. Between the outer wall of the crystallizer **7** and the flowing slurry is a heat transfer surface **8**. A fluid refrigerant or a film of an evaporating refrigerant of any suitable kind flows at a sufficient temperature to refrigerate (by indirect heat exchange) and sub-cool the solvents in the film, i.e., lower the temperature below the freezing point of the solution in the film.

The removal of the heat of crystallization and the removal of the necessary heat to maintain the temperature of the slurry at the proper freezing temperature is carried by the sub-cooled solvent to zone **12**. A slurry containing inter alia, the concentrated solution, is withdrawn from crystallizer **3** through outlet **10**, the crystal content separated therefrom and the concentrate sent to storage.

FIGURE 2.19: SUB-COOLING IN BOUNDARY FILM AREA

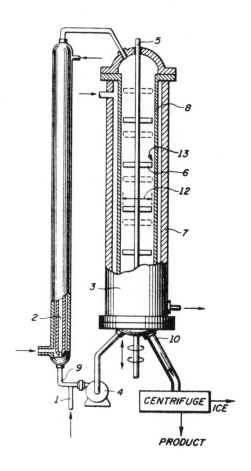

Source: H. Svanoe; U.S. Patent 3,328,972; July 4, 1967

An important feature of the process is the creation and maintenance of the boundary film. It is known (*Principles of Chem. Eng.,* Walker, Lewis and McAdams, 1923, page 134) that "When a liquid is in contact with a solid, there is strong evidence to show the presence of an adhering relatively stationary film of fluid on the surface of the solid, a film that becomes thinner as the velocity of the fluid parallel to the surface increases, but which breaks away from the solid only at very high velocities, if at all". It has been found that during the concentration of a solution by freezing by prior art processes, crystals are generated in the "stationary film". If crystal generation could be prevented while at the same time the solution be properly refrigerated by indirect heat exchange, many of the difficulties encountered by the prior art should be eliminated.

By extensive research, crystal generation has been eliminated in the film and the crystallization transferred to the crystallization and crystal growing zones from which the crystals can easily be withdrawn. Contrariwise the crude and awkward mechanical means of the art invariably require the use of scrapers or other means of removing the crystals from the heat transfer surfaces to which they are prone to adhere so tenaciously. The resulting comminution of the crystals by the scrapers occludes the solution being concentrated. Frequent complete freeze up of apparatus used in the art points up, with the difficulties described supra, the problems this process avoids.

In accordance with the process, means are provided to subject the boundary film to subcooling and to intense turbulence that prevents the formation of crystals on the heat exchange surface although normally crystallization would occur with or without scraping under such sub-cooling. Agitators are provided in the crystallization zone, the periphery of each is surrounded by and defines the inner limits of the boundary zone. The o.d. of the boundary zone is defined by the i.d. of the heat transfer surface. The agitators whip into and disturb the continuity of the film of the boundary zone without touching the heat exchange surface.

Example: Orange juice, concentrated for use in preparing frozen juice, is prepared by squeezing oranges followed by customary separation of the pulp and concentrating the juice by the following process. The expressed juice containing about 12% solids, as feed, is chilled to about 0°C, is passed through inlet 1 (Figure 2.19) into a slurry containing from 20 to 40% ice and about 40% solution of orange juice and the resulting slurry subjected to sub-cooling below the freezing point of the solution, i.e., to about –8°C.

The sub-cooling is effected in the boundary film extract and the extract transferred by turbulence from the boundary layer to the crystallizer for release of the sub-cooling by crystal growth on the crystals in the slurry. The concentrated extract is separated by centrifuging; the crystals washed with dilute orange juice and the resulting washwater returned to the crystallizer with the feed.

Concentration of Undercoated Extract

J.W. Pike; U.S. Patent 3,285,022; November 15, 1966 describes a process of continuously introducing a dilute extract, undercooled below its freezing point and within the metastable state, into a concentrating extract and ice slurry, releasing the undercooling to heat of crystallization in growth of ice on the crystals present in the slurry and thereby concentrating the extract.

The water in the extract is changed from a liquid phase solvent to a solid phase by deposition of ice on the crystals of ice present in the slurry, thus expanding the size of the crystals and concentrating the extract. By maintaining carefully controlled conditions as described below during the heat transfer of the undercooling, dense pure ice crystals are formed without occluding the solute. Moreover, the solute retained on the surface of the crystals can be readily washed from the crystals after their separation from the concentrated extract.

The practice of the process involves, as a preliminary step, cooling the extract to a metastable state. This state has been defined as a peculiar state of peudo-equilibrium, in which the system has acquired or lost energy beyond that required for its most stable state, yet has not been rendered unstable. Thus, by using great care an extract undercooled below its normal freezing point will not crystallize. In this condition it has lost heat energy to the extent that it would normally be expected to crystallize spontaneously; and only a slight disturbance will precipitate that change, the disturbance being provided from some external source. While in the metastable state, spontaneous crystallization does not obtain until the metastability is disrupted by the triggering of crystal formation generally due to the creation of a source of nucleation thereby reverting metastability to stability. In the process a source of nucleation, e.g., ice crystals in the crystallizer serve as the external disturbance that precipitates the change. The following example uses Figure 2.20 as a reference diagram.

FIGURE 2.20: CONCENTRATION USING UNDERCOOLED EXTRACT

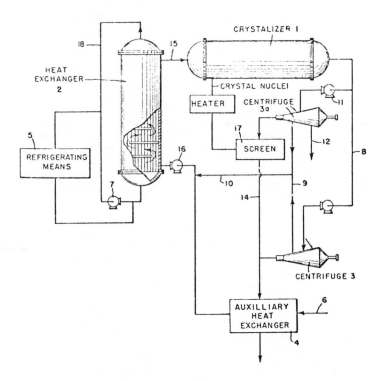

Source: J.W. Pike; U.S. Patent 3,285,022; November 15, 1966

Example: Orange juice for sale in the form of frozen juice or as a concentrated juice is prepared by squeezing oranges followed by the customary separation of the pulp and removing water from the resulting juice. In the process, the juice, of 12% concentration by weight with an initial freezing point at 28°F, is first chilled in auxiliary heat exchanger 4; is then forced at a rate governed by the variable speed pump 16 into head exchanger 2; is cooled therein from the stable monophase state to a metastable monophase state at a temperature of approximately 25°F by contact with the heat transfer surfaces of the heat exchanger and is finally quickly transferred through line 15 to crystallizer 1 containing a slurry of extract and ice crystals at a temperature of 27°F. There are present in the heat exchanger from 50 to 500 square feet of heat exchange surface per 1,000 pounds of water subsequently removed as ice from the extract per hour in the crystallizer which accomplishes the refrigeration.

A feature of the process is the control of the heat removed from the extract in heat exchanger 2 for the purpose of undercooling the extract to from 0.5° to 10.0°F, and preferably 1.0° to 5.0°F, below the normal freezing point of the extract and into its metastable state. The concentration and kind of extract determines its normal freezing point and the degree of undercooling may approach but not reach below the metastable range as the extract leaves the heat exchanger. For optimum operation, the rate of heat withdrawn by the brine or other refrigerant used is so adjusted and arranged by means of the flow volume and rate of extract and the flow volume, rate and temperature of the circulating refrigerant past the heat exchange surfaces and out of contact with the extract that the metastable state of the extract is attained and not disturbed and its crystallization inhibited until the extract meets the slurry in the crystallizer.

Any suitable type of refrigerant may be used. For example, the well known ammonia vapor pressure type is used to refrigerate circulating brine in line 18 and through heat exchange surfaces of the heat exchanger, pump 7 being of a variable speed type to permit the control of the amount of heat withdrawn from the heat exchanger and from the extract therein.

It has been found that control of crystallization is dependent on the quantity of nuclei present on crystallization. With too many nuclei present, crystal size is decreased and the reverse is also true. Adjusting the quantity of nuclei is subject to meticulous control by maintaining the nucleating source under the proper temperature. This may be accomplished, for example, by the heater 20 in line 21. If the quantity of nuclei is too great, the nuclei fed by line 21 to the crystallizer may be decreased by heating and thereby reducing the nuclei in the heater. If too few, the nuclei fed by line 21 to the crystallizer may be increased in flow volume by lowering the temperature of the nuclei feed to or in the heater.

Recycling of Crystals to Upstream Crystallization Stage

D.D. Shaul; U.S. Patent 3,285,025; November 15, 1966; assigned to Phillips Petroleum Company describes a multistage crystallization process wherein crystals separated from the mother liquor in the final crystallization stage are recycled to an upstream crystallization stage and the crystals in the final crystallization stage are refluxed with an upstream process stream.

With reference to Figure 2.21, ice crystals are formed within the crystallization zone 11 and are separated from the mother liquor and withdrawn from the crystallization zone via conduit means 12. The mother liquor comprising a recoverable product (alcohol and sugars) in concentrated form is withdrawn from the crystallization zone via conduit means 13.

The mother liquor withdrawn from the crystallization zone is passed via conduit means 13 to a final downstream crystallization zone comprising chiller 14 and purification column 16. Although only one upstream crystallization zone is herein illustrated, it is within the scope of this process to employ additional crystallization zones between the initial and final crystallization zones wherein each of the said intermediate crystallization zones can be operated as described in connection with crystallization zone 11 and wherein the feed to each of the said intermediate crystallization zones comprises the mother liquor withdrawn from an upstream crystallization zone.

The final crystallization stage as herein illustrated comprises the process steps of chilling a liquid feed mixture to form crystals of at least a higher melting component, separating the crystals of the higher melting component from the mother liquor, and refluxing the crystals with a reflux liquid. As illustrated, mother liquor withdrawn from the crystallization zone

11 is passed via conduit means **13** to a chiller **14**. Chiller **14** can comprise any conventional apparatus wherein the temperature of the feed can be lowered so as to produce a slurry of crystals and a means for passing the said slurry of crystals therefrom. Conventional chilling apparatus comprises a jacketed vessel equipped with a surface scraper and with a cooling medium passed through the jacket in indirect heat exchange with the feed to the chiller. Within chiller **14**, water is crystallized to form a crystal slurry which contains from about 10 to 55 and preferably about 15 to 45 weight percent solids. While it is desirable to concentrate to as high a degree as possible the formation of crystal solids, if the solids content is too high the slurry becomes quite stiff and becomes too difficult to pass from the chiller.

FIGURE 2.21: RECYCLING OF CRYSTALS TO UPSTREAM RECRYSTALLIZATION
STAGE

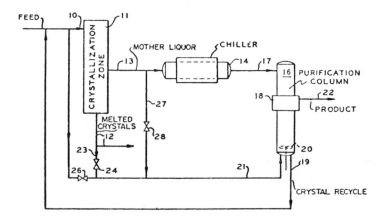

Source: D.D. Shaul; U.S. Patent 3,285,025; November 15, 1966

The slurry of ice crystals is passed from chiller **14** to purification column **16** via conduit means **17**. A compacted mass of crystals is forced through the column; a filter section **18** is provided in an intermediate portion in purification column **16** so that mother liquor can be separated from the crystals and withdrawn from the column; and the compacted mass of crystals refluxed with a liquid passed countercurrently to the mass of crystals.

The mass of crystals within purification column **16** is refluxed with a refluxing stream passed to purification column via conduit means **21** from a source hereinafter described. Mother liquor containing alcohol and sugars in a highly concentrated state is withdrawn from filter section **18** via conduit means **22**. Ice crystals containing occluded mother liquor is withdrawn from purification column **16** via conduit means **19** and recycled to an upstream crystallization zone. As illustrated, the ice crystals are recycled via conduit means **19** and conduit means **10** to an upstream crystallization zone **11**. It is within the scope of this process to recycle the ice crystals withdrawn from the final crystallization zone to other intermediate crystallization zones wherein the multistage crystallization process includes more than two stages.

An advantage of recycling the crystals to an upstream crystallization zone is that process refrigeration requirements are reduced. If the recycle stream was liquid, additional refrigeration would be required to form crystals from the recycle stream. In addition thereto, process heat would be required to melt the crystals separated from the mother liquor in the final crystallization stage.

A further advantage of the process is that by recycling the separated crystals, the normal high purity requirement of the crystals in the final crystallization stage is eliminated. Thus control of the final crystallization stage can be directed to and based solely upon the recovery of a mother liquor containing a desired product concentration.

Separating Components by Intermediate Density Layer

L. Rosenstein and M.H. Gorin; U.S. Patent 3,213,633; October 26, 1965; developed a process for separating a less concentrated solution from a relatively more concentrated solution which includes the steps of forming solids in a solution of intermediate concentration by direct contact with a vaporizable liquid refrigerant having a density intermediate that of the solids and the residual solution, separating the solids from residual solution by flotation or gravitation in a body of refrigerant and subsequently forming a liquid from the solids by contacting the solids with compressed refrigerant vapors.

The process is applicable to systems where a component of a solution is separated from the solution by the formation of solids and residual solution by transferring energy from the solution. Thus, the recovery of relatively demineralized water from aqueous solutions such as seawater by partial freezing or by refrigerant hydrate formation, or both, may be effected by the process. The practice of this process is applicable whether the solvent, the concentrate, or both, be considered the desired products. The method is therefore applicable to a process for preparing frozen concentrates such as orange juice. The patent contains full descriptions of the method and apparatus and uses as an example the recovery of potable water from seawater.

Heat Transfer Surface with Low Surface Energy

The prior art describes processes in which the solvent of a solution is frozen, crystals are formed and the resulting crystals separated, thus either concentrating the solution or liberating the solvent from the solution for use as a food or drink concentrate. In carrying out such processes the solution may be brought into contact wtih a heat transfer surface such, for example, as the external surface of an internally cooled drum which is immersed in the solution to be concentrated, or the internal surface of an externally cooled cylinder.

Usually the heat exchange surface is maintained below the freezing temperature of the solution being treated, the ice is formed on the heat exchange surface, and removed from the surface by scraping. In contradistinction to such processes the method of *R.H. Hedrick; U.S. Patent 3,335,575; August 15, 1967; assigned to Struthers Scientific and International Corporation* effects the freezing of aqueous solutions by an indirect heat exchange process and the use of heat transfer surfaces in which the heat of crystallization is released not on the heat transfer surface by nucleation and crystal growth on the surface, but by crystal growth on crystals freely moving and well dispersed in the solution being concentrated.

A process and means have been found that prevent the deposition of the solvent as crystals on heat transfer surfaces. The discovery is based on the work (energy) required to form a deposit on the surface correlated with the surface energy of the heat transfer surface while in contact with a slurry of ice crystals uniformly dispersed throughout an aqueous solution. It has been found that if the surface energy of a heat transfer surface is less than the work required to form ice deposits, none will form on the surface providing the surface is also in contact with a slurry of crystals.

An aqueous solution at a temperature below its freezing point and in the presence of nuclei will form or grow crystals. The heat of crystallization in the solution will be released principally either in the creation of nuclei or as crystal growth. The nuclei may be added to or formed in the solution or may form on the heat exchange surfaces. In accord with the process it has been found that the energy required to form crystals can be controlled by regulating the temperature difference between the average temperature of the solution and the temperature of the heat transfer surface.

Studies were carried out using tin, anodized aluminum, aluminum, and aluminum-brass alloy, copper, and stainless steel as heat transfer surfaces. The permissible temperature differences between refrigerated crystal solutions and the various heat transfer surfaces were determined using orange juice, beer, and coffee as the experimental solutions. Tin and anodized aluminum were found to give the best results and are recommended for use on the surface of heat exchangers.

Separation of Solute from Frozen Crystal Column

A.T. King; U.S. Patent 3,628,344; December 21, 1971; describes apparatus and a process for concentrating the solids content of a solids-containing solution or suspension by forming seed crystals of the vehicle or solvent and, by accurately controlled refrigeration and circulation of such solution, promoting growth of said seed crystals into larger crystals, and separating the concentrated solute from such larger crystals by causing a column of these crystals to rise, while the circulation system is closed to the atmosphere, and draining the concentrated solute from the rising column of crystals while gently washing the crystals, if necessary, and removing the ice crystals and concentrated solute separately from the system. The process is especially adapted to making beverage concentrates and fruit juice concentrates.

DEHYDRATION

DRUM DRYING

Gasification Prior to Dehydration

S.I. Strashun and W.F. Talburt; U.S. Patent 3,241,981; March 22, 1966; assigned to the U.S. Secretary of Agriculture describe a process for the dehydration of fruit juices. The principles of this process are primarily concerned with control of the factors of dehydration whereby to ensure extensive expansion (that is, from 10 to 25 times in volume) of the liquid during dehydration and to maintain this expansion throughout the dehydration. It has been found that a primary factor in ensuring extensive expansion is the step of gasifying the liquid prior to application of dehydrating conditions. This gasification greatly enhances expansion and is so effective in this regard that it will cause extensive expansion hence successful dehydration of liquids which could not otherwise be dehydrated under the same conditions, or which could only be dehydrated by using high levels of vacuum or by adding drying aids.

By utilizing this step of gasification and control of other factors in accordance with this process, successful dehydration of fruit juices is attained in that the film of liquid will consistently expand to a large degree and remain in an expanded condition throughout the dehydration procedure. As a result, the dehydration proceeds rapidly and efficiently and yields a free-flowing, porous product which exhibits a very high rate of rehydration when contacted with water to make a reconstituted juice. In addition, no damage to the color, flavor or vitamin content of the material is involved.

The liquid foodstuff to be dehydrated is first prepared by reaming, pressing, macerating, crushing, comminuting or extracting with water the edible portions of fruit or vegetables as, for example, orange, grapefruit, lemon, lime, apple, pear, apricot, strawberry, raspberry, pineapple, grape, prune, plum, peach, cherry, tomato, celery, carrot, spinach, lettuce, watercress and so forth. The liquid preparation may be clear, contain suspended pulp, or may even be thick like a puree.

The liquid preparation is introduced into an evaporator where it is concentrated so that it will be in proper condition for the subsequent dehydration step. The concentrate is then introduced into an agitator. A gas is also introduced into the agitator, this gas being thoroughly whipped into the concentrate to form an intimate dispersion of the gas in the concentrate. Although air is the most convenient gas to use, it is often preferred to use nitrogen, carbon dioxide or other inert, nontoxic gas whereby to minimize oxidative or other deleterious effects. To reduce the size of the gas particles in the concentrate, the concentrate (after having the gas dispersed by the use of agitators or the like) may be passed through a colloid mill.

The gasified concentrate is introduced into the feeding vessel of a dehydrator connected to a source of vacuum to maintain the interior of the dehydrator at a pressure of 1 to 3 mm Hg. There is also provided a flexible metallic belt which traverses over a heated drum and a cooled drum. As the gasified concentrate enters the feeding vessel, it is exposed to the vacuum whereby frothing occurs as some of the gas in the concentrate is liberated. The concentrate now in the form of a liquid froth or foam is applied in a thin film, having a thickness on the order of 0.005 to 0.1 inch, to the underside of the belt.

The optimum thickness of film to be employed in any particular instance will depend upon many factors such as the nature of the material being dried, the moisture content of the film, the speed of traversal of the belt, the temperature applied by the drum, and so forth. With many fruit juice concentrates, a film thickness of 0.006 to 0.20 inch gives efficient results. The means for applying this film comprises a roller which is positively rotated in a counterclockwise direction and which is spaced from the belt a distance equal to the film thickness desired. Wipers or scrapers may be provided to accurately define the thickness of the film.

The thin film of frothy concentrate applied to the underside of the belt is moved toward the drum which is hollow and through which steam or other heating medium is circulated to maintain the drum at a dehydrating temperature. In the case of orange juice and other fruit juice concentrate, excellent results are obtained with a temperature of 175° to 300°F.

Before arriving at the dehydrating drum, the applied film is preferably subjected to what may be termed a predrying. This takes place where the film is subjected to irradiation from radiant heaters which are metallic rods heated to glowing temperature by electrical resistance coils embedded therein or which may be infrared lamps or the like. The significance of this predrying can be explained as follows. To obtain complete dehydration in the short time that the belt is in contact with the drum, it is necessary to maintain this drum at a high temperature, on the order of 175° to 300°F.

If the film without predrying is applied to the hot drum, unfavorable results are often obtained. Thus, as the film is initially heated by the drum, it expands to a desirable degree but as the expanded film travels about the drum it may collapse, that is, shrink to about its volume before expansion. This phenomenon is caused by the expanded film assuming too high a temperature while its moisture content is still high. In effect, the expanded film melts and loses its vapor bubbles which theretofore gave it an expanded structure.

The predrying treatment has the effect of removing part of the moisture content of the film at a relatively low temperature, whereby when the film contacts the hot drum its moisture content is decreased and its viscosity is increased to such an extent that it will maintain its expanded structure even though subjected to the high temperature of the drum. In effect, the predrying stage has the effect of removing moisture from the film to increase what may be termed its pseudo-melting point, that is the temperature range in which the expanded film will collapse.

The belt carries the predried film about the drum whereby the principal dehydration takes place. The dehydrated film still in its expanded condition then passes about another drum where the film is cooled so that it will lose its plastic character and become relatively brittle and easy to remove. The cooled product is removed from the belt by a scraper which may be provided with means for oscillating it in a horizontal plane to give increased dislodging effect. The cooled product falls from the scraper into a hopper from whence it can be removed to a container, which is provided with a valved conduit for connection to the source of vacuum so that it can be evacuated prior to opening of the valve. Radiant heaters are provided so that the surface of the film away from the belt is properly dehydrated. In some instances, where such heating is not provided, the upper surface of the film is dehydrated to a lesser extent than the bottom surface of the film, with the result that the final product tends to roll up on the scraper. In the dehydration of some fruit juices, purees, etc., it may be necessary to make some provision for returning volatile flavoring materials which are vaporized during the concentration and/or dehydration. In the case of tomato and apricot products, such provisions are not necessary as the dehydrated product retains its natural flavor and odor. In the case of orange, apple, pineapple, strawberry, raspberry and many other fruit products, provision should be made to restore flavoring substances to obtain a high quality product.

The restoration of flavor may be carried out in several ways. In one technique, the volatile flavoring component is mixed with molten, supercooled sorbitol and the mixture allowed to crystallize. The sorbitol containing absorbed flavoring material is then incorporated with the dehydrated juice to furnish the approximately original amount of flavoring component. The use of sorbitol to absorb the flavoring component is preferred as thereby the flavor is stabilized and prevented from vaporizing.

Example: (A) Aeration of Concentrate — To a lot of orange juice concentrate was added 1.5% of its weight of sodium carboxymethylcellulose using vigorous agitation to disperse this drying aid into the concentrate and also to draw air into the mixture and disperse it thoroughly therein. The aerated concentrate (60°Brix) was then dehydrated in the apparatus previously described. Operating conditions were as follows:

Temperature of drum	233 °F
Belt speed	40 ft/min
Contact time between belt and drum	10.2 sec
Thickness of film (approximate)	0.010 inch
Pressure in dehydrator	2.8 mm Hg
Production rate of dehydrated product	33 lb/hr

It was observed that the film or orange juice concentrate expanded 20 to 25 times in volume during dehydration and maintained such expanded volume throughout. Thus, dehydration proceded rapidly and efficiently, the product was readily removed from the belt by the scraper, and the product was in a porous condition so that on agitation with water for a few seconds it formed a reconstituted juice.

(B) No Aeration of Concentrate — In a comparative experiment, the orange juice concentrate was mixed with a previously prepared solution of sodium carboxymethylcellulose using enough of this solution to add 1.5% of this drying aid. In this case, the mixing was gentle to avoid incorporating air into the concentrate. The resulting nonaerated concentrate (60°Brix) was applied to the dehydrator using the same conditions as in (A). It was observed that the dehydration was unsuccessful in that the concentrate film did not expand significantly, with the result that the product stuck to the belt and could not be removed with the scraper. Eventually the belt became fouled with a brown, hard layer of overheated material.

(C) No Aeration but Additional Drying Aid — In another comparative experiment, the drying aid was added in solution form as in (B) with gentle agitation. In this case however the proportion of sodium carboxymethylcellulose was increased to 3.25%. The resulting nonaerated concentrate (60°Brix) was applied to the dehydrator using the same conditions as in (A). It was observed that dehydration was successful, the concentrate expanded 20 to 25 times in volume and remained expanded throughout. The dehydrated product was porous, easily removable from the belt and exhibited a very high rate of rehydration when contacted with water.

Addition of Amylolytic Enzyme

Fruit juice or fruit concentrate is not readily dried by conventional techniques. This is due to the relatively large amount of natural sugar present in fruit juice. Thus, when fruit juice or concentrate is dried on a drum drier, the sugar present prevents the formation of a sheet which can be easily removed by the drier's doctor blade or scraper. Instead of being able to remove a continuous dried sheet from the drier as with other types of foods, the dried fruit juice yields a gummy mass after heating which collects at the doctor blade and disrupts the drying operation.

In the drying of high sugar content food other than fruit juice, the same problem has been encountered. To overcome the problem with other foods, starch thickeners have been added to the food slurry to be dried. The starch thickened mass of high sugar content food, after being heated to gelatinize the starch, can then be dried on a drum drier for example, relatively free from the foregoing problem. It has not been feasible to use this same approach with fruit juices however, since the starch thickener, after reconstituting the dried juice, imparted a thick consistency to the juice wholly unlike and uncharacteristic of fresh juices.

L.H. Anderson; U.S. Patent 3,117,878; January 14, 1964; assigned to Gerber Products Co. describes a process which solves the problem of dehydrating juices and permitting their reconstitution to their characteristic liquid form by combining an amylolytic enzyme with the dried, starch thickened juice. When water is added to the combination starch thickened juice and enzyme product, the starch is hydrolyzed by the enzyme to a sufficient degree to impart the desired consistency to the reconstituted product.

Thus, the process provides a method for making a juice drink from dehydrated fruit juice which comprises drying fruit juice containing a starch thickener, combining an amylolytic enzyme with the juice after the drying step, and reconstituting the dried juice by combining it with water. The reconstitution is conveniently carried out with the use of tap water. When tap water is added to the juice-enzyme mixture with moderate agitation, the product is ready for use normally in 1 to 2 minutes.

One suitable way of carrying out the method is to form a slurry with the selected fruit juice or concentrate with a starch thickener. Any of the common starches may be used for this purpose and include naturally occurring starches which are separated from the seed such as in corn, wheat, waxy maize, sorghum, and rice; those separated from the root such as tapioca, potato, and arrowroot; or those obtained from the stem, such as sago. One suitable operable range for the quantity of starch to be added is from 35 to 45% by weight of the fruit juice.

Suitably, the mixture of starch and fruit juice is heated with agitation to gelatinize the starch. The mixture is then suitably dried to a moisture content of 1 to 5%, although here again the precise moisture level after drying is subject to considerable variation. Under the foregoing conditions, it is possible to drum dry fruit juices to form a continuous sheet that is conveniently handled for subsequent operations. The dried product in accordance with this method is then combined with an amylolytic enzyme. The quantity of enzyme to be used depends on the particular starch present, the quantity of starch employed, and the consistency of the final product that is desired. Generally, the enzyme may be added to the dried, thickened juice in an amount by weight of 0.5 to 0.8% and an acceptable product will be obtained.

The dried product mixed with the enzyme is then ready for use by the consumer. The consumer merely need add a sufficient quantity of water to replace that which has been removed in the processing and a juice closely approximating that of the preprocessed fresh variety is obtained.

In general, any amylolytic enzyme may be combined with the dried juice. Although diastatic enzymes have been found to be extremely satisfactory, enzymes of bacterial origin which will liquefy a starch paste may be used in this process. Beneficially the enzyme selected should convert the starch in the dried juice to a relatively high percentage of sugars which thereby add to the overall nutritive and taste properties of the reconstituted juice beverage. However, any amylolytic enzyme which will liquefy the starch is contemplated as being within the scope of this method. The process is applicable to any fruit juice or to combinations thereof. The following examples illustrate the process.

Example 1: The enzyme known as Rhozyme H-39 may be employed in this and the succeeding example. Rhozyme H-39 is a diastatic enzyme of bacterial origin, active up to 60° to 80°C, and for use with up to 60% starch materials. One part of the enzyme will liquefy 20,160 parts of starch in 1 hour at 40°C at a pH of 7.

A slurry was prepared from pineapple concentrate (60°Brix), 760 grams, and Tenderfil Tapioca, 200 grams. Sufficient water was added to form a slurry. The slurry was then heated to 190°F and placed on a drum drier at 30 lb steam pressure (260° to 265°F surface temperature). The dried product was removed from the drum as a sheet, chilled to 40°F or less, and mechanically flaked. 20 grams of the flakes, 10 grams of sugar, and 100 milligrams of enzyme were intermixed. The mixture was then combined with 118 cc of water. A pineapple juice drink having a consistency substantially that of fresh pineapple juice was obtained.

Example 2: A slurry was prepared from: Pineapple concentrate (61°Brix), 350 grams; grapefruit concentrate (57°Brix), 50 grams; citric acid, 4.4 grams; and Tenderfil Tapioca, 100 grams.

A slurry was obtained by combining the above ingredients with the necessary amount of water. The slurry was then heated to 190°F and placed on a drum drier at 30 lb steam pressure (260° to 265°F surface temperature). The dried product was removed from the drum drier in sheet form and chilled down to about 40°F. The chilled sheet was then broken into flakes. A sample was prepared by taking 13 grams of the flakes, 11 grams of sugar, and 100 mg of enzyme. The sample was combined with 118 cc of water and a pineapple-grapefruit drink was obtained having a liqueform consistency characteristic of juices.

FOAM-MAT PROCESSES

Cellulose Ethers and Soy Protein as Foam Stabilizers

The foam-mat drying process consists essentially of three steps, namely: (1) formation of a stable foam containing the product which is to be dried, (2) air drying of the foam to form a thin porous sheet or mat, and (3) compression of the dried mat followed by disintegration to yield a free-flowing powder. The foam-mat drying process is a very simple and inexpensive process. One difficulty that has heretofore been experienced with this process, however, is the lack of stability of the foam during the heating cycle. If the foam does not remain stable, cellular breakdown occurs causing serious impairment of the drying operation.

R.C. Gunther; U.S. Patents 3,119,698 and 3,119,699; January 28, 1964; both assigned to Gunther Products, Inc. describes a method for employing in the foam-mat drying process a water-soluble enzyme modified soy protein in intimate association with a water-soluble cellulose alkyl ether or a water-soluble cellulose hydroxyalkyl ether, or a water-soluble cellulose in which the hydroxy groups of the cellulose are etherified with both alkyl and hydroxyalkyl groups. Examples of suitable alkyl groups which may be present in the preparation of the water-soluble cellulose ethers are methyl, ethyl, hydroxyethyl, and/or hydroxypropyl groups. One specific example of a suitable water-soluble cellulose ether is the water-soluble cellulose methyl ether known as Methocel.

The water-soluble cellulose ethers which are effective for the purpose of this process are all characterized by the fact that they form fluid solutions at room temperature, the viscosity of which decreases when the solutions are heated until the gelation temperature is reached, and decreases again when the heated solutions are cooled. The ability to gel on heating may be called thermal gelation and this in combination with the ability to become fluid again on cooling may be called reversible gelation.

This unique property of reversible thermal gelation in combination with the properties of the enzyme modified soy protein allows the fluid mixes of products which it is desired to prepare in dry form to be whipped to the desired foam density with air or other gases and the foams produced to be stabilized on drying. The particular advantage of the reversible nature of the gelation property lies in the fact that these water-soluble cellulose ethers can be used to stabilize foams prepared from juices, such as prune, grape, and the like, in which the reconstituted juice must have good clarity with no coagulated or gelled insolubles present.

Especially good results have been obtained by employing either the dimethyl ether derivatives of cellulose (Methocel MC) or an alkyl ether of cellulose which contains both methoxyl substitution and hydroxypropoxyl substitution in the cellulose chain (Methocel HG). The particular concentration of the cellulose ether used will depend upon the type and viscosity of the cellulose ether and upon the particular system being stabilized. For all practical purposes, however, it may be stated that the concentration of the water-soluble cellulose ether may vary from 0.025 to 5.0% based on dry solids present in the system.

As previously indicated, an enzyme modified soy protein is another essential substance employed for the process. Such soy proteins are made by steeping soybean material in acidified water to remove the bulk of the solid nitrogen-free extract, subjecting the remaining material to hydrolysis with an enzyme, separating the solubles from the insolubles and concentrating the solubles. A suitable method for manufacturing an enzyme modified soy protein for the purpose of this process is described in U.S. Patent 2,489,173.

For the preferred practice of the process a pepsin modified soy protein (prepared as described in U.S. Patent 2,489,173 at a pH of 5.0) is used. This substance is the essential ingredient of the substance hereinafter referred to as D-100 whipping agent (Gunther Products, Inc.). The quantity of the enzyme modified soy protein should be sufficient for whipping (i.e., to entrap air or other gas with the substance being treated). Generally, 0.1 to 5% by weight of the dry solids is sufficient and 0.4 to 1.5% by weight of the dry solids is preferred. The foamed products will usually have a density within the range of 0.15 to 0.60 g/cc.

The advantage of employing a water-soluble enzyme modified soy protein in a foam-mat drying system is shown by the fact that orange juice in the presence of methylcellulose shows absolutely no whipping properties until a small amount of the vegetable protein whipping agent is added, whereupon excellent foaming properties are achieved. Tomato paste in the presence of the dimethyl ether of cellulose but in the absence of any water-soluble enzyme modified soy protein shows practically no whipping tendencies even after prolonged beating. The addition of a small amount of enzyme modified soy protein, however, allowed the same mix to beat up very readily to more than twice the original volume.

Example 1: To 200 grams of concentrated, unsweetened orange juice (40% solids) was added 0.25 gram Methocel-65 HG (4,000 cp) (10 grams of 2.5% solution) and 0.9 grams of D-100 vegetable protein whipping agent (3 grams of 30% solution). The mixture was stirred for a few minutes, then whipped on a Hobart Kitchen Aid mixer equipped with a wire whisk for 4 minutes. A firm, light foam was produced which weighed 0.23 g/cc.

This foam was spread to approximately 1/4" to 3/8" thickness on a Teflon coated fiberglass mat and dried in an oven at 155°F. Drying time required was approximately 1 hour. The mat produced showed no signs of breakdown during drying. It could be readily crushed and the powder readily reconstituted in water to give an orange juice identical to the original juice.

Example 2: 200 grams prune juice (22% solids) were mixed with 0.375 gram Methocel-65 HG (4,000 cp) (15 grams of 2.5% solution) and 0.3 gram D-100 whipping agent (1 gram of 30% solution). The mix was whipped with a wire whisk to produce a firm foam with a creamy consistency. The foam had a density of 0.21 g/cc. A small sample dried at 170°F and a larger sample dried on Teflon at 160°F produced excellent products with no sign of breakdown or discoloration. The resulting powder could be reconstituted very readily in water to give a clear, excellent tasting juice.

Example 3: 0.6 gram of D-100 whipping agent (2 grams of 30% solution) and 0.25 gram of Methocel-65 HG (1,500 cp) (10 grams of 2.5% solution) were added to 200 grams grape juice (concentrated and sweetened, 45% solids). The mix whipped 2 minutes in the Kitchen Aid mixer. The mix whipped extremely fast to produce a very light and very firm, almost rigid, foam having a density of 0.18 g/cc. This foam was oven dried at 160°F on the Teflon coated glass fiber mat in approximately 3 hours. The dried product showed no cellular breakdown or weep of any kind. The product was easily crushed to a fine deep purple colored powder which redissolved in water very readily to give a juice indistinguishable from the original grape juice.

Use of Two Component Mixture

It has been demonstrated that the flavor of dehydrated foods can be enhanced if they are rehydrated in the presence of certain enzyme preparations. It is postulated that the enzyme acts upon flavor precursors present in the dehydrated product, forming natural flavor. In a sense, the enzyme preparation may be considered as developing the latent flavor present in the dehydrated product. Such enzymes may therefore be termed as flavor-developing enzymes.

A disadvantage of the procedure above is that it requires the use of purified enzyme preparations. These substances are made from fruit or vegetable materials and require considerable manipulation, such as extraction with organic solvents, precipitations, centrifugations, and other mechanical or chemical treatments. Because of these cumbersome procedures the process in question is expensive and offers problems from the standpoint of compliance with regulations governing the wholesomeness of food products.

Another disadvantage of this method is that the enzyme preparation does not contain the various flavor-developing enzymes in the same proportions in which they existed in the natural tissue. As a result, when the enzyme preparation is used to restore flavor, one obtains a predominant note or aspect of the overall flavor rather than obtaining the complete pattern of the natural flavor. By proceeding in accordance with the process of *A.I. Morgan, Jr. and S. Schwimmer; U.S. Patent 3,170,803; February 23, 1965; assigned to the U.S. Secretary of Agriculture*, the disadvantages outlined above are completely obviated.

A typical embodiment of the process involves the preparation of dehydrated foods which exhibit enhanced natural flavor when prepared for consumption. These products contain two distinct ingredients as set forth below.

Ingredient A: This ingredient used in major proportion, is a dehydrated food prepared by conventional methods. In the preparation of this material the natural produce has been subjected to substantial heating and as a consequence the dehydrated material is deficient in natural flavor. This material might be described as one which contains a flavor precursor or latent natural flavor. This ingredient might also be described as a dehydrated food which has been prepared by a process where enzyme-destructive heating has been applied to the food during the course of its processing.

Ingredient B: This ingredient, used in minor proportion, is also a dehydrated food but of characteristics totally different from that of Ingredient A. Thus Ingredient B is a dehydrated food which has been prepared by a process where no enzyme-destructive heating is applied to the food during the course of its processing. Typically, Ingredient B is prepared from natural produce, for example, raw fruit, raw vegetables or other food material containing active enzymes, by subjecting it to freeze drying.

This ingredient, not having been subjected to enzyme-inactivating heating programs, contains an essentially full complement of the enzymes appropriate to the product in question. As a consequence, Ingredient B can be considered to contain the specific enzymes required to convert the latent flavor of Ingredient A into patent flavor. Thus, when the product, containing Ingredients A and B in admixture, is rehydrated for use, the desired natural flavor will be developed in the reconstituted product.

The simplicity of the technique of the process is evident from the above description. Preparation of Ingredient A is simply an application of standard dehydrating methods and preparation of Ingredient B is simply an application of the lesser-used but well-known freeze drying method. Once Ingredients A and B are provided, they merely need be mixed together to provide the product of the process. It is recognized that preparation of Ingredient B requires application of a relatively expensive dehydration method, namely, freeze drying. However, it is to be emphasized that this ingredient is used in a minor proportion. Consequently, the cost of preparation of Ingredient B is a minor influence on total cost. Moreover, despite the simplicity of this technique, it is equally as effective as prior procedures using purified enzyme preparations and completely obviates any problems concerning wholesomeness of the products. Moreover, since Ingredient B is prepared without applying any enzyme-isolating technique, it contains the full complement of enzymes as needed for restoration of the complete pattern of natural flavor.

The proportions of Ingredients A and B which are blended together to yield the product of this process, may be varied depending on such factors as the level of flavor retained in Ingredient A, the level of flavor desired in the product, the effectiveness of the enzymes in Ingredient B as regards their ability to develop the latent flavors in Ingredient A, etc. In all cases only a minor proportion of Ingredient B is needed because the restoration of flavor is essentially a catalytic process. In general, Ingredient B is used in a proportion of from 0.1 to 10 parts thereof per 100 parts of Ingredient A. In many cases, a proportion of about one part Ingredient B per 100 parts Ingredient A gives excellent results.

Ordinarily in preparing the products, Ingredients A and B are both prepared from the same kind of food product. For example, both are prepared from tomato juice, orange juice, cabbage, or whatever food is selected. However, it is possible to prepare one ingredient from one kind of produce and the other ingredient from a different but related kind of produce. The point here is to select ingredients so that the enzyme components of Ingredient B will have the ability to bring out the latent flavor contained within Ingredient A. An example in this regard is the use of orange as Ingredient A and lemon, lime, or grapefruit as Ingredient B. However, although such combinations are possible, it is usually preferred for best results and for accurate definition of flavor to employ the same kind of produce for both ingredients.

Example 1: Ingredient A was dehydrated tomato juice prepared by the foam-mat drying method as disclosed in U.S. Patent 2,967,109. Thus, to 100 parts of tomato juice concentrate (30% solids) was added one part of glycerol monostearate. This material was whipped into a foam having a density of about 0.4 g/ml. The foam was extruded through a die in the form of $1/8$" diameter spaghetti and subjected to contact with a current of air at 160°F for 12 minutes and then to a current of air at 130°F for 3 minutes. The porous dehydrated foam contained about 3% moisture.

Ingredient B was prepared by mincing fresh tomatoes, freezing them in a blast freezer and subjecting the frozen material to a vacuum until dry. The product was made by blending 100 parts of Ingredient A with one part of Ingredient B. As a test, the product and a sample of Ingredient A by itself were reconstituted, using about 10 parts dehydrated material per 100 parts water and holding at 37°C for 3 hours. It was found that the product had more of a fresh tomato taste than did Ingredient A.

Example 2: (1) Orange juice was concentrated under vacuum to 55% solids content. One hundred parts of the concentrate were mixed with 0.4 part of solubilized soya protein and 0.1 part of low-viscosity methylcellulose. The mixture was beaten in air to produce a foam having a density of 0.35 g/ml.

(2) One lot of the foam prepared as described above was spread out as $1/8$" diameter extrusions on a belt moving through an air stream of 200 ft/min velocity. The air temperature decreased from 180° to 130°F during a 12 minute drying period. The crisp, dry extrusions, containing 3% moisture were collected and crumbled. This was Ingredient A for the purpose of this example.

(3) Another lot of the foam prepared as described in Part (1) was spread on trays, then

frozen in a blast freezer. The frozen foam was then placed in a vacuum drier where, while in the frozen state, it was exposed to a pressure of about 0.2 mm of mercury until its moisture content was about 3%. This material was Ingredient B for the purpose of this example.

(4) One hundred parts of Ingredient A were then blended with one part of Ingredient B.

Use of Surface Active Agent to Stabilize Foam

Generally, in the method of dehydrating foamed food material, the procedure is followed where a suitable food concentrate is prepared in which a gas, usually air, is incorporated by whipping, resulting in a rather stiff foam. Conversion of the food into foam and the stability thereof is aided by the introduction of an edible foam stabilizer. The foam is then deposited as by casting or extrusion onto a drying surface and thereafter appropriately dried to an extent which may depend on the material but generally until a moisture level usually in the range of 1 to 4% is reached. The dried foam may then be flaked or ground and where desirable may be compressed into pellets or other forms without significant loss of ready solubility in cold water.

The use of various surface active agents such as the monoglycerides of the higher fatty acids, for example, glycerol monolaurate, glycerol monomyristate, glycerol monopalmitate, glycerol monostearate and glycerol monooleate, as foam stabilizers in aqueous systems is known. As such, they have been used in the process known as foam-mat drying though they are not limited to this application. These compounds can be used alone or in combination with a hydrophilic colloid, such as methylcellulose.

J. V. Fiore; U.S. Patent 3,323,923; June 6, 1967; assigned to American Machine & Foundry Company has found a group of compounds, not heretofore known as useful for this purpose, which offers certain definite advantages in the stabilization of foams. The compounds of the process are: ester derivatives of the monoglycerides of the higher fatty acids; polyglycerin; and esters of polyglycerins. Examples of the first group are those ester compounds having the following generic formula:

$$
\begin{array}{cccc}
H_2 & H & H_2 & O \\
| & | & | & \| \\
C\text{—}C\text{—}C\text{—}O\text{—}C \\
| & | & | \\
OR' & OR'' & R''' \\
\end{array}
$$

where R' and R'' represent hydrogen or an organic ester substituent derived from mono- or polycarboxylic acids containing up to 12 carbon atoms or from an inorganic acid and R''' is an alkyl substituent having at least 11 carbon atoms. The ester groups referred to above may be derived from the monocarboxylic acids such as acetic, or the polycarboxylic acids such as tartaric.

An especially suitable compound in stabilizing food foams and in producing an excellent product of fine taste is the diacetyl tartaric acid ester of glycerol monostearate available commercially, for example, as Emcol D-66-1 (Witco Chemical Co.). Examples of the polyglycerin compounds of the second group are such as: diglycerin, triglycerin, tetraglycerin, etc. which are included in the term polyglycerin, i.e., glycerin polymers which are produced in a manner as described in U.S. Patents 2,022,766 and 2,023,388 by the alkaline polymerization of glycerin under suitable conditions.

It will be understood that a polyglycerin in mixtures of this kind is not a single compound but a mixture of compounds. It is further understood that any polymeric glycerin isolated and purified from such a mixture would also be included in the term polyglycerin as used herein. Compounds of the third group useful as stabilizers in accordance to the process are the esters of polyglycerin which include those derived from mono- or polycarboxylic acids as well as those from inorganic acids or mixtures of one or more of the aforementioned acids.

Polyglycerin stearate prepared in a manner similar to that described in U.S. Patents 2,022,766 and 2,023,388 and available from Witco Chemical Co. as Emcol 18, works excellently as a foam stabilizer to produce a foam and product therefrom of exceptionally advantageous characteristics.

In utilizing the compounds in the preparation of foam material to be dehydrated in accordance with the process, a liquid concentrate of the material to be dehydrated is first diluted or concentrated, depending on the material, to a fairly viscous condition and converted into a stable foam by incorporating therewith a minor proportion of the foam stabilizing agent of the type described above together with a substantial volume of air or other gas. The foam so produced is then exposed to heat in the form of a relatively thin layer until it is dry.

The advantages in the technique of drying material in the foam condition include, for example, rapid processing by increasing the surface area of the liquid concentrate thereby facilitating dehydration and production of a dehydrated product of high porosity such as is obtained in freeze drying, puff-drying, etc. It is apparent that the greater the foam stability, especially under the high temperature conditions of dehydration, the better these purposes will be achieved. In practice, foams made with the improved stabilizing agents described offer the following advantages over the various stabilizing agents, including the monoglycerides which have been employed for this purpose heretofore:

(1) Less collapse on the drying belt, tray or other support, during heating and drying; this results in:

increased drying rates,
easier scraping of the dried product from the support, and
higher porosity products which therefore have greater solubility.

(2) Greater ease of incorporation into the food material to be foamed and subsequently dehydrated. The monoglycerides, previously recommended for use in foam-mat drying, have critical gelatin characteristics which preclude their direct addition to food materials to be whipped at room temperature or below. As illustrated in the subsequent example this problem does not exist with the group of materials designated by the process.

(3) Flavor and taste advantages.

The proportion of foam stabilizing agent introduced into the liquid containing the material to be dried may vary over fairly wide limits and may depend on various conditions, for example, the properties of the liquid, the nature of the material to be foamed, etc. In general, the proportion of agents may vary from 0.01 to 10% by weight based on the weight of solids in the liquid subjected to foaming.

Ordinarily, amounts of from 0.05 to 8% are adequate. Normally it is desirable to use the lowest proportion of foam stabilizing agent compatible with the production of a foam stable at room temperature for a minimum of 2 hours. In any particular case, pilot runs may be readily conducted with different proportions of a given agent in a given liquid, noting the stability of the foam by casting a small quantity of the foam on a drying conveyor belt and conveying it through the drying zone at dehydration temperatures. A suitably stable foam will substantially retain its height throughout the drying stage. Further advantages which are derived from use of the foam stabilizers claimed herein will become obvious from the example which follows.

Example: This example demonstrates the ease with which the compounds claimed herein can be used. For example, no special techniques are required to disperse polyglycerin stearate (Emcol 18) and to form stable emulsions therewith as contrasted to the monoglycerides which frequently require the preparation of a pony or intermediate premix into which the stabilizer is first dispersed prior to introduction into the general mass to be dehydrated.

Polyglycerin stearate, Emcol 18, is powdered by grinding and added slowly to boiling water contained in a high speed mixer, A Cowles Mixer or Waring Blendor. The boiling water is stirred while sufficient powdered material is added so as to yield a 3 to 5% aqueous solution by weight. Mixing is then carried out until a consistency similar to shaving cream is obtained. The emulsions thus formed are extremely stable and can be stored under refrigeration for several weeks without separation.

These emulsions are added directly to the four materials to be foamed, tomato paste, tomato juice, orange juice and tea concentrate. The foam obtained is extremely stable and insensitive to overwhipping. The table below lists materials foamed with the preferred representatives of both classes of compounds discussed herein. The foams were prepared in a Kitchen Aid Mixer using emulsions obtained as described for Emcol 18 above.

Material Foamed		Percent Foaming Agent (based on food solids)	Emcol 18 [1]		Emcol D–66–1 [1]	
Type	Percent Solids (dry basis)		Foam Density (g./cc.)	Time Req.[2] (min.)	Foam Density (g./cc.)	Time Req.[2] (min.)
Tomato Paste	30	0.75	0.52	20	0.52	20
Tomato Juice	25	0.50	0.36	25	0.37	11
Orange Juice	60	0.50	0.20	7	0.35	15
Tea Concentrate	54	1.00	0.25	15		

[1] All foams were stable over 60 min.
[2] For the desired foam density.

Vacuum Process to Prevent Foam Formation on Reconstitution

The foam-mat dehydration process which has been frequently used gives the best results when a foaming agent or other substance of a similar nature is used. The use of these foaming agents causes the formation of extremely small (microscopic) bubbles which produce a large surface and permit rapid and more complete drying. Certain physical treatments of the liquid also permit the formation of fine-bubble structures. Treatments to form these fine-bubble structures have several advantages, including the removal of moisture to a more complete degree under less severe conditions of time and temperature. This permits the retention of more flavor and aromatic character to certain juices, particularly fruit juices, and permits the preparation of powders having a high degree of storage stability.

However, the powders thus produced often contain incorporated microscopic air bubbles. Upon reconstitution of these powders, these microscopic air bubbles cause the formation of air sols or colloidal dispersions of these air bubbles dispersed throughout the solution. These bubbles impart to the reconstituted juice an unnatural, white, cloudy or milk appearance. After the reconstituted product stands a very short time, this air sol rises and collects on the surface as a dense layer of foam. The presence of this milky appearance and particularly the presence of the foam are detrimental to the physical appearance of many reconstituted products and adversely affect their commercial acceptance.

In accordance with the method of *R.E. Berry, O.W. Bissett and C.J. Wagner, Jr.; U.S. Patent 3,379,538; April 23, 1968; assigned to the U.S. Secretary of Agriculture*, the disadvantages outlined above are avoided by a procedure which basically involves the following steps:

(1) The dried pieces are first prepared by one of the common foam-mat processes.

(2) The minute air bubbles contained therein are then removed by the application of a high vacuum. The length of time required to permit the diffusion of the gases from the dried pieces to a point of equilibrium is dependent not only upon the size of the pieces but also upon the extent of the vacuum applied, and may be readily determined by those skilled in the art.

(3) After the absorbed gases have been removed by the vacuum treatment,

the vacuum may be retained by sealing the container; or the vacuum may be released by means of a nontoxic water-soluble gas, such as carbon dioxide, and the tendency to foam upon reconstitution will be inhibited.

In general, in carrying out the process, a microscopic air bubble-containing dehydrated food product, prepared by a foam-mat process, is deposited into an open container. The food product may be subjected to a warm-rolling treatment prior to being deposited into the container, and may be in the form of a powder, flake or granule. When a powder is used, the particle size ranges from 0.015 to 0.025 inch.

The open container with its contents is then subjected to a vacuum ranging from 1 to 5 mm Hg absolute pressure, and the vacuum maintained until a state of equilibrium is obtained, but not exceeding 72 hours. The container may then be directly sealed to maintain the equilibrium, or, as an alternative, the vacuum may be released with a water-soluble gas, such as carbon dioxide, sulfur dioxide, nitrous oxide, and ethylene oxide to give an absolute pressure ranging from 38 cm Hg to 760 mm Hg, and the container then sealed to maintain the equilibrium.

Example: Three portions of the dried product obtained from orange juice concentrate (treated by the warm-rolling process) are placed under vacuum (1 mm Hg absolute pressure) for 24, 48 and 72 hours, respectively. Each of the three samples shows a noticeable improvement in the appearance of the reconstituted juice and the reconstituted juice from the 72 hours sample closely resembles the juice from a reconstituted concentrate. These reconstituted products are commercially acceptable and are clearly superior to a juice reconstituted from a powder which has been packed under nitrogen gas. There is a distinct improvement in appearance as the time under vacuum increases up to 72 hours.

Deacidified Citrus Juice

R.E. Berry and C.J. Wagner, Jr.; U.S. Patent 3,723,133; March 27, 1973; assigned to the U.S. Secretary of Agriculture have developed a process by which fruit juices are deacidified and converted to a dehydrated form. In this form the product can be mixed with other acid citrus products to produce a blend in either liquid or dehydrated powder form, thereby converting the unacceptable product to one with lower acidity and commercial acceptability.

Citrus fruit juices and products are manufactured by commercial methods from fruit which varies in maturity and flavor quality throughout the processing season. Thus, there are early fruit products which are rather high in acidity in October and lower in acidity in November and December, midseason varieties which are high in acidity in December and January and lower in acidity in subsequent months, and late season varieties which are high in acidity until about March or April and become progressively lower in acidity until June. As a consequence of these variations in natural characteristics of available fruit, the juices and products from these fruits vary in acid content during the season. High acidity products in general are not considered to be of the best quality for consumption. Quality is affected to a large extent by the Brix/acid ratio.

F.E. Nelson et al, *Abstracts of USDA Citrus Research Conference,* Pasadena, Calif. page 17, December 3, 1968 described a method whereby acidity in grapefruit products would be lowered by partial neutralization with calcium hydroxide, the precipitate removed, and the clarified partially deacidified juice would be blended with high acid grapefruit juice to adjust their acidity. Other recent technological advances in dehydration methods, particularly foam-mat drying, have made it possible and feasible to prepare dehydrated solids from high-sugar-containing materials such as citrus juices, in an economical manner commercially.

If deacidified juice could be converted to a dehydrated form, this would give it a higher degree of storage stability and lessen weight and storage requirements and cost. This dehydrated product then could be made available for blending with other juices and products to adjust their acidity without adding any unnatural ingredients. In all such cases the material blended would be of a natural consistency and only trace amounts of artificial or synthetic material would be included.

In general, this process can be described as a citrus product prepared from deacidified orange juice which is dehydrated and then blended with high-acid products. The method, briefly, consists of obtaining single strength orange juice or other citrus juice, centrifuging to remove suspended solids, neutralizing the clarified supernatant with calcium or other suitable metal hydroxide, recentrifuging to remove the precipitated calcium citrate or other metal citrate, recombining with originally removed suspended solids, concentrating this deacidified whole juice, and dehydrating the resultant concentrate. This powder is then blended with high acid orange juice, or other selected high acid juice, from early season fruit, immature fruit, orange concentrate of relatively low Brix to acid ratio, and high dehydrated powders.

For example, a single strength orange juice was prepared from frozen concentrate orange juice by the addition of water to form a 12.5°Brix solution (same density as aqueous 12.5% sucrose solution) with a Brix/acid ratio of 16.7:1. This juice was centrifuged at 4,000 rpm using a pilot model basket centrifuge with a three minute process cycle, ten seconds flush, operate 0.5 second and feed 25 seconds. After centrifugation, the serum was pasteurized by heating it to 191°F at 0.5 gal/min. This pasteurized serum was stored in a cold wall tank. The sludge separated during the first centrifugation was stored in closed containers at 40°F.

Dry, finely divided calcium hydroxide was added to the centrifuged serum at the rate of 0.33 gram $Ca(OH)_2$ to 80 grams of single strength serum. This was allowed to stand with stirring for several hours, then the solution was screened through a 60 mesh (U.S. Sieve Size) screen to remove undissolved calcium hydroxide. Additional finely divided calcium hydroxide was added to adjust the pH to about 7.0. This was centrifuged under the same conditions as before.

The precipitate of calcium citrate removed during this centrifugation was discarded. The neutralized clarified serum was mixed with the suspended solids sludge which had been separated during the first centrifugation. Before this mixing, the pH of the serum was 6.8, and after mixing the suspended solids back into the juice the pH was lowered to 6.5. This neutralized recombined citrus juice was then concentrated on a high vacuum falling film evaporator to 51.5°Brix and mixed with the appropriate amount of foaming agent and dried by foam-mat drying.

The resultant dry product was evaluated in several different ways. A small portion of it was reconstituted with water to form a juice of about 12°Brix. This was tasted by a panel of five members and judged to be very low in acidity, mild and bland, and tasted somewhat like papaya juice or peach juice. In another test, a sample of orange juice powder prepared from a highly acid concentrate, when reconstituted with water to a 12.5°Brix juice, resulted in a solution having a pH of 3.44 and containing 1.427 grams citric acid/100 grams juice. The Brix/acid ratio of this material was 8.76:1.0.

When this dried powder was mixed with the deacidified orange juice powder in the ratio of two parts acid juice powder to one part deacidified juice powder, and the dry mixture was reconstituted to 12.5°Brix by the addition of water, the resultant juice had pH 3.9, contained 0.95 gram citric acid/100 grams juice and the Brix/acid ratio was 13.16:1. When this was compared to the reconstituted juice from the original powder by a taste panel, the sample containing the added deacidified juice powder was judged to be very greatly improved in organoleptic quality.

In another example, single strength fresh orange juice was prepared from immature Valencia oranges. The pH of this juice was 3.25, it contained 1.736 grams citric acid/100 grams juice, and had a Brix/acid ratio of 7.19:1. When this immature Valencia juice was mixed with deacidified instant orange juice in the ratio of two parts green Valencia juice to one part deacidified juice powder and the resultant solution adjusted by the addition of water to 12.5°Brix solution, the resultant juice had a pH of 3.73, contained 1,097 grams citric acid/100 grams juice, and had a Brix/acid ratio of 11.39:1. This sample was also judged by the taste panel to be much more palatable and an acceptable product whereas the original green Valencia juice from which it had been made had been judged entirely unpalatable.

Tests on the deacidified juice powder itself, when reconstituted to 12.5°Brix solution with the addition of water, indicated pH 6.57 and a citric acid content of 0.009 gram/100 grams juice.

SPRAY DRYING

Countercurrent Spray Drying

It has been established as a rule that for heat sensitive materials of all types (and for many foodstuffs heat sensitiveness commences at a temperature as low as 35°C) the concept of countercurrent spray drying is unworkable and impractical. For reasons of equipment efficiency as well as for economic reasons, temperatures ranging from 100° to 160°C must be employed and, therefore, it is quite obvious that an incoming air at this temperature will destroy or completely burn the product in only fractions of seconds.

Even when the drying air is fed at a temperature of 50°C the air damages the dry powder since in all known countercurrent drying processes the dispersed droplets explode when contacting the low saturated drying gas and then shrink into a flattened skin which later on, during the course of the dehydration, agglomerates into the conventional type of particle having an exterior crust of skin and inner cavities closed to the exterior.

The dehydrated particles obtained by the dehydration process according to the process of *P. Hussmann; U.S. Patent 3,415,665; December 10, 1968; assigned to Uta-Patentverwaltungsgesellschaft mbH, Germany* when magnified, present a wrinkled and shriveled appearance which may be designated as porcupine-like or hedgehog-like appearance. The exposed surface areas of the particles are extensive in proportion to the surfaces of generally smooth surface particles of about the same diameter and are very considerably larger than the surface areas of particles obtained according to conventional spray drying.

These are of a spheroidal form with vapor holes through the particle shell; they have a relatively smooth surface and body with a mass of fine and larger vapor holes through the particle shell and body. The product comprises fully spherical granules with holes reaching deeply into the interior of the spheres. The particle does not evidence an outer skin, and it is free of an outer crust. Further, the particle is essentially free of cavities, or holes, that are closed to the exterior. As a result, the particles are free of air traps, or of such traps for other gases.

The holes or crevices of openings of the particles are open to the exterior and thus connected with the exterior surfaces of the particles. The powders of the process may be considered as instant powder or product because the powder will essentially instantly dissolve without leaving any significant residue, even in cold water.

In order to obtain the desired structure in the dehydrated product it is necessary that the treatment of the material during the first part of the dehydration be extended or continued beyond the time necessary for dehydrating the product to the desired degree of water content until there is formed a corn or grain from the dispersed droplets. It is an important aspect of the process that the residence time of the material to be dehydrated in the drying zone exceeds the time necessary for obtaining a product of the desired residual humidity. Thus the contact time of the material to be dehydrated with the specified conditions exceeds that required for the degree of dehumidification.

Moreover, in accordance with the process, it is necessary that in the first zone of the dehydration, there be maintained an atmosphere of such high humidity that the dispersed droplets do not, as it is customary, explode during the dehydration and then shrink into a flattened skin which later on, during the course of the dehydration, agglomerates into the conventional type of particle having an exterior crust of skin and inner cavities closed to the exterior.

In the first stage of the dehydration process the dispersed droplets are subjected to such a limited dehydration in an atmosphere of highly humid gases of relatively low temperatures that the droplets of the material being treated forms itself without exploding into a porous corn, free of crusty skin. Moreover, in this first stage the volatile substances that may have been extracted into the drying gas from a preceding particle that was dried are then in turn extracted, transferred or washed out from the humid atmosphere into another particle to be dried.

Accordingly, for thse two reasons, the contact time or treatment period of the products with the moving countercurrent dehydrating gas must be prolonged beyond the time necessary for the drying of the products to the extent desired. In this manner, in the upper stage of the drying zone, in the area of the highly saturated humid gases, the product of new structure can be formed and, as a second reason, to provide a so-called washing zone in which the volatile materials which have been extracted from the materials in the lower zone are again absorbed in the materials.

Thus, there prevail two main zones; an upper zone, the absorption zone and a lower zone, the adsorption zone. In order to form these effective zones, it is necessary to carry out the process with a slowly moving countercurrent of drying gas in a drying zone, or tower of certain unusual height under the conditions specified. It is an important aspect of the process that a certain relationship be maintained between the material to be treated and the drying gas, its humidity when fed into the drying zone, that at point of exit and its upward velocity in the zone.

In accordance with the process the liquid starting material is dispersed into a countercurrent of gas, in determinable droplet size, at an inlet feed velocity in such a way that preferably the diameter of the drying tower is essentially constantly covered with a dense layer of the dispersed starting material. Accordingly, the starting material is sprayed into the tower in such a way as to form a dense screen of falling particles. In this manner the escape of dust from dried material is substantially eliminated and the humidity saturated air is brought into intimate contact with the dense rain of drops which reabsorbs vapors and aroma carried in the updraft of air.

Accordingly, there prevails within the tower a column of falling drops initially falling in a dense rain into the entire area immediately below the spray device, their distribution becoming increasingly heterogeneous as the drops encounter the moving current of air or gas and decreasing in weight as the evaporation progresses. The gradual and progressive decrease in weight is another characteristic of the process. It promotes the retention of the integrity (physical and biochemical) of the product. It is another aspect of the process that a pre-dried, gas-forming drying material which has a low humidity is fed into the bottom of the tower.

The drying gas has a low degree of humidity and is of moderate low temperatures; it has a regulatable inlet feeding velocity. In this manner the drop height of the material treated and thereby the height of the tower can so be determined and related to the upwardly moving velocity of the drying gas.

Thus the material and the gas are maintained in contact until, at the top portion of the tower, exiting gas has a humidity between 65 and 95% of saturation. Under such conditions the material reaches the bottom of the tower already in a corn-like form, in which it is then removed from the tower. The spraying device or nozzle system for forming the droplets is preferably mounted in the tower at some distance from its top. A distance of 2 meters to 10 meters is preferably selected. Numerous tests have shown that a distance of 3 meters to 5 meters from the top of the tower is particularly advantageous in a tower of the diameter and height used in the process.

By having the spray nozzles below the top of the tower, space is provided above the nozzles for the air that does not contact the product to mix with the moist air so that the drops initially contact only moist air. The velocity with which the droplets leave the nozzles is between about 0.1 m/sec and 3.0 m/sec and preferably lower than 2 m/sec. Beyond the practical aspect, the initial low velocity with which the droplet is fed into the highly humid atmosphere contributes to minimizing the development of electrical charges on the droplet and its deleterious effects on the product.

Feeding of the material into the tower is performed with such means adopted to disperse the material to be dried into a substantially similar droplet size. There can be used, for instance, dual material delivery nozzles or cup-like sprays. However, any nozzles that produce a rain of drops or droplets of a generally uniform average selected size with low friction may be employed. Fundamentally, the process is independent of the droplet size of the material to be dried.

However, it has been found that it is highly desirable that the lower limits of the drop size be maintained at about 50 microns since at sizes below that there occurs a denaturization of the material as a result of the electrostatic charges which adversely affect the nature and the quality of the product. As a rule, the particle size should not be below 200 microns. To promote instant solubility, particle size should normally not be below 400 to 500 microns. Particle sizes up to 2,000 microns in diameter are possible.

The drying gas which is used with the process is brought and maintained by pretreatment, a predrying, at a humidity not exceeding about 10% preferably about 8%. When the temperature of the inlet gases is maintained at about 35°C, the relative humidity of the dehumidified gas is at about 3 to 4%.

Example: There were transformed 1,100 kg of orange juice into a powder having a residual moisture content of 12%. Preliminary experiment had indicated that droplets of 500 microns were most advantageous. The orange juice was divided into such droplets with the aid of pressure nozzles arranged below the top of the drying tower. Three large size nozzles each having a capacity of 365 kg/hr were used, the combination being capable of handling 1,100 kg/hr.

In place of three large nozzles, eleven smaller nozzles, each of 100 kg/hr capacity could have been used. The most effective dehydrating period was determined to be 70 seconds in a tower 50 meters high with a rate of descent of 0.65 m/sec, and with the nozzles 4.5 meters from the top of the tower. Because of its high fructose and glucose sugar content, orange juice is very hygroscopic. The temperature of the drying air entering the tower was 20°C. The air leaving the top of the tower contained 10% of water per cubic meter, this being close to 85% saturation taking into consideration the temperature drop caused by evaporation. For evaporating about 1,000 kg of water from 1,110 kg of orange juice, a total of 100,000 cubic meters of air were required.

The cross-sectional area of the tower was about 195 m², and its diameter was 15.75 meters. The drying air was introduced tangentially at the bottom of the tower with the aid of fans through a circular feed line. The tangential air feed slits had a total discharge area of 30 to 60 m². In this manner about 115 kg of dehydrated orange juice having a moisture content of about 7% were recovered at the bottom of the tower using a revolving scraper and screw conveyor.

Dehydration of Droplets from Filament Carrier-Structure

The process of *C.P. Huysmans; U.S. Patent 3,419,062; December 31, 1968; assigned to Lever Brothers Company* provides a concentration process in which a liquid containing material to be concentrated is attached to a carrier-structure and dried in the form of droplets.

In a preferred embodiment the carrier-structure consists of taut filaments. Several filaments may be arranged parallel or substantially parallel to each other and may be spaced apart at a desired distance, for example by grooves in guide rolls. Alternatively, the carrier-structure may consist of a plurality of filaments in a supporting frame. Clearly the strength of the filaments must be sufficient to withstand applied tension necessary for maintaining the shape of the carrier-structure.

Conveniently droplets of the liquid to be dried are applied to the carrier-structure which is then transferred to a drying zone where concentration of the liquid occurs, although the droplets may, of course, be applied to the carrier-structure while it is actually in the drying zone. In a preferred embodiment the droplets are applied to the carrier-structure which then passes through a drying zone and, after emerging from the drying zone the dried material is removed from the carrier-structure. Usually the carrier-structure will proceed in a horizontal direction through the drying zone, although the actual disposition of the carrier-structure may be varied, consistent with maintaining the liquid in droplet form.

Figure 3.1a is a vertical cross section of the drying apparatus for carrying out the process, the section being taken along the line I—I in Figure 3.1b. Figure 3.1b is a top view of part of the drying apparatus. Figure 3.1c is a device for applying droplets to a carrier-structure and Figure 3.1d is a schematic representation of a device for detaching dried material from the carrier-structure.

FIGURE 3.1: FILAMENT CARRIER-STRUCTURE APPARATUS

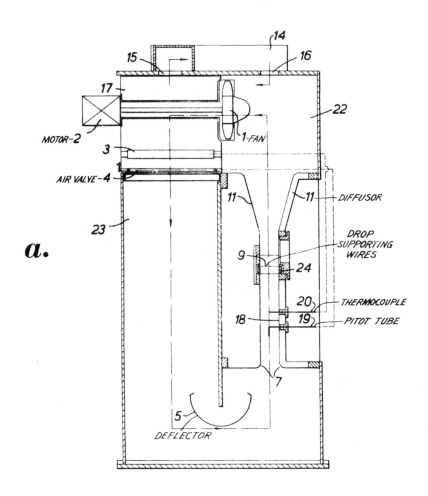

(continued)

FIGURE 3.1: (continued)

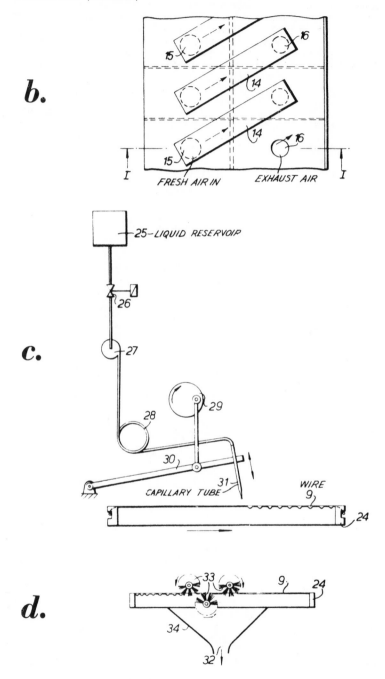

Source: C.P. Huysmans; U.S. Patent 3,419,062; December 31, 1968

In Figure 3.1a **1** represents a fan, powered by a motor **2**. The velocity of the air is regulated by a hand-set valve **4**, while its temperature can be varied by an electric heater **3**. After conditioning to the desired temperature and velocity in compartment **17**, the air flows downward through the space **23** and then upward through the duct **18** with the rounded entrance **7**. The deflector plate **5** helps to achieve uniformity in the flow of air. The duct **18** is about 10 times as high as it is wide and imparts a streamlined flow of air through the set of wires **9**. These wires are stretched in a frame **24**, which is moved at right angles to the plane of the drawing. The air leaves the duct **18** via a diffusor **11** with an opening angle of 15°. From the diffusor the air enters the chamber **22**, from which it is sucked into compartment **17** by the fan **1**.

The air velocity is measured by a pitot tube **19**, and the air temperature is sensed by the thermocouple **20**, which regulates the power input of the air heater **3**. Figure 3.1b gives an idea of the various sections or compartments into which the apparatus is subdivided, these sections being so delimited by the horizontal dotted lines. The ports **15** and **16** serve as entrance and exit for the air in each section. The air flows from one section to the next by duct **14**, which duct is provided with a valve to regulate the intersectional flow of air.

The following parameters are measured and regulated: wet and dry bulb temperature measured with thermocouples; dry bulb temperature regulated by varying electric current through heater; wet bulb temperature regulated by supplying fresh dry air through air entrance port; and air velocity measured with pitot tube regulated with handset valve.

In Figure 3.1c, a reservoir **25** contains the liquid to be dried or concentrated; **26** is an electromagnetic valve, **27** a pump, **28** a flexible hose, **31** a capillary tube, **29** an excenter actuating the bar **30**, to which the capillary tube **31** is attached. **9** is one of the wires stretched in frame **24**.

In Figure 3.1d, **9** is one of the wires stretched in the frame **24**, **33** are rotating brushes. The detached solid particles fall into the funnel **34** and are evacuated through the opening **32**. The performance of the process is illustrated by the following example.

Example: Orange juice was first depectinized and filtered to obtain a clear liquid. Subsequently 10 grams dextrin maltose (50% dextrin and 50% maltose) per 100 cm^3 juice were added and the liquid was treated in an apparatus, as described above, which was 1.80 meters in length and contained 5 sections. The filaments were of stainless steel, 0.6 mm diameter, and were spaced 3 mm apart from center line to center line. The drying time within the apparatus was 2.5 minutes and the conditions in the various sections of the apparatus were as follows.

Section	- - - - Temperature, °C - - - -		Air Velocity, m/sec
	Dry Bulb	Wet Bulb	
1	130	60	6
2	95	50	12
3	70	45	12
4	60	30	12
5	50	25	12

Terminal drying was carried out by transferring the frames carrying the filaments to a drying room through which dry air of 40°C was circulated. After 30 minutes the droplets were completely dry and were scraped from the filaments. The dry product obtained could be easily reconstituted.

Use of Perforate Collecting Screen

R.E. Meade; U.S. Patent 3,520,066; July 14, 1970; assigned to The Pillsbury Company describes a process for drying fluids by spraying into a drying atmosphere, directing the drying atmosphere and dispersed droplets of the fluid toward a perforate collecting screen and allowing the droplets to dry to the point where they are in a tacky condition when they reach the screen. The tacky bodies when they contact one another become bonded together to form a self-supporting porous mat. A portion of the drying atmosphere is passed through the porous mat collected upon the screen to dry it as it forms. The screen (typically an endless conveyor belt) can be used, if desired, to transport the mat into a zone where cool air is forced through it to further rigidify the mat.

FIGURE 3.2: FLOWSHEET FOR SPRAY DRYING PROCESS

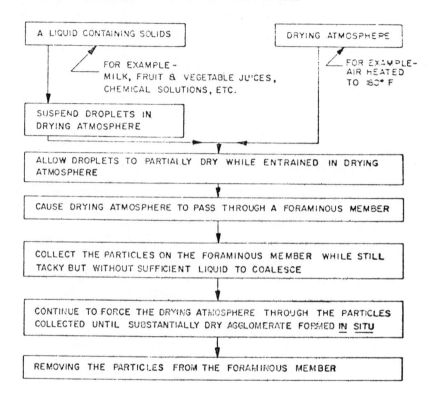

Source: R.E. Meade; U.S. Patent 3,520,066; July 14, 1970

Referring to the flowsheet in Figure 3.2, the process is begun with a fluid to be dried which is composed of a liquid containing a solid material either dissolved or suspended therein as a starting material. Examples of such starting materials are vegetable and fruit juices, milk, chemical solutions such as aqueous or nonpolar solutions of any of a variety of materials and in general a solution, slurry or suspension of any material which is to be dried by the removal of a solvent or suspending liquid. An additional starting agency comprises a gaseous drying atmosphere.

The drying atmosphere will normally consist of air heated substantially above room temperature or of air having a relatively low humidity level or of heated relatively low humidity air. The moisture present in the drying atmosphere is substantially below its saturation point.

As a first step in the operation, the fluid to be dried is dispersed into the drying atmosphere as droplets small enough so that the liquid component of the fluid droplets will be readily evaporated. For most practical applications, it is preferred that the droplets be comparable to those produced in commercially available spray dryers. Generally, the smaller the diameter of the droplets, other things remaining equal, the more rapidly will moisture be removed.

Next, the drying atmosphere together with the entrained droplets is directed toward a foraminous collecting member. While the surfaces of the particles are still in a tacky condition, but do not contain sufficient liquid to enable them to coalesce and form a relatively impermeable continuous material, the drying atmosphere passes through the foraminous member and the suspended particulate material is collected upon the foraminous member and upon the particulate material previously collected or upon both.

The particles are thus brought together so as to contact one another while the surfaces thereof are in a tacky condition and bonds are formed at the points of contact between the particles to produce relatively highly porous lacy reticulum in which a substantial portion of the agglomerate thus formed consists of communicating spaces or pores between the contacting and bonded particles.

The ability of the particles to form bonds (fuse) will depend, of course, upon the nature of the product itself but in addition will depend largely upon two other operating conditions, the temperature of the particles at the time they strike the surface of the accumulated material and their moisture content. Thus, at a constant temperature greater moisture contents will promote greater fusion.

During the drying operation, as the droplets pass through the dryer, the temperature of each droplet will be limited by its moisture content and by the wet bulb temperature of the drying gas which, in a typical case, for example, may be between 125° and 130°F. The phenomena taking place during the falling rate phase will be described. Once the particles have been deposited on the collection screen, a sudden change will take place in the relation between the particles and the surrounding air. The air will then begin to stream over and around the particles and through the minute microporous interstices between the particles in the agglomerate.

As this streaming takes place, moisture removal from the particles will occur at a much higher rate. Removal of the last traces of removable moisture proceeds at a characteristically low rate. This is commonly referred to as the falling rate drying period. In accordance with this process, after the movement of the particles has been arrested by deposition on the bed or screen, a substantial increase in the velocity of the drying gas relative to the particles is established. This provides a more effective means for removing the last traces of removable moisture than is attained during the falling rate phase in a drying process of the type in which the particles are entrained in the drying gas and thus moving at substantially lower velocity relative to the particles.

The flow, of drying atmosphere through the bonded particles continues until the remaining moisture or other liquid present on the surface of the particles is removed and the particles are thereby firmly bonded to one another at their points of contact. In this way a deposit of bonded particles builds up upon the foraminous member with the drying atmosphere passing through the deposit to dry it and the particles which have been deposited upon the foraminous member serving as a means for collecting freshly deposited particles. When the spraying operation is finished and the accretion of material on the foraminous member is dried to the desired moisture content, it can be removed from the screen in any suitable manner.

It has been found quite surprisingly that the particles do not pass through the foraminous member but instead accumulate in a porous, self-supporting mat. The mat includes side, upper and lower surfaces and is relatively large in size compared with the particles of which it is composed and the pores between the particles communicate with each other to form channels that extend from the upper or influent to the lower or effluent surface of the mat. The lower surface is positioned adjacent to the foraminous collecting member. The mat in general has both a width and breadth of at least several inches, i.e., from 2 to 3 inches. The thickness of the mat should be at least the combined thickness of a multiplicity of dried particles but will often be several inches in thickness. Drying in this manner has a number of highly unique and advantageous benefits. The primary benefits are:

First, filtration of air-entrained particles from the drying medium is accomplished by those particles already deposited in the mat, thus, reducing and in some cases eliminating the need for auxiliary filters in the stream of exit drying gas. Since this phenomenon in the course of a drying operation has heretofore been unknown, it will be referred to as auto-filtration.

Second, greater drying efficiencies can be achieved than was heretofore possible. While the precise reason for this result is not known with certainty, it is believed to be, in part, due to the accelerated evaporation due to the streaming of the drying medium around and through the particles having been deposited in the mat and, in part, to the increased driving forces across the solid and gaseous interface.

Third, greater product dryness is accomplished with the process because of the increased time of exposure of the material to the drying atmosphere.

Fourth the process is capable of drastically reducing the undesired accumulation of the product on the walls of the dryer. This allows the application of the process to products which were heretofore difficult or impossible to dry by conventional spray drying techniques or for that matter, by any previous drying process. It also increases the product quality because of the reduction of heat damage.

Fifth, the product that is being dried is placed, while in a practically dried state, in a form which can be transferred from the drying zone to one or more additional zones where further treatment may be performed.

Sixth, the process places the product in a physical form (a porous, self-supporting mat which can be further processed if desired to provide products having advantageous properties).

Preparation of Foamed Liquid or Concentrate

D. Rhodes; U.S. Patent 3,749,378; July 31, 1973; assigned to General Foods Ltd. has described an apparatus for foaming liquids such as juices, capable of controlling the fineness and density of the foamed liquid consisting of a mixing zone in which gas is introduced into the liquid under pressure and a second zone containing a plurality of spaced, flat annular plates which define numerous paths through which the foam must pass. The foamed liquid may be dried by freeze drying or spray drying. The apparatus is particularly useful in a process for producing a spray dried product.

According to the process there is provided a mixing device for producing a fine foam which comprises an inlet for gas and an inlet for liquid, leading into a mixing zone; the mixing zone is connected to a second zone containing a plurality of spaced plates which form numerous narrow paths through which the coarse foam passes. The foamed liquid is discharged through the outlet of the second zone as a fine foam.

The inlet for the gas preferably contains a gas injection device for introducing the gas into the mixing zone in a plurality of fine streams to ensure satisfactory dispersion of the gas within the incoming liquid to produce a course foam. A preferred injection device comprises a diffuser injection ring containing a plurality of fine holes as illustrated in Figure 3.3.

The flat plates used in the device of this process for providing the fine foam are preferably thin annular plates made from a corrosion-resistant metal. The size and capacity of the device may be varied within wide limits depending upon the particular application and the size of the installation within which it is to be used.

FIGURE 3.3: LIQUID FOAMING DEVICE

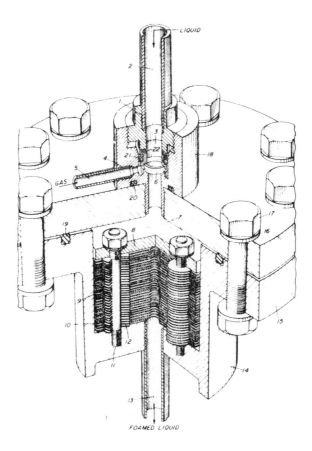

Source: D. Rhodes; U.S. Patent 3,749,378; July 31, 1973

A great advantage of the device is that it contains no moving parts and by altering the number, thickness and/or spacing of the plates and carefully controlling the rate of flow of gas and liquid extract and the pressure thereof, a foam of any desired fineness and density may be obtained for spray drying. Another advantage is that the device may be easily installed in an existing plant without any major or expensive alterations to pipe work or other apparatus. The process also provides a process for producing a foam composition which comprises dispersing a gas in an aqueous extract or emulsion of the desired product in a device as hereinbefore described and drying the resulting fine foam by known techniques such as spray drying, freeze drying, etc.

The gas used in the process may be any gas which does not interact with the extract or emulsion and suitable examples are nitrogen, carbon dioxide and nitrous oxide. The preferred gas is nitrogen. Carbon dioxide does not give the same low bulk density products at the same initial foam density as nitrogen.

By virtue of the fine dispersion of gas provided by the device, the process produces spray dried powder of low bulk density where small gas bubbles are entrapped within the walls of the spray dried particles as can be seen by examining them under the microscope. Using a fixed rate of extract flow and spray drying conditions, the quantity and type of gas used in the process determines the final bulk density of the spray dried product, which may therefore be adjusted as desired.

It is often advantageous to dry an extract in a concentrated form as a means of reducing the overall cost of an expensive process such as freeze drying. Concentrated extracts result in a dry product of high density as compared to products prepared from more dilute extracts. The apparatus of this process can be used to foam a concentrated extract as a means of lowering the density of the product obtained when drying concentrated extracts.

The device, illustrated in Figure 3.3 comprises an inlet 1 adapted to receive a pipe 2 for introducing liquid extract into a mixing zone 3. A second inlet 4 is adapted to receive a pipe 5 for introducing the gas for foaming. The gas is injected into the mixing zone through an injector ring 6 which contains a plurality of fine holes.

The injection of the gas into the liquid extract produces a coarse foam in the mixing zone and this foam is passed under pressure into a second zone 7 where it is deflected by a circular top plate 8 into and through the annular space between the wall of the zone 9 and a plurality of flat annular plates 10. The annular plates are mounted on studs 11 and spaced apart by washers 12. By virtue of the pressure drop between the inlet and outlet of the device, the course foam is directed through the narrow spaces between the annular plates resulting in efficient dispersion of the gas throughout the liquid to produce a fine foam which is ejected through the outlet pipe 13.

In the preferred embodiment as illustrated in Figure 3.3 the second zone is designed by a body portion 14 having a flange 15 through which it is bolted to a plate 16 by a plurality of bolts 17. The mixing zone is defined by a hollow cylinder 18 mounted on the plate 16 and sealing of the various zones is ensured by O-sealing rings 19, 20, 21 and 22.

By appropriate spacing of the annular plates it is possible to increase or decrease the liquid pressure drop over the device and thus adjust the shear and dispersion of the gas. The preferred number of plates, plate thickness and spacing for a particular product may be readily determined in a few trial runs.

VACUUM DRYING

In-Package Desiccation and Conditioning

In commercial processes of dehydration, volatile constituents are removed from the product lowering the flavor level and quality of the dehydrated product so that upon its reconstitution it has a bland, flat taste. Previous processes for handling dehydrated fruit juices have been able to only partially restore or return these flavoring constituents to the product without increasing the moisture content of the dehydrated product to such an extent that coalescence or melting of the product would destroy its value.

According to a preferred embodiment of the process of *C. Kortschot; U.S. Patent 3,185,581; May 25, 1965; assigned to Plant Industries, Inc.* the dehydrated fruit juice or other edible product is removed from the dehydrating apparatus in friable, pulverulent or particulate form and is placed in an air tight package or enclosure which may contain moisture absorbing or desiccating material. The product at this stage has a low moisture content but the moisture contained therein is unevenly distributed throughout the product.

The product then has more moist portions that will coalesce at lower temperatures and drier portions that will not coalesce unless the product is allowed to attain higher temperatures. To prevent the coalescence of any portions of the product it is cooled to a temperature that is substantially below the coalescence point of the most moist or more moist particles of the product. When the product has been so cooled a minor amount of moisture containing flavoring ingredients such as liquid or solid flavorings, nutritive sweetening agents, anticaking agents, bodying agents, water-soluble fruit essences or water-soluble vegetable juice essences may be added if care is taken to hold the temperature of the product below the coalescence point of the most moist areas of the product including that moisture added by the moisture containing flavoring ingredients. The critical temperature below which the product must be kept at this point depends on the method of drying, the characteristics of the particular product and the amount of moisture added in the moisture containing flavoring ingredients and is determined by statistical analysis and laboratory samplings, using ordinary methods.

The product is stored for a period of time at a temperature that is below the coalescence point of the most moist particles or areas of the product. All of the product remains in its solid state and the moisture retained by the product begins to distribute itself more uniformly throughout the product under the driving force of the difference in vapor pressures of the more moist and less moist areas of the product. Thus, after a period of time the critical storing temperature of the product, that is, the coalescence point of the most moist portion of the product will have increased.

As the moisture distributes more homogeneously throughout the product the storing temperature is gradually or by steps allowed to increase but is always kept below the coalescence point of the more moist portions of the product. The allowing of an increase in storage temperature carries with it a subsequent saving in the cost of depressing the temperature of the product below the ambient or normal storage room temperature.

If the initial total moisture content of the dehydrated product was low enough, the moisture will be distributed throughout the product while its temperature is depressed until the critical temperature, the coalescence point of the more moist portions of the product is above average room or ambient temperature and the temperature of the product can ultimately be allowed to rise to the ambient temperature without danger of any of the product becoming liquefied, gummy or caked.

Even if the total moisture content of the dehydrated product is initially so high that the product could not be stored at room temperature after the moisture level of the product was allowed to come to equilibrium during a low temperature preconditioning period according to alternatives of the method of the process, desiccating or moisture absorbing material are included in the container.

Edible moisture absorbing materials may be intimately mixed with the product or a nonedible desiccant may be enclosed in the container by keeping it separate from the product. The nonedible desiccant is enclosed in a pouch or pillbox permeable to water vapor. Examples of desiccating and moisture absorbing materials used are high surface area, open cellular solids; anticaking agents; nutritive sweetening agents; solid flavoring materials and bodying agents. The water that they remove from the product may be adsorbed, absorbed or combined as water of crystallization.

When amounts of these inclusions are properly adjusted the moisture content of the most moist portions of the product can be lowered by redistribution and removal during the low temperature preconditioning period so that the product can ultimately be stored in hermetically sealed containers, at average room temperatures without the product becoming liquefied, gummy or caked.

In addition to the inclusion of desiccating or moisture absorbing material in the product enclosure during the low temperature preconditioning period, or as an alternative therefore, a dry gas which most economically is dry air at atmospheric pressure is passed into intimate contact with the product. The temperature of the dry gas must be programmed in such a way that the temperature of the product is below the point of coalescence.

Example: A puff drying process for pineapple juice consisted of dehydrating the juice in a continuous high vacuum belt dehydrator to give an end product of 2.0 to 2.5% average moisture content. The dehydrated juice was extremely hygroscopic and had to be handled in a dehumidifying atmosphere of 15% relative humidity or less, at a temperature below 75°F. The product was packaged in hermetically sealed containers at 2 to 2½% average moisture content with a desiccating pouch to provide in package desiccation to reduce moisture content below 1%.

No commercial means of addition of natural flavoring essence was satisfactory and the product often caked, produced sticking spots or gummy spots due to the melting or coalescing of the more moist portions of the product before the average moisture level had been reduced sufficiently by the desiccant. According to the method of the process it is possible to dehydrate pineapple crystals to an average moisture content of 2½%, lower the temperature of the product to 0°F or below and add an amount of pineapple essence solution containing moisture in the amount of 1% by weight of the dried pineapple juice crystals.

As the moisture content of the more moist areas of the pineapple crystal product is reduced by transfer of moisture to desiccants and moisture absorbing ingredients included in the product package and the evening out of the moisture content among the several crystals, the storing temperature of the superior, full flavored pineapple crystals product may be gradually raised to average room temperature. This product when stored at room temperature remains friable and can be readily reconstituted to pineapple juice of improved quality and flavor and characteristics.

Slush Drying for Flavor Retention

Liquid foods are dehydrated by subjecting them to a vacuum and to a temperature only low enough to freeze part of the water content to produce a slush. A high drying rate, coupled with good flavor retention is provided.

A particular object of the process of *S.K. Chandrasekaran and C.J. King, III; U.S. Patent 3,716,382; February 13, 1973; assigned to the U.S. Secretary of Agriculture* is the provision of a high drying rate coupled with good retention of volatile flavoring principles. Basically, the process utilizes a principle which may be termed slush drying because the liquid food is maintained in the form of a slush, a mixture of ice and liquid, during the dehydration.

FIGURE 3.4: SLUSH DRYING APPARATUS AND STUDIES

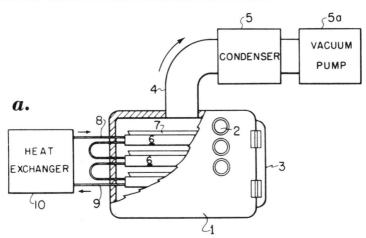

(continued)

FIGURE 3.4: (continued)

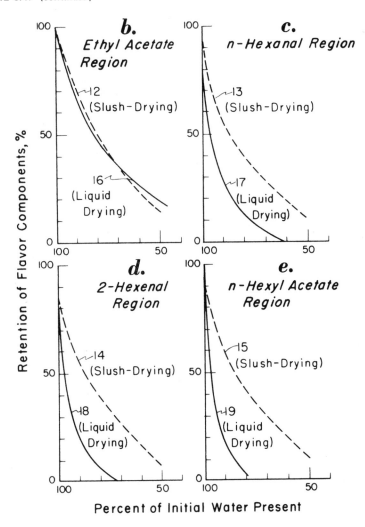

Source: S.K. Chandrasekaran and C.J. King, III; U.S. Patent 3,716,382; February 13, 1973

In a practice one may use various types of apparatus, for example, conventional freeze drying equipment, with proviso that means be provided so that the temperature of the material under dehydration can be so controlled that it is maintained in the form of a slush. The practice of the process using such equipment is described below in connection with Figure 3.4a.

The apparatus shown in Figure 3.4a includes chamber 1 provided with glass ports 2 and vacuum-tight door 3. For maintaining the interior of chamber 1 under vacuum there is provided conduit 4 communicating with condenser 5 and vacuum pump 5a. During operation of the device, the interior of the chamber is held at a pressure of about 50 mm Hg or less. Condenser 5 is continuously refrigerated so that the water vapor leaving the chamber via conduit **4** is continuously removed from the system as frost or ice.

Within the chamber are a series of shelves **6** of hollow construction so that a heat transfer medium can be circulated through them. The material being dehydrated is contained in trays **7** which rest on the shelves. For circulating the heat transfer medium there are provided pipes **8** and **9** communicating with the interior of the hollow shelves. The pipes, in turn, are in communication with adjustable heat exchanger **10**. With this system the medium is heated to the extent necessary to continuously supply the heat of evaporation and sublimation while maintaining the material in trays **7** in the form of a slush.

The temperature required to maintain the material as a slush cannot be stated in terms of so many degrees because it will vary depending primarily on the solids content of the material under dehydration, and this in turn will change as the dehydration progresses. In any particular case the proper temperature to apply can be determined by pilot trials on samples of the material, or by observing the material during the course of the dehydration (for example, through windows **2** in the apparatus) and adjusting heat exchanger to control the temperature of the material as is necessary.

In general, the material under dehydration is kept at such a temperature that 20 to 70% of the water present in the material is frozen (ice), the remainder is liquid. This liquid remainder will not be pure water but rather an aqueous solution containing the sugars and other water-soluble components of the material under treatment. It is obvious that since both ice and liquid water are present in the material under treatment, the removal of water takes place by concurrent sublimation and evaporation. The dehydration procedure as described is continued for the time necessary to attain the desired degree of dehydration of the starting material. The process is of wide applicability and can be used for the concentration of liquid foods of all kinds.

Example: Slush Drying — Samples of apple juice (17% solids content) were dehydrated in a vacuum dehydrator maintained at an absolute pressure of about 0.5 mm Hg. During the dehydration, the juice was maintained in the form of a slush, a mixture of ice crystals and liquid. The initial juice and the products were analyzed by vapor phase chromatography to determine their content of volatile flavor components. To cover the wide boiling point range of the flavor components naturally present in apple juice, measurements were made in four areas as follows:

> ethyl acetate region, including methanol, ethanol, ethyl acetate, isobutanol, and acetal;
> n-hexanal region, including n-hexanal and n-butyl acetate;
> 2-hexenal region, including ethyl 2-methylbutyrate, 2-hexenal, and n-hexanol; and
> n-hexyl acetate region, comprising essentially n-hexyl acetate.

Liquid Pool Drying — In this case the samples of apple juices were retained in the liquid state (55° to 60°C) during the dehydration which was carried out at atmospheric pressure. Chromatographic analyses were made of the products.

The results of the above are shown in Figures 3.4b through 3.4e which are graphs of the percent of initial water in the material under treatment versus the percent retention of flavor components. In these graphs the dotted lines (curves **12, 13, 14, 15**) represent the slush drying treatment; the solid lines (curves **16, 17, 18, 19**) represent drying from the liquid state.

It is evident from Figures 3.4c, 3.4d and 3.4e that the slush drying procedure yielded an improved retention of flavor components in three of the important flavor areas, namely, the n-hexanal, 2-hexenal, and n-hexyl acetate regions.

OTHER PROCESSES

Drying Tower for Heat Sensitive Liquids

P. Hussmann; U.S. Patent 3,190,343; June 22, 1965; assigned to Birs Beteiligungs- und Verwaltungsgesellschaft AG, Switzerland has developed a process for dehydrating aqueous dispersions, suspensions or solutions of solids in which the material to be dried is dispersed in the upper region of a high tower in the form of a dense umbrella of droplets descending in the tower through a countercurrently flowing stream of relatively cool or cold drying air, the air being introduced in the lower region of the tower in a highly dehumidified state, for instance, with a water content of 0.35 g/m³, at a temperature not exceeding 60°C. In view of the low temperature of the drying gas, the residence time of the material in the tower must be relatively long and the volume of drying gas must be accordingly large.

In all embodiments of the process, use is made of a drying tower where the throughput of the material to be dried, its droplet size and distribution, the drying gas velocity and temperature are so correlated that the material falling through the dehumidified and upwardly streaming drying gas reaches the tower bottom in the form of porous and fully spherical granules, which remain on the bottom without collapsing or adhering to each other.

This granular structure of the dried material makes it possible to introduce the gaseous drying agent into the tower through the bottom, even if it carries a layer of dried powder up to 20 cm thick, and without imparting turbulence to the powder layer. The powder remains lying on the tower bottom until it has reached the desired degree of dehydration and is then conveyed on the shortest possible path to the vacuum packing station (which does not form part of the process).

Alternatively, the powder may be removed from the bottom of the tower as soon as it may be mechanically or pneumatically conveyed to a sieve-like support on which it is additionally dried to the desired degree of dehydration without turbulence.

Since this drying method uses relatively cool air and so requires drying towers of large volume and correspondingly large volumes of drying gas, the process also provides for operation of the drying tower with as little heat requirement as possible and with a maximum recovery of the required heat. For this purpose, the drying tower is connected with a special air conditioning plant. Drying towers useful for the practice of this process must have a height in the range of 50 to 200 meters, tower heights of about 70 meters having been found most useful for most purposes.

Figures 3.5a and 3.5b illustrate a structural embodiment of the plant for conditioning the drying air in the indicated manner, Figure 3.5a being a vertical section of the tower and Figure 3.5b showing a horizontal section thereof. To facilitate a schematic showing of the conduits, the elements **2a**, **2b** and **3a**, **3b** are shown in Figure 3.5a one behind the other, while they are illustrated adjacent one another in Figure 3.5b. In practice, they are arranged only at one of the two locations. Elements **6** and **7** also are positioned at the same location.

The drying air enters the drying tower at inlet opening **9** and passes upwardly to outlet opening **11**. The liquid material distributing means (not shown) is mounted in the tower below the drying gas outlet opening. The tower, which may have circular or rectangular walls, is surrounded by a jacket formed by an inner and outer tower wall defining a space therebetween. This space is divided into outer cells **4** and inner cells **5** by an intermediate zigzag wall which has a heat-insulating lining facing the interior of the tower.

It is preferred to make all the walls of cement which has a considerable heat-storing capacity. The fresh air for drying as well as for regeneration of the adsorption medium is passed into the plant from the atmosphere through the outer cells **4** of the tower jacket. The heater is subdivided into two branch conduits. In one of the operating cycles, the fresh air, which has been preheated by passage through jacket cells **4**, is led through the upper branch conduit into a regenerated adsorption medium packing **2a** consisting of two vertical packings arranged in parallel. The other portion of the preheated fresh air is conducted into a heat storage device **3a**. The entry valve of the lower branch conduit then remains closed.

FIGURE 3.5: DRYING TOWER FOR SPHERICAL, POROUS GRANULES

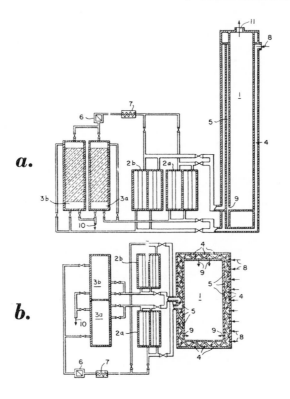

Source: P. Hussmann; U.S. Patent 3,190,343; June 22, 1965

In the following operating cycle, a portion of the fresh air coming from cells **4** is conducted by the lower branch conduit to adsorption medium packing **2b** which is similar in structure to packing **2a**. The other portion of the fresh air is then led from the lower branch conduit to heat storage device **3b**. At this cycle, the entry valve of the upper branch circuit remains closed.

Depending on the cycle, the dehumidified air coming from packing **2a** or **2b** is conducted to the inner cells **5** of the tower jacket and is led up and down these cells by variously placed fans. Finally, the dehumidified and conditioned drying air is introduced into the tower through opening **9**. The fresh air further heated in heat storage devices **3a** or **3b** is led through the flue of the heating element of another heat exchanger **6**, where it is additionally heated, and is finally directed into a heat exchanger **7** where it is brought to the requied regeneration temperature.

This hot air is then directed to the adsorption medium packing requiring regeneration, when it is passed into one of heat storage devices **3a** or **3b** to heat the same. The regenerating air then passes from the heat storage devices into the atmosphere through flue **10**. The inlet openings for cells **4**, which admit the fresh air thereto, and for cells **5**, admitting the dehumidified and conditioned drying air, are provided with suitable filters.

If the temperature of the adsorption packing used for dehumidifying the air exceeds a predetermined value, for instance 50°C, a thermosensitive relay may automatically operate suitable valves in the air conduits to direct the fresh air to a previously regenerated adsorption packing and to direct the regenerating air to the exhausted packing. The control of the next cycle may then be taken over by a thermostat in the regenerated packing. However, the cycle control may also be effected in an obvious manner by a thermostat in the conduit directing the conditioned air to cells **5**.

By using a tower wall jacket as heat storage and balancing device, it is possible to equalize the air temperatures so as to obtain a drying air of nearly constant temperature throughout the operation of the tower. The entire air circulation through the drying plant may be effected by fans mounted in the fresh air inlet openings of the outer wall of the drying tower.

The instant powders obtained by these procedures have all the properties of the solids contained in the starting material. They are not denatured and they show no change of taste. They may be considered as instant products because the powders will instantly dissolve without leaving a residue, even in cold water, if they are colloidally soluble or, if they are only dispersible, they will be instantly dispersed or wetted, while swelling.

Separation of Juice into Fractions Before Dehydration

R.J. Bouthilet; U.S. Patent 3,365,298; January 23, 1968 has developed a process for preparing a solid fruit beverage base which, when dissolved in water, provides the flavor characteristics of natural fruit. The base concentrate combines fruit oils, proteins and water-soluble fruit constituents held in pellet form by a binder.

While the previous methods of stabilization have merit, it would seem more sensible to separate the ingredients of the juice and to recombine the ingredients only just before consuming as one virtually does in a fresh squeezed drink. Recombination is a relatively simple matter. Of the vital constituents in a juice such as orange juice, many are cheaply available as pure compounds, for example, citric acid, potassium citrate, ascorbic acid, pectin and carotenes, these being identical in every respect to that in the fruit.

If one separates only a very few ingredients from the orange, a preparation can be made to duplicate in every way the ripe orange juice and improve it by providing a preparation which is more stable than the fresh juice. The flavors may be fixed by physical isolation in solids such as gums to give more lasting stability mixed in a dry powder. The most common way of accomplishing this is to simply mix the flavor with a concentrated solution of the gum and spray dry.

The little coated particles are similar to the particles found in a whole fruit and are called oil sacs. When pectin is used as the gum for the fixing of flavor, the nature of the particles is similar almost to the fruit. It is obvious then, if the separate components of the fruit be separated before they are allowed to interact, the quality of the beverage is closer to fresh than otherwise possible.

In the dehydration of juices, it is not enough to isolate intact ingredients, but it is necessary as well to isolate the whole mixture from the air. Even in dried powdered products, ingredients react slowly with air to lose quality. In the preparation of pellets such as are used here, the technique of tablet making involves the compression of dry powdered ingredients into solid pellets. Two ingredients are essential to provide good tablets, one being a binder and the other a lubricant. The binder may be in the form of some of the well-known gums, while the lubricant may be in the form of a solid fat or oil such as are commonly known and used. In the event that the pellet is to be required to dissolve quickly, a disintegrant is used. Disintegrants are similarly commonly in use, the disintegrants usually being a hydrophilic substance which quickly swells when wet.

The steps in the method involve first, the inactivation of the enzymes of the fresh fruit. The second step comprises the separation of the ingredients into homogeneous compounds. The next step involves fixing the ingredients in gums, and the fourth step involves drying the stable ingredients (or suitable substitute identical ingredients from an outside source, such as the pure compounds previously described), and lastly compressing the stabilized ingredients into pellets preferably having a minimal practical surface. As an illustration, a sample of a dehydrated beverage concentrate may be prepared in the following manner.

Step 1: 25 lb of whole fresh washed oranges of mixed varieties were ground in a colloid mill to a fine suspension. This suspension was frozen to a slush in a Sweden Soft Ice Cream Machine, and then mixed intimately with 2 gal of isopentane, chilled to dry ice temperature. The solvent was separated from the ice and when evaporated at low temperature yielded an orange oil with the odor and flavor of fresh orange juice. (For purposes of clarity in this illustration, this oil is designated as fraction 1.) This oil was mixed with a suspension of water-soluble gum and spray dried to yield an orange juice flavor powder, the type prepared by commercial flavor houses. (This orange juice flavor powder is designated as fraction 1-X.)

Step 2: The residue left in the ice in the above fractionation was dried in vacuo and extracted with 20% alcohol. This was then redried by lyophilation to yield a mixture of the water-soluble constituents of orange juice. Upon analysis this mixture was found to contain organic acids and their salts, dextrose, sucrose, trace substances as a source of ash, and ascorbic acid. Sugar is the predominant ingredient. This fraction was called fraction 2.

Step 3: The residue from the alcohol extraction in Step 2 was heated on a boiling water bath for 30 minutes to denature the proteins, then dried in vacuo to yield a mixture of proteins and gums (polysaccharides) essentially pectin. This when dry was ground to a fine powder. It is called fraction 3.

Step 4: The preparations from the preceding steps were combined in the following ratio: 33 parts of fraction 2, 6 parts of fraction 3, and 3 parts of fraction 1. 20 parts of this mixture when mixed with 80 parts of water yielded a beverage similar in many respects to fresh orange juice.

Step 5: A sample of the dry powder from Step 4 was compressed into cube shaped pellets. The resultant cubes when aged and stored retained their flavor and in all respects were an improvement on beverages prepared from frozen orange juice or any orange-type beverage drink.

FREEZE DRYING

FLUIDIZED BED PROCESSES

Fluidized Bed with Auxiliary Particles

There is a need for a process that will substantially reduce the time required for freeze drying, while preserving appearance and taste in the reconstituted food. *W.H. Mink and H. Nack; U.S. Patent 3,239,942; March 15, 1966; assigned to The Battelle Development Corporation* developed a process for freeze drying foods by immersing a frozen food in a fluidized bed of solid, discrete particles while maintaining either an absolute pressure in the fluidized bed chamber of not more than about 4 millimeters of mercury, or an atmosphere of dry gas such that the vapor pressure does not exceed about 4 millimeters. A temperature greater than $-15°C$ is maintained in the fluidized bed chamber. The food is removed from the fluidized bed when the desired residual moisture content is reached. Figure 4.1 is a drawing of apparatus in which the process is practiced.

In this process, a bed of solid, discrete particles 11 is subjected to an upward gaseous current 12, the size and weight of the particles and the velocity and nature of the current being so chosen that the force exerted by the current is sufficient to counterbalance the gravitational force on free particles and to expand the bed, thus allowing movement of the particles, but being insufficient to convert the bed into a stream of particles. A bed of solid, discrete particles subjected to, and expanded by, such an upward gaseous current in the manner described is referred to as a fluidized bed. A perforated plate 13 supports the bed material and assists in distributing the fluidizing gas 12 over the total base area of the unit. While a fluidized bed, per se, is well-known and used in many areas of technology, the treatment of food in a fluidized bed by immersing the food therein is first disclosed in U.S. Patent 3,035,918. When applied to freeze drying, surprising results are obtained.

Since a food produce is involved, that portion of the system 14 coming in contact with the food must be constructed of a material suitable for food preparation. The particle to be fluidized is selected because of its ability to be fluidized, its stability at the temperature at which the bed is operated, and its safeness from a health standpoint. The fluidized bed particles may comprise a material suitable for flavoring or seasoning of the food being treated. There are many materials that meet these requirements for purposes of this process. Among the materials that are suitable as fluidized bed particles are sodium chloride, calcium chloride, tricalcium phosphate, limestone, monosodium glutamate, sugar, rice, beans, lentils, or any material that is a solid of appropriate particle size at the temperature of operation and is generally regarded as safe as a food additive or is, in fact, an edible food. In fact, the bed particles may even comprise dried particles of the same food being dried.

145

FIGURE 4.1: FLUIDIZED BED WITH AUXILIARY PARTICLES

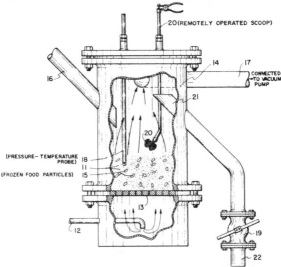

Source: W.H. Mink and H. Nack; U.S. Patetn 3,239,942; March 15, 1966

The bed particles need not be edible so long as they do not contaminate the food being treated. Appropriately sized beads such as stainless steel, glass, copper, cast iron, etc. may be used. Since NaCl is stable over most operating temperatures, is available in various particle sizes, is generally added to most foods, and is readily available, it is the most desirable of the potential bed materials.

Bed particles do not adhere to the surface of food being treated when the surface is maintained in a frozen condition until substantially dried. The gas used to fluidize the particles in the bed must not render the food to be treated inedible. Many gases are suitable for this purpose. Included among these are air, nitrogen, carbon dioxide, and flue gas. Where it is desired to inhibit oxidation of the food being treated, a nonoxidizing gas should be used. Nitrogen and carbon dioxide are most suitable in this instance. To minimize processing costs, the fluidizing gas may be circulated in a closed system and may be recycled through the bed. Since it is not desired to add water to the product being treated, the fluidizing gas should be maintained in a reasonably dry condition. This is readily accomplished by passing this gas through a suitable drying agent, or following an appropriate drying procedure before it is recirculated through the bed of particles.

The food 15 to be freeze dried by this process is first frozen. The method works best when the food to be freeze dried has at least one dimension not greater than two inches. Liquids can be frozen by known techniques in appropriate size, or can even be reduced in size. Where the natural size of the food being treated is greater than this, the time required for freeze drying is reduced by reducing the size of the food being processed so that at least one dimension is two inches or less. The frozen food 15 is immersed in a fluidized bed of solid, discrete particles 11. The food should be completely immersed in the bed of particles. The frozen food may be fed either continuously or in batch fashion into the fluidized bed. This can be accomplished through a port 16, which in a batch operation need not be equipped with a vacuum lock arrangement.

In a batch-type operation, the frozen food may be immersed in the fluidized bed at atmospheric pressure. After the frozen food is in the fluidized bed, the pressure is reduced to the desired level. Where the fluidized bed chamber is maintained at a reduced pressure, the frozen food to be freeze dried is fed into the fluidized bed chamber by means of vacuum locks. In this situation, the feed may be continuous or batch, as desired. The phase diagram of water defines a pressure-temperature region where sublimation will occur, i.e., ice will change directly to vapor without passing through the liquid phase. The sublimation of ice is the foundation for the entire freeze drying concept. The phase diagram of water shows that, at a vapor pressure of not greater than about 4 millimeters of mercury, ice will sublime to vapor. Thus, during the drying step of the process, the vapor pressure in the fluidized bed chamber cannot be greater than about 4 millimeters of mercury. A vapor pressure not greater than about 4 millimeters can be maintained by keeping the absolute pressure in the fluidized bed at not greater than about 4 millimeters of mercury, or by using a dry gas for fluidizing the bed of particles. The pressure can readily be reduced by means such as a tube **17** connected to a vacuum pump or other vacuum source. The only pressure limitation imposed on this process is that imposed by the phase diagram of water.

The drying steps of this process are carried out at a pressure and temperature at which solid ice will sublime. However, practical considerations, such as the size and cost of vacuum equipment, dictate that the absolute pressure in the fluidized bed chamber not be reduced below about from 1 to 10 microns of mercury. While the process can be carried out at atmospheric pressure, lower temperatures and a dry fluidizing gas are necessary to achieve a vapor pressure less than about 4 millimeters, and consequently longer drying times usually result. For example, temperatures in the ranges of $-15°$ to $+5°C$ are most effective in drying under these conditions. In practicing this process, conventional vacuum techniques and equipment are used to achieve the desired system pressure.

It has been observed that operating at a reduced pressure does not interfere with the fluidization of the bed particles and that fluidization of the bed particles does not prevent operating the system at a reduced pressure sufficient for freeze drying. Of course, the depth of the fluidized bed must not be so great that the pressure drop from the top to the bottom of the bed results in a pressure at the bottom of the bed that exceeds about 4 millimeters of mercury. The critical bed depth for any given bed particle can readily be determined by means of a pressure-temperature probe **18** that can measure the pressure or temperature at any given bed depth. This result was not predictable from the known state of the art. While the frozen food **15** is immersed in the fluidized bed of solid, discrete particles **11**, with vapor pressure in the fluidized bed chamber **14** of not more than about 4 millimeters of mercury, the heat of sublimation is supplied to the food to remove the ice as water vapor.

The particles in the fluidized bed are heated by any known means. For example, these particles may be heated by the fluidizing gas, through the vessel walls, by coils immersed in the bed and carrying steam or hot fluids, or by heating the particles themselves through radiated heat, dielectric heating, or induction heating. The food **15** to be dried is contacted on all sides by the bed particles **11**. It is this intimate contact of a solid with a solid that produces heat transfer rates that are vastly superior to those obtained by any other known method of freeze drying. Even when the only heat supplied is from the fluidizing gas at normal room temperature, about $20°C$, drying times superior to those obtainable by known processes are achieved. When additional heat is provided by elevating the temperature of the fluidized bed particles, drying times are reduced still further, without affecting taste or appearance of the food.

The dried food may be removed from the fluidized bed chamber either continuously or in a batch-type arrangement. In a batch-type arrangement, the system is brought to atmospheric pressure and the food removed. On a continuous basis, the food is removed through a system of vacuum locks **19**, so that the fluidized bed chamber is maintained at a reduced pressure. One method of continuous removal of dried products is by means of a remotely operated scoop **20** that picks up the dried food from the fluidized bed and deposits it in the exit port **21**. The scoop **20** would be made of a material sufficiently coarse to permit drainage of the bed particles **11**, but fine enough to retain the food **15** that has been dried.

Where oxidation of the food would reduce its quality or shelf life, the chamber **22** from which the food is removed after drying is brought to atmospheric pressure by means of a nonoxidizing gas. Gases such as nitrogen and carbon dioxide are especially suitable for this purpose. The dried food and the container in which it is to be packaged are flushed with an inert gas and the food is sealed in the package. It is also undesirable to have substantial quantities of moisture contact the food prior to the time that it is to be reconstituted. Thus, the gas used to bring the removal chamber to atmospheric pressure and to flush the food and container before packaging is maintained in a substantially dry condition. There are standard methods for the removal of moisture from gases and any of these may be applied here for this purpose.

Fluidized Bed Employing Frozen Foodstuff Particles

The process of *C.E. Dryden, W.H. Mink and H. Nack; U.S. Patent 3,269,025; August 30, 1966; assigned to The Battelle Development Corporation* eliminates the necessity of immersing food in a fluidized auxiliary bed of solid, discrete particles as described in U.S. Patent 3,239,942 by eliminating auxiliary fluidized particles and by having the foodstuff, per se, in a particulate form making up the fluidized bed. The process comprises fluidizing discrete, frozen solid particles of a material by a substantially dry gas while maintaining the particles in a frozen state and under a water vapor partial pressure of less than 4 millimeters of mercury on the fluidized particles. In many applications, the process also includes preparing the materials in the form of discrete frozen solid particles suitable for the fluidizing step.

The process also includes the freeze drying of water-containing materials in the form of eutectic compositions and, when treating such materials, the fluidizing, in addition to being carried forth at a vapor pressure of less than 4 millimeters of mercury, is carried forth at a temperature below the eutectic temperature of the composition being dried.

A sequence of steps comprising one embodiment of the process is as follows: (1) freezing a particulate portion; (2) comminuting to free-flowing frozen-solid powder particles; (3) introducing into a fluidization chamber; (4) fluidizing with a gas while maintaining the particles in a frozen-solid state and under vapor pressure of less than 4 mm Hg; and, (5) removing dried particles. In another embodiment, a mass of discrete frozen solid particles of a suitable size for fluidization already is present in a suitable fluidization apparatus, and in this embodiment the method comprises the preceding steps 4 and 5.

In practice of the process, frozen solid, discrete particles of material are placed in a fluidization chamber. The introduction of the particles may be either continuously or in a batch fashion. In a batch-type operation, the frozen particles introduced into the chamber are brought under a suitable reduced pressure and fluidization of the particles commenced by introduction of the fluidizing gas. In most instances, it is desirable that the fluidizing chamber and/or the fluidizing gas be cooled to a temperature below the temperature of the frozen, solid, discrete particles before the particles are introduced into the fluidization chamber. Means are known to the art, such as surrounding of the fluidization chamber by a refrigerant, for bringing the fluidization chamber to a sufficiently low temperature. Similarly, the fluidizing gas introduced may be precooled by passing it through a heat exchanger to lower the temperature of the fluidizing gas to a low enough temperature.

Where the fluidization bed chamber is maintained below atmospheric pressure, the frozen, solid, discrete particles may be fed into the chamber by means of vacuum locks. In this situation, the feed may be continuous or batch, as desired. In like manner, the freeze dried particles may be withdrawn by means of vacuum locks from the fluidization chamber. Thus, it will be readily apparent that the process is readily adaptable to either continuous or batch operation, as desired.

Example: A commercially available frozen orange juice concentrate is thawed sufficiently for removal from its container, then rapidly frozen at a temperature lower than –25°C, and crushed to a fine, free flowing, frozen solid, orange juice concentrate of a temperature of lower than about –25°C. This crushed, frozen solid concentrate, while still frozen solid, is charged to a precooled fluidization column of a temperature lower than –25°C. The column is evacuated and the charged concentrate fluidized by introduction of a precooled substantially dry nitrogen gas of a temperature lower than about –25°C. Fluidization is carried forth for about 12 hours with the fluidized concentrate maintained at a temperature lower than about –25°C and under a reduced absolute pressure of less than about 4 millimeters of mercury. At this time the resulting product, a dehydrated orange juice concentrate, is removed from the column. The dehydrated orange juice concentrate is thawed and found to have a water content significantly lower than the commercially available orange juice concentrate.

Rehydration of this dried concentrate is readily accomplished by mixing with water. The reconstituted orange juice is found by a taste panel to be substantially indistinguishable from a similarly reconstituted orange juice prepared from the original commercially available frozen orange juice concentrate.

Fluidized Bed Process Employing Liquids

G.F. Sachsel and W.H. Mink; U.S. Patent 3,319,344; May 16, 1967; assigned to The Battelle Development Corporation have discovered a method whereby liquid foods may be frozen, fluidized, and sublimed substantially simultaneously without the necessity of first freezing the liquid and then crushing the frozen liquid into fluidizable particles or of freezing the liquid in the form of fluidizable particles. The method and apparatus not only eliminates the necessity of the extra step of providing frozen liquids in particulate form but also provides the frozen liquid in a particularly desirable small particulate form which sublimes much faster and completely than has heretofore been envisioned. Liquid foods may be sprayed into a vessel having a low gaseous pressure therein and a counter-current gaseous flow to effect freezing, fluidization and sublimation of the sprayed liquid.

Figure 4.2 is an illustrative cross-sectional view of a fluidizing vessel-spray apparatus that falls within the scope of the process. In the apparatus of the drawing a vessel **10** is provided with a fluidizing distributor plate **12** positioned between a fluidizing gas plenum chamber **14** and a main fluidized bed chamber **16**. Distributor plate **12** is a perforated plate of conventional design disposed to divide the fluidizing gases entering chamber **14** from gas inlet **18** into multiple dispersed jets which flow upwardly into the main chamber **16** and effect proper fluidization of particles within the vessel. Chamber **16** of vessel **10** is provided with an outlet **20** that leads to a vacuum source such as a vacuum pump of conventional design (not shown). A conduit **22** projects into chamber **16** of vessel **10** through an opening in the top of the vessel and terminates within chamber **16** into a spray nozzle **24**.

The apparatus of the drawing is provided with optional equipment designed to enhance its operation. Such optional equipment consists of a water jacket **26** positioned around chamber **16** of vessel **10**. Jacket **26** is formed with a liquid coolant inlet **28** and outlet **30**. Such a jacket enables the operator of the device to more closely control the temperature within chamber **16**. Another optional adjunct consists of a pressure probe conduit **32** which extends into vessel **10** and enables one to insert a pressure probe into chamber **16** and adjust the input of fluidizing gas and the vacuum pumps (not shown) to maintain the desired degree of fluidization and pressure within the chamber **16**.

One method of carrying out this process is to provide a bed of inert particles within chamber **16** of vessel **10**. Such inert particles should be of a size that is readily fluidized preferably being within the usual fluidized bed particle range of from about –8 to +325 mesh. A vacuum is drawn within chamber **16** by the vacuum pumps disposed to withdraw the atmosphere from within chamber **16** through the exhaust outlet **20**. Fluidizing gas is introduced into the plenum chamber **14** through inlet **18** in sufficient volume to cause jets of gas to flow upwardly into chamber **16** through the perforations of distributor plate **12** and fluidize the inert particles. A pressure probe (not shown) of convenient construction inserted into chamber **16** through conduit **32** enables the operator to accurately ascertain the pressure within the chamber. He may then proceed to adjust the degree of vacuum pump activity and the amount of fluidizing gases introduced into plenum chamber **14** via inlet **18** to effect fluidization while maintaining the desired pressure within the chamber **16**. It will be understood that the desired pressure level within chamber **16** is not atmospheric pressure but instead is a pressure at which a solid ice phase can exist in equilibrium with the vapor phase. When pure water is being considered, this pressure is equivalent to about 4 mm of mercury. The practice of reducing the total gaseous pressure within chamber **16** is a practical and preferred means for providing an environment such that the partial pressure of the water vapor will not exceed the desired value. Another potential mode of operation is to introduce a dried (low water vapor content) gas through inlet **18**. A third means of providing conditions which will permit the desired partial pressure of water vapor is to combine a relatively low vapor content fluidizing gas with a lowered atmospheric pressure.

Where an evacuated system, such as vessel **10**, is employed, wherein the total chamber pressure is reduced to 4 mm of Hg, even if the atmosphere is 100% water vapor, the partial pressure will not exceed 4 mm of Hg and ice crystals will sublime. The preferred and practical mode of operation is to create a vacuum (via outlet **20**) within chamber **16** and leak fluidizing gas into the vessel through inlet **18** by means of an appropriate valve (not shown). The leaked-in gas is regulated to provide fluidization within chamber **16**. A sufficient vacuum is retained within chamber **16** to maintain a vapor pressure equivalent to 4 mm of mercury or less. In the operation of the apparatus of the drawing, liquid food such as orange juice, coffee, tea, etc., is introduced into chamber **16** through conduit **22** and spray nozzle **24**.

FIGURE 4.2: APPARATUS FOR FLUIDIZED BED PROCESS

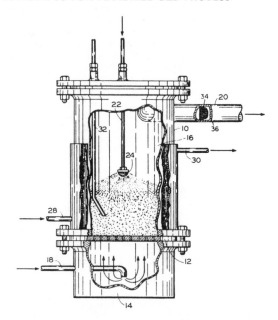

Source: G.F. Sachsel and W.H. Mink; U.S. Patent 3,319,344; May 16, 1967

Spray nozzle **24** is preferably one that is disposed to provide a fine spray onto the fluidized bed of inert particles. Such spray should be directed downwardly and outwardly; however, care should be taken that droplets do not impinge on the sidewalls of vessel **10** prematurely or prior to their solidification. In accordance with the process, since the vapor pressure within chamber **16** of vessel **10** is at or below the equivalent of 4 mm of mercury the water base liquid spray droplets will either solidify or vaporize as they enter chamber 16. Where a fluidized bed of inert particles is employed within chamber 16, as shown by the single figure of the drawing, the liquid spray will coat the individual particles with frozen liquid food which immediately begins to freeze dry. Where inert particles are not employed within chamber 16, the spray and fluidizing gases may be regulated so that the spray droplets freeze to form a sleet-like fluidized bed. The frozen moisture of individual particles immediately begins to sublime. The spray from nozzle 24 is preferably very fine and as stated above should not cause the liquid to impinge on the side of vessel 10 prior to freezing. The spray itself will, of course, tend to change the total pressure and the pressure of water vapor within chamber 16 so that compensating vacuum and fluidized gas flow adjustments may be required.

The freeze dried product which coats inert particles may be recovered from the fluidized bed by removing the particles from the bed and agitating to abrasively separate the freeze dried product from the inert particles. It has been found that such particles generally abrade one another while in the fluidized state to remove the freeze dried coating while within the bed of vessel 10. Such freeze dried organic materials are of light weight and fine size and consequently flow from vessel 10 through outlet 20. To collect and recover the fines it is expedient to position an appropriate filter (shown in the breakaway portion 36 of outlet 20 at 34) within the conduit leading from outlet 20 to the vacuum pumps. By regulation of total pressure, spray velocity and fluidization gas velocity, freeze spraying and sublimation may be effected irrespective of temperature. It is desirable to elevate the temperature within chamber 16 to facilitate sublimation or vaporization of the ice crystals; however, if too high a temperature is employed the sublimed food may burn or scorch.

Electromagnetic Induction Heating

A. van Gelder; U.S. Patent 3,253,344; May 31, 1966 provides a process for the dehydration of products such as solutions, suspensions, colloidal suspensions, and pulps of any kind, by subjecting such products to a series of steps to transform the same into a dried powder-like end product which can be reconstituted with either cold or hot water into a form having substantially the same properties as the original product.

Initially it is desirable to prepare the product by bringing it into a state of solution, suspension, colloidal suspension, and/or pulp, consisting of finely divided solids and liquids. Thus, if the end product is dehydrated orange juice, the juice is prepared by conventional squeezing. Products capable of being processed by the method need not be limited to products brought into a state of solution, but also include concentrations of such products where part of the moisture or other substances have been previously removed, and larger particles or chunks of the products.

The second step of the process consists of dividing the product into small particles preferably by introducing the product into any type of commercially available spraying equipment by means of nozzles or rotating disks, bowls, or rotors of any size or shape capable of dividing the product into small particles.

The third step of the process is to freeze the small particles of the product to produce a powdered snow-like product. The third step may be combined with the second step by locating the spraying equipment inside of a chamber and subjecting the particles to a flow of cold gases having a temperature sufficient to freeze the particles substantially instantaneously upon contact therewith. An alternate method of freezing is to bring the particles into intimate contact with cold surfaces which are maintained at a sufficient temperature to cause the particles to freeze while the particles are being constantly agitated to prevent their sticking to the surfaces. The prepared material can also be frozen by immersion into a cryogen and then pulverized into powdered form, although this adds an extra step. Any method of quick freezing is entirely satisfactory which will produce a frozen powder or snow-like product.

The next step in the process is introducing the frozen particles into a low temperature mixing chamber containing small pieces of metal, preferably in the form of spheres or balls, which may be made of any suitable metal and are preferably coated with Teflon or any other suitable type of material to prevent the frozen particles from sticking to the metal or the coating. The mixing chamber and metal spheres or balls are preferably cooled to a temperature below the freezing point of the particles before the particles are introduced in order to prevent the particles from melting upon coming into contact with the spheres. The spheres and the frozen particles may be thoroughly agitated (though this is not necessary) to further prevent the frozen particles from sticking to the spheres during the period of residence.

It is also possible to combine this step with the previous step, in that the particles may be frozen while spheres are being cooled in the same mixer, during which time the mixer is agitated in order to keep the particles from sticking to the spheres until the particles are frozen, at which time the agitation of the mixer continues to thoroughly distribute the spheres throughout the frozen particles.

In the next step of the process the frozen particles and spheres are introduced into a chamber in which a high vacuum is drawn. While the frozen particles and the spheres are being subjected to the high vacuum, the spheres are subjected to electromagnetic forces which will produce induction heat in the spheres, and this heat is transferred to the frozen particles by means of conduction and radiation. This heating of the particles creates a differential vapor pressure between the particles and the vacuum which effects evaporation of the moisture in the particles and results in their dehydration. It will be appreciated that the intimate contact between the frozen particles and the spheres causes a uniform heat transfer from the spheres to the frozen particles, thereby resulting in rapid dehydration of the particles.

It has been found that this process enables a much greater quantity of material per unit volume to be processed than normally found in freeze vacuum drying due primarily to the intimate contact between the spheres and the frozen particles to thereby make the process much more economical than other processes heretofore used. The final step in the process is releasing frozen particles and spheres from the vacuum chamber and screening the frozen particles from the spheres. The frozen particles are then packed or subjected to further treatment, as may be desired, and the spheres are preferably cleaned and returned to a suitable receptacle for reuse.

The essential elements of this process can be applied to products having a larger particle size and not in the form of suspensions, colloidal suspensions and pulps. Also, while the dehydration described takes place in the presence of a pressure lower than atmospheric, simple dehydration by induction heated means at atmospheric pressure is included.

Process at Atmospheric Pressure

In accordance with the process of *G.J. Malecki; U.S. Patent 3,313,032; April 11, 1967; assigned to U.S. Secretary of Agriculture* freeze drying is conducted not under vacuum but at ordinary (normal) atmospheric pressure. Many significant advantages are achieved in a practice of this process including faster rate of dehydration, more uniform dehydration of individual particles, and a substantial saving in equipment costs because the apparatus may be of lighter and simpler construction.

In the preferred embodiment of this process, the liquid starting material is formed into frozen droplets by conducting the freezing in cooperation with the drying step. In brief, the technique involves using cold gas emanating from the drying zone as the refrigerant to freeze the incoming spray of liquid material to be dried.

Having formed the frozen particles, these are arranged to form a bed thereof. A predried gas is injected upwardly through the bed to maintain it in a fluidized condition and to dehydrate the particles while they are maintained in the frozen state. It is especially to be noted that this dehydration step is not under vacuum, but is conducted at essentially nor-

mal atmospheric pressure. Despite the absence of a vacuum, the desired result of dehydration is attained because the injected gas, being in a predried condition, has a moisture vapor pressure below the moisture vapor pressure exhibited by the material under
treatment. This difference creates a driving potential which causes the ice in the material to sublime (pass directly to the vapor state). The evolved moisture vapor is carried
away by the stream of gas.

Also, under the conditions of strong turbulence and intimate contact between the dry
gas and the suspended frozen particles in the fluidized system, moisture removal becomes
very efficient. Furthermore, the movement of the dry gas and particles sweeps moisture
vapor away from the particles much more effectively than is obtained in a vacuum system. This efficient removal of vapor from a turbulent surface markedly accelerates the
drying rate.

With reference to Figure 4.3a orange juice is sprayed from nozzle **4** into upper (freezing)
chamber **1a**. Cold nitrogen (or air, CO_2, N_2O, etc.) at about minus 40°F is rising countercurrently from below fluidized bed **9** and in zone **1a**, freezes the falling droplets of
juice to solid particles. These solid particles drop down to zone **1b**, forming bed **9**.
The size of the droplets is regulated, preferably to about 0.05 to 0.1 mm in diameter,
and the flow of gas is adjusted accordingly to maintain the fluidized state in bed **9**, as
well as to maintain proper freezing of the incoming liquid droplets.

FIGURE 4.3: FREEZE DRYING AT ATMOSPHERIC PRESSURE

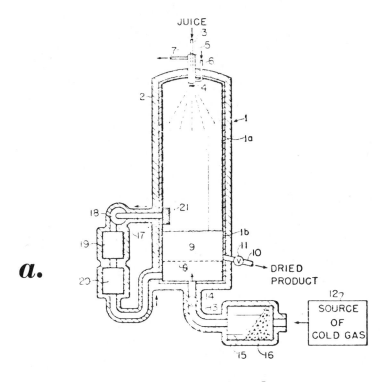

Preliminary Freeze Dryer

(continued)

FIGURE 4.3: (continued)

b.

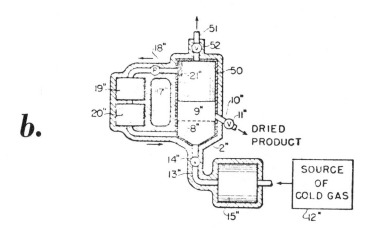

Fluidized Bed for Final Drying

Source: G.J. Malecki; U.S. Patent 3,313,032; April 11, 1967

The rate of cooling gas flow should be large enough to freeze all the droplets to below the eutectic point of the material under treatment, but not so large as to carry away the majority of the smaller size droplets. In order to be able to correlate the rate of flow of gas through the freezing chamber, there is provided the recirculation system of conduit 17 and associated components. Any excess or deficiency of gas going into the freezing chamber 1a can be removed or supplemented by this recirculation or by-pass system. During operation heat exchanger 20 may be activated to heat or cool the recirculating gas stream to the appropriate temperature level (about minus 40°F, in this particular example).

As noted hereinabove, the gas flowing through bed 9 effects a sublimation of ice from the frozen particles. The evolved vapor is carried away by the gas stream and eventually absorbed by drier 19. The process may be continued until the orange juice particles are completely dried, or preferably, the process is continued until their moisture content is about 10%. This product is then withdrawn via conduit 10 and may then be further dried by the system shown in Figure 4.3b.

The apparatus shown in Figure 4.3b is intended for the freeze drying of material which was preliminarily dried in apparatus according to Figure 4.3a, or in a conventional vacuum freeze drying unit. The device includes a drying chamber 50, provided with a conduit 51 and a valve 52 located at the top of the chamber. The various other parts of the apparatus are as in the modification of Figure 4.3a and are indicated by the same reference numerals with a double prime sign.

In operation, the frozen, partly-dried particles are introduced into chamber 50, forming bed 9". Cold dry gas is circulated through the bed, keeping it in a fluidized state and effecting the dehydration. During the operation, heat exchanger 20" may be activated as required so that the gas reentering the drying chamber is warm enough to effect the sublimation of ice yet not so warm as to cause thawing of the frozen particles. Fresh, dry, cold gas (N_2, air, CO_2, etc.) as may be needed is fed into the system from source 12" via conduit 13", drier 15", and valve 14". Excess gas may be vented via valve 52, valve 11", or both. After the product has been dried to the desired extent, it is withdrawn via conduit 10" and valve 11". In a preferred system of applying the process, the dehydration is conducted in two phases. It is initiated in the device of Figure 4.3a and when the material is partly dry it is transferred to the device of Figure 4.3b and the drying completed therein. The primary advantage to be gained by this procedure is that the porous structure of the particles is set by the preliminary drying. Therefore, a higher gas temperature (with higher rate of dehydration) can be applied in the final drying without damage to the particles. Thus, for example, whereas in a particular instance the initial dehydration may require a temperature as low as –30°F, the final dehydration may be at a more elevated temperature of about –5° to –20°F.

SPRAY DRYING

Spray Drying Liquid Concentrate

According to the method of *F.P. Hanrahan; U.S. Patent 3,222,193; December 7, 1965; assigned to U.S. Secretary of Agriculture* a liquid food is pasteurized, concentrated to about 40 to 50% solids to produce a liquid food concentrate, the concentrate is forced under a first pressure into a mixing zone, an inert, relatively insoluble gas at a pressure in excess of the first pressure is injected into the concentrate in the mixing zone to produce in the mixing zone a concentrate uniformly supersaturated with respect to the gas, and the gas-concentrate mixture is conducted to a spray drying zone and spray dried.

In the process there is a marked decrease in the bulk density of the particles to be dried compared to the density of the particles in the normal spray drying process. This lowered density is obtained by spraying a concentrated liquid food into the drying chamber as relatively large droplets of foamy or puffed material.

The process provides a method of foam preparation by injecting gas into the liquid to be dried an instant before the newly formed foam is actually sprayed. When gassing or foam production in the concentrate before drying is achieved as in the process the particles remain in orbit for relatively long periods of time, thus providing unique drying results. The process is demonstrated to be applicable to spray drying acidic liquid foods such as tomato, grapefruit, and orange juices, and represents an improved spray drying process for liquid foods in general.

Concentrates for use in the preparation of food products are prepared by conventional procedures of pasteurization, homogenization if required, and removal of water by standard economical procedures such as vacuum pan evaporation, to a degree of concentration which will allow free pumping, preferably to about 40 to 50% solids. Pumping is facilitated by forewarming (preheating) the concentrate, preferably at a temperature between approximately 130° and 190°F.

Example 1: Tomato juice, pasteurized and concentrated to 45% solids, was spray dried as follows. The concentrate was heated at about 130°F and pumped with a high pressure reciprocating pump operating at 1,800 psig into the gas injector and mixing chamber. Nitrogen gas was injected into the gas injector and mixing chamber using 2,000 psig pressure at a uniform rate. The combined flow of gas and whey concentrate mixture was sprayed into the dryer.

The spray dryer was a commercially available nine-foot model of a cyclone type. The concentrate flow rate into the mixer was 60 gallons per hour and the gas flow rate was 120 standard cubic feet (at 2,000 psig) per hour. The nozzle opening was 0.040 inch diameter. The temperature of the dryer air was 260°F.

The product was a free-flowing powder, although the temperature of the dryer air caused discoloration. As demonstrated in the following example, acidic fruit juices can be dried in this process using dryer air at markedly lower temperatures.

Example 2: Concentrated grapefruit juice obtained from a commercial source was adjusted to 45% solids and forewarmed to 130°F. The forewarmed concentrate was pumped with a high pressure reciprocating pump operating at 1,800 psig into the gas injector and mixing chamber. Nitrogen gas was injected into the gas injector and mixing chamber using 2,000 psig pressure at a uniform rate. The combined flow of gas and grapefruit juice concentrate was sprayed into the dryer described in Example 1. The concentrate flow rate into the mixer was 25 gallons per hour and the gas flow rate was 120 standard cubic feet per hour. The nozzle opening was 0.025 inch diameter. The temperature of the drying air was 190°F. The grapefruit juice powder had a moisture content of 2 to 3% and particle size ranging from 30 to 100 microns.

Example 3: Orange juice concentrate at 45% solids was spray dried following the procedure and conditions of Example 2 and gave an orange juice powder with moisture content and particle size similar to that of the grapefruit juice powder. Microscopic examination of the particles from the various examples showed them to be generally sphere-shaped, foamed or puffed material or agglomerates of two or more spheres of foamy solids.

The products of the process have the advantages of larger particle size, important in ease of reconstituting the dried product, and of more complete removal of water under any given condition of dryer temperature, thus providing a more stable product.

Quick Freezing Using Liquid Nitrogen Followed by Lyophilization

A.P. Rinfret, C.W. Cowley and W.J. Timson; U.S. Patent 3,228,838; January 11, 1966; assigned to Union Carbide Corporation describe a method and apparatus for quick-freezing orange juice in droplet form and lyophilizing the frozen droplets. The resulting product was reconstituted with water to yield juice of satisfactory taste. The following example illustrates the process.

Example: Droplet Freezing of Orange Juice in Liquid Nitrogen — 40 ml of orange juice were frozen in droplet form. Droplets of diameters from 0.5 to 2 mm were formed by spraying from a container under a few pounds air pressure. The frozen droplets were then stored in liquid nitrogen to await further treatment.

One or two cubic centimeters of the frozen droplets from each freezing unit were transferred from the liquid nitrogen to small flat trays in flasks kept at –77°C. The flasks were attached to the lyophilizing unit containing liquid nitrogen and immersed in methyl Cellosolve baths at –77°C in Dewar flasks. The Cellosolve bath was then allowed to warm over the ensuing 24 hours while the orange juice droplets were being dehydrated under a pressure of about 25 to 35 microns.

The flasks were then removed from the Cellosolve bath while still attached to the lyophilizing unit. Shortly thereafter the flasks reached room temperature and were then removed from the apparatus. The dried droplets were placed in a desiccator. A sample of the dried droplets was reconstituted with water and tasted. The orange juice flavor appeared intact.

Rapid Freezing of Liquids to Eliminate Structural Damage

One of the important steps in the freeze drying process is the freezing of the material which is to be dried. The freezing has been accomplished in a variety of ways, including freezing in conventional refrigeration units before placement of the material in the drying installation. Also, freezing of the material is sometimes done directly in the drying chamber itself by, for example, producing a sudden pressure drop within the chamber to cause surface evaporation freezing of the material. Other freezing methods have been utilized which provide a desirable enlargement of the surface area on the frozen material.

The enlarged surface area provides a greater surface from which sublimation can occur, thereby reducing the time required to complete drying of the material. One method of this type involves freezing of liquids in rotating containers wherein the centrifugal forces cause the material to be frozen in relatively thin layers against the inner walls of the containers. Also known is a method in which the liquid material to be frozen is dispensed in a thin layer on a refrigerated surface from which the material is detached by a scraping operation after having been frozen thereon. Still another method introduces liquid material drops onto the surface of a cold liquid medium having a low freezing point such as, for example, methylene chloride, fluorinated hydrocarbon derivatives, petroleum distillates, etc. The frozen pellets formed in this way provide large surface areas for sublimation. However, none of the above methods has proven entirely satisfactory for freezing certain sensitive materials. With such materials, the above methods of freezing apparently produce some type of structure changes in the material to be dried resulting in an inferior final product. Also, many prior methods entail high refrigeration costs or produce a frozen material which requires relatively long drying times and are thereby economically impractical for high-volume freeze-drying installations.

The object of the method of *K. Kautz; U.S. Patent 3,281,950; November 1, 1966* is to provide a process for freezing materials to be freeze dried which is rapid and economical in its execution, which does not produce structural damage in the material being frozen and which results in a frozen material which can be completely freeze dried in relatively short drying times.

In this process a liquid or fluid substance to be freeze dried is introduced into a gas-tight chamber containing a cooled gas. The fluid substance is preferably introduced in the form of a spray composed of small droplets. The nozzle mechanism used to introduce the substance into the gas-tight chamber is adapted to provide substance droplets of a certain maximum size. The maximum size is related to the size of the chamber, the point of substance introduction, and the temperature and pressure of the gas contained so as to effect freezing of the substance droplets by contact with the cooled gas before reaching the inner wall surfaces of the gas-tight chamber.

The freezing process requires an extremely short time, and the frozen particles produced thereby are without any form of structural damage. The frozen particles are easily handled and can be readily filled into the various types of material containers used in conventional freeze drying installations. Furthermore, the frozen particles offer extremely large sublimation surfaces and a multitude of hollow passages into the interior of the accumulated material. These factors allow rapid drying of the material by conventional freeze drying methods. Materials which can be frozen and dried in this manner include various organic and inorganic materials which are liquid or fluid in their natural form or which can be changed into liquid or fluid form by means of suitable solvents. Suitable materials include fruit juices.

In a preferred embodiment of the process the quantity of cooled gas contained in the gas-tight chamber is such as to provide a substantially greater than atmospheric pressure. The high pressure increases the molecular contact between the cooled gas and the substance introduced and correspondingly increases the heat transfer therebetween. In this way, the time required to freeze the substance droplets can be reduced. It is also desirable in many applications to utilize within the gas-tight chamber an oxygen-free cooling gas. In this way, undesirable oxidation of the substance being frozen can be prevented.

In this regard, an inert gas such as, for example, nitrogen can be advantageously utilized. An improved result can also be obtained with some organic substances by using a gas such as, for example, sulfur dioxide, which actually provides a preservation effect on the substance being frozen. In other applications, the use as a composite cooling gas formed by a mixture of suitable oxygen-free gases such as, for example, nitrogen and sulfur dioxide is effective. A suitable boost gas can be combined with the fluid substance before injection of the mixture into the gas-tight chamber by a suitable spray nozzle. The boost gas serves as a dispersing agent for the fluid substance producing substance droplets of the required size. In this way, simple injection nozzles may be utilized without a requirement for a mechanical structure, such as impact surfaces or centrifuges, to induce dispersion of the fluid substance.

To further aid in the dispersion of the fluid substance and to also produce desirable cooling of the fluid substance during injection into the gas-tight chamber the boost gas can be compressed before combination with the fluid substance. This desirable effect can also be accomplished by causing compression of the already combined boost gas and fluid substance before introduction of the mixture into the gas-tight chamber.

The compression of the boost gas before injection of the mixture into the gas-tight chamber is especially desirable where the substance being processed is an especially viscous material such as, for example, molasses. The process can also utilize the cooling gas itself as the boost gas to be combined with the fluid substance. To this end, a closed gas circulation loop which includes the gas-tight chamber can be provided for continuously withdrawing the cooling gas from the chamber, combining it with the fluid substance and injecting the resulting mixture back into the gas-tight chamber. In this operation, the above described compression step can be practiced by providing a compressor in the closed loop either before the combination of the boost gas and fluid substance or after the combination, but in any case before injection of the mixture into the gas-tight chamber.

One Step Spray Process

This process relates to freeze drying, and more particularly to a spray freeze drying system wherein solids containing liquid is pressure sprayed into a vacuum freezing chamber, whereupon the atomized droplets of liquid freeze and fall as frozen particles into a vacuum drying chamber. Perfectly dry particles of the solids emerge from the drying chamber, without having been wet during the drying process. When employed with substances amenable to spray freeze drying treatment, such as fruit juice, the spray freezing process, when followed by freeze drying provides a number of advantages.

In the first place, handling costs are reduced, because the process lends itself to continuous operation. No loading trays or the like are required, because the solid bearing liquid is pumped continuously into the freezing chamber. The dried particles, which can have a very fine texture, reconstitute with water to provide a product superior in taste to similar products dried by other processes.

With the system employed by *E. Thuse, L.F. Ginnette and R.R. Derby; U.S. Patent 3,362,835; January 9, 1968; assigned to FMC Corporation* the total time during which the product is under treatment, commonly referred to as the residence time, is but a fraction of the residence time employed in other freeze drying processes. Since during the drying process, the ice core becomes surrounded with a shell of dried solids, if this material is heat sensitive (and heat must be supplied to reduce the residence time to a commercially acceptable value) then undue prolongation of the residence or treatment time may result in partial deterioration of certain qualities of the dry product, such as taste, enzyme content, or the like.

The spray freeze drying system is essentially a one step process, in that the solids bearing liquid is spray frozen in one unit of the system, whereupon the frozen particles pass directly to a freeze drying unit of the system, and hence out of the system through an air lock.

The basic elements of the freeze drying system are illustrated diagrammatically in Figure 4.4. The major elements of the system include a freezing chamber 10 connected to a drying chamber 12, the outlet of which is connected to an air lock 14, that delivers dried material to a receptacle 16. The freezing chamber 10 includes a pressure withstanding vessel 18, which is fitted with a false hopper bottom 20.

Surrounding a major portion of the side wall of the vessel 18 is an annular array of internally lined or jacketed refrigerated condenser coils 22, which are of sinuous construction in accordance with conventional practice. It is these coils that abstract the heat of melting and of vaporization from the liquid product. Refrigerant is circulated through the coils 22 from a refrigeration unit illustrated generally at 24, the details of which are conventional and form no part of the process. In the refrigeration system, a refrigerant inlet line

26 leads from the refrigeration unit to the condensing coil 22 by way of an expansion valve 28. The usual refrigerant return line 30 returns the refrigerant to the refrigeration unit, for condensing and recompressing in the usual and conventional manner. A temperature gauge 31 indicates the condenser coil temperature.

FIGURE 4.4: ONE STEP PROCESS FOR SPRAY FREEZE DRYING

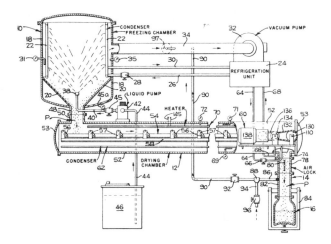

Source: E. Thuse, L.F. Ginnette and R.R. Derby; U.S. Patent 3,362,835; January 9, 1968

Since the drying process must be carried out under a relatively high vacuum, a vacuum pump 32 is connected to the vessel 18 of the freezing chamber 10 by means of an exhaust line 34. The vacuum pump primarily removes noncondensible gases, such as air or the like, because the water vapor sublimed from the product during the freezing operation is condensed to form frozen particles by the refrigeration coils 22. A gauge 35 indicates the pressure in the freezing chamber.

The liquid to be freeze dried, such as coffee extract, fruit juices, or the like is atomized into a fine spray within the freezing chamber 10 by a spray nozzle 38. The nozzle is supplied with the liquid by means of a pressure line 40, a pump 42, and a supply line 44, which receives liquid from a reservoir 46. A valve 45 controls the spray nozzle pressure, as indicated by a gauge 45a. The outlet of the freezing chamber 10 is in the form of a neck 48, which makes an air tight joint with a neck 50 projecting upwardly from the inlet end of the drying chamber 12.

The drying chamber 12 comprises an elongated drying vessel or tube 52 closed at each end with removable end plates 53. In order to support the product particles during the drying operation, and to conduct the product through the drying chamber 12, a longitudinally extending pan or tray 54 is mounted in the drying chamber. The pan 54 is supported along its length on angularly disposed links 56 which are pivoted at their lower ends to the pan 54, and which are suspended from posts 57 projecting upwardly from longitudinally extending angle irons 58 that are mounted within the drying chamber 12.

The pan 54 is given a vibratory movement by a vibrating drive assembly indicated generally at 60, the details of which will be described presently. In order to condense the water vapor that is sublimed from the frozen particles of product P, as they progress along the pan 54 in the drying chamber, a condenser 62 is mounted below the pan 54. As shown, the condenser 62 is in the form of sinuous coils connected to a refrigerant inlet line 64, by means of an expansion valve **66**. A refrigerant return line **68** is also provided and the refrigerant is circulated through the condenser **62** by the refrigeration unit **24** previously referred to. The condenser temperature is measured by a thermal device and indicated on a gauge **69**.

In order to supply the heat of sublimation necessary to dry the product **P**, as it progresses along the pan **54** in the drying chamber **12**, a longitudinally extending heater assembly **70** is mounted above the pan **54**. The heater **70** is in the form of an electrically heated blanket of conventional construction, and its temperature is measured by a thermal device and indicated on a gauge **71**.

A high degree of vacuum is maintained in the drying chamber **12** because of the connection to the freezing chamber **10** by way of necks **48** and **50**, previously described. The vacuum pump **32** normally removes only noncondensible gases from the drying chamber **12**, because the water vapor sublimed from the product **P** during the drying process is condensed by the condenser **62** in the drying chamber **12**. The dried product falls through an outlet neck **74**.

Experience with the freeze drying of solid bearing liquids has shown that the geometry of the link mounting for the pan **54** is somewhat critical. If these geometry factors are under selected, the product will not move fast enough through the drying chamber to give the desired short residence time within the chamber. If the factors are over selected, the product will be vibrated out of the pan or if not, will advance too rapidly through the drying chamber so that the product will not be completely dried by the time it reaches the air lock **14**, at the delivery end of the pan.

With heat sensitive products, which also tend to be somewhat sticky, certain critical dimensions and speeds for the vibrating assembly have been developed. In the apparatus, it has been found that the angle which the links **56** make with the horizontal plane should be substantially 65°. As a result, the average direction of pan motion is at the same angle of 65° with the vertical plane. Although the length of the links **56** is not critical, at the angle of 65°, a length of two inches for the links has been satisfactory. The horizontal amplitude of vibration is ¼ inch total, which means that the eccentric **114** has a ⅛ inch offset or stroke.

The speed of rotation of the vibrator shaft **110** is 500 rpm. This imparts a maximum horizontal acceleration to the particles or product **P** of 0.80 g, and a maximum vertical acceleration to the particles of 0.37 g. Thus, although the particles progressively advance along the pan, they do not jump or dance clear of the pan, or from one another, during the process.

Quick Freezing to Produce Porous Ice Chunks

A. van Gelder; U.S. Patent 3,477,137; November 11, 1969; assigned to Sun-Freeze, Inc. describes a method for the preparation of liquids, with or without entrained solids, for subsequent dehydration, by feeding the product into a closed chamber under high vacuum with rapid vapor removal so that there is instantaneous freezing of the material into porous ice chunks, which are simultaneously broken into smaller sizes from pea size to powder, the frozen form being porous in nature throughout.

The frozen pieces are then moved through the chamber subjected to the same vacuum vapor removal, care being exercised to insure that no more than 80% of the moisture content is removed by the time it reaches refrigerated storage or passes on for further and final dehydration. The entry of the material must be from the bottom of the treating chamber through an elongated opening, the feed being drawn by the suction of the low pressure in the chamber, interrupted only, if desired, by a proportioning device.

A cube of ice has only six exposed sides. Should this cube be porous, a very large surface area becomes exposed. It is therefore an object of this process to produce ice-containing solids of great porosity so that when they are subjected to heat under high vacuum, the water vapor can pass from any part of the cube to its surface easily, thereby providing more rapid dehydration.

Figure 4.5 shows a schematic vertical layout of the plant for making and holding the frozen porous product which is preliminary to vacuum dehydration with an extension into two units shown in broken lines.

FIGURE 4.5: QUICK FREEZING TO YIELD POROUS ICE CHUNKS

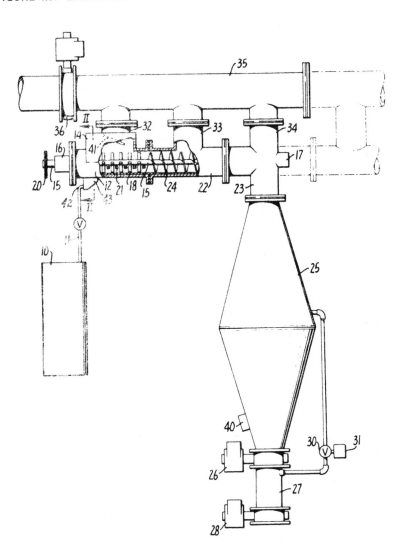

Source: A. van Gelder; U.S. Patent 3,477,137; November 11, 1969

Operation of the plant is as follows. The liquid, whether it is clear, colloidal or solids in suspension, is fed from the supply tank 10 upwardly through the line 11 into the feed chamber 43, through the elongated slot 44 and into the chamber 12 and swept by the pins 18. If the flow is to be metered a proportioning pump may be used, but this is not usually necessary. At this point the liquid passes from room temperature into the vacuum maintained in the system of from 2,000 to 100 microns of mercury. A vacuum above or below this range is exceedingly difficult to handle and make the apparatus function, and certainly operating outside of this range affects the efficiency of the unit.

At the moment of entry through the slot 44 there is a flash freezing or instantaneous freezing, the product almost literally explodes into ice clusters or chunks of a porous nature, to the extent that at least 15% of the vapor is eliminated from the product at the moment of entry into chamber 12. The rapid freezing is caused by a massive and rapid evaporation which process removes the heat from the liquid resulting in a differential vapor pressure between the liquid and the vacuum.

This evaporation continues until the dew point of the operating pressure is reached. For example, at a pressure of 100 microns of mercury the product will continue evaporating until it has reached a temperature of about minus 40°F which temperature is reached almost instantaneously upon delivery to the tube. Of course, the removal of water vapor continues in chambers 12, 22 and 23 until the frozen product has 80% or less of the moisture removed. In liquids with entrained solids if more than 80% of the moisture is removed then the product becomes taffy-like and cannot be moved.

On the other hand, when a liquid is undergoing treatment, if more than 80% of the moisture is removed, it becomes so light and feathery that it is removed by the vapor flow through 33 and 34 and is lost. The vapor from chamber 12 is taken off through the connection 32 to the manifold 35 and then to the condenser. There is a momentary buildup of ice chunks, the expanded volume of which is temporarily accommodated by the box 14. The water vapor in leaving the ice chunks so rapidly creates vapor channels throughout and the entire chunk becomes sponge-like with a noticeable porosity.

The rotation of the pins 18 in combination with the stationary pins 21, continuously breaks up any buildup of the chunks, which are readily friable, into granules sized from powder to pea size. Each granule, like the chunk, is laced with channels left by the removal of the vapor so that the particles themselves are also porous. Because of the explosive and ebullient nature of the instantaneous freezing of the product, a baffle 45 is provided at the top of chamber 14, shielding the opening to vapor take-off 32, to prevent inadvertent removal of the frozen product and separate the frozen product from the vapor take-off.

The manner of delivery of the product to the chamber 12 is of unexpected and critical importance. In the first place the slot 44 provides a self-clearing or releasing means which does not freeze up and stop operation. Certain areas within the slot may freeze and block part of the passage for a short time but the warmer entering liquid through the remainder of the slot soon frees the material and thus self-cleaning is accomplished.

This phenomenon is aided by the observed nature of the instantaneous freezing of the entering material. The instantaneous freezing under high vacuum is so violent and explosive that only the top portion of each increment of feed is thus frozen, leaving a liquid base forming the next increment. This means that there is always liquid feed in the chamber 43 and very nearly always in the feed slot 44.

Under the operating conditions defined herein it would be quite impossible for the feed to be otherwise than at the bottom or otherwise than a slot. The material enters the chamber 12 at substantially zero velocity and is instantaneously subjected to the operating conditions. There is no appreciable or deleterious buildup of a frozen skin inside the chamber 12 or frozen chunks within the chamber and blades or spikes 18 and 21 are not primarily scrapers but perform their real function of breaking up the immediately formed ice chunks into smaller sized pieces and particles. The broken ice chunks in the form of frozen particles or pieces are then delivered by the screw conveyor **24** through the chamber **22** where they are again subjected to removal of water vapor under vacuum. It is to be observed that there is constant movement of the particles and pieces through the chambers **12** and **22** due to the vapor velocity plus the continued decrease in specific gravity. The vapor from chamber **22** leaves through the connector **33** to the common manifold **35** and then to the condenser (not shown). The capacity of this equipment is determined by the speed at which the water vapor can be removed.

Therefore, the larger the vapor removal opening, the greater the capacity of the equipment. This same movement by screw conveyor **24** through chamber **23** continues and at the same time is being subjected to vapor removal under vacuum with high velocity. As indicated earlier, no more than 80% of water vapor is removed, and so this is not to be construed as a dehydrating method or apparatus.

Upon delivery at the end of chamber **23** the frozen porous particles drop into a holding tank or bin **25** and pack down in the bottom thereof. Any heat coming from the outside of the tank **25** may cause some melt but this melt is refrozen and the water vapor of the refreeze is removed through the tank as this tank is under the same vacuum and connected by connector **34** to the common exhaust manifold **35**.

The delivery of the frozen porous product from the tank is accomplished through the air lock valve **26** into the passage **27**. Since the tank **25** is already under the same vacuum conditions as the entire system, in order to equalize the vacuum in the tank with that of the conveyor line **27**, it is necessary to have a valve **30** operated by a solenoid to keep the negative pressures equalized in the system. It is important to note that the product delivered at **23** can be connected directly to a continuous dehydrating system.

The pressure of the pack in the bottom of the tank **25** is sufficient to block the free flow of the frozen porous particles into the line **27**. A vibrator **40** may be attached to the outside of the tank adjacent the air lock valve **26** to loosen any packing of the material. The frozen porous products in granular form are released through air lock valve **28** for subsequent treatment and dehydration.

Snowflakes Dropped Directly to Conveyor

E.L. Rader; U.S. Patent 3,616,542; November 2, 1971 describes freeze drying equipment and methods in which a liquid such as a fruit juice is sprayed into a refrigerated chamber, maintained under a high vacuum, and is frozen into small preferably snow-like particles or flakes before the liquid can fall onto any surface in the chamber, following which the frozen particles fall downwardly onto a conveyor in the lower portion of the chamber, and are advanced slowly along the conveyor while heat is supplied to the particles in a manner subliming moisture from them.

In the apparatus, the liquid is sprayed into a freezing region, and frozen into small particles, in a relation and under conditions such that most of these particles (desirably all of them) fall downwardly directly onto a conveyor in frozen form, and without being permitted to first contact any other surface in the apparatus. Thus any possibility of even gradual buildup of frozen material on a surface such as the lower funnel or chute portion of the freezing chamber is avoided.

The conveyor then advances the particles generally horizontally through a sublimation region and toward a discharge end of the apparatus, with heat being supplied to the particles as they move slowly along the conveyor, to thereby sublimate moisture from the particles while they remain frozen. The conveyor desirably vibrates, in order to periodically bounce the particles upwardly away from the conveyor surface, to thereby continuously expose a maximum amount of the surface area of the particles, and attain maximum freedom for evaporation of liquid from all of the particle surfaces.

Spray Drying with Steam Current

There exist processes for drying by spray freezing, in which the liquid to be dried is sprayed in the form of fine droplets into a partially evacuated chamber in which the pressure may for example, be of the order of 100 to 500 microns of mercury. On entering the low-pressure zone, the fine particles freeze during their fall and should normally be in solid state by the time they come into contact with a wall of the chamber. The frozen particles are then dried by subliming the liquid diluent in a suitable freeze drying chamber.

In practice, operation of the process described above has certain disadvantages which have considerably restricted its industrial application. Thus, the formation of fine particles involves an atomization of the liquid under high pressure. The particles are formed in a stream which originally moves at high speed and since its path lies in a vacuum, there is no resistance to their falling motion within the chamber. As a consequence it frequently happens that the liquid particles hit one of the walls of the chamber before they have been frozen to a solid state and thus stick to the wall, which leads to losses in production.

To overcome this particular problem, attempts have been made to lengthen the trajectory of the particles, as by increasing the height of the chamber or by spraying the liquid upwards rather than downwards. Neither of these improvements has proved to be entirely satisfactory for efficient industrial operation since dry products could only be obtained from dilute solutions generally not containing more than about 20% by weight of solids. Problems of a different nature had also arisen in that the rapid cooling of the liquid on entering the vacuum caused it to freeze and frequently plug the nozzle through which it was sprayed.

A.R. Mishkin and W.S. Symbolik; U.S. Patents 3,633,283; January 11, 1972; and 3,620,776; November 16, 1971; both assigned to Societe D'Assistance Technique Pour Produits Nestle SA, Switzerland describe a process for drying liquids, containing up to 60% by weight of solids, which comprises spraying the liquid into a zone of subatmospheric pressure in a current of a gaseous fluid thereby to form frozen particles of the liquid and subsequently freeze drying the frozen particles.

The method provides an apparatus suitable for carrying out the process comprising a freezing chamber, means for maintaining subatmospheric pressure within the chamber, means for spraying a liquid into the chamber simultaneously with a current of a gaseous fluid, means for evacuating and condensing vapors generated within the chamber and at least one freeze drying chamber.

As shown in Figure 4.6a the apparatus comprises a vertical freezing chamber 1 of metal construction, with cylindrical walls and conical bottom. The dimensions of the chamber may, for example, be three meters in diameter and ten meters in height. At the upper end of the freezing chamber is mounted a spray system comprising a two fluid nozzle 2 and feedlines 3 and 3a for supplying, respectively, the solution to be dried and the gaseous fluid which is preferably steam.

At the bottom of the chamber is a hopper 4 if the chamber is directly connected to a freeze drying chamber 25 or an airlock if the freeze drying chamber is not directly connected. This chamber 25 may be of any desired type or construction, and in particular, it may be a continuous or batch unit, including the usual ancillary equipment such as condensers, heating platens, vacuum pumps and the like.

Ducts 6 connect the lower part of the chamber to condensers 5, disposed symmetrically. These may be 2, 4 or 6 in number, depending on their dimensions and those of the chamber. A valve 7 is mounted on each duct so that each condenser may be individually isolated for cleaning or defrosting without necessarily breaking the vacuum within the chamber. The condensers 5 are also connected by ducts 8 to a vacuum system 9 comprising one or more pumps of adequate capacity to maintain an absolute pressure within the freezing chamber of 50 to 500 microns. When steam is used as the gaseous fluid, the pumping

FIGURE 4.6: SPRAY DRYING WITH STEAM CURRENT

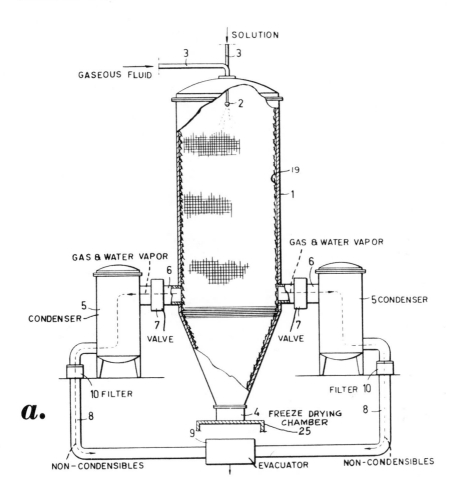

Freezing Chamber with Ancillary Equipment

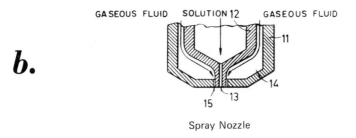

Spray Nozzle

Source: A.R. Mishkin and W.S. Symbolik; U.S. Patent 3,633,283; January 11, 1972

system need not be excessively large since the water vapor formed can be condensed out of the system and need not be pumped. A filter 10 is mounted on each duct 8 between the condenser and vacuum system to trap any fine particles which may have been sucked out of the chamber.

Freezing of the particles of liquid formed at the upper end of the chamber 1 should be rapid. When the liquid to be dried is a coffee extract containing 30 to 50% by weight of dissolved coffee solids, the particles should be frozen solid after a free-fall lasting about 0.5 to 1.5 seconds. Particles of a tea extract of similar concentration require about 0.5 to 1.0 seconds.

Furthermore, in order to obtain an even dispersion of the liquid, that is, a uniform particle size, it is generally necessary to spray at a high pressure. This would lead to a jet of high-velocity particles, directed downwardly and encountering no notable resistance during the fall. Under these conditions, the time of fall within a chamber of reasonable dimensions would be too short to ensure complete freezing of all particles.

The liquid is sprayed at a relatively low pressure, and dispersion is obtained by the action of a current of gaseous fluid, preferably steam, which is sprayed from the same nozzle as the liquid. The fluid, for example, steam, is sprayed in the form of an annular curtain surrounding the liquid jet, and the paths of the jets meet at a short distance from the nozzle, and the liquid jet is broken up into fine particles on impact with the jet of steam. The particles then have a sufficiently long path of fall within the chamber 1 to ensure their complete freezing.

Figure 4.6b shows a preferred spray nozzle. It comprises an outer sleeve 11 which surrounds a central spray jet 12. The jet 12 is fed with solution through line 3 which is sprayed through orifice 13, for example, at a pressure of 0.2 to 0.4 kg/cm^2 in the form of a conical sheet. Steam, supplied to the nozzle by line 3a, passes through the annular space 14 between the sleeve 11 and the spray jet 12, for example, at a pressure between 0.5 and 2.5 kg/cm^2, and enters the chamber through the annular orifice 15. As shown in the drawing, the orifices 13 and 15 lie in the same horizontal plane.

According to a feature of this process, the annular curtain of gaseous fluid is injected into the chamber more or less vertically and thus it meets the conical sheet of liquid at a short distance below the nozzle, which prevents the liquid from spreading outwards in the direction of the sidewalls of the chamber. Furthermore, this particular arrangement of the steam and liquid jets prevents formation of frozen liquid deposits at the nozzle opening which would lead to an irregular particle size and ultimate plugging of the jet.

In order to ensure that no liquid particles stick to the inside walls of chamber 1, a permeable flexible member 19, for example of nylon net, may be disposed within the chamber. Such a lining may be shaken to dislodge any attached particles, and it also serves as a filter preventing particles from entering the ducts 6. In operating the process, three factors have to be considered in order to determine optimum conditions of freezing, notably the absolute pressure within the chamber and the solids concentration and temperature of the solution being dried.

The absolute pressure within the chamber, measured in microns of mercury, should be maintained below the vapor pressure of the eutectic present in the solution which freezes at the lowest temperature. In general, the pressure will usually be below 500 microns, but may be lower in certain cases.

The density of the finished product may be adjusted by incorporating a small amount of a gas, such as nitrogen or carbon dioxide in the spray solution, but in general this is not necessary. Sublimation of the frozen diluent present in the solution to be dried commences in the freezing chamber and the resulting vapors are evacuated from the chamber and condensed, together with those generated when the liquid boils on first encountering the low pressure within the chamber. Sublimation of the diluent is completed in a freeze drying chamber. When the freeze drying installation is directly connected to the freezing chamber, some of the ancillary equipment, notably condensers 5 and vacuum system 9 may be shared by both the freezing and the freeze drying chambers. The process and apparatus described herein are especially suitable for drying sensitive materials such as fruit juices and the like containing 20 to 60% by weight of soluble solids.

CONTINUOUS PROCESSES

Minimum Aeration and Elimination of Foaming

Continuous vacuum drying equipment has been built and has been used commercially for drying at temperatures above the freezing point. It typically comprises a straight, flat, continuous belt (for supporting and conveying the material during drying) that reverses direction by passing over a drum or roll at each end and is contained within a vacuum chamber.

This equipment has not been used successfully for freeze drying because of the lack of a satisfactory feeding method. The feed must be frozen before exposure to the vacuum of the chamber in order to minimize volatile flavor losses. Furthermore, for liquid feeds, prefreezing eliminates foaming which interferes with subsequent heat transfer. The primary object of this process is to feed material continuously to a freeze dryer and, moreover, to prefreeze the material to the desired operating temperature before exposure of the material to the vacuum of the chamber.

The purposes of the process of *R.M. Stinchfield; U.S. Patent 3,218,731; November 23, 1965; assigned to Arthur D. Little, Inc.* are to feed material continuously to a freeze dryer, to prefreeze the material to a desired operating temperature before exposure to the vacuum of the chamber, to positively exclude air from entering the chamber when the feed material is liquid and to minimize air introduction when feed material is solid, to eliminate undesirable foaming which occurs when liquid feeds are introduced unfrozen, and to provide intimate contact of the feed material with the belt or other continuous surface for better subsequent heat transfer.

In accordance with this process the liquid feed material is introduced through an extended flat housing disposed along a short portion of the top of the dryer belt or other continuous surface forming therewith a freezing chamber. The feed is frozen on the belt or surface while in the housing and before being subjected to the vacuum of the vacuum chamber, even though the belt upon which it is deposited is contained within the vacuum chamber.

Refrigeration means are positioned beneath the belt and opposing the extended flat housing. The housing is provided with top and three sides, but no bottom. However, in use, it is open only at the end toward which the belt is traveling because the three sides are in a sliding seal contact with the belt.

The liquid feed is frozen prior to emerging through the open end of the housing, at which point it acts as a pressure seal to prevent air or excess feed from entering the vacuum chamber. An added advantage of this process is that the feed material has intimate contact with the belt by being frozen to it and will thus have better heat transfer characteristics in the subsequent drying.

Figure 4.7a represents a side view partly in section of the apparatus. Figure 4.7b represents a top view of interior of the apparatus taken along line 2—2 of Figure 4.7a. Figure 4.7c represents an end sectional view of the apparatus taken along line 3—3 of Figure 4.7a and Figures 4.7d, 4.7e and 4.7f show sectional details of various arrangements and modifications of the housing and refrigerating means.

Vacuum chamber 11 is provided with a continuous belt (or equivalent continuous surface) 15 moving over roll 17 which is mounted on axes 19 and driven in any appropriate manner. The belt is of good heat conductivity, e.g., of aluminum or stainless steel. A similar roll (not shown) is located at the other end of the chamber, together with any suitable means such as a scraper blade for removing the dried product. This dried product may be taken out of the vacuum chamber through any suitable air locks. Adjacent the end of the belt near roll **17** is located refrigerating means shown generally by the numeral **21**. This is provided with inlet **23** and outlet **25** for introducing and removing refrigerating fluid **27**. On the opposite side of belt **15** is the extended flat housing generally represented by the numeral **31**, and forming with belt **15** a freezing chamber. This housing is fed through conduit **33** projecting through the wall of the vacuum chamber **11**.

FIGURE 4.7: MINIMUM INTRODUCTION OF AIR AND ELIMINATION OF FOAMING

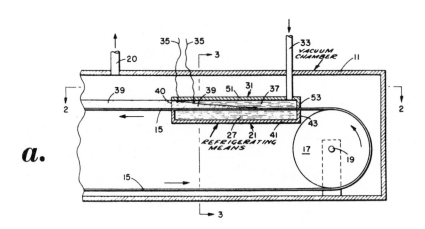

a.

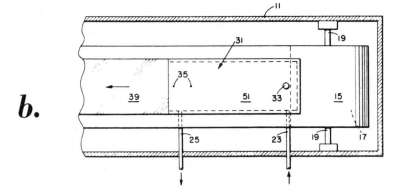

b.

(continued)

FIGURE 4.7: (continued)

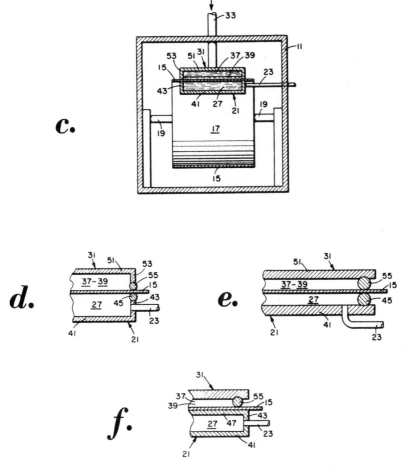

Source: R.M. Stinchfield; U.S. Patent 3,218,731; November 23, 1965

Thermocouples **35-35** may be provided if desired at appropriate places along the top of housing **31**. The feed enters in the form of liquid **37** and becomes frozen as it travels along the belt and through the housing toward the exit end **40** thereof. This frozen product is represented by the numeral **39**. The refrigerating means **21** consists generally of a bottom plate **41** and sides **43** which confine the refrigerating fluid **27** against the bottom of the belt **15**.

The sides **43** may be provided with low friction edges **45** (Figures 4.7d and 4.7e). These low friction edges, as shown in Figure 4.7e, may constitute the entire side wall of the refrigerating means **21**. Alternatively the refrigerating means **21** may be entirely enclosed as shown in Figure 4.7f. Such a refrigerating means would have a top plate **47** attached to walls **43** all around. The housing **31** consists of a top plate **51** and sides **53** which extend all around except at exit end **40**. As in the case of the refrigerating means, these sides may have low friction edges **55**, which may constitute part of the sides as shown in Figure

4.7d or the entire sides as shown in Figures 4.7e and 4.7f. The top 51 may be made of transparent material in order to observe the progress of the liquid and frozen product through the housing; however, this is not necessary and the thermocouples 35 can be used instead to determine the condition of the feed material as it progresses through the housing.

It is obviously important that the sides of the housing should fit tightly against the belt, in order to prevent escape of liquid or gases into the vacuum chamber. The placement of refrigerating means 21 directly opposite the housing 31, as shown, is a preferred method of accomplishing this result. The low friction edges 45 and 55 may be made of polytetrafluoroethylene or similar low friction materials. The feed liquid may be precooled, even to slush form, prior to introduction through feed conduit 33. It may also be under partial vacuum, but insufficient to effect any substantial evaporation of the water phase. The housing 31 must obviously be long enough and the refrigerating means 21 adequate, to effect freezing of the liquid feed before it reaches the end 40 of the housing. At that point the frozen feed 39 will fill the end of the housing and effectively block any escape of liquid or gas from within the housing out into the vacuum chamber.

Desiccation of Frozen Particulates at Early Stage

A primary object of the method of K.H. Seelandt; U.S. Patent 3,290,788; December 13, 1966 is to provide a process and apparatus for low temperature desiccation of soluble, or primarily soluble and insoluble organic materials in liquid solution which is susceptible to continuous operation. A related object is to provide a method of initially freezing the liquid material into frozen particulate solids and ice, while simultaneously removing some of the liquids contained water; and yet further to freeze the particulates in such a manner as to concentrate the remaining water (ice) at or near the outer periphery of the frozen particulate solid, while partially desiccating the particulates interior.

A further object is to spray and freeze the liquid material so that pores, vents and cracks occur in the outer periphery of the particulates to facilitate later water vapor removal. Another object is to freeze the liquid material instantaneously at very low temperatures to effect transport of water from the interior of contained cells while forming the water into ice in the interstices between the cells, thereby avoiding cell rupture due to expansion of frozen water (ice) within the cells as occurs at slower freezing rates.

Still another object is to provide an improved freeze drying process which is capable of effecting the desired drying in a minimum amount of time. Yet another object is to provide a freeze drying process which will produce extremely porous, discrete, amorphous or spherical particulate solids having a large surface area and a low bulk density, which are capable of being rehydrated without any loss of flavor and aroma.

A still further object is to provide a freeze drying process wherein the radiant heat for sublimation is provided at a specific wavelength which will pass through most organic products, but not through ice; thereby permitting a maximum of intensity of heat for sublimation to be applied throughout the freeze drying operation without danger of scorching or burning the organic material and thereby facilitating speedier sublimation of the ice. A yet further object is to provide means for accelerating water vapor removal from the particulate surfaces during the freeze drying operation.

A feature of the process is to provide a method and means whereby soluble, or primarily soluble and insoluble organic materials in water or other liquids are freed of the bulk of moisture or liquids in an early stage, and particulate matter surfaced with ice is recovered substantially free of moisture or liquid in a later stage.

Another feature of the process is to provide a process as defined in the preceding paragraph wherein a high velocity jet stream of gas having a temperature below the freezing point of the organic liquid solution is utilized to disintegrate the organic liquid solution into a fine mist of moisture forming a very substantial portion of the liquid, and into particulate solids coated with ice. A related feature is to remove the moisture mists in the form of microcrystalline particles of ice at an early stage of the process, and to remove the frozen particulate solids at a later stage of the process. A further related feature of this process is to concentrate the organic material and ice at or near the outer periphery of the frozen particulates and to remove the surrounding ice at a later stage in the process. A still further feature of the process is to provide effective steps and means for the removal of residual moisture in the particulate matter.

Still another feature of the process is to provide processing apparatus and method steps for providing an economical super-cooled process gas, and recuperating the gas by substantially removing its contained moisture while maintaining a super-cooled temperature to facilitate reuse of the recuperated super-cooled gas in the process.

A still further feature of the process is the provision of fluid bed apparatus including: a hollow vessel having heat transfer means including a wall structure means within the vessel defining a plurality of columns; grid means adjacent to the heat transfer means; means for introducing a particulate substance into the vessel through an inlet means; means for fluidizing the substance in the heat transfer means; means for heating the wall structure means; and means for removing the substance from the vessel through an outlet means. A related object of the process is to utilize a fluid bed apparatus described above in a process for desiccating organic materials.

The methods and apparatus embodying the process have four distinctly different operational stages which can be described in chronological sequence as: the liquid transport and discharge stage; the liquid freeze-disintegration-evaporation stage; the final desiccation stage, which may be by gas ejection-sublimation, by vacuum radiation-sublimation, by fluidized bed evaporation, or by combinations of each of these steps; and, a fourth stage embodying the gas supply and recuperation system.

Examples are cited in the patent for the process as applied to strained orange juice and strained tomatoes to yield the desiccated solids which readily reconstituted to the corresponding juices.

Continuous Process Using Induction Heating

The process of *A. van Gelder; U.S. Patent 3,316,652; May 2, 1967; assigned to Sun-Freeze, Inc.* provides a method and apparatus for the dehydration of products such as solutions, suspensions, colloidal suspensions and pulps of any kind, by subjecting such products to a series of steps to transform the same into a dried powder-like end product which can be reconstituted with either hot or cold water into a form having substantially the same properties and characteristics as the original product. For example, if the product to be dehydrated is orange juice, the dried powder would be reconstituted with cold water in order to provide a mixture having substantially the same taste, coloring, texture, enzyme and vitamin content as the original orange juice.

Initially it is desirable to prepare the product for treatment and bring it into a state of solution, suspension or colloidal suspension consisting of finely divided solids and liquids. The product used here for illustrating and describing the process is orange juice and the juice is prepared in any conventional manner such as squeezing.

With reference to Figure 4.8, the juice 10 with its natural pulp is fed into an attrition mill 11 where the solids, whether in suspension or solution, are reduced to finely divided form. The juice with its finely comminuted solids is then fed into an homogenizer or colloid mill 12 for further preparation where it is converted to a suspension which flows into a holding tank 14. Preferably the holding tank, if circumstances require, is cooled by refrigeration. From tank 14 it is pumped by a proportioning pump 15 to an atomizer or spray nozzle 16. The atomizer or spray nozzle 16 may be stationary or rotating and of any suitable size as is conventional in this art. The controlled flow from the proportioning pump 15 is necessary in order to feed the material at a rate so that it freezes instantly

FIGURE 4.8: CONTINUOUS PROCESS USING INDUCTION HEATING

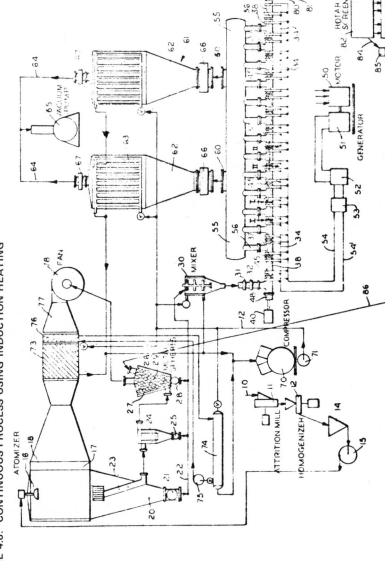

Source: A. van Gelder; U.S. Patent 3,316,652; May 2, 1967

upon atomization. The atomizer **16** is preferably a high speed rotary atomizer capable of dividing the fluid into small particles. It is located within a cylindrical vessel or chamber **17** which is cooled internally by a flow of cold air or other gas, tangentially introduced at **18** to cause a spirally rotating pattern within the chamber **17**.

The gas introduced is precooled well below 0°F by apparatus which will hereinafter be described, so that the atomized small particles of the product are instantaneously frozen upon contact with the cold gas. Any method of quick freezing of these particles is entirely satisfactory and it should be noted that generally, the quicker the freezing process the better the final product. Atomization of the homogenized material is not necessary as any means for reducing it to a frozen powder or snow-like product is quite satisfactory for the performance of this step.

The frozen particles spiral downwardly by gravity into the conically shaped bottom portion **20** of the chamber **17**. From here they are continuously discharged through an air lock device or star valve **21** into the line **22**. The cold air or other gas is discharged from the chamber **17** by means of a duct **23** which is connected to a separator **24** where any entrained or remaining particles of the frozen product are separated from the cold gas.

The collected frozen particles are removed from the separator **24** by means of a star valve **25** at the bottom of the separator and pass into the main line of flow **22**. The cold air discharged from the separator **24** is delivered to another chamber **26** which is made with a perforated spaced inner jacket **27** of substantially the same shape and slope as the outer shell of the chamber **26**. Within the perforated jacket **27** are pellets made of a suitable conducting material such as metal, carbon, graphite and the like, and preferably in a form of spheres or balls **29**, although other geometric shapes which provide a substantial surface area may be used.

Regardless of the shape, it is preferable to coat such conducting spheres or balls **29** with a suitable plastic material such as Teflon in order to prevent any possible contamination to the product and to prevent the product from sticking to the pellets themselves. The pellets may be solid or hollow but are shown in the drawings as spheres as a matter of convenient reference. The spheres **29** are cooled in the chamber **26** by the cold gas from the separator **24** so that they attain a temperature below the freezing point of the frozen particles which are in the line **22**. This is so that when the spheres **29** contact the particles in the line the particles themselves will not melt upon the contact.

A predetermined quantity of the spheres **29** is measured out of the chamber **26** through the valve **28** and into the line **22** so that they are delivered together with the frozen particles to the mixer **30**. The mixer **30** is cooled likewise to a temperature below the freezing point of the particles to maintain their frozen state. It is also under continuous agitation with the spheres **29** to maintain a uniform proportion between the spheres and the particles and to maintain the particles in a frozen state.

The spheres **29** are used for the purpose of obtaining a large surface area in direct contact with the frozen particles being processed. For example, when the pellets or spheres are one-half inch in diameter and arranged side by side in layers, one cubic foot of these would represent a total surface area of 75.36 square feet. The interstices available for the product would represent some 46% of the same cubic foot occupied by the spheres.

Should the ratio be changed so that 60% of the cubic foot would be occupied by the product then the possible surface area of the spheres for contact with the product would be 64.81 square feet. Thus, it is plain that by changing the proportion of the spheres per cubic foot, it is possible to mathematically change the surface area available for contact with the frozen particles. The maximum surface area of spheres for the maximum volume of frozen particles, i.e., not less than 60%, is the operating requirement for this process.

The frozen particles and the spheres **29** in proportion from the mixer are discharged into the vacuum apparatus through two air locking systems **31** and **32** which are preferably butterfly valves or slide valves. The upper or first air lock **31** operates in sequence with the second air lock **32**. As air lock **31** opens dropping the frozen particles and pellets into the small chamber while the second air lock **32** remains closed, air lock **31** then closes and second air lock **32** opens to allow the product and the pellets to pass into the vacuum chamber **33** in which a high vacuum is maintained.

The vacuum chamber **33** is preferably a long tube which may be placed either horizontally or vertically, but preferably in the horizontal position. It is made up of a succession of T-shaped segments **34** made of glass or any other suitable dielectric material. The cylindrical segments are T-shaped with a radial vent or take-off pipe **37**. These segments are removably joined in a linear series with couplings (not shown) to provide air and bubble-tight seals preserving the vacuum within the chamber **33** while at the same time providing a means for quick access for disassembly of any of the T-sections **34** for purposes of cleaning or replacement as needed. The tube, of course, is sealed at both ends by caps **48**.

The radial vent **37** is of sufficient cross-sectional area to allow all evaporative products to escape from the chamber **33** at the lowest practical velocity and with the minimum turbulence. Inside the segmented lengths of the chamber **33** there is means for continuously conveying the product being processed and the mixed spheres through the length of the chamber.

Each screw section **38** is removably joined in a continuous helicoidal pattern to each other screw section by means of any suitable coupling. The helical or screw type conveyor has the advantage of continuously causing the spheres **29** to rotate or tumble and move while still contacting the material under treatment, so that as the mixture is moved through the chamber **33** new surface areas of the material are continuously exposed to the particles. The conveyor means, regardless of type, however, is preferably formed of a dielectric substance including suitable plastics and the like when the strength requirements permit. The drive mechanism **40** is a variable speed drive so as to permit control of the speed of conveying the mixture through the chamber **33**.

Chamber segments **34** have induction heating means surrounding the same in the form of coils **45** which are wrapped around the exterior thereof. The induction heating means may be a pancake coil wrapped around only a portion of the segments **34**. The coils may be tubular so as to permit the circulation of a coolant therethrough in order to maintain the coils at a constant temperature with the desired constant electrical resistance, allowing large currents to pass through the relatively small coils without undue heating.

Oscillating electrical current is passed through the electrical conducting coil means by means of a transformer at controlled frequencies. The frequency may be at line frequency or higher by means of electrical generators with frequencies up to 20,000 cycles per second, or by means of radio-frequency generators to about 1 megacycle per second. The heat to the system may be controlled manually or automatically by variations in the vacuum pressure or product temperature within the chamber **33**. To supply the required current motor **50** is provided which drives generator **51**. Although the coils **45** are shown electrically connected by lines **54** and **54'** in parallel, they may also be connected in series as this is dependent upon the particular application involved.

As the frozen product particles and spheres pass through the vacuumized tube **33** the spheres **29** are subjected to the variable electromagnetic forces emanating from the induction coils **45**. The emitted energy passes through the dielectric walls of the chamber segments **34** inducing secondary eddy currents in the spheres **29** which causes them to heat. This heat is transferred through the close contact by conduction and radiation to the frozen particles of material as they are being carried along in continuous contact with the spheres through the vacuumized chamber **33**.

The vacuum causes the boiling point of the product to be lowered by decreasing the vapor pressure. To keep the product frozen the vacuum pressure must equal the saturated vapor pressure of the product below its freezing point. It is therefore desirable that the vacuum pressure be as low as possible commensurate with economy of operation. The application of heat to the frozen product under vacuum causes the product to boil or lose its moisture by sublimation. The very large surface of heating area provided by the spheres in the intimate contact with the large surface area of the particles enables a large amount of heat to be absorbed by the particles in a very short time producing a rapid and efficient dehydration which is even further enhanced by the agitation produced during passage of the mixture through the chamber 33.

The vapors and moisture from the dehydration from within the chamber 33 pass through the ducts 37 and their air and bubble-tight connection with the corresponding manifold radial members 56, into the manifold 55. The manifold has a sufficient cross-sectional area to maintain the velocity of the vapor at a reasonable level. From the manifold they pass through the large ducts 60 into the condenser system 61 through the operation of the vacuum pump 65.

The water vapor is relieved of its moisture in the condenser system by precipitation and frost formation on the refrigerator coils or plates 63. The condenser coils or plates 63 have a surface temperature below that of the dew point temperature of the product caused by the vacuum pressure. The condenser system 61 is connected to a vacuum system by lines 54 which lead to the vacuum pump 65.

To make this process continuous, two or more condenser systems 61 are operated in parallel, one being in operation while the other is being defrosted from the ice precipitation on the refrigerated coils or plates 63 caused by the moisture coming from the vapor. To accomplish the isolation of the condenser from the vacuum system while it is being defrosted, each condenser is isolated from the manifold 55 and the pump 65 by two valves 66 and 67. These are preferably butterfly valves or slide valves. It is apparent that suitable control means are provided to control the temperature of the refrigerated coils or plates 63, to stop the flow of refrigerant to the coils, to switch on the defrosting device operated by means of electricity and to close and open the valves 66 and 67.

It is further apparent that conventional control means may be used so that one or more of the condensing systems is in operation while one or more are being defrosted. While one type of condensing system is shown, it is to be understood that any suitable system for removing the moisture vapors may be used in connection with this process so long as it is available for operation on a continuous basis.

The refrigeration for the system is supplied by a compressor 70 operably connected to a refrigeration condenser 71 which is cooled either by air, water or evaporation. The refrigerant is circulated directly through line 72 with suitable valving to the condenser coils or plates 63, to the mixer 30, and to the refrigeration coils 73. The refrigerant is also circulated through a heat exchanger 74 through appropriate valving. The brine in the heat exchanger is pumped by pump 75 to the condenser 76 in the cooling chamber 77. The cold air or gases supplied to the freezing chamber 17 is cooled by means of one or more refrigerating coils 73 in the cooling chamber 77 which is maintained at a temperature well below the freezing point.

The secondary refrigerated coil 76 is maintained at a temperature just above freezing to remove excess moisture from the air or gas which would otherwise accumulate in considerable quantity on the freezing coil 73. A fan 78 provides the required volume and pressure of air and gas and has its outlet operably connected to the chamber 77. Its inlet end is operably connected to the chamber 26 thereby making the entire cooling system one continuous unit.

The final steps in the process include the releasing of the dehydrated particles and spheres from the vacuumized tube 33 through air locks 80 and 81 which operate sequentially in the same fashion as the admitting air locks 31 and 32. The dehydrated particles at room temperature and atmospheric pressure are separated from the spheres 29 in the rotary screen 82 or in any other suitable manner. The dehydrated product is delivered to means

83 for conveying it to other stations for packaging and storage. The spheres are recovered from the rotary screen by line 84 and are cleaned in any suitable manner at 85. The cleaned spheres are then returned to line 86 to the perforated container 27 in chamber 26 for continuous recycling through the system.

Continuous Freeze Drying of Thin Sheet on Moving Belt

J.L. Mercer and L.A. Rowell; U.S. Patent 3,648,379; March 14, 1972 disclose a method and apparatus for the continuous freezing and freeze drying of solids-containing aqueous liquids to obtain a freeze dried product. The feed liquid is frozen as a thin sheet on a continuously moving belt and is broken to form discrete pieces which are further reduced in size prior to freeze drying. The frozen particles are moved on a chilled multistage vibratory conveyor in an evacuated chamber wherein refrigerated condensers and radiant energy sources cooperate with the conveyor to sublimate the ice content of the frozen particles to form a freeze dried product.

The vibrating conveyor is constructed to minimize transfer of vibratory forces as well as the effects of changes in length of the conveying sections as a result of temperature change. The system operates continuously to receive the liquid feed, to discharge the freeze dried product, and to separate and remove ice collecting on the condensers. The system functions to accomplish the freezing and freeze drying operations in the relatively short period of from 40 to 110 minutes.

Carbon Dioxide Refrigerant

A continuous process is provided for the freeze drying of an aqueous solution whereby the solid content in the solution is recovered as finely divided product of low unit weight per unit of volume. Carbon dioxide is utilized as the refrigerant because it is relatively inert and can be brought into direct contact with various foodstuffs without the formation of undesirable compounds which would adversely affect the taste, odor or color of the dried product.

Further, the relatively high vapor pressure of carbon dioxide at ambient temperatures makes its complete removal from the dried product feasible. Additionally, carbon dioxide can be maintained in the liquid state at temperatures above the freezing point of water at relatively low pressures, e.g., about 600 pounds per square inch absolute. The adiabatic expansion of liquid carbon dioxide results in the conversion of the liquid to a mixture of solid carbon dioxide and gaseous carbon dioxide.

The process of *A.S. Guerard; U.S. Patent 3,673,698; July 4, 1972* includes mixing of liquid carbon dioxide with the solution to be processed. For example, this can be accomplished by mixing the liquid carbon dioxide at a pressure of about 600 pounds per square inch absolute and at a temperature of about 40°F with the solution to be processed so that freezing of the water in the solution does not occur. Following creation of the commingled feed and carbon dioxide at a temperature above the freezing point of water at the existing pressure, the pressure on the mixture is then rapidly reduced as by release through an expansion valve.

To achieve this, the mixture can be flashed into a vessel wherein the gaseous carbon dioxide is also separated from the solid crystals which form. The finely divided crystals which are formed consist of carbon dioxide and frozen feed stock. The solid crystals are then fed to a second vessel wherein the water ice and carbon dioxide are removed as by a suitable procedure. The final crystalline material is of such small particle size that the solid material behaves as a liquid, thereby making possible the utilization of the fluid bed technique to fluidize the crystals.

Dry gaseous carbon dioxide is passed through the fluidized bed, the water present as ice subliming to water vapor which is carried away by the carbon dioxide gas which is fed to maintain the fluidized bed and the carbon dioxide which sublimes from the crystals.

Referring to Figure 4.9, the solution to be converted to a solid state is contained in feed tank **6** where it is maintained in a homogenous state by the mixer **7**. Additional material is provided through the fill connection **8** as desired. Liquid material is withdrawn from the feed tank through line **9** and is passed through a heat exchanger **11** wherein heat exchange occurs with a stream of water vapor and carbon dioxide vapor in line **12**. The feed material in line **9** is cooled by heat exchange **10** to about 40°F. The material in line **9** is forced by pump **14** through line **16** to a mixer **17**.

FIGURE 4.9: CARBON DIOXIDE REFRIGERANT

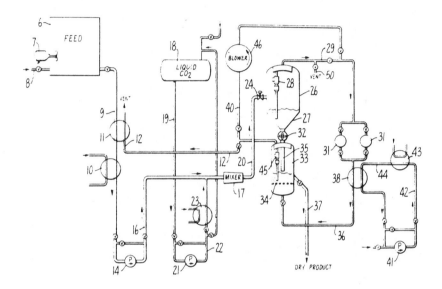

Source: A.S. Guerard; U.S. Patent 3,673,698; July 4, 1972

Liquid carbon dioxide is derived from a tank **18** and is fed through line **19** to a pump **21** which in turn forces the liquid carbon dioxide on through line **22** through heat exchanger **23** into line **16** ahead of the mixer **17**. Mixer **17** serves to mix the two liquid streams quite thoroughly before they are passed through line **20** to expansion valve **24** provided immediately adjacent a first pressure vessel **26**. In pressure vessel **26**, crystals are formed of solid carbon dioxide, water ice and the frozen solid contained in the water fed to the process.

The crystals settle in the cone shaped bottom **27** of vessel **26**. The carbon dioxide which does not solidify is removed through cyclone separators **28** and is passed through line **29** to dryers **31**, a portion being vented as desired as at **50**. Preferably the dryers are provided in parallel and contain a conventional drying agent such as silica gel, phosphorus pentoxide, activated alumina, calcium sulfate, or magnesium perchlorate, as well as those materials conventionally known as molecular sieves which are aluminosilicates or zeolites, the crystal of which contains minute pores and which have the ability to absorb relatively large volumes of water vapor. The dryers are operated sequentially, one being reactivated while the other is in use.

The crystals which collect in the bottom **27** of vessel **26** are fed through a power operated star valve **32** and pipe **35** into a second vessel **33** which includes a grid or screen **34** adjacent the lower end thereof. Dry carbon dioxide gas from the driers **31** is fed through line **36** into the bottom of vessel **33** to pass upwardly and fluidize and maintain the solid particles on the screen **34** in a fluidized state. Conventional cyclones or centrifugal separators **45** are provided in vessel **33** to prevent removal of solids from vessel **33**. A portion of the sublimed water vapor and carbon dioxide vapor is vented through line **12** from the upper portion of the vessel **33** while the solid dried material is removed as the product through line **37**.

That portion of the mixed stream of sublimed water vapor and carbon dioxide which is not vented through line **12** is removed through line **40** and is passed to line **29** to ensure the presence of an adequate quantity of carbon dioxide for sublimation of the ice in vessel **33**. Line **40** derives its stream of water vapor and carbon dioxide from cyclone separators **45** in vessel **33**. Blower **46** is provided to increase the pressure in line **40** to a value equal to that in line **29**.

The temperature of the stream of carbon dioxide gas issuing from the driers **31** through line **36** is controlled by utilizing heat exchanger **38**. Methanol, glycol or other low freezing point liquid is forced through a circulatory system which includes pump **41**, line **42** passing to an heat exchanger **43** and then through line **44** to heat exchanger **38** to regulate the temperature of the dry carbon dioxide stream passing on to vessel **33**.

In a typical operation, utilizing a relatively heavy aqueous coffee infusion or syrup for illustrative purposes, the syrup was fed continuously through line **9** by pump **14** and was delivered to line **16** at a pressure of 600 pounds per square inch absolute and 40°F. Carbon dioxide derived from vessel **18** at a temperature of –20°F and 200 pounds per square inch was fed to pump **21** and through heat exchanger **23** for delivery to line **16** at the same temperature and pressure, that is, 40°F and 600 pounds per square inch absolute.

The liquid mixture so formed was in the ratio of 1.8 pounds of carbon dioxide per pound of water present in the aqueous solution. The resultant mixture was then fed to the expansion valve and was permitted to flash in vessel **26** which was at a pressure of approximately 20 pounds per square inch. The pressure in vessel **26** exceeded that in vessel **33** by the amount sufficient to provide the pressure drop through the driers and piping. The dried coffee product was removed through line **37**.

FOAM DRYING PROCESSES

Use of Frozen Foam

In freeze drying a frozen product, such as frozen fruit juice, it is essential that consideration be given to the fact that the substance may contain as much as 25 or 30% soluble solids. It is also essential that no significant reliquefaction take place during the sublimation dehydration process, because this degrades the quality of the product and the product becomes plastic and/or frothy and difficult to handle.

L.F. Ginnette, R.A. Lampi and J.A. Abbott; U.S. Patent 3,309,779; March 21, 1967; assigned to FMC Corporation report that avoidance of reliquefaction is accomplished by placing the frozen material in a drying chamber in the form of a frozen foam. This foam, in effect, provides a series of interconnected paths, crevices, cracks or the like throughout the entire frozen body, for the ready evolution and escape of water vapor subliming from the ice cores. The result is that adequate heat can be applied to the ice cores of the product for rapid drying without causing the vapor pressure of the ice to substantially exceed about 560 microns of mercury corresponding to an ice temperature of –10°F. Thus, all the advantages of freeze drying are attained without the usual disadvantage in drying the products, namely, long drying time.

Addition of Higher Carbohydrate Solution

Certain fruit juices and syrups, such as apple juice, grape juice, honey, are difficult, if not impossible, to dry by usual methods. The difficulty seems to arise from their relatively high content of monosaccharides, notably levulose, which is highly soluble and highly hygroscopic. High temperatures cannot be employed without losing characteristic flavor. At low temperature the hygroscopicity of the sugars involved, together with their tendency to form viscous syrups, results in prolonging the time required for drying beyond practical limits.

When a fruit juice, such as apple, is dried at low temperature, either by freeze drying or vacuum drying, there is no great problem in removing water by evaporation or sublimation during the early stages of the process. However, when the concentration has reached the syrupy stage, the material becomes difficult or impossible to handle; it bubbles and foams, or loses its initial structure and collapses. While the juice can be dried with a prolonged process from this condition, the end product inevitably reaches the glassy state which can be collected only with difficulty and requires further processing before being usable.

Experience has shown that those materials such as apple juice and grape juice in which levulose comprises more than 25% of the total sugar solids, or those in which invert sugar or dextrose comprises more than 50%, give unsatisfactory yields by freeze drying.

Levulose is the most hygroscopic and soluble of the sugars. As such, it tends readily to inhibit or destroy the formation of a stable foam structure or matrix which is apparently essential for the production of a friable, easily soluble dry product. The establishment and maintenance of such a foam structure or matrix is highly beneficial because it provides increased surfaces for evaporation or sublimation of the water and greatly speeds the drying process.

Dextrose is neither as soluble nor as hygroscopic as levulose and consequently is not as active an antagonist in the preservation of the matrix. However, it does not contribute to the matrix strength and therefore must be considered as at least a passive antagonist.

In order to properly describe the method of this process it will first be necessary to define the nature of the additive employed. The term higher carbohydrates will be used to include any disaccharide as well as higher molecular weight sugars and soluble carbohydrate derivatives of starch hydrolysis. The principal common examples of the group are lactose and corn syrup solids having a relatively low dextrose equivalent.

Lactose is the most desirable of the disaccharides when used as a drying adjunct. Its low solubility promotes crystallization as the drying progresses thus forming adsorptive centers for volatile components as well as contributing rigidity to matrix structure. Its relatively low level of sweetness does not materially change the flavor of the product to which it is added.

The most practical source of other suitable carbohydrates as drying adjuncts is from starch derivatives such as corn syrup, or corn syrup solids. These are mixture of dextrins, polysaccharides, disaccharides and monosaccharides, the proportions depending upon the degree of processing or conversion. Those processed to a low degree of conversion are best suited for this purpose since they contain the least amounts of monosaccharide or dextrose. High conversion corn syrups, which may contain 45% or more of dextrose, are not very suitable. The higher molecular weight components are the desirable fractions since they are less soluble and thus provide the skeleton or framework which will support a stable foam or matrix structure.

In the process of *R.M. Stern and A.B. Storrs; U.S. Patent 3,483,032; December 9, 1969; assigned to Great Lakes Biochemical Co., Inc.* an appropriate amount of the higher carbohydrates is added to the juice or material to be dried, mixed and dissolved as completely as possible, after which drying is carried out in the usual manner. Freeze drying is the preferable manner in most cases, although vacuum drying without prior freezing may be satisfactory in those cases where the material is sufficiently concentrated to permit handling in this manner. To determine the amount of additive required, the proximate composition of the sugars in the material to be dried must be known. The amount of higher carbohydrates to be added depends upon the amount and ratio of the monosaccharides in the original juice.

Higher carbohydrates must be added so that this fraction, including any which may have been in the juice itself, will comprise at least 75% of the levulose or at least 25% of the total monosaccharide content, whichever is higher. This is the minimum amount which can be expected to be beneficial. Best results will be obtained if the higher carbohydrates in the treated juice are adjusted to about 125% of the levulose content or about 75% of the total monosaccharide content, whichever is higher.

While both lactose and corn syrup solids provide a suitable foam structure or matrix for the drying juice, they differ a little in their performance. Lactose, by its nature, tends to impart a more crystalline structure to the foam as it dries and, if used in relatively large amounts, will even restrict foam volume, yielding a rather hard, crystalline end-product. Corn syrup solids tend toward a more amorphous type foam, being increasingly so as the amount of dextrose increases, and exerting less of a limiting effect than lactose.

Example 1: Apple Juice — As indicated previously, untreated apple juice can be dried by freeze drying only with the greatest difficulty, if at all. It requires a long drying cycle and invariably dries only to the glassy state, which cannot be collected or harvested efficiently. While the end-product is soluble, it lacks the instant properties which are desired.

The following series of samples, using fresh, unconcentrated apple juice, demonstrate the favorable results which can be obtained by the use of high carbohydrate additives. In this series the drying equipment was operated at a platen temperature of 200°F for the first 3¼ hours after the initial pull-down to operating vacuum, followed by 2½ hours at a platen temperature of 125°F. Total cycle time was 6 hours. The control sample (no additive) did not dry completely, did not exhibit any puff or foam structure, was glassy with plastic, tacky body at end of cycle.

2% lactose had very slight foam structure, was tacky and not completely dry. 4% lactose had a slight foam structure, was very slightly tacky and not quite completely dry. 8% lactose was dry, had good foam structure and a light, friable body. 16% lactose was dry, had high foam structure and light, friable body. 2% corn syrup solids (24 DE) gave very slight foam, was slightly tacky and not completely dry. 4% corn syrup solids (24 DE) gave slight foam, was very slightly tacky and not quite completely dry. 8% corn syrup solids (24 DE) was dry, had good foam structure and light friable body. 16% corn syrup solids (24 DE) was dry, had good foam structure and light, friable body.

All of the above samples were soluble when reconstituted with water, but those containing 8 and 16% added carbohydrates were more rapidly dissolved than those at lower levels. Inasmuch as fresh apple juice contains approximately 6.6% levulose and about 1.6% dextrose, it will be seen that optimum results were achieved when the carbohydrate additive was equal to at least 120% of the levulose content, or at least 95% of the total monosaccharide content. It will also be observed that the added carbohydrates shortened the time required for drying the juice, a matter of some economic importance.

Example 2: Grape Juice — The sugars of grape juice are monosaccharides, fresh juice containing about 8% levulose and 14% dextrose. As might be expected, this composition indicates that problems will be encountered in drying due to a lack of foam-forming or structural elements. The addition of 20% lactose to grape juice gave very good results with respect to drying. As little as 4% lactose improved drying performance but not sufficiently to be of practical significance. Additions greater than 20% did not appear to have any increased advantages. Malto-Dextrin, a low DE corn syrup product, had about the same effect as lactose except that about half again as much was required for the same degree of improvement. High conversion corn syrup, as typified by material with a 63 DE value, resulted in excessive foaming and poor results. These high conversion syrups contain too much dextrose to be able to supply enough foam structural elements in a system such as that of grape juice. Grape juice is a typical example of the case where the total content of monosaccharides would be the determining factor in selecting the amount of higher carbohydrates to add.

SLUSH FREEZING

Formation of Hard Slush for Extrusion

It has been found by *B.E. Elerath; U.S. Patent 3,637,398; January 25, 1972; assigned to General Foods Corporation* that a fruit or vegetable extract can be prepared in the form of a hard slush and that the hard slush can be extruded in the form of ribbons which retain their shape and can be easily frozen before or after cutting without the necessity of using belt freezers.

Typically the final freezing can be accomplished by extruding the ribbons into a cold gaseous atmosphere at a temperature below the eutectic point of the extract. The gas used can be air but also it may be an inert gas which may afford additional protection to volatile aromatic constituents.

As used herein the term hard slush is intended to describe a mixture of concentrated extract and water ice wherein the ice has been frozen out of the original extract and the viscosity of the slush formed is such that it cannot be readily spread on a flat surface (e.g., a freezing belt). However, the hard slush can be extruded in ribbon form such that the ribbons will not tend to run or spread after extrusion.

The term ribbons as used herein is meant to describe any form such as ropes, rods, bars, etc., which can be continually discharged from an extruder. One of the many advantages of this process is that two dimensions of the final product can be uniformly formed on extrusion. The third dimension of the final particulate matter to be freeze dried is controlled by the means of cutting selected. The process eliminates the need for complex and costly belt freezing systems.

A preferred embodiment of this process is to continually freeze an extract containing 20 to 45% solids by weight of the extract in a continuous manner in order to produce frozen particulate matter suitable for freeze drying. A continuous system is preferred so that the slush being formed (mixture of extract and water ice) can be constantly agitated and moved in a homogeneous mass through an extruder.

It has also been found that small ice crystals are more desirable than large ice crystals in practicing this process, as with a given percentage of ice crystals in the slush, a harder slush is apparently obtained with the smaller ice crystals. Therefore, in practicing this process a continuous scraped surface heat exchanger is used.

The slush formed in the heat exchanger is forced through an extruder. The discharge end of the extruder is a die with openings which conform to the desired product shape. It is necessary in practicing this process to produce a hard slush, such that it will retain its shape after extrusion and be very nearly in a completely solid condition. It has been found that the ice content may be varied from about 20 to 60% by weight of the slush when the extract concentration varies from about 20 to 45% solids by weight of the initial extract.

The desired degree of hardness will result from a combination of increasing viscosity due to the ice crystals being formed and the increasing viscosity of the concentrated extract which constitutes the liquid phase of the slush. Normally the higher the initial solids content in the extract being frozen, the smaller the amount of ice which must be crystallized in order to form a hard slush. The range of concentrations of 20 to 45% solids in the initial extract was chosen for a variety of reasons. The upper limit was selected such that it is sufficiently below the eutectic composition of the extract to permit enough water to be crystallized out in the form of ice to obtain the necessary hard slush. The eutectic composition will vary for different extracts, but for fruit and vegetables extracts the composition is generally above about 70% solids by weight of the extract. Therefore, by eliming the extract concentration to an upper limit of 45%, it is possible to freeze out enough water in the form of ice crystals such that the ice content of the slush is at least 20%. A lower limit of extract concentration of 20% was selected in order to avoid having to freeze an excessive amount of ice in order to obtain a hard slush.

For most extracts, it is believed that 60% ice in the slush will give a satisfactory hard slush wherein the free liquid contains about 50% solids by weight of the extract. If one were to start with 20% extract and form a slush containing 60% ice, the solids concentration in the liquid portion of the slush would be 50%. Also, as a practical matter an initial solids content of less than 20% would be undesirable economically since the object of this process is to produce a product suitable for freeze drying. Freeze drying is an expensive form of dehydration and for most products it would be uneconomical to attempt to freeze dry an extract containing less than about 20% solids.

The hard slush is extruded in the form of continuous ribbons which may be cut before or after additional freezing. A preferred technique is to slice the ribbons into desirable lengths as they are discharged from the extruder and to allow the pieces thus formed to fall through a cold air tunnel in order to completely freeze the pieces to below the eutectic point of the extract.

An alternative method would be to allow the ribbons to completely freeze in a cold air stream and then pass the frozen ribbons through a cutter or grinder. This latter technique will produce particles with a more random size distribution and shape and may be desirable for some products. The shape of the pieces can also be varied by varying the shape of the openings in the extruder die as well as the size of the openings in the die.

This process also offers the possibility of several processing advantages in freeze drying. For example, the shape of the die opening can be irregular in order to achieve particles with a maximum surface area. The greater surface area should result in an increased drying rate and thus increase the productivity of a freeze dryer. Also, the shape of the extruded pieces could be varied to obtain a final dried product with a specific, desired density. Density control may also be achieved by foaming the extract prior to forming the slush or by foaming the hard slush prior to extrusion.

THERMAL SHOCK PROCESS

Discrete Frozen Citrus Fruit Cells

R.C. Webster and E.C. Parish; U.S. Patent 3,246,993; April 19, 1966; assigned to Air Reduction Company, Incorporated and H.P. Hood & Sons Incorporated describe a process for the preparation of frozen discrete citrus fruit cells and their use in combination with other food products. Figure 4.10 is a flow diagram of the process. In this procedure, the fruit is first peeled by any of the conventional peeling methods. This leaves some of the pithy lining of the peel on the outside surfaces of the section membranes (carpellary membranes).

The peeled fruit is then immersed in an extremely cold liquid, such as liquid nitrous oxide at a temperature of approximately -128°F. Liquid nitrogen or liquid air can also be used, or similar liquids of comparable low temperature. In the preferred method, the temperature of the liquid is at least as low as approximately -100°F. The term immersed is used herein to designate a covering of the fruit with a liquid for a limited period of time.

Ordinarily, the immersion will be a dipping of the fruit in the liquid, but it can be a covering of the fruit by spraying liquid on it. When the immersion is by dipping, a number of pieces of fruit can be treated simultaneously by placing them in a wire mesh basket. The period of the immersion should be long enough to freeze the fruit to a solid condition; but it can be longer. A period of nine seconds has been found sufficient with orange sections immersed in nitrous oxide at a temperature of about $-128°$F.

When the fruit is withdrawn from the low temperature liquid, it is found to have been shattered by thermal shock, i.e., extensive separation of the fruit has taken place along the segment walls and between individual juice cells. Sharp, crackling sounds are heard as the fruit is withdrawn from the liquid into an ambient atmosphere at room temperature. This shattering phenomena is not clearly understood. It must result from thermal shock, but it is not apparent to what extent the shattering shock occurs during the freezing, or while the extremely cold fruit is being brought into an atmosphere at much higher temperature.

Both the sudden freezing and the sudden transferring from the extremely low temperature to a higher temperature are believed to contribute to the shattering, but research on the process has not been carried far enough to learn the full extent to which the conditions can be varied while still obtaining such advantageous results.

If the shattering is entirely the result of setting up steep temperature gradients in the fruit, then it appears that some of the shattering occurs at the time of the freezing, and other at the time of withdrawal of the fruit from the low temperature liquid. The shattering occurs even though the fruit has been refrigerated to a temperature of about $34°$ to $36°$F at the time of immersion, and even though the fruit is withdrawn from the liquid to a medium of higher temperature that is considerably lower than room temperature.

When the process is not mechanized, it is an advantage to transfer the fruit to the ambient atmosphere at room temperature because this is the most convenient and economical way for carrying out the method. It is important, however, that further processing be done with the fruit in a solid frozen state; and when any substantial time is required after the dip, the process steps carried out during that time must be done at freezing temperature. Agitation of the shattered sections, while still frozen, causes them to crumble further into individual or discrete juice cells, but the juice cells themselves are not broken and are distinct from one another and individually intact.

Processing of the fruit while in this frozen condition and with the juice cells intact, permits them to be completely separated from each other and from the pithy material, carpellary membranes, seeds and vascular bundles. This eliminates from the frozen juice the substances which have been found to cause objectionable losses in stability and quality.

The agitation or separation can be carried out by passing chunks of adhering cells, on a belt under resilient rollers, or between such rollers. This detaches juice cells from one another and also from the membranes that cover the sections. The juice cells may then be separated from these carpellary membranes and from the pithy material, seeds, and vascular bundles by means of shaking sieve screens that let the juice cells go through them and stop the other parts of the fruit. Other methods of separation can be used.

The final mass of discrete juice cells is thus made substantially free of other constituents, and especially those other parts of the fruit that impair the keeping quality of the juice, probably because of their enzyme action. These frozen cells are packaged and are themselves an article of commerce, especially when sold in their frozen condition. When the frozen cells are to be kept for a long time, they are preferably packaged in an atmosphere of nitrogen or other gas that does not affect the cells; and this preserves the frozen cells against deterioration or change for longer periods. Other barrier gases that can be used are carbon dioxide, argon, helium, nitrous oxide and mixtures of these gases or other suitable inert gases.

When packaged in a gas atmosphere, the cells may be in a bottle or can, or any gas-tight container, and inert gas provides a barrier around the cells. It preserves the color of the frozen cells and prevents changes in taste, and other changes which normally occur over long periods of time, when the frozen cells are left exposed to contact with air.

FIGURE 4.10: FLOW DIAGRAM FOR FROZEN DISCRETE CITRUS FRUIT CELLS

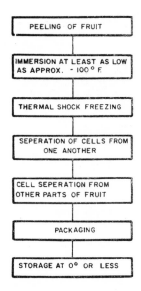

Source: R.C. Webster and E.C. Parish; U.S. Patent 3,246,993; April 19, 1966

When the frozen cells produced by the above process are added to frozen citrus fruit juice concentrates, they restore flavor loss which is commonly experienced with concentrated citrus fruit juice, and especially orange juice. The cells may be added, in a similar manner, to single strength juice which has not been concentrated. So used, they add pulp to the juice and given it a consistency which is more attractive to the consumer.

In related work *R.C. Webster; U.S. Patent 3,365,310; January 23, 1968; assigned to Air Reduction Company, Incorporated* describes a process where the flash-frozen fruit juice crystals prepared as above are subsequently dehydrated by sublimation. The crystal product is placed in a vacuum chamber, and, in a high vacuum, water in the product is transformed directly from ice to form a vapor, which is abstracted from the product and collected elsewhere, for example, on refrigerated plates located in the chamber. Controlled heating is applied to the citrus fruit product in the vacuum environment to create a temperature gradient allowing removal of the water from the product. The dried product can then be stored. Any of the standard dehydration apparatus well-known in the art may be utilized, such as the Food Machinery and Chemical Corporation freeze drying equipment known throughout the industry.

The frozen discrete citrus juice cells, in one preferred method of dehydrating, are placed in a vacuum chamber environment below 4 mm Hg, usually in a batch type arrangement for 16 or 24 hours. The moisture is abstracted from the individual discrete juice cells, from the boundary of ever receding high crystal zones of each cell. The possibility of chemical, enzymatic or microbiological action during drying is remote. Heat is normally conducted to the product during the drying procedure by conduction and radiation. The dehydrated discrete citrus juice cells are dried to a point where approximately 98% or more of the water is removed. Nitrogen or other inert gases may be used in the dehydration process during the break back process. As already stated, the chamber of the freeze dehydrator is under a high vacuum. There has been very little oxidation of the cells, due to the absence of oxygen. The cavities left between sublimating ice crystals are virtually void of air. If the vacuum is broken by breaking back with nitrogen or other inert gases, the cavities in the produce will be occupied with the gases and the oxygen included within the product practically negligible.

The inclusion of the breaking back concept aids in the packaging of the dehydrated discrete citrus fruit cells since oxygen will be practically excluded from the cells. The nitrogen or other inert gas used may be the effluent of the nitrogen or other inert gas previously used during the flash freezing operation described above.

The advantages of freeze-dehydration of citrus fruits by the process described in detail above are numerous. The flash freezing allows for the obtaining of discrete citrus fruit cells without substantial ice crystal growth which then may be dehydrated to produce a product, that is, dehydrated discrete citrus fruit cells. The dehydrated discrete citrus fruit cells retain their original size, shape and structure, and may be stored in the dehydrated state for almost indefinite periods of time.

The addition of water will produce rapid rehydration of dehydrated citrus fruit cells since the porosity of the dehydrated materials enables a rapid penetration of the water. The dehydrated citrus fruit cell may not only be stored for long periods of time without significant losses of produce quality, but storage of such dehydrated cells in bulk is greatly enhanced by the light weight of such cells after dehydration, since approximately 98% or more of the water has been removed.

The light weight just referred to, the lack of need of refrigeration, the substantial exclusion of oxygen from the dehydrated cells, the lack of enzymatic change and microbiological growth during drying, and the ease of rehydrating, among other reasons, not only make for ease of storing, but ease of distribution and consumption as well as distinct pleasantness in consumption.

APPARATUS

Vapor Velocity Limitation to Achieve More Rapid Drying

Rapid and economical drying of products containing a large percentage of water, e.g., 50% or more, can be accomplished by means of the process of *H.J. Togashi and J.L. Mercer; U.S. Patent 3,293,766; December 27, 1966; assigned to Cryo-Maid, Inc.* in which the product to be dried is first solidly frozen, preferably as quickly as possible, ground or shredded (if the product is not already in the form of discrete particles) to relatively uniformly sized pieces or particles while frozen, and subjected in the frozen condition to the action of a dehydrating zone in which the water is caused to be sublimed from the frozen particles at low temperature and pressure.

Contrary to the efforts of the prior art, the overall rate of production of dried products can be vastly increased without deterioration in quality by deliberately limiting the vapor velocity to only a small fraction of the maximum theoretical. Specifically, the vapor velocity should not exceed about 20% of the arithmetical average molecular velocity for the vapor under the conditions which exist in the flow path. When the flow velocity drops below 3% of the arithmetical average molecular velocity, no further advantage occurs, so that there is no reason for using a velocity below 3%. The dehydrating zone is characterized by the following features.

(1) A condensing surface (cryoplate) at very low temperature is provided immediately adjacent the product being dried without intervening serious restrictions to the flow of water vapor, thus preventing the build-up of water vapor molecules at any point within the zone. The flow path of water vapor from the point where it is evolved from the product being dried to the cryoplate condenser should be such that at no point in the travel of the vapor

does the average flow velocity exceed 20% of the arithmetical average molecular velocity at the existent conditions. It is preferred that the flow velocity exceed 3% of the arithmetical average molecular velocity, since no advantage is gained by going below this figure.

(2) The efficiency of the process is demonstrated by the fact that the average dynamic water load, i.e., the average rate at which the water vapor is evolved from a unit area of the drying surface or product pathway during the drying cycle is at least 0.25 lb/hr ft^2 for all products and may exceed about 0.4 lb/hr ft^2 if the material being dried exists in the form of pieces having a size smaller than about 4 mesh. Moreover, this high drying rate is achieved without adverse effect on the quality of the product, such as scorching or case hardening.

(3) Energy for supplying the heat of sublimation is preferably provided to the particles in the form of radiant energy, a substantial portion thereof, suitably at least about 50% and preferably about 80%, having a wavelength longer than about 2.5 microns. Although radiant energy is preferred, other methods of supplying heat to the particles, such as conductive heating and dielectric or microwave heating, may also be used.

(4) The frozen particles are agitated or vibrated or otherwise acted on so as to change the orientation of the surface of the particles. Thus, each particle presents a substantially constantly changing portion of its surface for absorbing energy from the energy source, thereby preventing localized hot spots while still permitting a high rate of energy absorption. In the process, the vibrations can also be used to advance the particles along a pathway through the dehydration system. The vibration and depth of the layer are correlated so that for practical purposes, each particle is in free communication with the energy source and the condenser. That is, shielding of one particle by others is largely avoided.

(5) At least about 20% of the area of the product pathway is cooled by external means to a temperature below about 32°F. This cooling unexpectedly improves product quality while preventing sticking and agglomeration.

(6) The temperature of the particles is maintained at all times sufficiently low that the particles are not permitted to thaw in any part (including those particles in contact with the pathway along which the particles move). Thawing of the particles is prevented by maintaining the pressure in the zone sufficiently low that the refrigerating effect caused by the sublimation of the ice crystals in the particles serves to keep them solidly frozen.

The patent further illustrates the apparatus and method of the process including a table which shows the treatment of various food products among which are fruit juices.

Reduced Drying Time and Increased Heat Utilization Efficiency

U. Hackenberg; U.S. Patent 3,234,658; February 15, 1966 provides a freeze drying method and apparatus, which reduces drying time, increases heat utilization efficiency and prevents damage to the freeze dried product caused by application of excessive heat.

Figure 4.11 shows a water vapor condenser **11** positioned in the upper portion of the freeze drying vacuum chamber **12**. The vacuum pump device **13** for evacuating the vacuum chamber is connected to the top wall thereof by the exhaust tubulation **14** while the refrigeration unit **15** is adapted to provide cooling for the water vapor condenser.

Positioned within the vacuum chamber and below the water vapor condenser is the cylindrical material drum **16** composed of, for example, a suitable metal and adapted for clockwise rotation. Diametrically straddling the cylindrical material drum in a horizontal plane are the radiant heat source **17** and the dried product removal device **18**. Passing through and electrically insulated from the vacuum chamber is a pair of electrical feed-throughs **19** which provide electrical energization for the radiant heat source. A plurality of heat zones **21** are adapted to provide progressively lower temperature heat source areas from bottom to top in the radiant heat source. The scraping device is adapted for counterclockwise rotation and is biased for linear movement in the horizontal plane toward the material drum so as to provide parallel tangential contact therewith. The cylindrical surface of the scraping device is provided with a brush-like covering **22** adapted to provide a product layer removal action as described below.

FIGURE 4.11: APPARATUS FOR REDUCED DRYING TIME AND INCREASED HEAT UTILIZATION EFFICIENCY

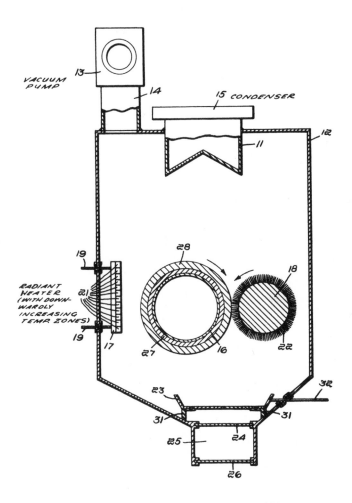

Source: U. Hackenberg; U.S. Patent 3,234,658; February 15, 1966

Positioned below the line of tangential contact between scraping device and cylindrical material drum is the dried product receptacle device **23**. Below the receptacle in the wall of the vacuum chamber is a vacuum valve **24** which opens an airlock chamber **25**. The bottom portion of the airlock chamber is formed by a second vacuum valve device **26** which opens to atmosphere. In the operation of this device the cylindrical surface of the material drum is provided with an inner ice layer **27** and an outer frozen core **28** composed of a layer of the material to be freeze dried. These frozen layers can be applied with the material drum positioned either within the vacuum chamber or while it is removed therefrom. Then with the vacuum chamber pressure reduced by the vacuum pump device, the water vapor condenser cooled by the refrigeration device 15, and the plural zoned radiant heat source energized via feed-throughs the frozen material covered drum and scraping device are energized to provide rotation thereof.

As a given exterior segment of the frozen material core 28 passes by the radiant heat source 21 its water content will be removed by sublimation. The water vapor resulting therefrom will move upward in the chamber in response to the pressure gradiant created by the water vapor condenser and vacuum pump device. However, upon reaching the scraping device the surface temperature of the material core will have decreased to approximately the equilibrium temperature appropriate to the steam pressure in the vacuum chamber. Therefore during the scraping operation there is produced little or no water vapor which would carry the dry loosened product toward the pumping components 11 and 13.

Upon contact with the scraping device the external dry product layer on the material core will be removed by the brush-like covering 22. As a result of the counter-rotational directions of the material drum 16 and the scraping cylinder device 18 (which is preferably adapted for faster rotation than the product core 16) the dry loosened product particles will be compelled downward tangentially to the product core 16 and scraping device 18 and into the product receptacle 23.

After the product receptacle has been filled in this way it can be automatically emptied through the opened valve 24 into the airlock chamber 25. The upper vacuum valve 24 will then again be closed to maintain vacuum within the vacuum chamber and the vacuum valve 26 opened to allow removal of the dried product from the airlock chamber. The purpose of the ice layer 27 in this operation is to prevent damage to the material drum by the scraping device upon removal of the entire frozen material layer 28.

To provide a greater compelling force for the detached product particles the product receptacle 23 can be insulated from the vacuum chamber 12 by insulating supports 31 and electrically energized via an electrical feed-through 32 which passes through and is insulated from the wall of the vacuum chamber. The electric field produced thereby will provide an attractive force on the neutrally charged product particles toward the energized product receptacle.

The removal of the dried surface layer on the material core 28 continually exposes a new frozen surface to the applied drying heat. The problems of inefficient heating, heat damage and water vapor flow restriction described above are substantially eliminated. Furthermore the fact that the drying material surface is moving by the heat source allows for much more uniformity in the heating of localized surface areas.

Proper heating is further enhanced by the provision of the decreasing temperature zones 21. The frozen surface which has been freshly exposed by the scraping device initially moves into the first zone of the radiant heating device which has been adjusted for maximum permissible heat input. As the dry layer begins to form on the product surface, this maximum permissible temperature is reduced because of the lower heat capacity of the dried surface layer. However, as this dry layer is forming it will be passing with the rotating material drum 16 into zones of properly selected lower temperatures.

The preferred embodiment described above also provides the very desirable function of preventing the detached dried material from being carried along in very fine diffusion with the sublimating water vapor. Such an occurrence would result in an undesirable loss of freeze dried product in addition to harmful contamination of the pumping device 13, water vapor condenser 11 and radiant heat source 17. This advantage is provided by scraping the dried material on a side of the rotating material drum opposite to the heat source and water vapor condenser and by arranging these units so that the gravitational force compels the detached product particle in a direction away from these devices. This result is enhanced by the similarly directed forces produced by the oppositely rotating material drum **16** and the scraping device **18** and by the electric field provided by the energization of the product receptacle.

Controlled Multipressure Drying

W. Nerge; U.S. Patent 3,234,661; February 15, 1966; assigned to Leybold-Anlagen Holding AG, Switzerland describes a process for vacuum freeze drying, and, more particularly, to the continuous vacuum freeze drying of substances which pass through a tubular vacuum freeze drying chamber having at least two compartments which are at least partially sealed or sealable with respect to each other.

Process controls for such processes are already known for following or surveying the progressive drying of the goods. This is accomplished by keeping the course or progress of the vacuum freeze drying process under surveillance by periodically, and for fixed periods of time, completely sealing the vacuum freeze drying chamber from the evacuating means and ascertaining the pressure increase which is obtained at the end of the period during which sealing has taken place.

By using this method, an accurate picture of the drying state of all of the goods in the apparatus may be obtained according to an integral value, and thus substantial progress has been achieved as compared to prior measuring processes wherein the state of only one or several representative samples is checked, for example, by using thermocouples.

When an attempt is made to carry out continuous vacuum freeze drying processes on a large industrial scale, considerable difficulties are encountered in adapting for this purpose the above-described advantageous integral method for determining the drying state of the goods. These difficulties are mostly due to the required arrangement and control of the sealing members which must bring about a momentary complete sealing of the vacuum drying chamber, or of an appropriately sealable compartment formed by a portion of the entire vacuum drying chamber.

A tubular vacuum drying chamber is provided in a continuous vacuum freeze drying apparatus. The chamber is provided with at least two partial chambers substantially or at least partially sealed from one another. The goods are preferably placed in transporting means. The continuous vacuum freeze drying process is carried out under continuous program control wherein the velocity of the goods being transported through any compartment is such that at predetermined measuring points of these compartments, predetermined pressure or temperature values are maintained by the evacuating means and heat exchange means.

In this process, instead of the previously required sealing time of the vacuum drying chamber, there is a residence time or time which the goods inserted in the apparatus must remain in the individual compartments. This period of time is dependent upon the velocity of the goods which are conveyed through the chamber. If at least a substantial amount of, or partial, sealing is achieved, then the pressure increase at a definite measuring point within the compartment represents an indication of the progress of the drying of the goods.

By making appropriate tests, pressure values may be obtained or ascertained which are coordinated with the desired orderly procedure of the vacuum freeze drying process at measuring points along the vacuum drying chamber.

Thus, in the practical application of this process, there is only need for maintaining these previously ascertained pressure values constant. This may be accomplished by appropriate control of the evacuating means or heat exchange means, respectively, which communicate with each compartment. This process provides a substantial simplification of the previously required apparatus and reduces the expense thereof, in particular eliminating the expensive sealing means as well as the switching device for the periodic actuation of these sealing means which was previously necessary. As the containers which receive the goods inserted into the apparatus take up substantially the entire cross section of the vacuum drying chamber, there is thus a partial or substantial sealing effect between the individual compartments, without additional sealing means being necessary, which makes possible the formation of a pressure gradient from one compartment to the next. This may be enhanced by providing special sealing means in addition to those which are provided by the containers.

In this process, there are conveying means for conveying the goods to be dried through the tubular vacuum freeze drying chamber. The conveying means include transport elements which take up a substantial amount of the cross section of the tubular chamber and thus provide a partial sealing between individual compartments which are formed thereby, which permits the formation of a pressure gradient between chambers.

Thus, the process may be performed in a vacuum drying chamber which is not subdivided and one which is of considerable longitudinal length. Appropriately fixed pressure and/or temperature values are to be maintained at several measuring points which are distributed along the length of the drying chamber.

However, it may be useful to increase the sealing effect of the cross section of the conveying means which include the transport elements which may be designed as transfer cars or sections of a conveyor belt, by additional sealing means provided on the wall of the vacuum drying chamber or on the transport elements.

It has proven to be particularly advantageous to increase the cross section of the transfer cars, or at least some of them, with respect to the chamber by providing screen-like elements which are preferably arranged at a uniform distance. By this means, there is appropriate subdivision of the vacuum drying chamber into at least partially sealed compartments defined by the screen-like elements, between which and the interior chamber wall a number of constriction gaps are formed.

Thus, pressure differences may be formed in the individual partial chambers or compartments by using suitably adjusted evacuating means, which pressure differences may be kept under constant surveillance by appropriately arranged measuring instruments.

In a practical example according to Figure 4.12, orange juice was dried by filling vessels **84** with juice, and freezing exteriorly of the chamber. This juice had a bulk density of about 0.6 kg per liter. In this manner it was possible to accommodate about 40 kg of goods to be dried on a car. There was room for 4 x 4 or 16 vessels **84** on a single car. In the particular example being considered the drying time amounted to 12.5 hours and the length of the chamber between the gate valves **4** and **5** was about 5 meters.

The velocity of the goods to be dried was 0.4 meter per hour with the motion of the conveying means in the apparatus according to Figure 4.12a taking place in stepwise manner, while in the apparatus according to Figure 4.12b a continuous motion thereof is possible.

The pressure in the chamber at the measuring points **12** through **16** will depend upon the nature of the goods to be dried. In the case of orange juice the operation was carried out with the following pressures:

Measuring Point	Pressure, mm Hg
13	4×10^{-1}
14	2×10^{-1}
15	8×10^{-2}

The pressures in the inlet and outlet locks **2** and **3** are maintained at 1×10^{-1} mm Hg and 8×10^{-2} mm Hg, respectively. The relatively small pressure drop from point **13** to point **14** is necessary in order to allow for the diffusion coefficient which is increased through the already dried layer. The low pressure at point **15** is caused by the later drying and gradation of pressure is accomplished by use of sealing means on the wall. It is possible to retain the pressure differences in the vacuum chamber **1** solely by the sealing effect of the cars and by the additional sealing means provided so that the particular advantage of

(continued)

FIGURE 4.12: CONTROLLED MULTIPRESSURE DRYING APPARATUS

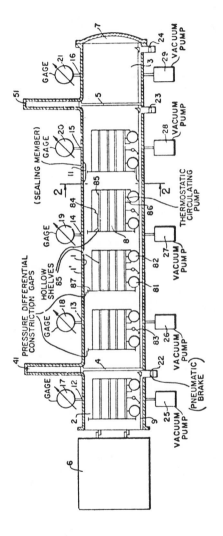

Stepwise Conveyance

FIGURE 4.12: (continued)

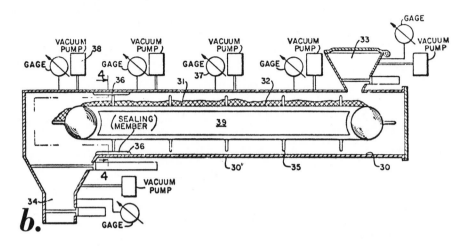

Continuous Conveyance

Source: W. Nerge; U.S. Patent 3,234,661; February 15, 1966

the process is that further complicated valve devices and sealing structures within the chamber are not needed. According to the pressure values noted above, control of the evacuating means and/or of the heating means is accomplished and performed with the object of retaining the pressure and/or temperature values constant in the program, the temperature and pressure being interrelated by a well-known principle, the interrelation being readily obtainable by reference to appropriate steam tables.

When the desired degree of drying has been attained, the transfer cars **8** will finally leave the vacuum chamber **1** through outlet lock **3** and will be emptied and readied for renewed filling in the process which is a cyclic process.

In the embodiment of Figures 4.12b, the control may be such that the speed of the conveying means is controlled, thereby to control the progress of the drying operation. In this manner, the drying process may be under constant surveillance.

Defrost System for Condenser Coils

In a freeze drying process, articles to be freeze dried are frozen and then placed within a hermetically sealed enclosure. Means are provided to heat the articles to be freeze dried while they are subjected to a reduced pressure thereby causing ice within the frozen articles to sublime. The moisture evolved by sublimation of the ice is withdrawn and passed to a condenser. The moisture vapors condense on the condenser coils and form ice.

The method of *R.K. Tyson; U.S. Patent 3,281,949; November 1, 1966; assigned to Pennsalt Chemical Corporation* provides a defrost system for melting accumulated ice on the condenser coils of the freeze drying apparatus.

Referring to Figure 4.13 in detail, wherein like elements are indicated by like numerals, the freeze drying apparatus of the process is generally designated by the numeral **10**. The apparatus **10** includes a hermetically sealed chamber **12** including a door **62** at one end. Supported within the chamber are a plurality of freeze drying shelves **14** arranged in a

FIGURE 4.13: FREEZE DRYING APPARATUS

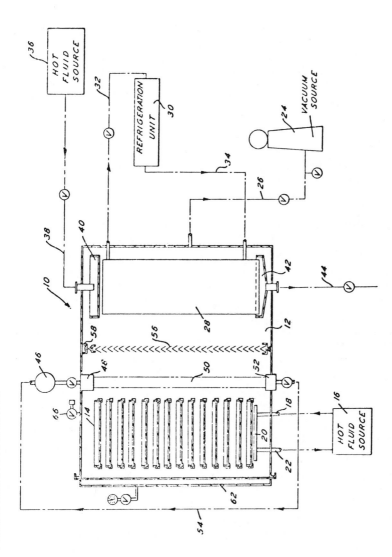

Source: R.K. Tyson; U.S. Patent 3,281,949; November 1, 1966

vertical array. The products to be freeze dried are adapted to be supported by the shelves. A hot source of fluid 16 such as steam is connected by means of an inlet conduit 18 to a heating means 20 disposed beneath each shelf 14. The heating means is conventional and includes a plurality of heating coils.

The hot fluid is circulated through the heating coils within the heating means and returned to the hot fluid source 16 by means of an outlet conduit 22. Although one heating means 20 is shown, it should be understood that a similar heating means is disposed beneath each of the freeze drying shelves. Connected to the chamber 12 by means of a vacuum line 26 is a vacuum source 24. The chamber 12 is adapted to be evacuated by the source 24.

The products to be freeze dried are first frozen and placed upon the shelves. The pressure within the chamber and the temperature produced by the heating means is such that the ice within the frozen products will sublime. That is, the ice will pass directly from a solid state to a vapor state. The water vapor evolved by the sublimation of the ice is adapted to be condensed by a condenser 28 within the chamber.

The condenser coils of the condenser are connected to a refrigeration unit 30 by means of a refrigerant inlet line 34 and a refrigerant outlet line 32. The refrigerant unit 30 is adapted to pump a suitable coolant through the line 34, condenser coils, and line 32. The moisture in the chamber will condense and freeze in the form of ice on the coils of the condenser 28. The ice formed on the condenser coils of the condenser must be melted after each freeze drying cycle. Otherwise, the condenser will be insulated by an ice coating and will not be able to operate effectively.

Accordingly, a weir 40 is mounted within the chamber 12 above the condenser 28. The weir is connected by a hot fluid inlet line 38 to a hot fluid source 36. A hot fluid, preferably a liquid, such as water or glycol is fed to the weir 40 and cascaded by the weir over the vertically arranged condensing coils of the condenser. Ice collected on the coils of the condenser is melted by direct contact with the evenly distributed hot liquid. The melted ice and hot liquid is caught in a drain pan 42 disposed beneath the condenser. The drained liquid leaves the chamber through a drain conduit 44 connected to the drain pan.

The condenser is adapted to be defrosted between each freeze drying cycle. Accordingly, the condenser is defrosted while the freeze dried products are being unloaded from the chamber. The unloading of the freeze dried products is accomplished by breaking the vacuum within the chamber by opening the chamber to the atmosphere through a valve 66 and opening the door 62. After the vacuum is broken within the chamber, a high velocity air curtain 50 is established between the condenser and shelves.

The air curtain 50 is established just prior to defrosting condenser 28. The air curtain prevents high temperature, moisture laden air evolved by the defrosting of condenser 28, from contaminating the unloading area. The unloading area will thus be maintained in a low humidity controlled environment.

The air curtain is established between a pair of ducts 48 and 52 mounted at the top and bottom of the chamber respectively. A blower 46 is adapted to shoot a high velocity stream of air through the duct 48. The air enters the duct 52 in the bottom of the chamber 12 and is recirculated by means of a recirculation duct 54.

In order to decrease the refrigeration load upon the condenser, a radiation shield 56 is provided between the freeze drying shelves and the condenser. The shield will block heat radiated from the heating means 20 and the shelves. The shield 56 comprises a plurality of inverted V-shaped plates which block radiation but allow the sublimed water vapors to pass through them to the condenser. The shield is slidably mounted on an overhead track 58 so as to afford easy access to the condenser for inspection and minor maintenance.

The operation of the freeze drying apparatus 10 is substantially as follows. Products to be freeze dried are supported upon the shelves in the chamber. The chamber is evacuated by means of the vacuum source **24**. A hot fluid is circulated through the heating coils of the heating means **20** beneath each of the shelves from the hot fluid source **16**. The ice which has frozen in each of the products disposed within the chamber is caused to sublime and passes directly into a vapor stage. This is accomplished by adjusting the pressure within the chamber and the temperature of the heating coils within the heating means to a combined value wherein sublimation will take place.

The sublimed moisture will pass through the radiation shield **56** to the condensing coils of the condenser **28**. After a time, ice will form and build up on the condensing coils. The shield prevents heat radiated from the heating means and shelves from increasing the refrigeration load on the condensing coils of the condenser. When the freeze drying cycle is completed, the vacuum within the chamber is broken by opening the valve **66** to the atmosphere. The blower **46** is then activated to establish a high velocity air curtain **50** between the condenser **28** and door **62** leading to the chamber **12**. The door may then be opened and the freeze dried products removed.

A hot liquid is then applied directly from the weir **40** over the condensing coils of the condenser to melt accumulated ice on the coils. The hot liquid and melted ice are collected in a drain pan **42** and removed through a drain conduit **44**. The air curtain **50** prevents high temperature, moisture laden air evolved by defrosting of the condenser from contaminating the unloading area. The apparatus is then ready for its next freeze drying cycle. The hot liquid flow is stopped following the melting of the ice to avoid overheating of the condenser metal. Accumulated ice on the condenser coils is removed as a liquid and not in solid chunks.

Use of Cryogenic Gas System for Initial Freezing

The process of *M.R. Jeppson; U.S. Patent 3,304,617; February 21, 1967; assigned to Cryodry Corporation* provides for a simpler and more economical plant than previously known, eliminates the need for conducting freeze drying within a high vacuum system, and provides for a much more efficient heat transfer to the interior of the product during freeze drying with a consequent reduction in processing time. A basic feature of the process is the use of a cryogenic gas system for initially freezing the product, for imparting heat thereto in the course of drying, and for withdrawing water vapor which is released as ice within the product sublimes.

The product is placed within a drying cabinet on a gas manifold which has a large number of perforated hollow needles that penetrate into the product. The manifold, and thus the injection needles, is connected with a supply adapted to deliver gas at an adjustable temperature. In a preferred form the supply is a Dewar of liquid cryogenic gas, liquefied nitrogen being an advantageous example inasmuch as it is a readily available by-product of steel making and of liquid oxygen rocket fuel manufacture and can therefore be obtained at a relatively low cost. The cabinet gas manifolding is connected with the supply through a first conduit which provides for the initial injection of liquid gas, or very cold vapor, directly into the product to effect rapid freezing.

Following freezing, the constituent water in the product is present in the form of minute ice crystals which, under appropriate temperature and pressure conditions, will convert directly to water vapor without passing through an intermediate liquid phase. In contrast to the prior practice, evacuation of the drying cabinet is unnecessary for establishing pressure conditions under which sublimation will occur. What is required is that the partial pressure of water vapor in the cabinet be reduced to a negligible value, the presence of dry gases such as completely dehumidified air being unobjectionable. Accordingly the use of a cabinet pumping technique which primarily withdraws only water vapor allows the process to be performed at atmospheric pressure or at any other desired pressure.

Cryogenic pumping is ideally suited for this purpose and is an advantageous technique within the context of the process in view of the availability of liquid gas. Thus the pumping of water vapor from the product is performed by communicating the cabinet with a pumping chamber into which the liquid gas is continually sprayed, collected and recirculated. Water vapor from the cabinet is thereby condensed and deposited on the wall of the pumping chamber in the form of frost. To counteract sublimation cooling and accelerate the drying process, heat is delivered directly to the interior of the product by injecting relatively warm gas either continuously or in periodic bursts. This is most conveniently accomplished by connecting the cabinet manifold with the gas supply through a second conduit which includes a heat exchanger. The injection of warm dry gas directly into the product largely avoids reliance on heat conduction across dry porous surface regions and thus provides much more efficient heat transfer.

In addition, the gas injection promotes drying by still another effect. The injected gas diffuses through the product to the surface thereof which gas flow promotes the removal of water vapor and does not itself have any appreciable effect on the product inasmuch as it is dry and inert. The partial pressure of the water vapor in the product is not increased but is decreased owing to the purging action of the injected gas.

Referring now to Figure 4.14, the product 24, after the customary preparatory processing, is impaled on the needles 23 within the cabinet 11. Following closure of the cabinet door 13, valve 58 is set at the described second position thereof to vent the cabinet and the gas supply valves 43 and 44 are also set at the described second positions thereof to feed cold liquid gas from Dewar 34 to the cabinet manifolds 17 and 28. Valve 51 is opened during this initial stage of the process to feed the liquid gas to the upper spray manifold 28. Owing the the injection of the cold gas directly into the product through the needles as well as the spraying of the exterior of the product with gas, constituent water is very rapidly frozen into minute ice crystals without any significant change occurring in the remainder of the product. Valves 43, 44 and 51 may then be closed to stop the flow of cold gas into the cabinet.

Following freezing of product, the pumping system is actuated by starting backing pumps 82 and recirculation pump 79, with the pumping gas supply valve 71 opened and the exhaust line valve 58 set at the third position thereof to connect the cabinet with the pumping chambers 63 and 64. To provide for the initial heavy pumping load, both chambers 63 and 64 may be operated by opening all the associated valves 86, 87, 88, 89, 91, 92, 93 and 94. As the load decreases in the later portion of the drying stage, the pumping chambers 63 and 64 may alternately be isolated by closing the associated valves to permit the removal of accumulated ice.

The injection of liquid nitrogen into the pumping chambers 63 and 64, through manifold 68, will rapidly freeze water vapor from cabinet 11, the excess gaseous nitrogen being withdrawn by backing pumps 82. Owing to the consequent reduction of the partial pressure of water vapor within the cabinet, the sublimation of ice crystals within the product is accelerated.

As has been discussed, the rate of sublimation will tend to progressively decrease owing to the further cooling which is inherent in the process. To maintain the sublimation at an optimum rate, the cabinet gas supply valves 43 and 44 are set at the third positions thereof. With these valve settings, gas from Dewar 34 is warmed by passage through heat exchanger 46 and is delivered by pump 54 to the cabinet manifold 17 and needles 23, the temperature of the gas being controllable by appropriate adjustment of the heat exchanger fluid supply 53. The emission of the warm gas from the passages in the needles efficiently delivers heat throughout the interior of the product resulting in a much more rapid drying than can be effected by applying heat only to the surface of the product.

When sufficient gas from Dewar 34 has been introduced into the cabinet and the pumping system, valves 40 and 96 are operated to disconnect the Dewar from valve 43 and to initiate the recirculation of exhaust gas from pumps 82. After all ice within the product has sublimed, gas supply valves 43 and 44 are closed to stop the injection of gas and the exhaust valve 58 is set at the second position to vent the cabinet. The cabinet 11 may then be opened and the freeze dried product 24 removed for packaging. To unclog the gas

FIGURE 4.14: APPARATUS FOR DIRECT INJECTION OF CRYOGENIC GAS

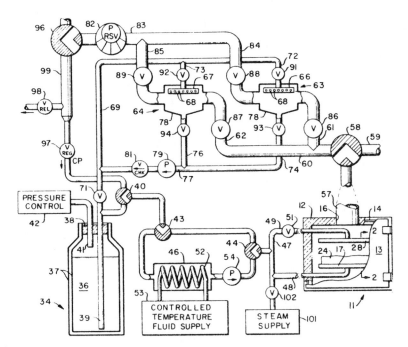

Source: M.R. Jeppson; U.S. Patent 3,304,617; February 21, 1967

emission passages of the needles, in preparation for a subsequent cycle of operation, valve
102 may be momentarily opened to supply high pressure steam to the needles. It will be
apparent that the apparatus may readily be modified for the freeze drying of liquids, such
as fruit juices, by minor modifications of the gas manifold **17** within cabinet **11** to provide
a fluid retaining wall around the needles.

STABILIZATION PROCESSES

ANTIOXIDANT COMPOSITIONS

Addition of O-Methyltransferase

It is well-known that when most fruits and vegetables are subjected to disorganization of their natural structure as by peeling, cutting, comminuting, pitting, pulping, freezing, etc., the produce suffers deteriorative changes including the development of dark and unnatural colors (browning), softening of tissue, and development of unnatural odor and taste. These deteriorative changes are attributed to various chemical reactions catalyzed by the enzymes such as polyphenoloxidase naturally present in the plant material. The disorganization of the plant structure disrupts the natural segregation of substrates and enzymes and thus permits the enzymes to contact various substrates with the results noted above.

More specifically, the browning of plant tissue is attributed to a mechanism wherein ortho-dihydroxy phenolic compounds such as catechol, caffeic acid, chlorogenic acid, or gallic acid, present in the plant tissue are oxidized through enzyme-catalyzed reactions to ortho quinones and the latter compounds polymerize, producing dark colored substances. In any preservation process, whether it involves dehydration, freezing, canning, or any combination of these, means must be provided for controlling these undesirable enzymic reactions if an acceptable product is to be produced.

Various techniques are used for preventing or inhibiting the reactions by what may be termed an attack on the natural enzymes in the produce. Thus, these procedures have the effect of destroying, denaturing, inactivating, or otherwise attenuating the enzymes which have the ability to catalyze the oxidation of the ortho-dihydroxy phenolic substrates. For example, it is common in the food industry to subject raw fruit or vegetables to blanching with steam or hot water whereby to inactivate the enzymes.

The treatment is generally effective but has the disadvantage that the produce is at least partially cooked so that it no longer tastes like the fresh food. Also, blanching causes a leaching out of valuable nutrient materials from the plant tissue. The use of sulfur dioxide and other sulfiting agents (for example, sodium sulfite or bisulfite) to inactivate enzymes is also well-known. Use of these reagents, however, has the disadvantage that the flavor of the food is adversely affected.

In accordance with the method of *B.J. Finkle; U.S. Patent 3,126,287; March 24, 1964; assigned to the U.S. Secretary of Agriculture*, raw plant material which is normally subject to enzyme-catalyzed deterioration is subjected to a treatment which so affects the substrates in the plant material that they are no longer responsive to the deteriorative enzymes. More specifically, the process causes such changes in the ortho-dihydroxy phenolic constituents (the browning precursors) that they no longer will form brown reaction products. An unusual aspect of the method is that it involves an attack on the browning precursors, rather than following the conventional pattern which involves an attack on the browning enzymes. It may be noted that in applying the process, the oxidative enzymes which cause browning are not destroyed. They remain active yet unable to carry out their usual function because the substrates on which they normally act have been chemically altered, or blocked.

In accordance with the process, the plant material is subjected to contact with an enzyme capable of causing chemical changes resulting in the blocking of one or both of the ortho-hydroxy groups of the browning precursors. A preferred enzyme for this purpose is O-methyltransferase which has the ability of converting hydroxyl groups to methoxyl groups. Thus, by applying O-methyltransferase to the plant material, the browning precursors are chemically altered by conversion of one or both of the ortho-hydroxyl groups to methoxyl groups. As a result, the browning reaction is blocked in its first stage since the precursors cannot form ortho quinones.

Suitable contact with the enzyme is attained by immersing the fruit in an aqueous dispersion of the enzyme. Where liquid materials such as juices, pulps, or purees, are being treated the enzyme is mixed directly with the liquid plant material. Since the enzyme in question acts as a catalyst, the amount used is not critical. For optimum results, it is preferred that the system of plant material and enzyme be maintained at a pH level of about from 7 to 9. Such pH levels can be readily attained by applying any conventional nontoxic alkaline material such as an alkali metal carbonate, bicarbonate, or phosphate, or an amine, in the amount as necessitated by the natural pH of the plant material.

Also, since the desired reaction involves conversion of hydroxyl to methoxyl, it is necessary that there be present at the locus of the reaction a source of methyl radicals. This may be provided by the natural components in the plant tissue or, if not present therein, may be supplied by addition of a methyl-donating compound, as, for example, methionine or S-adenosylmethionine.

The presence of magnesium ion is required for the action of the methylating enzyme, however, this ion is virtually always present in natural plant materials and need not be added. In any event, it does no harm to add magnesium ion, for example, in the form of a nontoxic magnesium salt to supplement the natural complement in the plant tissue. The temperature of the system of plant material and enzyme is generally held in the range from about $20°$ to $40°C$.

Methylation of the browning precursors does not take place instantaneously but requires a definite period of time which may be anywhere from 5 minutes to 3 hours, depending on such factors as the temperature, the type of produce, the nature of the browning precursors, and the amount of enzyme therein, etc. Thus, during the period of reaction it is necessary to maintain anaerobic conditions. Anaerobic conditions may be established in several ways.

One technique involves adding a minor proportion of ascorbic acid to the system. Another plan is to remove air from the system by subjecting it to vacuum or by flushing it with nitrogen or other nonoxidizing gas. If desired, one can use a combination of addition of a minor proportion of ascorbic acid together with removal of air by flushing with nitrogen. After the desired methylation has occurred, the plant material may be readjusted to its natural pH. This is readily accomplished by incorporation of the required amount of a nontoxic acid such as citric, tartaric, malic, phosphoric, gluconic, etc., or an acidic salt such as an alkali metal dihydrogen phosphate.

Example: Fresh apples were squeezed to prepare a juice and 0.01% of ascorbic acid was added to the juice to prevent browning before application of the treatment. Fifty volumes of this apple juice were mixed with 25 volumes of an O-methyltransferase preparation containing 89 mg protein/ml, 15 volumes of S-adenosylmethionine solution (0.008 M), 5 volumes of magnesium chloride solution (0.2 M), 5 volumes of tris-(hydroxymethyl) aminomethane hydrochloride solution (2 M). The resulting mixture, having a pH of 7.5 to 8, was evacuated to remove air and held in a closed vessel at 38°C for 2 hours. At the end of this time the pH of the solution was brought to 6 by addition of KH_2PO_4.

As a test, a sample of the above product and a sample of the original juice (diluted with water to same concentration as the product) were shaken in air for several hours, then examined. The treated juice had a pale straw color exactly like the freshly-prepared juice; the untreated juice was dark brown.

Addition of Enediols of 3-Ketoglycosides

The use of food antioxidants which serve to stabilize foodstuffs against discoloration, off-tastes and aromas is well-known in the art. Such compounds, by their presence, function by maintaining reducing conditions in food and thus preserve their taste and appearance.

R.W. Eltz; U.S. Patent 3,372,036; March 5, 1968; assigned to Sun Oil Company discloses a foodstuff composition containing an inhibitor against such deterioration. The process comprises incorporating into the foodstuff an inhibitor selected from the group consisting of the 2,3-enediols of 3-ketoglycosides and the higher fatty acid esters thereof. The inhibitor is a compound selected from the group consisting of 2,3-enediols of 3-ketomaltose, 3-ketosucrose, 3-ketolactose, 3-ketomaltobionic acid and 3-ketolactobionic acid and the fatty acid esters thereof.

These enediols of 3-ketoglycosides are readily obtainable by the oxidation and tautomerization of certain common sugars or sugar acids, as for example, the disaccharides such as maltose, sucrose or lactose, or the bionic acids such as maltobionic acid or lactobionic acid. Use of the enediols of 3-ketoglycosides are especially advantageous in conjunction with the use of preparations containing vitamin C, since these enediols, when present in amounts in excess of the vitamin C, serve to spare the oxidation of this vitamin, which itself is a known reducing agent, and thus permit this material to retain its vitamin activity.

Example: To one quart of bottled apple juice is added 700 mg of the 2,3-enediol of 3-ketomaltobionic acid. The juice is stirred until the acid is dissolved, the bottle is capped, and refrigerated for 20 days. At the end of that time the juice is examined and found to be light amber colored, clear in appearance and suitable in taste. A corresponding untreated jar of apple juice is much darker in appearance with a brown sediment and unpalatable odor and taste.

CHEMICAL PRESERVATION

Addition of Stannous Ions to Prevent Nonenzymic Browning

Previous efforts to eliminate or retard the nonenzymic, anaerobic browning of fruit juices include ascorbic acid addition, addition of sulfur dioxide and packaging in containers with exposed tin surfaces. Ascorbic acid addition is relatively expensive and not always effective. For example, in concentrated lemon juice ascorbic acid promotes rather than retards browning. Sulfur dioxide cannot be used in cans because of its corrosive action and further is limited in application by its characteristic odor.

In reconstituted, bottled lemon juice sulfur dioxide very effectively prevents browning but eventually gives rise to a unique and unpleasant off-taste described as "skunky." Acid foods react with tin surfaces to produce a reducing effect which prevents browning but at the same time gives rise to an unpleasant metallic off-taste and in some cases hydrogen gas is produced.

W.K. Higby and D.E. Pritchett; U.S. Patent 3,219,458; November 23, 1965; assigned to Sunkist Growers, Inc. found that the addition of small amounts of stannous ions to citrus juice products such as single strength lemon, orange and grapefruit juices, concentrated lemon, orange and grapefruit juices and concentrates for orangeade and lemonade, retards or inhibits browning of such products. It has further been found that not only can the juice concentrates be preserved in this manner, but that by the addition of greater amounts of stannous ions, the reconstituted beverages made from such concentrates are also preserved against darkening. Additionally, it has been discovered that optimum results are obtained by adding the stannous ions in the form of a solution of stannous chloride in concentrated hydrochloric acid.

A number of tin salts exist which can serve as sources of stannous ions for the purposes of the process, such as, for example, stannous chloride, stannous sulfate and stannous tartrate, which are water-soluble, and stannous oxalate and stannous oxide, which are soluble in hydrochloric acid. Stannous chloride is preferred since it is readily available as a reagent grade chemical of known purity and therefore suitable as such for use in foods.

In carrying out the process the stannous salt is simply added to the fresh citrus juice or concentrate. Stannous chloride forms an insoluble oxychloride upon standing, and upon dilution with much water it forms an insoluble basic salt. Relatively concentrated, freshly prepared aqueous or citric acid solutions of stannous chloride can be used in carrying out the process, but considerable care must be taken to avoid or minimize the formation of the insoluble oxychloride or basic salt, neither of which appears to be effective to prevent browning.

Superior results in minimizing the formation of the insoluble compounds are obtained by dissolving the stannous chloride in concentrated hydrochloric acid and subsequently diluting the solution with water, preferably deaerated. To keep to a minimum the amount of strong acid added to the juice, only enough hydrochloric acid is used to dissolve the stannous chloride to form a clear solution. Thus, clear solutions can be obtained with as little as 2.5 ml of hydrochloric acid for 5 g of salt, but 1 ml of acid is insufficient for such amount of salt.

Stannous ion additions as low as 25 parts per million retard browning moderately, increased amounts bringing about a marked retardation until a concentration of 200 to 300 ppm is reached. Beyond this level, relatively small additional gain is realized. Taste tests with lemonade indicate that stannous ions can be detected at about 250 ppm in the fresh product. After storage and reconstitution of concentrate for lemonade, 90 ppm of stannous ions can be detected as a metallic off-taste, but taste differences between the treated and control samples are obscured by the generally improved flavor of the treated samples. Improved retention of the original flavor is an added benefit to be derived from addition of stannous ions. A number of typical citrus juice products were prepared for testing as follows.

Concentrated Grapefruit Juice: 0.572 grams $SnCl_2 \cdot 2H_2O$ were dissolved in 0.29 ml concentrated HCl and then washed with a few ml of water into 3,773 grams of 5.25 fold concentrated grapefruit juice to give 80 ppm Sn^{++}. The concentrate was then pasteurized at approximately 160°F into enameled cans.

Concentrated Lemon Juice: 0.541 grams $SnCl_2 \cdot 2H_2O$ were dissolved in 0.28 ml concentrated HCl and then washed with a few ml of water into 3,557 grams of 5.7 fold concentrated lemon juice. The concentrate was then pasteurized at 170° to 180°F into enameled cans.

Single Strength Lemon Juice: 9.5 grams $SnCl_2 \cdot 2H_2O$ were dissolved in 4.5 ml concentrated HCl and then diluted to 100 ml with distilled water to provide a solution containing 0.050 grams Sn^{++} per ml. 3.12 ml of this solution was added to 1,000 ml (1,034 grams) vacuum deaerated lemon juice (pasteurized, natural strength 6.10% acid as citric, 8.95°Brix, specific gravity 1.03382). 0.1% sodium benzoate was also added to protect against microbial spoilage, and the juice was stored in bottles.

Single Strength Orange Juice: One ml of a $SnCl_2 \cdot 2H_2O$ solution made up by dissolving 2 grams in 1 ml concentrated HCl and diluting to 10 ml with water was added to 1,045 grams of vacuum deaerated orange juice to give 100 ppm Sn^{++}. The orange juice was preserved against microbial spoilage with 0.1% sodium benzoate and was stored in bottles.

The effect of the stannous ion on shelf life, from a color standpoint, of these products was determined by examining them for color, initially and at periodic intervals during storage. Color of single strength lemon juice, concentrated lemon juice, and concentrated grapefruit juice was measured on a filtered mixture of equal parts isopropyl alcohol and the juice product or a dilution of the juice product using the Klett-Summerson photoelectric colorimeter with the blue, No. 42 filter and a water-isopropanol blank single strength lemon juice or concentrated lemon juice diluted to single strength was judged to be unacceptable at a reading of 125. Concentrated grapefruit juice diluted 23 to 89 grams to 100 ml was unacceptable at a reading of 175. Color of single strength orange juice was estimated visually and samples more brown than orange were considered unacceptable. The results are set forth in the table below.

Effect of Stannous Ions on Color Storage Life of Some Citrus Juice Products

Product	Storage Temp, °F	Untreated Storage Life, days	Sn⁺⁺, ppm	Treated Storage Life	
				Days	Percent Improvement
Concentrated grapefruit juice	82	69	80	150	117
Concentrated lemon juice	82	62	80	183	195
Single strength lemon juice	82	97	150	299	208
Single strength orange juice	100	30	100	> 90	>200

An additional benefit derived from color preservation with stannous ions is improved retention of ascorbic acid. This appears to be true in all citrus juice products.

Benzohydroxamic Acid

J.J. Beereboom; U.S. Patent 3,446,630; May 27, 1969; assigned to Chas. Pfizer & Co., Inc. has found that benzohydroxamic acid when added to various types and forms of foodstuffs preserves these foods from the growth of undesirable microorganisms. The preferred concentration is from about 0.01 to 1% based on the weight of foodstuff. Of course, higher levels are also effective but tend to superimpose the flavor of benzohydroxamic acid on the natural taste of the food. Also used in the process are the nontoxic salts of benzohydroxamic acid which include the beryllium, magnesium, calcium, sodium, potassium, aluminum, zinc, iron, manganese, and ammonium salts. For convenience and economy, benzohydroxamic acid, its sodium and potassium salts are to be preferred.

The acid and its salts or mixtures thereof may be added to the food as the dry material or more conveniently from a water or an organic solvent solution, for example, ethyl alcohol solution. The foodstuffs preferred in the process which have been most successfully preserved by the addition of benzohydroxamic acid and its nontoxic salts are those which it is not economically feasible to freeze or to subject to cold storage and those foods whose flavor is lost on freezing, such as fruit and vegetable juices.

Example 1: Apple Cider – To one liter of fresh unpasteurized apple cider was added sufficient dry benzohydroxamic acid to give a total of 0.1% by weight. The cider did not develop microbial growth after two weeks storage at room temperature of about 25°C. Untreated cider from the same pressing spoiled within three days when stored under the same conditions. The experiment is repeated with the sodium and potassium salts of benzohydroxamic acid at levels of 0.1% by weight. After two weeks storage at room temperature (25°C), no microbial growth develops.

Example 2: Prune Juice – To one liter of fresh, unpasteurized prune juice was added sufficient dry benzohydroxamic acid to give a total of 0.05% by weight. The prune juice did not develop microbial growth after two weeks storage at about 25°C. An untreated control sample developed microbial growth within four days under the same storage conditions.

Disubstituted Benzoic Esters and Ketones

R. Ueno, M. Kashihara and T. Matsuda; U.S. Patent 3,767,827; October 23, 1973; assigned to Ueno Fine Chemical Industries, Ltd., Japan describe a process for the preservation of liquid foodstuffs which comprises adding to a liquid foodstuff a compound expressed by the formula

wherein R is an alkyl group of 3 to 8 carbon atoms and M stands for hydrogen, and alkali metal or ½ mol of an alkaline earth metal in an amount of 5 to 300 ppm.

As preservatives generally used for liquid foodstuffs there have been known benzoic acid, salicylic acid, dehydroacetic acid salts, para-hydroxybenzoic acid esters and sorbic acid salts. In these preservatives, it sometimes happens that a sufficient preservative effect cannot be expected when they are added in amounts within the range allowed by the Food Sanitation Law. Further, their effects vary depending on the kinds of foodstuffs to which they are added.

It has been found that aromatic carboxylic acid esters or aromatic ketones having two hydroxyl groups linked to the benzene nucleus have excellent antibacterial spectra and are generally characterized by very low toxicity because precursors of these compounds are existent broadly in the natural world and are usually harmless to the human body, and that these compounds have excellent solubility in liquid foodstuffs and are excellent in storage stability.

In this method it is critical that the compound should possess an alkyl group R having 3 to 8 carbon atoms. Those compounds having an alkyl group of up to 2 carbon atoms as R are not suitable because their antibacterial activity is very weak but their toxicity is high. On the other hand, those having as R an alkyl group of 9 or more carbon atoms are not preferred because of their low solubility.

Any of the compounds to be used can be readily dissolved in liquid foodstuffs. Further, the compounds have a structure quite analogous to the structure of a para-hydroxybenzoic acid ester, the use of which is evaluated to be safe and harmless by World Health Organization (WHO) and Food and Agriculture Organization (FAO), and the internal metabolism course of the compounds of the process is presumed to be similar to that of the para-hydroxybenzoic acid ester.

The compounds exhibit a high solubility in liquid foodstuffs and even when they are added at a relatively high concentration, e.g., 300 ppm, they do not precipitate during storage. Since the compounds have high antibacterial activity, sufficient effects can be attained when they are added to liquid foodstuffs in an amount of 5 to 60 ppm.

In the practice of this process, the compounds may be added in any stage during the preparation of liquid foodstuffs. They may be added in the form of an aqueous solution of a caustic alkali such as sodium hydroxide and potassium hydroxide.

The preservative effects and antibacterial activities of the compounds of this process vary depending on the kind of main saprogenous microorganisms of the liquid foodstuff, and the position of the hydroxyl group and the number of the carbon atoms of the alkyl group are closely concerned with the kind of the liquid foodstuff to which the compounds may be applicable effectively. Accordingly, a suitable compound is selected depending on the kind of the liquid foodstuff to be preserved.

Natural fruit juices are easily contaminated with microorganisms during the course from the juice-squeezing step to the canning or bottling step, and deteriorations such as occurrence of turbidness and gas formation are caused by molds, yeasts and acid-resistant lactic acid bacteria. Such deteriorations may be prevented by adding to juice benzoic acid at a concentration of 500γ/ml to some extent, but this preservative gives a peculiar unpleasant taste to the juice, and therefore, good results are hardly obtainable by use of this preservative.

Dehydroacetic acid as preservative for juice is defective in that since it is gradually decomposed in a juice product and loses its activity, deterioration is easily caused to occur when a bottle of the juice product is uncorked after long time storage. When the compounds of the process are used as preservative at a concentration of 10 to 50γ/ml, the abovementioned defects of the conventional preservatives can be overcome.

Examples 1 through 7: One platinum loopful of a putrefactive liquor (containing trained yeast, mold, acid-resistant lactic acid bacteria and other bacteria) was added to 50 ml of a fruit juice prepared by squeezing an orange (Onshyu variety) and adding sugar thereto in such an amount as would give a sugar content of 10%. Then a solution of a compound indicated in the table below in 1N aqueous sodium hydroxide was added to the juice, and the juice was allowed to stand at 30°C.

The growth of mold and occurrence of turbidness in the juice was examined. The results are shown in the table. Symbols "−" to "+++++" appearing in the table mean the absence of the mold or turbidity and the intensity degree of the mold growth or turbidity in the juice. The following are the structures for Compounds 1 through 7:

(1)   HO—⟨OH⟩—COOC₄H₉   (2)   HO—⟨OH⟩—COOC₅H₁₁

(3)   ⟨OH, HO⟩—COOC₅H₁₁   (4)   HO—⟨HO⟩—COOC₅H₁₁

(5)   HO—⟨OH⟩—COC₄H₉   (6)   HO—⟨HO⟩—COC₅H₁₁

(7)   HO—⟨HO⟩—COC₅H₁₁

Preservative	Amount added (γ/ml.)	Turbidness			Mold growth		
		3 days	7 days	10 days	3 days	7 days	10 days
Non-added control		+	++	+++	+	+++	+++++
Benzoic acid	500	−	± to +	++	−	− to +	+
Butyl parahydroxybenzoate	30	−	−	− to ±	−	−	−
Compound:							
1	30	−	− to ±	± to +	−	−	±
2	30	−	− to ±	± to +	−	−	± to ±
3	30	−	−	−	−	−	−
4	30	−	−	−	−	−	−
5	30	−	−	±	−	−	−
6	30	−	−	±	−	−	− to ±
7	150	−	−	±	−	−	− to ±

From the results shown in the table it can be seen that the compounds used are prominently effective for inhibiting the growth of mold and preventing the occurrence of turbidness in fruit juice, as compared with benzoic acid.

Polyphosphates

W.F. Kohl and R.H. Ellinger; U.S. Patent 3,681,091; August 1, 1972; assigned to Stauffer Chemical Company discovered that nutrient-containing materials, e.g., food materials of vegetable as well as animal origin can be preserved against microbial action of deleterious fungi, including molds as well as yeast and bacteria in an unexpectedly, highly effective manner by the incorporation therein of a small but effective amount of a substance comprising a medium chain length polymeric phosphate of the type:

$$X-O-\left[\begin{array}{c} O \\ \| \\ P-O \\ | \\ O-Y \end{array}\right]_{N_{ave}}X$$

wherein X represents hydrogen or an alkali metal including ammonium, which is preferably sodium or potassium; and Y represents an alkali metal including ammonium, which is preferably sodium or potassium: N_{ave} represents an average chain length between about not less than 14 and about 100. A preferred range comprises polyphosphates having N_{ave} between about 16 and 37. The term average chain length or N_{ave} as employed herein, is intended to represent a statistical average chain length or indication of the number of recurring units linked together comprising the anionic species. Such an average is determined by titration as described in Van Wazer et al, *Anal. Chem.*, 26, 1755-9 (1954).

It has been found that the medium chain length polyphosphates as described herein exhibit unexpectedly superior performance as microbial inhibitors in food preparations when compared with orthophosphates, pyrophosphates and hexametaphosphates employed in the past. It has also been found that the very long chain polyphosphates, e.g., average chain lengths of 1,000 to 2,000 are unsuitable for incorporating in certain food preparations because of solubility and viscosity considerations. There is also evidence that the long chain materials have decreased efficacy as compared with the medium chain length polyphosphates.

The terms metaphosphate, hexametaphosphate, and polymeric phosphates when employed in conjunction with examples illustrating hexametaphosphates as employed herein and in the prior art should be distinguished from the medium chain length polymeric phosphates having the N_{ave} as defined herein on the basis that such prior usage refers to N_{ave} from about 6 to a maximum of 12 when determined by the method of Van Wazer hereinbefore referenced. The term microbial as employed herein pertains to fungi, including mold and yeast, as well as bacteria. The inhibition of spoilage may be due to microbiostatic as well as microbiocidal action.

Suitable food materials which are retarded from spoilage by application of medium chain length polyphosphates include a wide range of solid as well as fluid food preparations. Fruit and vegetables illustrate typical solid foods which are benefited by surface application of these polyphosphates. It is pointed out, however, that potatoes are specifically excepted from this group as they do not appear to benefit by such treatment.

Food materials which are fluid during processing appear to be more readily retarded from microbial spoilage by application of medium chain length polyphosphates than solid foods. The greatest efficacy has been attained in clear juices such as apple juices and apple ciders. The polyphosphates can be readily incorporated in fluids by simple admixture or blending techniques known in the art.

In general, one skilled in this art would be able to readily determine an effective amount of medium chain length polyphosphates for a particular application. Broadly effective amounts will vary between about 0.1 and about 5% on a weight basis. However, a preferred range where the polyphosphates are blended into a fluid is between about 0.1 and about 2% and most preferably 0.5 and about 1.0% on a weight basis. When dipping, flooding or spraying techniques are employed, the preferred concentration of solution is between about 5 and about 20% by weight.

It has also been found that the medium chain length polyphosphates exhibit superior taste appeal when compared with known preservatives of comparable efficacy such as alkali metal benzoates, sorbates or propionates, in particular the sodium or potassium salts of these materials. This is particularly true in the case of apple cider. Taking into consideration both efficacy and taste, the combination of polyphosphate and sorbates or benzoates is preferred for the preservation of edible fluids, in particular. Combined concentrations of between about 0.2 and about 2% and most preferably 0.5 to 1.0% on a weight basis are employed.

When a combination additive such as sodium benzoate or potassium sorbate or sodium propionate and sodium polyphosphate (N_{ave} 25) is prepared as an article of commerce, the ratio of the benzoate, sorbate or propionate salt to polyphosphate is preferably between about 1:20 to 20:1 and most preferably between about 2:1 to 1:2 on a weight basis.

Example 1: In an experiment employing apple juice as the medium of microbiological spoilage, the effects of different inorganic phosphates were tested against a variety of fungi:

(1) *Aspergilus niger*
(2) *Penicillium italicum*
(3) wild yeast isolated from spoiled juice
(4) baker's yeast, *Saccharomyces cerevisiae*
(5) a blue-green mold isolated from spoiled apples

The following phosphates were added to portions of apple juice to a final concentration of 1%.

(1) disodium orthophosphate
(2) sodium acid pyrophosphate
(3) tetrasodium pyrophosphate
(4) sodium tripolyphosphate
(5) sodium hexametaphosphate (N_{ave} 9)

(6) sodium polyphosphate (N_{ave} 18)
(7) sodium polyphosphate (N_{ave} 20)
(8) sodium polyphosphate (N_{ave} 31)
(9) sodium polyphosphate (N_{ave} 35)

Inoculation of portions of the juice containing the phosphates was carried out by use of suspensions of spores from the molds, or suspensions of cells of yeasts, respectively. Incubation temperature was 25°C which condition assured good growth facilities as was seen in the controls which contained no phosphates, and in which heavy growth could be observed from 1 to 2 days after inoculation.

No inhibition was observed in the samples of juice to which had been added orthophosphate. It was further observed that tetrasodium pyrophosphate and tripolyphosphate acted as slight inhibitors for fungal growth. Especially good inhibition was achieved by the use of sodium hexametaphosphate (N_{ave} 9) and of sodium polyphosphate 18 to 35). The latter group acted as chemical preservatives in foods, and preserved the juices to which spores of molds or yeast cells had been added for up to 6 weeks.

Example 2: Taste preferences were evaluated in samples of stored apple cider. Samples of apple cider were preserved by various additive systems and tested for the consumer acceptance by taste panel analysis. The results of the taste panel analysis were as follows. Taste panels compared the flavor of apple cider samples containing preservatives with a reference sample which contained no additive. The reference sample was frozen apple cider which was thawed the day of the test. The taste panel members rated the samples according to the following descriptive terms:

	Assigned Numerical Value
Better than reference	5
Equal to reference	4

(continued)

Assigned Numerical Value

Slightly less desirable	3
Much less desirable	2
Completely undesirable	1

Numerical values were assigned to the descriptions, in order to facilitate statistical analysis of the data. The taste scores gathered on each sampling day varied somewhat. However, when weekly averages were taken, a definite trend could be established. The weekly averaged taste scores allowed a valid comparison of benzoate or sorbate versus mixtures of these preservatives with NaMP–25 (sodium polyphosphate with average chain length 25).

Average Taste Scores of Apple Cider

Additive	1st week	2nd week	3rd week	4th week	5th week
0.1% Na-benzoate	2.83	2.58	2.82	2.51	2.26
0.05% Na-benzoate plus 0.5% NaMP–25	3.20	2.98	2.84	2.77	2.43
0.1% K-sorbate	2.55	2.58	2.52	2.06	1.90
0.05% K-sorbate plus 0.5% NaMP–25	3.21	3.00	3.17	2.84	2.63

The higher values for each week and thus the preferred preservative systems were given by the combinations of sodium polyphosphate (N$_{ave}$ 25) with either sodium benzoate or potassium sorbate.

Ion Exchange Resin Treatment

C.F. Huffman; U.S. Patent 3,801,717; April 2, 1974; assigned to The Coca-Cola Company describes a process for bringing a fruit juice, natural beverage, or liquid food into contact with an ion exchange material for a short period of time and thereafter separating the juice, etc., from the ion exchange material. This short contact time with the ion exchange material increases the resistance of the juice to abuse so that the juice can then be heat-treated and stored without the formation of off-flavors to any marked extent.

Following treatment, the juice is separated from the resin and may be sent for further processing depending on the desired end use. For example, if a concentrated juice is desired, the juice may be subjected to evaporative conditions to remove water. If it is desired thereafter to prepare a dried product, the juice or concentrated juice may be dried according to conventional methods such as vacuum belt drying, micro-flake drying, freeze drying, spray drying, vacuum self-drying or foam mat drying.

It has been found that the best results are produced when a strong cationic ion exchange resin is used in contact with the juice, natural beverage, or liquid food. Suitable strong cationic ion exchange resins include Amberlite IR–120 and Dowex–50. While the objects of the process may be achieved by using a limited amount of ion exchange material, most desirable results are obtained when an amount in excess of the stoichiometric amount is employed. The precise amount of ion exchange material to be employed will depend on the composition of the product being treated, treatment conditions, resin particle size and subsequent processing of the product; but in general, it has been found that up to about one pound of wet resin per pound of soluble solids in the material being treated will give the desired results. A preferred range of resin to soluble solids is about 0.5 to 1.0 pound of wet resin per pound of soluble solids.

For example, when orange juice is brought into contact with an excess of strong cationic ion exchange resin, the pH of the juice changes from 3.7 to 2.0. When a lesser amount of resin is used, so that the pH of the juice becomes 3.0, the resulting juice has more resistance to browning and off-flavor formation than the untreated juice, but exhibits less resistance than when treated with an excess of resin. The resin material after use may be washed to remove materials that have accumulated on the resin. The washing medium may be water or other suitable liquid. At appropriate intervals, the resin may be regenerated with an acid solution such as a 5% solution of sulfuric acid of a 10% solution of hydrochloric acid. A treatment of juice in accordance with the process results in removal of amino acids and amines which have been associated by other investigators with the formation of off-flavors. In addition, metallic ions such as potassium, sodium, calcium and magnesium ions are removed by the ion exchange resin.

By eliminating off-flavors and undesirable aromas, it is possible to prepare such products as improved hot-packed, single strength orange juice, improved hot-packed, single strength lemon juice, as well as improved dried juice crystals or powders that may be subsequently reconstituted. The process makes possible the storage of improved bulk concentrated citrus juices at ambient temperature and the manufacture of improved concentrated or single strength juices for nonrefrigerated shelf storage.

Example: Forty-four pounds of 65°Brix orange juice concentrate were diluted to 45°Brix and Valencia oil (14.2 ml or 0.015% by volume) was added. The juice was further diluted to 18°Brix and was treated with 44.0 lb of Dowex–50W for ten minutes with stirring. The Dowex–50W was separated from the juice and the Brix of the juice was 15°. The pH was adjusted from 2.04 to 3.76 by the addition of 555 ml of 45% potassium hydroxide solution followed by a final Brix adjustment to 12.5° using spring water. The product was heat stabilized and then hot-packed in cans. The cans were cooled in water and stored at 70° to 80°F in a storage room.

A control sample of untreated juice was prepared in the same manner omitting the treatment with Dowex–50W and also omitting the pH adjustment. Following storage for approximately 48 hours, one can of treated juice and one can of control were opened and taste-tested. The treated sample was found to exhibit a good taste and had only a slightly cooked flavor. The untreated sample was found to exhibit a poor taste and had a decidely cooked flavor.

One week later, samples were taste-tested by a panel experienced in taste-testing orange juice and the panel exhibited a significant preference for the treated sample. Four weeks after the treated sample and the control sample were prepared, they were submitted to a panel of experienced taste-tasters that were not conditioned to testing orange juice. The panel also showed a highly significant preference for the treated sample. Three months later, one can of the treated juice and one can of the untreated juice were taste-tested. The treated juice exhibited a pleasant fruit odor whereas the untreated juice exhibited a strong cooked odor and taste.

CLARIFICATION OF FRUIT JUICES

Contact with Resinous Copolymer

Many essentially clear limpid beverages, or beverages intended to be of an essentially clear or limpid character, are liable to be obtained in their as-manufactured state with some degree of haziness or cloudiness that persists despite filtration, or to develop such a condition upon standing or being chilled, or both. It is quite common, of course, for beverages to be stored, sometimes under refrigeration, after their manufacture.

Besides, they are frequently chilled prior to consumption to enhance their palatability. Such haziness, including hazing on standing and chill haze, occurs frequently in the several essentially clear or limpid beverages that are derived from various fruits, berries and vegetables or mixtures thereof.

Typical of such beverages there may be mentioned cider (sweet or hard), such unfermented fruit juices as apple juice, grape juice, prune juice and the like, cranberry juice and other clear berry juices that are desired to be obtained and used in a transparent or translucent, haze-free condition.

It has been found by *M.E. Elder, C. Moore and W.F. Tousignant; U.S. Patent 3,146,107;*

August 25, 1964; assigned to The Dow Chemical Company that the substances which are responsible for producing the hazing phenomena in beverages can be removed by contact with and preferably by passage through a bed of a water-insoluble polymeric 2-oxazolidinone, 2-oxazinidinone or 2-oxazepidinone resin at a reaction temperature between its freezing point and the highest temperature tolerable without harm by the beverage, advantageously between about 4° and about 40°C and preferably between 20° and 30°C.

Thereby the haze and turbidity-inducing ingredients and their precursors in the beverage are removed by the resin particles, and the treated beverage is recovered by mechanical separation from the resin. The resins useful in the process are prepared by reacting an alkali metal salt of a 2-oxazolidinone, 2-oxazinidinone or 2-oxazepidinone having the formula

$$\begin{array}{c} \rule{1cm}{0pt}(CZ_2)_m\!-\!O \\ \rule{2cm}{0pt}| \\ \rule{1cm}{0pt}\rule[-0.3em]{0pt}{1em}N\rule{1cm}{0pt}C\!-\!O \\ \rule{1.5cm}{0pt}| \\ \rule{1.5cm}{0pt}H \end{array}$$

wherein Z is independently selected from the group consisting of H, alkyl groups having 1 to 4 carbon atoms and aryl groups having 6 to 10 carbon atoms and m is an integer from 2 to 4, and wherein only one aryl substituent group may be present, with a chloromethylated vinylaryl polymer having 0.75 to 1.5 chloromethyl groups per available aryl nucleus, cross-linked with between 0.9 and 5 mol percent, vinylaryl polymer basis, of a cross-linking agent having two nonconjugated vinylidene groups, in stoichiometric or substantially stoichiometric proportions until at least 60% of the benzylic chloride is replaced by an oxazolidinone, oxazinidinone or oxazepidinone group, as specified. The reaction may be represented as follows

$$[-CH_2\!-\!\overset{|}{C}H\!-\!C_6H_4CH_2Cl] \;+\; Na\underline{N\!-\!CO\!-\!O\!-\!CH_2\!-\!CH_2} \;\longrightarrow\; [-CH_2\!-\!\overset{|}{C}H\!-\!C_6H_4\!-\!CH_2\!-\!\underline{N\!-\!CO\!-\!O\!-\!CH_2CH_2}]$$

wherein the first reactant represents a polymeric vinylbenzyl chloride and the second reactant represents an equivalent amount of 3-sodio-2-oxazolidinone.

In practice, the beverage to be treated is contacted batchwise or in a columnar operation with the air-dried, water-wet or water-swollen water-insoluble resin beads or particles of the resins described above, with or without agitation, at a temperature between the freezing point of the beverage and 40°C, preferably at room temperature, and the beverage is mechanically separated from the insoluble resin.

For greater contact the resin beads or particles can be comminuted to increase surface area. Preferably, the beverage to be treated is passed through a bed of the water-insoluble resin beads and the clarified beverage is collected as effluent. In the process the haze-producing substances and their precursors are removed by the resin. The beverage may be treated at any desired stage of its manufacture or processing. With beer, for example, the treatment may be carried out when it is being racked down from the fermenters or prior to storage in the cold cellars. Because the resins used are insoluble in the beverages being treated, no deleterious materials are added to the beverages.

The breakthrough point, when haze-producing substances or their precursors appear in the effluent after the resin has been loaded with haze-producing substances, can be determined by continuous turbidimeter measurements, or by adding a minor amount, ca 20 volume percent, of a 0.1 weight percent aqueous solution of water-soluble resinous polymeric N-vinyl-2-oxazolidinone or its 5-methyl homolog, having a Fikentscher K-value between 10 and 100 (Cellulosechemie 13:60) to resin bed effluent and observing whether a precipitate forms. Haze-producing substances form a precipitate with such water-soluble resinous polymeric N-vinyl-2-oxazolidinones. At this point the exhausted resin beads can be regenerated by elution with any of the following reagents: dilute, ca 2.5%, bleach (NaOCl) solutions; dilute, ca 4%, acetic acid (vinegar); dilute, ca 5%, ammonia solutions.

Improved Pectinase Activity

Fruit substances, such as fruit juices, jellies and the like, are desirably clear and sparkling for maximum consumer acceptance. It is well-known that such fruit substances can be clarified to remove suspended colloidal pectic materials by adding pectolytic enzymes to such fruit substances and allowing the resulting mixture to stand until the suspended material is flocculated. Decantation or filtration results in a clarified liquid.

However, in order to achieve the desired degree of clarification, repeated filtrations are often necessary. Even after repeated processing with pectinase and filtration the fruit substances are sometimes found to remain somewhat cloudy. The pectinase used for clarification of fruit substances is a well-known material and consists essentially of a mixture of pectinesterase and polygalacturonase. As used herein, the term pectinase refers to such commercially available enzyme mixture.

In accordance with the process of *E.G. Bassett and R.L. Charles; U.S. Patent 3,335,012; August 8, 1967; assigned to Miles Laboratories, Inc.,* a composition useful for improved clarification of fruit substances consists essentially of a mixture of pectinase and at least 50 parts per million by weight based on weight of pectinase of a material selected from the class consisting of clupeine, salmine, sturine, poly-L-lysine and a basic, nonenzymatic protein-like factor derived from pectinase, the factor having the properties of electrophoretic mobility of about 1.09×10^{-5} cm^2/volt/sec at pH 9.4, molecular weight between 30,000 and 60,000, ultraviolet absorption spectrum having typical protein peak at 277μ and very strong absorption below 230μ, and visible absorption spectrum having a main peak at 310μ with smaller peaks at 320μ and 325μ.

Preferably the composition contains from 50 to 150 parts per million by weight of the added material based on weight of the pectinase. At least 50 parts per million by weight of the added material must be present before there is noticeable improvement in pectinase clarification activity. When more than about 150 parts per million by weight of the added material are employed, the clarification takes place rapidly, but generally there is no particular advantage to using the added material in amounts over 150 parts per million by weight.

The clupeine, salmine and sturine materials are protamines and are known to be available from fish. These protamines are technically different from protein albumins previously employed for clarification of beverages. The protamines are not coagulated by heat while albumins are readily coagulated by heat. Poly-L-lysine is an amino acid and is known to be commercially available.

The basic, nonenzymatic protein-like factor derived from pectinase can be obtained in several ways. An aqueous solution of pectinase can be mixed with ammonium sulfate, in an amount of from 25 to 65% of the amount required for saturation of the solution with ammonium sulfate, to form a precipitate of the desired factor. The precipitate is then separated from the supernatant liquid.

This factor can be added in the required amounts to pectinase in a solid form or in a liquid form. The liquid form is prepared by dissolving the solid factor in water. Any enzymatic activity in the factor is preferably eliminated prior to its use. Removal of enzymatic activity is accomplished by boiling the raw material pectinase solution for 10 to 30 minutes prior to precipitation of the factor or by boiling an aqueous solution of the factor for a similar period of time. If desired, solid factor free of enzyme activity can then be obtained from this solution by evaporation of liquid.

The preferred method of obtaining the factor derived from pectinase comprises boiling an aqueous solution of pectinase for a time sufficient to destroy the enzymatic activity of the solution, cooling the solution to room temperature, removing insoluble matter from the solution (such as by filtration or centrifugation), exhaustively dialyzing the solution against water to form a gelatinous precipitate, extracting the desired factor from the precipitate with an aqueous alkaline medium containing at least 0.05 M of an alkaline buffer, adding a nonaqueous polar solvent to the resulting extractant solution in an amount of 65 volume percent concentration to form a precipitate, separating the precipitate from the supernatant solution, adding a nonaqueous polar solvent to the supernatant solution in an amount of 80 volume percent concentration to form a precipitate of the desired factor product, and then recovering the solidified product. The mentioned dialysis procedure is conveniently carried out against running tap water for 48 hours followed by dialysis against running distilled water for 24 hours.

Illustrative examples of alkaline buffers useful in the above process are sodium carbonate, sodium citrate-citric acid and the like. The preferred extractant is 0.2 to 0.6 M sodium carbonate. Illustrative examples of nonaqueous polar solvents are ethanol, methanol, acetone and the like. Ethanol is the preferred nonaqueous polar solvent. With the exception of process steps involving boiling of solutions, all the above described process steps are conveniently carried out at normal room temperatures.

Example: An aqueous solution (250 ml) of commercially available pectinase containing 10 weight percent pectinase (25 grams) was fractionally precipitated with ammonium sulfate. Solid ammonium sulfate was added until the solution contained 65% of the saturation amount (107.5 grams). A heavy precipitate formed. After standing for 20 minutes at room temperature, the precipitate was separated from the solution by centrifugation at 1,000 rpm and dissolved in water at room temperature. The resulting solution was found to contain only a small part of the original pectinase activity.

This solution was then heated to boiling to destroy all traces of enzyme activity and was designated as nonenzyme factor. To the 280 ml of ammonium sulfate-containing solution remaining from this precipitation, an additional 30 grams of solid ammonium sulfate were added to 80% of saturation. After standing for one hour at room temperature, a second precipitate which formed was separated by centrifugation at 1,000 rpm and redissolved in water at room temperature.

The resulting solution was found to contain most of the pectinase activity present in the starting solution. This solution was designated as factor-free pectinase. The strength of the solutions of nonenzyme factor and factor-free pectinase were such that a mixture of 1 ml of each is equivalent in properties to 1 ml of original pectinase solution. The original pectinase contained 170 parts per million by weight nonenzyme factor.

Various mixtures of factor-free pectinase and nonenzyme factor were prepared and tested for clarification ability on 50 ml samples of apple juice at 50°C. The time to produce substantially complete flocculation (measured from time of addition of mixture to apple juice) was used as indication of clarification ability. The results are shown in the table below.

	Run		
	1	2	3
Factor-free pectinase, ml	1	1	1
Non-enzyme factor, ml	1	2	3
Flocculation time, min	11	9	5

It can be seen from the above data that when the nonenzyme factor is added to pectinase, the flocculation time substantially decreases. Run 1 simulates action of commercial pectinase. Run 2 shows action of 1 ml additional factor (an added 150 to 170 parts per million by weight). Run 3 shows an added 300 to 340 parts per million by weight of factor.

Pectin Transeliminase Treatment

In various fruits, such as apples, grapes, citrus fruits and the like, there are contained considerable amounts of pectic substances, the elution and incorporation of which into fruit juices are caused by mashing or pressing the fruits. It has been known that the eluted pectic substances present in the fruit juice maintain the stability of the colloid system present in juice, thereby making the juice turbid, or because of being extremely rich in viscosity the pectic substances make it difficult to carry out the treatments required in a process of manufacturing product fruit juices, such as steps of pressing and filtering fruits or mashed products thereof or the steps of filtering the pressed juices from fruits, thereby prolonging the operation time or lowering the yields of product fruit juices.

Moreover, the pectic substances act frequently as contributory causes for a jellification during the course of operating the concentration step and the like. It has further been known that degradation of the pectic substances results in a liberation of flavor constituents bonded to the pectic substances, whereby excellent flavors are imparted to the resultant fruit juices.

The pectic substances referred to herein are composed mainly of polymers consisting of α-1,4-galacturonide units, which are classified into pectic acid and pectin depending on the state of the carboxyl radicals present in the galacturonic acid. The pectic acid is a polymerized product of the galacturonic acid containing free carboxyl radicals, while the pectin is that of the galacturonic acid in which the carboxyl radicals have been partially methyl esterified. The pectic substances contained in fruit juices are composed mainly of the pectin having usually about 60 to about 90% of the carboxyl radicals esterified, and they contain scarcely any pectic acid in which the carboxyl radicals have not been esterified at all.

Previously, pectin esterase (PE) and polygalacturonase (PG) were used to degrade fruit pectins but they were extremely difficult to remove from juices after their action had ceased, thus adversely affecting the flavor of the juice.

Studies by *T. Yokotsuka and S. Ishii; U.S. Patent 3,666,487; May 30, 1972; assigned to Kikkoman Shoyu Co., Ltd., Japan* have resulted in the finding that pectin transeliminase (herein referred to as PTE), which is entirely different in action and function from such pectolytic enzymes as PE and PG, will act independently and satisfactorily upon the pectin, whereby the treatment of fruit juice becomes easy, the juicing step is improved, the yield of juice pressed out of fruit is increased and the clarification of product fruit juice can be accomplished. This is ascribable to the fact that PTE reacts with an α-1,4-galacturonide bond, thereby effectively degrading the pectin.

The method comprises adding PTE to a material to be treated, such as mashed fruit or juice, at any stage of mashing, pressing and filtering, and treating such material with the PTE under the conditions of pH 3 to 6, temperature of $40°$ to $60°C$ and treatment time of from scores of minutes to ten odd hours, thereby degrading pectin contained in the resulting fruit juice. The juice is then heated to inactivate the PTE and solids removed by filtration or centrifuging to give a clear product fruit juice.

Example 1: A cultured product obtained by solid-culturing *Aspergillus sojae* 48 ATCC 20235 in wheat bran for two or three days was extracted with 5 times as much water, and the extract was then centrifuged to give a transparent crude enzyme-suspension. A precipitate formed by addition to the enzyme-suspension of ammonium sulfate in an amount necessary for attaining a 40% saturation was removed. Subsequently, a precipitate formed by addition of ammonium sulfate in an amount necessary for attaining a 75% saturation to a supernatant liquid of the enzyme-suspension was collected by centrifugal separation.

The precipitate thus collected was dissolved in a small amount of distilled water and the solution was passed through a column (2 x 140 cm) packed with Sephadex G-25 to remove the ammonium sulfate, and then an eluted fraction of enzyme protein was lyophilized to enzyme powder. The enzyme powder was dissolved in 0.01 M acetate buffer solution adjusted to pH 4.0, and adsorption was effected by means of a column packed with CM-cellulose, the column being equilibrated with the buffer solution. PTE adsorbed to the column was eluted with 0.1 M acetate buffer solution adjusted to pH 5.0. After repeating this operation, the eluted fractions of PTE were collected and concentrated. Subsequently, the gel formed was filtered off using a column packed with Sephadex G-100. In this manner, there was obtained an ultracentrifugally and electrophoretically homogeneous purified PTE that is absolutely free from other enzymes.

One liter of apple (species: Jonathan) juice was treated with 150 units (protein content: 0.5 mg) of the purified PTE obtained according to the above method at 40°C for 60 minutes. Thereafter, the enzyme-reaction was stopped by heat treatment. The reaction product was cooled and then centrifuged at 3,000 rpm for 5 minutes to give an extremely clarified apple juice having a light transmission value of 97.00 at 660 mμ. On the other hand, a control treated, without addition of the enzyme, in the same manner as above failed completely to give a clear apple juice.

Example 2: Thirty units of purified PTE obtained according to exactly the same procedure as in Example 1 was added to 100 ml of grape (species: Delaware) juice. After the reaction at 50°C for 30 minutes, the reaction product obtained thereby was then treated in the same manner as in Example 1 to give a clarified grape juice having a light transmission value of 96.5 at 660 mμ. A control treated without addition of the enzyme in the same procedure as above, however, failed to give a clear grape juice.

Example 3: A cultured product obtained by culturing *Aspergillus inui* 05 in a mixed medium comprising wheat bran and rice bran for 3 days was dried and then ground. One liter of mandarin (species: Unshu) juice was treated with 2 grams (PTE content: 724 units) at 40°C for 18 hours to give a clear mandarin juice.

Example 4: Twenty mg (PTE content: 94.4 units) of an enzyme obtained from a cultured product of *Aspergillus sojae* 48 ATCC 20235 by salting out using ammonium sulfate was added to 500 ml of pear (species: Nijusseiki) juice, and the mixture was treated at 40°C for 20 minutes to give a clear pear juice.

Controlled Depectinization

The method of *J.-P. Richard; U.S. Patent 3,795,521; March 5, 1974* provides a continuous process for the production of stable juices from fruit and vegetable products which comprises extracting the juice from the product and removing cellular debris, adding pectinolytic enzymes to the juice to obtain a mixture of juice and pectinolytic enzymes of controlled concentration, continuously passing the mixture through a heated enclosure at a controlled temperature and flow rate, continuously filtering the mixture leaving the heated enclosure, and continuously passing the filtrate through a pasteurization stage, the juice leaving the pasteurization stage being ready for enclosure in containers.

The calculation of the optimum concentration of pectinolytic enzymes in the juice to be treated and the determination of the optimum time/temperature combination (less than one minute at 87° to 88°C in the case of apples) for the depectinization of the medium and for the coagulation of the proteins to be simultaneously the best, are carried out by measuring the viscosity variation of the medium before and after depectinization. The measurement of the viscosity of the juice before and after depectinization during the process is then used to control the flow rate of enzymes into the juice in such a way that a predetermined desirable enzymes concentration is introduced into the juice to be treated.

In addition or alternatively it may be used to control the time and/or temperature of the depectinization process. By controlling these variables in desired combinations it is possible to preselect the degree of clarity and the yield of the finished products, to achieve the optimum depectinization and to select an optimum filtration temperature.

FIGURE 5.1: CONTROLLED DEPECTINIZATION

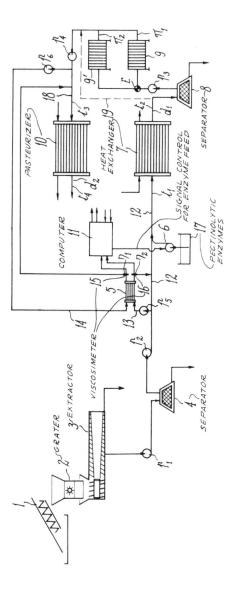

Source: J.-P. Richard; U.S. Patent 3,795,521; March 5, 1974

Referring to Figure 5.1 a production line for fruit or vegetable juices comprises a supply system 1 for fruits or vegetables, such as a feed screw for example, a grater 2, where applicable (for those cases where it is intended to obtain juices from fruits or vegetables which require preliminary grating), and an extractor 3 in which the juice is extracted from the fruits or vegetables, thus favoring the rupturing of the cells of which the fruits or vegetables are composed, the juice obtained being however full of cellular debris containing in particular cellulose fractions and pectin fractions.

Following the extractor 3 is an apparatus 4 suitable for separating the juice from the cellulose fractions which it contains. This apparatus for example may be a centrifuge, a sieve or a continuous decanter. The juice from the apparatus 4 is then passed on line 12 to a heated container through which it continuously passes in this case a heat exchanger 7 in which a depectinization operation is carried out.

The depectinization operation is made necessary by the fact that the pectin fractions contained by the juice prevent the filtering of the latter, as they are the principal cause of the clogging of the filters. A portion of the juice passing along line 12 is taken off on a bypass line 13 by pump p_5 and passed through a heat exchanger 5 before being returned to the line 12.

A pump 6 under the control of a servo control unit 11 pumps a controlled quantity of pectinolytic enzymes from a reservoir 17 into the juice in line 12. The depectinized juice obtained at the outlet from the heat exchanger 7 is continuously passed through a decanter or other separator 8 and is then filtered on a plate or cloth filter 9–9' by means of a filtration addition, such as for example kieselguhr. The filtered juice obtained is conveyed on line 18 for pasteurization which is carried out continuously in a heat exchanger 10.

At the outlet from the heat exchanger 10, the juice needs no further treatment and is transmitted to a conditioning unit, or for storage under sterile conditions, or for immediate bottling or canning.

If it is desired to obtain a juice having controlled and stable turbidity rather than clarity, it is sufficient to modify the conditions for concentrating with enzymes and the depectinization time/temperature combination so that coagulation in particular, but not solely coagulation, takes place not during heating in the exchanger 7 but during the pasteurization or cooling of the juice.

A portion of the filtered juice in line 18 is extracted on line 14 by a pump p_6 and passed through the heat exchanger 5 to heat the untreated juice in line 13 before being returned to line 18. The treated and untreated juices leaving the heat exchanger then have approximately the same temperatures and their respective viscosities are measured by two viscosimeter probes 15, 16, the viscosity measurements being supplied to the controller 11 and the difference in these measurements being used as a control parameter.

Preferably the difference in viscosity $\eta_2 - \eta_1$ (η_2 is viscosity before depectinization and η_1 is viscosity after depectinization and filtering) is used to control the addition of enzymes by controlling the pump 6 so as to maintain a predetermined constant viscosity difference. Times and temperature in 7 and 10 will be within desired limits; the viscosity measurement can also be used to control the flow rate of steam to 7 and 10 and/or the juice flow rate instead of or as well as the enzymes dosing pump 6. Control may also be carried out to maintain the final viscosity η_1 within a desired range.

Because of the importance of the coagulation phenomenon (coagulation of the proteins present) and of the two viscosity minima resulting therefrom, the control system is made to control both the flow rate d_1 through the heat exchanger 7 and the temperatures t_1 and t_2 at which the juice enters and leaves the heat exchanger, so as to control both the flow and thus the time of treatment and the pressure of the steam, and thus the temperature of treatment (t). The temperature difference $t_4 - t_3$ and the flow rate d_2 applied to the heat exchanger 10 are also maintained constant by means of the servo control system 11.

To summarize, the dosing pump **6** is subjected to control under the automatic and continuous measurements of the viscosities η_1, η_2 and their difference in such a way that the quantity of enzymes injected into the circuit keeps $\eta_2 - \eta_1$ substantially constant and η_1 within a predetermined range. In addition the temperatures and flow rates applied to the two heat exchangers are also kept constant by means of the regulating system **11**.

Finally, if **9** and **9'** are polishing filters functioning alternately, the change will be made automatically from **9** to **9'** by means of the automatic valve **E**, when the pressures π_1, π_2 alternately reach the limiting clogging value. In the case of a continuous filter, the problem will clearly be simplified.

Example: Into a pilot installation constructed in accordance with the process, there are introduced, into the supply screw **1**, 250 kg per hour of apples which, after washing, are treated in the grater **2** and the extractor **3**, which, in the present case, is constituted by a continuous press. The juice obtained is then conveyed to the apparatus **4**.

The juice freed of cellulose fractions is then transmitted into the heat exchanger **7**, which may with advantage, but not restrictively, be a plate-type heat exchanger; the temperature of the juice t_1, before its entry into the heat exchanger, is 20°C.

In the example described here, the average concentration of enzymes supplied by the pump **6** under control of controller **11** is 7.5 grams/hectoliter of juice treated, it being understood that the concentration of enzymes in the medium will vary as a function of viscosity measurement, within limits which may lie between 3 and 8 grams/hectoliter of juice, without these limits being critical.

The capacity of the heat exchanger **7** is 200 ml and the contact time for combination of the juice to be treated and the enzymes is from 2 to 4 seconds. The juice treated leaves the heat exchanger at a temperature t_2 of the order of 87° to 88°C, at flow rate d_1 of 175 liters per hour.

After decanting into the continuous decanter (which may also be a centrifuge or a sieve) **8** the juice is filtered at the same temperature in filters **9**, **9'**, from whence it is conveyed to pasteurization by the duct **18**, while it is at a temperature t_3 of the order of about 70°C. Pasteurization is carried out in the heat exchanger **10**, from where the completed juice leaves at a temperature t_4 of 90° to 92°C to be immediately bottled or dispatched for storage in sterile tanks.

CLOUD STABILIZATION

Clouding and Coloring Agent from Citrus Peel

When preparing juices from citrus fruits, one is concerned not only with the liquid juice including the constituents dissolved therein. In order to obtain a satisfactory result, it is essential that the final juice is cloudy to a rather high degree. The cloudiness is provided by minute particles of tissue matter and cell contents, and the degree of cloudiness depends on the amount of such minute particles suspended (or colloidally dissolved) in the juice.

It has been proposed to increase the degree of cloudiness by adding various substances to remain suspended in the juice. Such addition involves disadvantages, especially because it involves the addition of alien matter to the juice. Besides the cloudiness, it is also desirable that the juice should have a color which is intense and which resembles the natural color of the citrus fruit from which the juice is derived.

The natural juice itself, i.e., such as pressed from the fruits, has some color, but in some cases it is desirable to intensify it by aid of coloring matter of the same composition and origin as the natural pigments, etc., i.e., by aid of the natural coloring matter recovered from the fruit. Likewise, it is desirable to employ natural, genuine pigments or coloring matter as well as natural, genuine cloudifier or cloudiness-causing matter for soft drinks and similar beverages.

According to the method of *K.J.S. Villadsen; U.S. Patent 3,404,990; October 8, 1968; assigned to Aktieselskbet Grindstedvaerket, Denmark*, the starting material is citrus fruit peels and/or rags, this material being the waste material left over after pressing off the citrus fruit juice from citrus fruits by conventional processing thereof. These peels, together with which some rags will usually be present, may or may not be boiled, particularly in order to remove bitter-tasting principles therefrom.

The water used for this purpose may be discarded. Whether boiled or not, the peels and rags are subjected to a comparatively coarse comminution, after which water is added, usually in an amount from 1 to 5 parts by weight, and the peels and/or rags are boiled in this water for a suitable period of time, or at least heated to a temperature near 100°C. The cell walls and solid constituents of the material are thereby softened to a considerable degree and even some hydrolysis may take place.

This boiling operation facilitates the liberation of the substances and minute particles responsible for the desired cloudiness and/or color. Subsequent to the boiling operation, the boiled material is subjected to a pressing operation, whereby a liquid is liberated from the peels and/or rags, the liquid containing suspended therein (or colloidally dissolved therein) the minute particles of cloudifier and coloring matter.

The liquid, however, may contain also larger particles suspended therein, such as cell and tissue debris and even whole cells and the like, and in order to remove the latter, the suspension of which is not stable in contradistinction to the stable suspension or colloidal solution of the minute particles referred to hereinbefore, the liquid pressed off from the peels and/or rags is subjected to a conventional treatment such as screening or centrifuging in order to remove the coarser particles. Since a rather large amount of water, for instance four parts by weight, is usually employed in the boiling of the comminuted peels and/or rags, it will normally be necessary or desirable to concentrate the liquid obtained. This concentration may be carried out in any conventional manner, usually by evaporation.

The degree of concentration will depend on various circumstances; if, for instance, the agent is to be employed in the same factory as the one in which it has been prepared, only a small degree of concentration is needed or in some cases none at all. If, however, the cloudifying and coloring agent is to be shipped for use elsewhere, a more concentrated suspension will be required in order to reduce transportation and container costs.

A suitable degree of concentration will in many cases be from 15 to 40% of dry matter content. At some stage of the overall process, a sterilization may be, but, usually a pasteurization, is carried out. This may be carried out prior to or subsequent to concentration. It is preferred to perform pasteurization as the last step before filling the material into containers, because the pasteurization may cause some loss of cloudifier, and it has been found that this loss is reduced to a minimum level if pasteurization is carried out after concentration.

The liquid thus produced is usually rather viscous, owing to the fact that pectic substances are extracted into the liquid by the hot water during the boiling operation. Such a high viscosity can be avoided by adding a pectolytic enzyme to the liquid at a convenient step, prior or subsequent or both prior and subsequent to the concentration. The enzymatic treatment may conveniently be carried out at 10° to 55°C for 1 to 24 hours. The enzymatic treatment is preferably carried out for ½ to 5 hours at 35° to 55°C prior to the concentration step.

This enzymatic treatment causes the pectic substances to be degraded, whereby the viscosity decreases. The enzymatic treatment should be concluded before pasteurization, since the latter is carried out at a temperature which destroys the enzyme.

Example: From 100 kg of oranges of the Valencia variety, 40 kg of juice were first obtained by conventional methods, e.g., pressing. Furthermore, 50 kg of peels were obtained; the remainder was discarded or subjected to processing not pertinent to the process.

The 50 kg of orange peels were boiled for 30 minutes with 50 kg of water. The water used for boiling was discarded and 59 kg of moist peels were obtained. The 59 kg of moist peels were ground and mixed with 59 kg of water, to which 590 grams of citric acid and 59 grams of pectolytic enzyme were added.

This mixture had a pH value of 3.2 and was left standing for 4 hours at 22°C during which period the pectolytic enzyme acted on the material. At the end of the enzymatic treatment, the mixture was pressed, and thereby 96 kg of cloudy liquid (orange peel liquid) were obtained. The orange peel liquid was subjected to centrifuging, concentration and finally sterilization by means of pasteurization.

Cloud Fortified Citrus Juices

All extracted citrus juices contain what is known as cloud which is a natural stable turbidity maintained in suspension by action of pectinous substances naturally occuring in the fruit. This cloud is deemed by many to impart much of the flavor of fresh juice as well as desirable appearance. It is largely in the form of colloidal materials and fine or microscopic particles of pulp. Not only is this cloud desired by consumers, but it is also deemed desirable by distributors who prefer as much stable cloud as reasonably possible.

An important feature of the process of *P.L. Douglas; U.S. Patent 3,647,475; March 7, 1972; assigned to Brown International Corporation* resides in incorporating into an extracted normal or single strength juice, such as lemon juice, a quantity of the albedo, or inner white layer of the rind or peel, in finely divided form (which is here termed comminuted form) and which is retained in stable suspension like the original cloud. This added albedo fraction contains pectin and pectinous substances, like other portions of the fruit, and creates colloidal conditions maintaining the fine comminuted particles in stable suspension. Not only is the cloud in the resultant juice improved by the fortification, but the vitamin C content is increased. This is true of all the citrus fruits.

As indicated in the flowsheet of Figure 5.2, a quantity of the selected fruit, such as 2,000 parts by weight of lemons, is extracted at room temperature in any standard or preferred juice extraction apparatus 10, from which the extracted or initial or single strength juice is passed as by a pipeline 12 to an apparatus 14 known as a finisher (or the like). This apparatus may be a well-known paddle finisher, or a screw-type finisher (such as a Chrisholm-Ryder finisher) or other finisher as desired.

The finisher 14, which also usually operates at room temperatures, performs the function of separating or straining out the coarse solids in the form of pulp or rag from the desired juice. Typically 2,000 parts by weight of fruit yields about 1,000 parts by weight of juice mixture that is passed to the finisher 14 which in turn separates about 100 parts by weight of rag or pulp that is discarded by any removing means 15.

The resultant 900 parts by weight of desired finished juice is then withdrawn, as by a line 16. Optionally, the line 16 may include a heat exchanger 18 for either warming or cooling the juice as may be desired. The line 16 then feeds the juice to a mechanical comminutor, macerator or disintegrator or other appropriate apparatus 20, such as heretofore indicated, for incorporating finely divided or comminuted albedo into the juice in whatever proportion desired.

As illustrated, the peel from the extractor 10 is passed by a conveying means 22 to a standard or other preferred shaver or other separator 24 by which the inner albedo layer is removed from the outer flavedo layer containing the oil. The flavedo layer is passed from the shaver by means 25 for disposition. The shaved albedo is then passed by a conveyor 26 to the disintegrator 20.

FIGURE 5.2: PREPARATION OF CLOUD FORTIFIED CITRUS JUICES

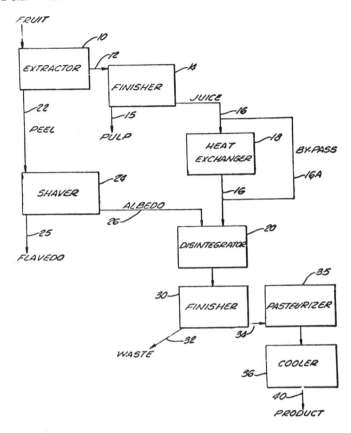

Source: P.L. Douglas; U.S. Patent 3,647,475; March 7, 1972

Thus, in this particular example, the disintegrator **20** works upon a mixture of about 60% of juice (900 parts by weight) and about 40% of shaved albedo (600 parts by weight). This apparatus may include grinding means, or chopping means, or any other form of disintegrating or macerating means that will yield a desired quantity of sufficiently finely divided or comminuted albedo distributed in the juice in colloidal or suspended form maintaining stability.

To maintain the required stable suspension, the resultant finely divided particles shall have particle sizes which are here considered colloidal in character and microscopic in size. The juice mixture, after required treatment in the disintegrator or comminutor apparatus **20** is passed through another finisher **30**, desirably of the screw finisher type by which substantially all materials coarser than the indicated colloidal or microscopic particles are separated and removed for further use or waste by a takeoff **32**.

Oversize particles that might pass the finisher, and which would otherwise settle, would be removed by further filtering or centrifuging or other appropriate means. The finished juice is then conducted, as by a pipeline **34**, to a pasteurizer **35**, and thence to a cooler **36**, whence it is removed at **40** for packaging. Pasteurization is effected at the usual pasteurization temperatures around 190° to 200°F for between about 15 seconds and about 2 minutes, before cooling, depending upon the kind of fruit. This treatment retards microbial activity and destroys pectic enzymes.

Addition of Polygalacturonase

A search of the prior art reveals that all citrus juice, even that sold as fresh chilled juice, is generally subjected to some form of heat treatment. The theory has been that this treatment is necessary not only for the destruction of spoilage organisms, but also for the inactivation of enzymes which bring about clarification of the juice. Without the heat treatment the loss of cloud lowers the quality of the juice before spoilage occurs.

At the pH of citrus juices a more severe temperature treatment is required to inactivate the pectinesterase than is necessary for the prevention of microbial deterioration. In addition there is no quick practical way to measure the degree of cloud stability being produced. Thus, there is a tendency to exceed the minimum temperature requirements to remove any possibility of clarification. The result of excessive heat treatment is a partial or complete loss of the fresh natural flavor and the development to some degree of a cooked off-flavor.

Recent developments in the art of sterilization, notably in the use of cold chemical sterilizing agents such as diethylpyrocarbonate (DEPC), promise to eliminate the need for heat as a means of preservation. Such sterilizing agents, which require no heat for their action and which are converted within hours to harmless end products, would be ideal for the protection of the delicate flavor notes of citrus juices.

A process is disclosed by *R.A. Baker and J.H. Bruemmer; U.S. Patent 3,754,932; August 28, 1973; assigned to the U.S. Secretary of Agriculture* wherein the natural cloud of fruit juice is stabilized and the juice is protected against clarification. This is accomplished by the addition of an enzyme preparation containing polygalacturonase activity and protease activity to the fresh juice immediately after it has been extracted. The addition of these enzymes in the proper concentrations produces a juice having a stable cloud equal to or superior to the cloud of freshly extracted juice.

No further treatment is necessary to remove or inactivate the added enzymes. Such juice or concentrate could then be protected against microbial deterioration by treatment with a cold process chemical sterilizing agent. The main object of the process is to provide a method of stabilizing the cloud of citrus juices to preserve the appearance of fresh, canned, and concentrated citrus juices.

The problem of clarification in orange juice may be attributed indirectly to the action of the native enzyme pectinesterase on juice soluble pectin. If allowed to act, this enzyme removes methoxy groups from the pectin molecule, producing demethylated pectin. It is this reaction product which, by precipitating as calcium pectate, causes cloud loss. It is assumed that the calcium pectate occludes the cloud particles and removes them from suspension.

This method attacks the chain of reactions leading to cloud loss at a different point. No attempt is made to inhibit pectinesterase activity. Instead, polygalacturonase, an enzyme which destroys demethylated pectins by hydrolysis is added. Thus, the formation of a calcium pectate precipitate is prevented by the removal, by hydrolysis, of demethylated pectins before it can combine with calcium.

For example, in three experiments in which Pectinol 41-P (a commercially available pectinase containing a high level of polygalacturonase) was added to fresh juice at the rate of one part in 2,000 and stored 24 hours at 80°F, the levels of water-soluble pectins, calcium pectates, and protopectin were reduced by 36, 53 and 75% respectively. Since pure preparations of polygalacturonase are not easily obtainable at the present time, commercially available pectinases which are mixtures of pectic enzymes must be used.

These commonly contain pectinesterase (PE), polygalacturonase (PG), and polymethyl-galacturonase (PMG). For the purposes described herein it is desirable to use a preparation having a high ratio of PG activity to PE activity. In addition it has been found that the presence of substantial PMG activity is detrimental to the function of the pectinase as a cloud stabilizer.

Examination of a number of commercial pectinases revealed that those having the highest ratio of PG activity to PMG activity were the most effective in stabilizing cloud. Several of these pectinases have provided good control of cloud loss at a concentration of one part to 500 parts of juice.

It is to be understood that any enzyme preparation containing polygalacturonase activity, either alone or in combination with other enzymes which are not antagonistic to the poly-galacturonase action whether derived from plant, fungal or bacterial sources, will satisfy the conditions of this process.

Another modification which can be employed is the addition of a proteolytic enzyme such as ficin, papain, or bromelin in addition to the polygalacturonase. The addition of a protease enhances the breakdown of calcium pectate by polygalacturonase. Juice treated thus has a stable cloud of greater turbidity than the cloud of freshly extracted juice.

DEAERATION PROCESSES

Deaeration of Juice in Final Package

F. A. Parodi; U.S. Patent 3,125,452; March 17, 1964; assigned to Stabil Internacional SA, Uruguay describes a process for stabilizing vegetable juices by charging the juice into its final container, deaerating the juice by boiling the juice in the container at a temperature below its boiling point at atmospheric pressure, sealing the container and sterilizing the juice in the container at a temperature below its boiling point at atmospheric pressure.

"Vegetable" as used herein is used in its broad scientific sense and refers to the plant kingdom. The process, although preferably applied to citrus fruit juices such as orange, lemon, lime and/or grapefruit, is also applicable to a wide variety of vegetable juices including grape, apple, pear, sugar cane, tomato and carrot. The process is even applicable with great success to such exotic Brazilian fruits as caju and guarana.

The flavor of vegetable juices, especially citrus fruit juices, is extremely sensitive to the temperatures used during the sterilization step. It has been discovered that when the temperature of the final sterilization step does not exceed the boiling point at normal atmospheric pressure of the liquid under treatment, the flavor of the final product compares very favorably with the flavor of the untreated natural juice. In fact, the flavor of the final product is virtually identical with that of the natural fruit juice.

The process, therefore, comprises the steps of charging the juice into its final container, applying vacuum to the container to boil the contents thereof while maintaining the temperature of the contents lower than the boiling point of the contents at normal atmospheric pressure, the juice being deaerated during this boiling operation, sealing the container while preventing air from entering therein, and heating the container to a temperature below the boiling point of the contents at normal atmospheric pressure for a period of time sufficient to sterilize the contents of the container.

During the sterilization step, the juice is heated at a temperature below about 100°C and preferably at a temperature between about 83° and 95°C. The optimum range is between about 85° and 92°C. When sterilizing at 85°C, for example, 7 to 9 minutes are generally sufficient. When sterilizing at 90°C, 6 to 7½ minutes are generally sufficient. The preferred temperature range during the ebullition step under reduced pressure is about 50° to 60°C with the ideal temperature being about 55°C. Lower temperatures are inefficient because of the need for establishing greater vacuum and also because of the greater time requirement. Temperatures significantly in excess of 60°C tend to undesirably alter the taste and flavor of the final product.

Example: 200 grams of freshly pressed orange juice were heated to a temperature of about 60°C, charged into a 220 cc bottle adapted to be stoppered and sealed with a crown cap. The bottle represented the final container for the orange juice. The container with the juice therein was subjected to a vacuum, the liquid in the container boiling vigorously when the pressure in the bottle was reduced to 76 mm of mercury.

The contents were maintained boiling for a period of about four seconds and while maintaining the container under vacuum conditions, the container was tightly stoppered with a crown cap, the entrance of atmospheric air being prevented prior to and during the sealing.

The container was then placed in a water bath having a temperature of 85°C for seven minutes during which time the container was continuously agitated. This heating sterilized the juice. The container was then removed from the bath and allowed to cool slowly to room temperature.

This product was stored at room temperature for a period of six weeks. At the end of this period the contents were found to be in excellent condition without any signs of fermentation. The product had the same taste and flavor as the natural freshly pressed orange juice.

Deoxygenated and Heat Stabilized Juice Pulp

T.W. Harwell; U.S. Patent 3,301,685; January 31, 1967; assigned to Union Carbide Corporation provides a process for producing a stable juice pulp comprising separating the juice into a pulp fraction and a liquid fraction; subjecting the pulp fraction to a stripping operation wherein an inert gas is passed through the pulp fraction so as to preferentially displace the oxygen present in the pulp fraction; increasing the temperature of the pulp fraction to a temperature sufficiently high to effect the desired stability and maintaining the pulp fraction at that temperature until the desired stability is effected; and cooling the stabilized pulp fraction preferably below 60°F.

It is preferred to maintain the pulp fraction in an inert atmosphere throughout all process steps subsequent to the stripping operation. The effect of maintaining the pulp fraction in an inert atmosphere is to most efficiently avoid recontamination of the fraction with oxygen from the air, and other equivalent methods of avoiding recontamination with oxygen may be employed, although usually with somewhat less efficiency.

There is also provided a juice pulp characterized by a pulp content of at least 15% by weight and an oxygen content of less than one part per million, and a juice product containing at least one weight percent of such a pulp and further characterized by a light transmissivity of less than 50% after storage for 24 hours at a temperature of 80°F in a substantially inert atmosphere.

In order to eliminate or minimize the adverse organoleptic effects of heat on the pulp fraction of the juice due to the presence of oxygen, the process removes oxygen from the pulp fraction by stripping it with an inert gas and then preferably continuously maintains the deoxygenated pulp fraction in an inert environment during the heat stabilization step and throughout all subsequent processing. The deoxygenated and heat stabilized pulp fraction may be packaged by itself for use in ades, blends, or other products or may be mixed with the liquid fraction of the juice.

The pulp fraction may also be subjected to additional processing steps, such as heating or evaporation to remove water therefrom. Similarly, the liquid fraction of the juice may be subjected to additional processing steps, such as concentrating, stabilizing, or deoxygenation prior to being recombined with the pulp fraction, or the final recombined mixtures of the pulp and liquid fractions may be processed further, such as by deoxygenation or stabilizing. The stabilizing temperature employed to achieve physical stability may be as high as the temperature of pasteurization for the particular juice pulp being treated, which is generally defined as a temperature high enough to destroy all pathogenic organisms and most other organisms in the vegetative form, i.e., high enough to effect partial sterilization.

However, lower temperatures lead to better retention of the desirable flavor components. Of course, the process may be used to completely sterilize the pulp fraction, or even to completely destroy or inactivate the enzymatic substances in the pulp which cause deterioration during storage.

Example: Freshly extracted orange juice was passed into a heavy pulp finisher equipped with 0.125 inch mesh cylindrical screen to separate the juice into a heavy pulp fraction and a liquid fraction. The finisher was adjusted to produce a pulp fraction containing 50% by weight pulp and a liquid fraction containing 15% by weight pulp. Pulp contents were determined by the conventional vibrating screen test, vibrating a 24-ounce sample on a 20-mesh screen for one minute.

From the finisher, the pulp fraction of the juice was passed into a stripping column and passed downwardly therethrough at a temperature of 75°F and a flow rate of 30 gallons per hour. The stripping column was 6 feet high and 4 inches in diameter. Nitrogen was passed into the bottom of the stripping column at a rate of 10 cu ft/hr and introduced into the pulp fraction therein through a 2-inch diameter porous disc having 10 micron openings.

The oxygen content of the pulp fraction was checked at various points by removing the gases from a sample of the pulp by evacuation and then analyzing the removed gases for oxygen content by a modified Orsat analysis and by use of dissolved oxygen polarographic equipment. The oxygen content of the pulp fraction was found to be 0.60 ml/100 g before stripping and 0.01 ml/100 g after stripping.

The deoxygenated pulp fraction was withdrawn from the bottom of the stripping column and passed through a preheater (coil immersed in hot water) which increased the temperature of the pulp fraction to 125°F. The preheated pulp fraction was then passed into a heater where it was quickly heated to a stabilizing temperature of 225°F and maintained at that temperature for 15 seconds. From the heater, the hot pulp was passed on through a cooler (coil immersed in cold water) which reduced the temperature of the pulp fraction to 50°F.

The deoxygenated and stabilized pulp fraction was then passed into a finisher, which removed enough liquid therefrom to increase the pulp content to 75% by weight. The concentrated pulp was then blended with the original liquid fraction and additional single strength juice and packed under nonoxidizing conditions in 6-ounce cans. These cans were stored at 0°F and periodically subjected to taste tests along with a similar product prepared from pulp which had been heat stabilized but not deoxygenated or processed under nonoxidizing conditions. The results of the comparative taste tests on these two products are shown in the following table.

Product	Gel Value	Percent Light Transmissivity	Floating pulp, gm./6-oz. can	Taste Tests After Storage							
				30 Days at 0° F.		60 Days at 0° F.		90 Days at 0° F.		6 Months at 0° F.	
				Flavor Score	Percent Pref.	Flavor Score	Percent Pref.	Flavor Score	Percent Pref.	Flavor Score	Percent Pref.
N₂ Processed Heat Stabilized and N₂ stripped pulp added	0	15	9.1	72	33	73	47	70	60	69	100
Air processed Heat stabilized pulp added	0	12	11.6	74	67	73	53	62	30	42	0

The percent preferring does not total 100% in every case because some members of the taste panel show no preference between certain samples. It is clear from the above table that the preference for the product prepared from the deoxygenated pulp increased radically as the storage period increased. Also, the flavor score of the product prepared from the deoxygenated pulp remained substantially constant while the flavor score of the product prepared from nondeoxygenated pulp decreased rather rapidly. The light transmissivity of each of the samples listed in the table was measured after storage for 24 hours at a temperature of 80°F in a substantially inert atmosphere.

STERILIZATION

Disinfection of the Surface of Pruinose Fruits

With grapes and other pruinose fruits, the conventional procedure for sterilization, based on considerations of conventional vinification, is not to treat the actual fruit before it is converted into juice; instead, endeavors are made to inhibit fermentation in the must stage by treating the must by pasteurization or refrigeration, by mutage with sulfur dioxide, and by carbon dioxide. These methods are expensive and lead to a change in the aroma and flavor of the juice, amongst other things.

According to the method of *P. Serviere; U.S. Patent 3,178,297; April 13, 1965,* yeasts and microorganisms are destroyed on grapes before pressing, so that the natural qualities are retained and there is no further fermentation. The process comprises contacting the fruit with an aqueous solution of certain substances.

The substances belong to a variety of well-known anionic detergents, namely, the ammonium or amine salts of mineral acid esters of fatty alcohols containing from 8 to 18 carbon atoms; in a preferred embodiment, ammonium or amine alkyl sulfates are used. It has been found, in particular, that ammonium lauryl sulfate gives very good results in the treatment of grapes by the process.

The process helps to provide sterilized fruits which after pressing yield a juice which, provided it is kept away from further anaerobic contamination, cannot ferment or undergo spontaneous conversion, and the process combines all the advantages of the prior art disinfection procedures with retention in the juice of all the natural qualities of the fruit from which the juice has been prepared. The juice thus prepared is completely free from alcohol and, because of its purity and its exceptional organoleptic qualities, has a marked absence of the baked flavor distinctive of pasteurization, the aroma depending solely upon the variety of vine used.

Also, since storage is so easy, qualities can be improved by aging, and blends can be prepared in which sugar and acidity are well balanced. The compounds used for sterilization are of reduced cost and the whole process is cheap to carry out on an industrial scale.

In tests carried out during the development of the process, it was found that the substances selected in this process are efficient because of their outstandingly good adaption to the conditions and mechanism of the disinfection of grapes. For instance, a grape is covered with a bloom, i.e., a nonwettable film which covers the skin and which has the classical constitution of vegetable waxes (cerotic acid, ceryl alcohols and myricyl alcohols).

The bloom retains the different substances, such as dust, stains, anticryptogamic products and more particularly vinifying yeasts and microorganisms which are deposited on the surface by the wind and insects or by handling. The bloom forms a water-repellant fat which by adsorption becomes associated with the water-repellant hydrocarbon part of the detergent so that the same penetrates the bloom. Once contact has been made with the microbe or yeast, the bactericidal part of the molecule, mainly the ammonium ion, comes into action. Finally, the hydrophilic polar group of the detergent or acid group is directed towards the aqueous phase and facilitates the wetting and unsticking of the bloom and subsequent removal of the detergent and also of the bloom which is carried away by the washing water.

Example: The technique of manufacturing and stabilizing grape juice comprises a number of stages: picking the fruit, destruction of the microorganisms, washing the fruit, pressing and conservation. For picking, the same conditions apply as for picking table grapes. They must be harvested before becoming excessively ripe; the bunches must not be crushed; and they must be transported without heaping in wide baskets. Withered or open grapes must be sorted out, and complex bunches divided. Yeasts and microorganisms on the fruit are destroyed before pressing by the bunches being immersed in the solution according to the process.

To this end, an 0.5% aqueous solution of ammonium lauryl sulfate, with 8 hours contact time, is preferably used. In the experimental cultures the yeasts and microorganisms (including the highly resistant pathogenic staphylococcus) are destroyed in two hours. This contact time must be increased fourfold to give a sufficient margin, allowing for wetting and unsticking of the bloom. The treated fruit is washed in water in which the alkyl sulfate is readily soluble.

After washing in a spray to remove the foam, the grapes are immersed in a bath of running water from 3 to 5 hours, the time varying with the rate of flow and the movement of the water. It is not essential to use a sterile water but a drinkable water must be used.

There is nothing special about pressing; it is only necessary to act quickly to prevent oxidation of the juice. Treading, stalking and pressing are performed as for white vinification, but the grapes are first drained or, and preferably, dried in hot air, for hot air drying bursts the skin cells and helps to release the anthocyans which are an important factor in aroma and coloring.

The resultant juice cannot ferment spontaneously and it can be stored by keeping it away from any chance of recontamination by the yeasts and microorganisms and by destroying the saprophytic flora which is supplied by the washing water and which occurs during pressing. To prevent recontamination, wetting must be performed outside a vinifying cellar, and the sorting and bunch-preparing steps must be separated from the following steps.

Final stabilization is achieved by removing the saprophytic flora by anaerobic storage. Hermetically sealed tanks are used for this, from a simple carboy to steel fruit juice tanks and to a closed vat with greasing of the openings. The vessels must be completely filled to obviate a large layer of air at the top.

Acid Treatment

G. Alderton; U.S. Patent 3,328,178; June 27, 1967; assigned to the U.S. Secretary of Agriculture describes a method for sterilizing a material contaminated with microbial spores which comprises contacting the material with an acid in a concentration insufficient per se to cause any substantial direct destruction of the spores, maintaining the material in contact with the acid for a period sufficient to obtain stripping of metal ions from the spores whereby to cause a substantial reduction in the thermal resistance of the spores.

The acid-treated material is restored to substantially its original pH, and without any substantial delay is subjected to heat at a temperature and for a time sufficient to produce an essentially sterile product, the combination of temperature and time of heating being substantially less than would be required to attain sterility in the absence of the acid treatment.

Example: Fresh frozen peas were thawed, pureed, heated at 100°C for one hour and centrifuged. The separated juice was filtered and autoclaved for 20 minutes under a steam pressure of 15 lb per sq in to provide a sterile, clear pea juice.

One portion of the pea juice was acidified to pH 2.5 by addition of hydrochloric acid (136 ml juice to 9 ml of 1.02 N HCl). Also, spores of *Bacillus stearothermophilus* were added to provide a level of one million spores per ml. The mixture was allowed to stand overnight (about 16 hr) at room temperature. The next day the acid treated, inoculated pea juice was treated with sufficient 1 N sodium hydroxide to restore it to its original pH of 6.0.

Another portion of the pea juice was inoculated with the same amount of the spores but without acidification, thus to provide a control. This was kept cool to prevent germination of spores. To provide comparative conditions, an equivalent amount of water and salt (NaCl) was added to the control.

Two-ml portions of the treated juice and control juice were sealed into thermal death time tubes and these were heated for various times in an oil bath maintained at 120.6°C. There were ten tubes for each of the juices and for each time of heating. After heating, the tubes were cooled quickly and each was plated on glucose-tryptone agar. After incubation at 55°C for 6 days the colonies on each plate were counted. The results are tabulated below:

Sample	Heating time, min.	Results
Acid treated and neutralized..	10	2 plates had 2 colonies each. 8 plates had no colonies.
Do........................	15	No colonies on any of the plates.
Control....................	20	All 10 plates had 20–50 colonies each.
Do........................	25	3 plates had one colony each. 7 plates had no colonies.
Do	30	No colonies on any of the plates.

Use of Hydrogen Peroxide to Prevent Spoilage

It has been suggested that hydrogen peroxide could be added to potable liquids to sterilize the liquids in order to prevent spoilage during storage or shipment. It is generally necessary to remove the residual hydrogen peroxide usually remaining in potable liquids so treated because of statutory requirements relating to potable liquids and because of undesirable side reactions which can occur to impair the quality of the potable liquid if left in contact with hydrogen peroxide for prolonged periods of time.

Satisfactory means have not been available for removing such residual hydrogen peroxide and consequently hydrogen peroxide sterilization of potable liquids has not gained wide acceptance. By way of illustration, one known means for removing residual hydrogen peroxide from potable liquids involves adding soluble catalase to the liquid to take advantage of the catalytic effect of catalase on the decomposition of hydrogen peroxide to produce water and oxygen.

The water produced is innocuous and the oxygen is readily evolved from the liquid. However, the disadvantage of this method resides in the difficulty in recovering the soluble catalase with resulting high consumption of catalase and contamination of potable liquid with unremoved catalase.

H.R. Schreiner; U.S. Patent 3,282,702; November 1, 1966; assigned to Union Carbide Corporation has developed a process for removing hydrogen peroxide from a potable liquid containing hydrogen peroxide which involves (1) contacting the hydrogen peroxide-containing potable liquid with an enzymatically-active, water-insoluble, catalyst composition composed of catalase chemically bonded to a normally solid, water-insoluble polymeric carrier having at least one electrophilic functional group capable of replacing an active hydrogen atom in an amino group to form a carbon-to-nitrogen linkage, the catalase being chemically bonded to the polymeric carrier via a covalent linkage formed from nucleophilic functional groups on the protein moiety of the catalase and the electrophilic functional groups on the polymeric carrier, and (2) separating the potable liquid from the catalyst composition. The catalyst composition catalyzes the decomposition of the hydrogen peroxide initially present in the potable liquid thereby freeing the potable liquid of the hydrogen peroxide without introducing another contaminant into the potable liquid.

Separation of the potable liquid whose hydrogen content has been reduced by contact with the catalyst composition employed in the process can be achieved in any convenient manner. By way of illustration, when the process is conducted in a batchwise manner by agitating a mixture of the liquid and the catalyst composition, separation is readily achieved by decantation or filtration.

As a further illustration, when the process is conducted in a continuous manner by passing the liquid through a vertical column packed with the catalyst composition, separation is readily obtained by permitting the liquid to flow from the bottom of the column under the influence of gravity. The patent describes techniques for preparing the catalyst compositions and develops an equation evaluating the performance of columns containing these compositions.

FLAVORS FROM FRUIT JUICES

ESSENCE RECOVERY BY CONTINUOUS CONDENSATION

Recovery of Volatile Flavor Components

E.M. Byer and A.A. Lang; U.S. Patent 3,118,775; and U.S. Patent 3,118,776; January 21, 1964 describe procedures for recovering volatile fruit flavor constituents from juices which are being concentrated. U.S. Patent 3,118,775 describes the process as it applies to fruit juices typified by those from tomatoes, strawberries, boysenberries, grapes, prunes, apples and the like. U.S. Patent 3,118,776 describes the process at it applies to citrus fruit juices, and will be used for exemplification. The process recovers the specific fraction of volatile constituents from citrus fruit juices by a series of steps, which comprise the following.

(a) Causing the citrus fruit juice to flow rapidly, preferably in a thin, continuous film, over a heat exchange surface which is under a substantially reduced subatmospheric pressure, typically less than 1½" of mercury, in a closed system to partially concentrate the juice by separating it into a major juice concentrate portion and a minor volatile portion condensed to include flavor-producing volatile constituents boiling at temperatures higher and lower than that of water and to exclude noncondensible gaseous constituents. The temperatures employed to effect such separation will be dependent in great measure upon the identity of the citrus juice being processed. The juice temperature generally does not exceed 120°F at any point in its flow over the heat exchange surface and, more ideally, the citrus juice is caused to travel at temperatures above 40° and below 80°F.

(b) The aforesaid volatile fraction produced by the first step is thereafter subjected to condensation continuously, at such temperatures that the volatile flavor-producing constituents are collected as a two-phase oily-watery mixture. Advantageously, the temperatures at which this oily-water mixture may be collected by condensation may be only moderately reduced, typically 30° to 70°F. Usually, it is found that the desired condensate collected is in the neighborhood of 5 to 15% by weight of the juice initially introduced to the evaporation system or third effect vaporization chamber.

(c) The aforesaid two-phase mixture is thereafter separated into a minor subfraction containing desirable high as well as low boiling flavor-producing constituents and a major subfraction containing mainly previously condensed water and an undesirable quantity of oily flavor-producing constituents. It is this minor subfraction which has been found offers the desirable flavor enhancement to the juice concentrate. Such separation can be carried out by azeotropic distillation of the two-phase mixture under absolute pressure of less than 1½" of mercury at temperatures of 50° to 100°F or by any other process yielding substantially the same minor subfraction, as will be described hereinafter.

The desirable subfraction which is collected comprises a major proportion of a watery phase and a minor proportion of an oily phase. This minor subfraction may be collected by condensation at temperatures of 30° to 70°F. Preferably the minor subfraction is further subdivided by allowing the watery and oily phases to separate one from another upon standing, the watery phase being continuously removed from the bottom of this separation while accumulating an oil level on the surface; upon sufficient oil accumulation, this oil is drained off separately and mixed with a suitable high boiling organic material, typically cold press citrus oil. It is preferred that this minor subfraction be collected by condensation in a closed system, where no external vapors are introduced to the minor subfraction.

The minor subfraction of use generally represents about 0.5 to 1.5% by weight of the whole juice. The specific subfraction of citrus juices like orange and grapefruit is relatively colorless and has a light, cloudy appearance stemming from the emulsification therein of the minute quantity of oily material associated therewith, which minute quantity makes a desirable flavor contribution. The specific subfraction of use is ideally recoverable by evaporation at only moderately elevated temperatures and by condensation at temperatures ranging above 30°F and upwardly to 70°F when employing absolute pressures in the neighborhood of less than ½" of mercury; however, this fraction may also be condensed at temperatures below 30°F by means of a brine solution or other refrigerating means which, depending on the temperature of condensation, may cause icing in the collection vessel and which permit recovery of the fraction as a snow rather than liquid.

The foregoing process for recovering the volatile fruit flavor fraction desired may be carried out under subatmospheric pressures at only moderately elevated temperatures in the initial whole juice concentration step; the juice concentrate portion may be subsequently introduced to further heat exchange equipment wherein it may be caused to again travel in the form of a thin film over one or more heat exchange surface also maintained under subatmospheric pressure but at higher temperatures whereby the more concentrated juices will be reduced in viscosity and thereby more effectively concentrated. Thus, most citrus juices call for moderate evaporating temperatures at least in the initial stages of concentration and, hence, it has been found useful in the process to employ highly volatile so-called refrigerent gases, typically ammonia, which when compressed contain sufficient latent as well as sensible heat to boil the desired volatile constituents.

Since the desired flavor fraction is collectable by condensation at temperatures above 30°F., a continuous heat exchange cycle employing such refrigerant gases is ideally suited to the process; thus, after the compressed refrigerant gas has surrendered its heat to the juice or juice concentrate, it can be employed in its liquid state to remove sensible heat as well as the heat of condensation from the distilled fraction, the heat of which can be reused to heat the liquid refrigerant for subsequent cycles. The heat of a compressed refrigerant gas may be utilized directly to boil further quantities of juice or it may be employed indirectly through transfer to another medium such as water which could serve in boiling the juice or the concentrate.

For citrus juice concentration it is preferred that the noncondensibles not be collected so that the redistilled condensate employed for flavor enhancement is relatively free of those materials like carbon dioxide and oxygen which impair the flavor values of the concentrate even at temperatures below 0°C. Thus, in the case of orange and grapefruit juice it is preferred that the noncondensibles and the difficultly condensible volatile vapors be evacuated from the initial concentration of the juice in a nonoxidizing atmosphere and discarded, thereby freeing the first two-phase oily-watery mixture collected of interference from such noncondensibles and highly volatile constituents stemming from their high gas velocities and resulting in more stable juice concentration fortified with the specific flavor fraction of the process. In this connection it is noteworthy that the citrus juice concentrates fortified with this flavor fraction have been characterized by their improved freedom from oxidative changes and the accompanying ability to avoid use of costly nitrogen packaging.

Ideally, the specific flavor fraction of use may be mixed in liquid form with the juice concentrate thereby offering the advantages of a simple plant recirculation. However, it has been found that a rather prolonged shelf life for flavor-enhanced concentrate is achieved when the specific flavor fraction of use is frozen into individual portions or pieces, typically cubes or discs, which are introduced to the juice concentrate in the can or other package just prior to freezing. It appears that, by maintaining the specific flavor fraction in a frozen condition separate from the frozen concentrate, the flavor values of the product are maintained over an unusually long period of time.

Volatile Flavor Fraction with Controlled Oxygen Level

E.M. Byer and A.A. Lang; U.S. Patent 3,117,877; January 14, 1964; assigned to General Foods Corporation describe a further process where care is taken to control the oxygen content of the various juices. The method involves the recovery of a specific flavor fraction for use from volatile constituents of fruit juices and the incorporation of this fraction in a concentrated juice portion under conditions wherein the oxygen content of such juices and said flavor fraction is at an extremely low level, typically less than 0.20 ml oxygen per 100 grams of juice concentrate containing the flavor fraction. The maximum oxygen level specified herein uses a juice concentrate product having a Brix level of $42°$ as a reference point.

The minor subfraction obtained as detailed above in U.S. Patent 3,118,775 and U.S. Patent 3,118,776 is added to a citrus juice concentrate under such conditions that the residual oxygen level in the packaged concentrate is less than 0.20 ml oxygen per 100 grams of juice concentrate at $42°$Brix. It has been found that at such drastically reduced oxygen levels the stability of the flavor fraction in storage is prolonged for an unusual period of time.

A preferred embodiment of the present invention involves the incorporation of this volatile fruit flavor fraction into concentrate to which raw or dilute juice commonly referred to in the citrus industry as "cut-back" juice has not been added; to this practice the oxygen level in a final juice concentrate having a Brix level of $42°$ can be reduced as low as 0.02 ml per 100 grams of concentrate. The total gas level in such a concentrate can be reduced to 0.10 ml per 100 grams of concentrate. Single strength fresh juice (cut-back) may also be combined with the concentrate to which the fruit flavor fraction has been added; in this practice oxygen levels of 0.17 ml and less have been observed in the packaged product.

This level of oxygen can be materially reduced in cases where the citrus juice or other fruit juice concentrate has cut-back juice added to it, by subjecting the cut-back juice to an oxygen-stripping operation which makes use of an inert gas such as nitrogen to remove oxygen from the cut-back juice prior to its being blended with the concentrate. In cases where the cut-back juice is not employed the juice concentrate is nevertheless protected from pickup of oxygen in subsequent operations by carrying out the concentration in multi-effect evaporators which are substantially air tight, it having been found that the conventional pumps, valves and lines to the various high vacuum evaporators may serve (if they are not properly sealed) to aerate concentrate with sufficient oxygen to impair the storage ability of a juice concentrate containing the specific flavor fraction of use.

The presence of even a trace quantity of oxygen, say above the level of less than 0.20 milliliter oxygen per 100 grams of juice concentrate at the reference Brix level of $42°$ will result in a noticeable deterioration of the flavor values stemming from the use of the specific flavor fraction of use. Accordingly, the various stages of the customary juice concentration operation, viz., the high vacuum evaporators, the mixing and storage tanks, and the can filling machines as well as the lines interconnecting these stations should be designed to preclude the ingress of oxygen into the juices.

In the course of packaging juice concentrate with the specific flavor fraction of use it may also be found to be desirable to take precautions that a low oxygen containing atmosphere is present in the headspace of the can prior to sealing; such a condition can be created by the forming of a vacuum in the headspace, or by sweeping the headspace with an atmosphere of nitrogen or some other inert gas.

Apparatus for Flavor Enhanced Concentrates

E.M. Byer and A.A. Lang; U.S. Patents 3,310,409 and 3,310,410; March 21, 1967; both assigned to General Foods Corporation describe modifications of their process outlined in the previous three patents. (U.S. Patent 3,310,409 applies to juices such as tomato, strawberry, boysenberry, grape, prune and apple; while U.S. Patent 3,310,410 applies to citrus juices.) Figure 6.1a is a schematic view of a typical plant operation for citrus juice concentration and flavor recovery. (A similar plant operation is used for the juices other than citrus.) Figure 6.1b is a schematic view of the system whereby the concentrate and flavor fractions are combined.

In operation fresh dilute juice delivered to the system through pipe **40** will be evaporated and concentrated through the successive stages of evaporator units **10C**, **10B** and **10A** and eventually delivered by circulation pump **42A** through product pipe **48A** to additional evaporators for further concentration and subsequent combination with other juice constituents for aromatizing the juice, as will be hereinafter described; the boiling juice vapors produced in the third effect evaporator **10C** are removed therefrom through vapor duct **64** and delivered to a tube-type vapor condenser **82** in heat exchange relationship with the vapors, cold liquid ammonia circulating through the tubes of the condenser **82** bringing about condensation of the vapors around the tubes in condenser **82**, wherefrom the condensed vapors are collected at sump **84**, delivered through pipe **85** to pump **86** and pipe **88** which delivers the juice vapor condensate to means for further concentration.

FIGURE 6.I: STABILIZED, FLAVOR ENHANCED CONCENTRATES

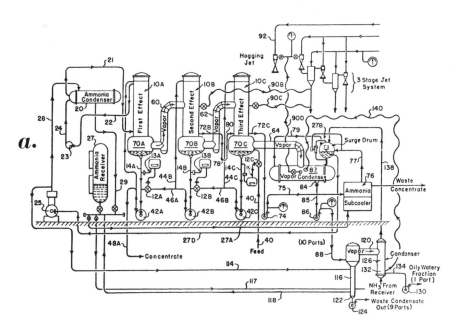

(continued)

FIGURE 6.1: (continued)

b.

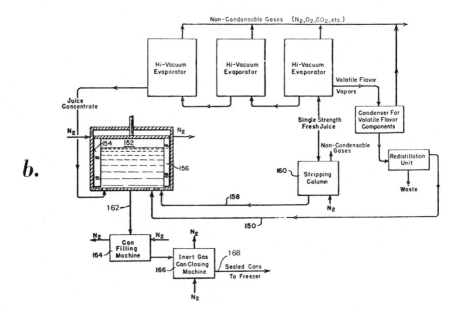

Source: A.A. Lang and E.M. Byer; U.S. Patent 3,310,410; March 21, 1967

The juice vapors condensed in the third effect evaporator **10C** are removed through pipe **72C** and are circulated by pump **74** through line **75** to an ammonia subcooler generally shown at **76**. Liquid ammonia from receiver **27** reaches the subcooler **76** through line **27A**, ammonia subcooler **76** serving to further cool liquid ammonia by having the relatively cooler waste condensate in line **75** brought into heat exchange relation with the liquid ammonia. Thus the temperature of ammonia circulated through line **77** and level control means **27B** to vapor condenser **82** is lowered and the efficiency of the vapor condenser is increased. Heat from juice vapors in condenser **82** is transferred to the liquid ammonia, the latter being recirculated back to pump **25** as a gas through line **79** and suction line **27D**.

The liquid phase recovered by the condenser **82** is essentially the vapor condensate of fresh dilute juice and is substantially free of the difficultly condensable vapors and noncondensable gases such as nitrogen, carbon dioxide and oxygen. This liquid phase is recovered in the course of initial concentration of fresh juice by subjecting the juice to reduced subatmospheric pressures generally less than $1\frac{1}{2}$" of mercury absolute and ranging typically downward to about $\frac{1}{2}$" of mercury and below. The vapors of fresh dilute juice are evaporated at temperatures which will not occasion degradation of the various desirable essences evaporated and generally will be at a temperature above 70°F and not exceed about 140°F; the range of temperature sensitivities varying, of course, for various juices.

The liquid phase contains various constituents (predominately water) many of which boil at temperatures higher as well as lower than that of water. In general, this liquid phase will be recovered as a minor proportion by weight of the fresh juice being subjected to evaporation in the third effect evaporator **10C** and, typically, in the case of citrus juice, will be in the neighborhood of 5 to 15% by weight of the fresh dilute juice.

This liquid phase is subjected to a redistillation to recover a desired oily-water fraction.

Thus, the liquid phase in pipe **88** is introduced to an evaporator unit where it is caused to travel in the form of a thin film along a preferably elongated heat exchange surface which is in heat exchange relationship with a hot gas or liquid, typically, hot ammonia gas. One form of evaporator comprises a tube-type evaporator having a plurality of vertically arranged elongated tubes suitably nested at their upper and lower extremities and adapted to receive the liquid phase delivered thereto from pipe **88**.

Hot ammonia gas from compressor **25** is delivered through inlet pipe **114** communicating with shell **116** surrounding the nest of tubes, hot ammonia gas being thereby placed in heat exchange relation with the liquid films forming within the tubes and thereby bringing about transfer of sensible heat and latent heat of evaporation to the liquid phase; hot ammonia gas condensing around the tubes is contained within and removed from the shell as a liquid through liquid ammonia pipe **118** communicating with ammonia receiver **27**.

Substantially all of the low boiling constituents (relative to the boiling point of water) together with certain high boiling constituents are volatilized in the tubes and conducted through duct **120** to vapor condenser **126** where they are condensed. The nonvolatilized portion contains high boiling constituents which are collected in a suitable sump generally shown as **122** and pumped as at **124** to a suitable waste.

Generally the waste from the liquid phase will be a majority by weight of the liquid phase being treated in the evaporator, typically, 85 to 95 parts by weight of the liquid phase. Condenser **126** is preferably of the tube-type and has the vapors condensed therein by means of liquid ammonia delivered thereto by line **117** from receiver **27**, the liquid ammonia being fed at a temperature in the neighborhood of $30°F$; the vapors condensed around the tubes of the condenser **126** are collected as an oily-watery fraction and are removed therefrom by means of pump **130** communicating with condenser shell **132** through pipe **134**.

An ammonia gas line **138** connects the shell of condenser **126** with the shell of the surge drum of level control means **27B** wherefrom gas is recirculated through line **27D** to compressor **25**. A vacuum line **140** connects the shell of condenser **126** with vapor condenser **82** from which it derives its vacuum, the latter being under negative pressure from the vacuum system generally indicated at **92**. The liquid phase entering the redistillation unit within shell **116** is subjected to a reduced absolute pressure generally between 1½" and ½" of mercury and below. The temperature of the liquid phase entering the redistillation unit will typically be about $60°F$ and generally should be at a temperature where the low and high boiling constituents are maintained in the liquid phase.

The temperature of the liquid phase in the redistillation unit should be above that temperature where, at the particular pressure employed, approximately 10% of the liquid phase will be volatilized and recovered as an oily-watery condensate fraction in condenser **126**. The yield of oily-watery fraction condensate will be dependent upon a number of variables including the total area of the heat exchange surface to which the liquid phase may be exposed, the temperature on the surface, the absolute pressure existing in the redistillation unit and the duration of exposure of the liquid phase to any particular temperature. Any volatile constituents vaporized in the course of redistillation and not collected by condenser **126** will be circulated through vacuum pipe **140** to vapor condenser **82** whereby such vapors may be condensed and recycled to the redistillation unit.

It is a feature of the process that the oily-watery fraction of use is combined with juice concentrate and cut-back juice in a manner which does not materially increase the oxygen content of the juice concentrate product. Referring to Figure 6.1b the oily-watery fraction pumped from the redistillation unit by pump **130** is delivered through line **150** to a mixing tank **152** where the cut-back juice and juice concentrate from pipe **48A** are blended.

As will be seen from Figure 6.1b the blend tank **152** is enclosed and has incorporated therewith suitable agitators **154** and **156** which gently blend the liquids fed thereto so as to eliminate splashing and any accompanying incorporation of air into the surface of the juice which might otherwise occur should the liquids be sprayed into the blend tank as has been customary in the juice concentrate industry.

Accordingly, juice concentrate pipe **48A**, cut-back juice supply pipe **158**, and line **150** empty below the surface of liquids in the blend tank, preferably at the bottom of the tank **152**, eliminating splashing and accompanying air incorporation. Though it is not necessary to purge the headspace of the blend tank of oxygen it may be desirable to do so as shown by sweeping nitrogen gas through the blend tank. Although it is a feature of the oily-watery fraction that it provides most of the balanced flavor requirements for enhancement of a juice concentrate it may be desirable for some applications to employ single strength fresh juice (that is cut-back juice) combined with the juice concentrate. When cut-back juice is used, it should be treated in the stripping column **160** where nitrogen gas is fed at a sufficient rate to remove oxygen and carbon dioxide from the cut-back juice. The nitrogen stripped cut-back juice is then in a condition for blending with the other juice constituents.

The blended substantially oxygen-free juice in blending tank **152** is conducted by line **162** to a can-filling machine **164** the juice in which may also be protected by nitrogen purging. The cans are thereafter delivered to a can-closing machine **166** and passed to a freezer as at **168**. During the can sealing operation nitrogen may be introduced into the headspace in the can in order to assure an inert atmosphere, although the can-sealing operation may be carried out under normal conditions without materially increasing the oxygen content of the final product.

ESSENCE RECOVERY BY DISTILLATION

Recovery of Essence-Bearing Vapors

In the processing of fruit juices or liquids in order to reduce the liquids into a concentrate of nonvolatiles for storage and subsequent reconstitution and consumption, considerable efforts and equipment are involved in recovering the flavor bearing materials released from the liquid being concentrated. Accordingly, the concentrated vapor stripped fruit juice is chilled and delivered to a receiver while the essence bearing vapor and condensate are delivered to a flavor concentrate recovery section wherein they are stripped of the flavor concentrate.

The recovery equipment includes a plurality of pumps, condensers, coolers, fractionating columns and reboilers necessary to concentrate the flavor bearing portion of the vapor. Additional equipment is also involved in scrubbing the vent gases exiting from the fractionating columns for recirculation of recovered volatiles through the fractionating columns.

The recovery process of *R.W. Cook; U.S. Patent 3,293,150; December 20, 1966* eliminates the expense and operational instability involved by use of the recovery equipment of prior processes by utilizing the stripped liquid in a heat exchange operation, which stripped liquid is otherwise removed from the system without being used in any manner in conjunction with the flavor concentration. Also, a pressure regulating system is utilized in the recovery process which, in conjunction with the circulation of the stripped liquid through the concentrating section, enables the separation of the flavor concentrates from the essence bearing vapor. The concentrate is delivered to the stripping column after being further condensed to remove the majority of condensibles therefrom which condensibles form part of the flavor concentrate delivered to a flavor concentrate container.

A reflux liquid is also delivered in counter current flowing relation to the essence bearing noncondensibles for filtering through the stripping column so as to form part of the flavor concentrate. The stripping column accordingly delivers noncondensible, flavor free waste gas to a pressure regulator which not only vents the noncondensible gas, but creates a predetermined pressure differential between the vapor inlet and noncondensible gas discharge causing vapor flow through the recovery stage. Further, the use of the vapor stripped feed liquid in heat exchanging relation to the essence bearing vapor for concentration eliminates the need of reboilers or other heat sources or the large condensers otherwise necessary in previous processes for concentrating the essence bearing vapor.

Also, by virtue of the use of the flavor concentrate stripping equipment including vapor fraction and reflux condensers interconnected below and above the stripping column respectively, reflux vapor may be delivered to the stripping equipment eliminating reflux splitting equipment and simplifying the vent gas scrubber equipment as heretofore used. The recovery equipment of this process includes the use of metering nozzles for determining the flow rate of vapors into the flavor recovery section to provide a constant rate of flow therethrough for operational stability purposes.

A brief description of the operation of the apparatus is given below in conjunction with Figure 6.2. The essence bearing vapor delivered from an initial state enters the heat exchanger **18**, passes upward therethrough whereupon a more concentrated flavor vapor fraction is drawn outward therefrom through outlet vapor conduit **42**. The flavor concentrated vapor fraction is delivered at a constant rate of flow to the condenser **66** which separates therefrom the majority of the condensible components. The vapor and a condensate mixture is then delivered by conduit **80** to a discharge chamber **82** of the stripping assembly **84**. Also, delivered to the stripping assembly is a reflux fluid derived preferably from the vapor inlet **10** and metered by metering nozzle **95** into the stripping assembly.

Vapors from the delivery chamber **82** pass upward through the condenser **96**; subsequently, the remaining noncondensibles pass through the stripping column portion **102** for removal of flavor bearing materials from the noncondensibles releasing noncondensible waste gas into the chamber **114**. The reflux fluid passes into the condenser **118** for condensation thereof and to exchanger **124** for further cooling from which it is delivered to chamber **114** whereupon the reflux liquid passes through the stripping column portion **102** in countercurrent flow for scrubbing contact with the noncondensibles. Accordingly, the flavor bearing materials are collected within the delivery chamber **82** for delivery to the essence container **86**.

FIGURE 6.2: APPARATUS FOR RECOVERING ESSENCE BEARING VAPORS

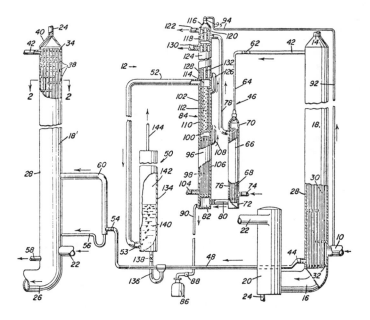

Source: R.W. Cook; U.S. Patent 3,293,150; December 20, 1966

The noncondensible waste gas on the other hand, is received in the chamber **114** and vented through the discharge conduit **52** for delivery to the vacuum pressure regulating device **50** by means of which the desired pressure differential for the recovery process is maintained to effect flow of the vapors through the recovery stage.

The condensate from the heat exchanger **18** may be recovered for delivery to a next stage of the system by being flashed through an orifice **54** whereupon additional vapor is released therefrom for delivery to the next stage heat exchanger **18'** through the conduit **60** while the liquid is delivered thereto by conduit **56**. Also, the liquid vapor mixture leaving the bottom of the heat exchanger **18** is separated by the separator **20** and the vapor phase may be delivered to the inlet of the next stage heat exchanger **18'** while the further stripped liquid may be delivered by conduit **24** to the liquid inlet of the next state heat exchanger **18'**.

Recovery Under Conditions Preventing Hydrolysis of Esters

For many years it has been recognized that fresh fruit and vegetable juice contained flavoring and aromatic constituents which are extremely characteristic of the particular fruit, plant extract or the like. It has also been recognized that the natural, fresh flavor and aroma of fruit, berries, and other foods are deleteriously affected by the normal concentrating, heating and sterilizing steps, with cooked and off flavors and with a loss of the aroma and flavor which characterizes fresh, mature fruit. Some attempts have been made in the past to recover the relatively volatile flavors and components found in plant products for the purpose of reintroducing them into the final concentrate or canned, cooked or sterilized fruit in order to impart thereto the flavor and aroma of the fresh, natural fruit.

Prior attempts to obtain a fraction in which it was hoped that the flavoring and aromatic constituents would be present in concentrated quantity were not successful and were fallacious in their method of operation. Prior workers looked for an oily material as a source of the flavor.

E.J. Kelly; U.S. Patents 3,223,533 and 3,223,534; December 14, 1965; both assigned to Libby, McNeill and Libby obtains the flavoring and aromatic constituents in a nonoily, water-soluble and miscible form which is virtually colorless, transparent, mobile, burns with a clear blue flame and has a remarkably low freezing point, well below 100°C and as low as −180°C.

In addition it has been found that oily contaminants are present with the flavor and aromatic constituents in certain citrus products, which even in extremely small proportions impart unpleasant taste and odor characteristics. Also it has been found that the flavor concentrate itself is a solvent for such oily contaminants so that if the oily contaminants are not removed prior to concentration of the flavor and odor constituents then separation becomes extremely difficult if not impossible.

One of the reasons for the failures of the prior art was the fact that the prior workers did not realize the importance of maintaining conditions of temperature and pressure below 65°C and 190 mm of Hg when dealing with fruit juices, citrus juices and other source materials. It has been found that the conditions of operation should be such as to prevent or minimize hydrolysis of the esters and ethers of acetic acid into acids, alcohols and secondary reaction products. It has also been discovered that the esters and ethers of acetic acid constitute important components which impart the characteristic fresh, natural flavor and aroma elements to the concentrate and to the products in which it is subsequently used; colorimetric determination of the ethyl ester of acetic acid (ethyl acetate) content of a concentrate provides a ready mode of evaluation.

Although some prior patentees have referred to what they termed a "100 fold essence" which they allegedly obtained, such term had no true meaning other than the volume of the condensate taken out of the system was $1/100$ of the juice fed into the system. For example, Patent No. 2,457,315 speaks of pumping 50 gph of apple juice into a single stage evaporator, evaporating 10% of such juice, passing the vapors into a fractionating column and condensing the vapors from such column, all at atmospheric pressure.

Uncondensed gases were vented from the condenser and the condensate was drawn off at $1/100$ of the rate at which fresh juice was fed into the evaporator, this condensate being termed a "100 fold essence." It is evident that in such process the condenser would be fed with vapors composed essentially of water and therefore the condensate would also consist essentially of water since the water will be condensed first. The mol fraction or concentration of the flavor constituents in vapors sent to such prior condenser is far below 0.5% and the vapors would exhibit all of the properties of water vapor. The partial pressure of the volatile constituents at no time approach saturation pressures. At no time would the prior patentees eliminate the water and then condense the more volatile constituents under conditions which effectively utilized partial pressure phenomena and Dalton's law.

Dew point conditions (with respect to the flavoring and aromatic constituents) were never reached; the mixtures of air, gases and vapors sent to the condenser contained excessive amounts of water vapor. As a result, the so-called "100 fold essence" was simply a mathematical and volumetric determination and did not actually contain any appreciably increased quantity of flavoring components.

The fallacy of the prior method of identifying the "essence" becomes apparent when one considers that orange juice appears to contain only about 30 ppm of true essence, so that only about 1.5 to 1.6 lb of water-free essence can be obtained from 52,000 lb of citrus juice. The products made by the method of this invention actually contain one thousand times as much flavoring constituents as the original source material or juice, even in the unpurified, aqueous solution form in which they are normally obtained. Moreover, it is to be remembered that ethyl acetate has a vapor pressure of 760 mm absolute at about 77°C, whereas water at the same temperature has a vapor pressure of 7 lb gauge.

Contrary to prior suggestions that the concentrated or flavor-stripped juice be used as an absorbent or scrubber for the noncondensed gases or vapors prior to venting such residual gases (in an attempt to recover some of the flavoring components from said gases), it has been found that such flavor-stripped juices are not good absorbents; instead, pure water (or dilute, aqueous solutions of ethyl alcohols or sucrose) have been found much more effective. Also contrary to prior practice which was concerned solely with removing water in order to obtain a small volume of liquid to be fractionally distilled, the present method after initially obtaining a small volume liquid actually adds water to separate the oily contaminants prior to fractional distillation since simple condensation does not separate the oily contaminants from the flavor constituents.

Generally stated, therefore, the present process departs from the prior art and relates to a method of obtaining flavoring constituents from aqueous source materials (such as juice of fresh, natural, deciduous and citrus fruits and berries) by conducting all of the operations under temperature and pressure conditions which will not cause hydrolysis of esters of acetic acid, the temperatures not exceeding 65°C and preferably being below 43°C and absolute pressures not over 190 mm of Hg and preferably as low as 30 mm Hg.

Any such source material in the form of water vapor and noncondensable gases containing minute quantities of volatile odor and flavor constituents is subjected to a temperature below about 43°C and an absolute pressure of not over 115 mm Hg in a condensation zone to condense not less than 70%, and preferably 80% by weight of water contained in said source material. After the water has been separated from the residual vapors and gases, such vapors and gases are subjected to dew point conditions for flavor and odor constituents and are readily condensed in accordance with Dalton's law.

These flavor and odor constituents are obtained in the form of aqueous solutions having the characteristics described hereinbefore containing in excess of 40 grams per liter of such constituents. Ordinarily, the final product contains 30,000 to 60,000 ppm of the volatile flavor-and aroma-imparting constituents, this being a readily handled and utilized product which is not as unstable as the pure essence; more concentrated forms have to be handled at very low temperatures because of their volatile character.

When the source material in the form of a gaseous mixture of water vapor and odor and flavor constituents contains traces of oily contaminants, it is first scrubbed with chilled water. Then it is cooled and scrubbed again with chilled water. The oily contaminants are then removed from the scrub water. The water and scrubbed gaseous mixture are then fractionally distilled to produce the gaseous mixture from which the flavor and odor constituents may be fractionally condensed.

The essence obtained from the juice of citrus fruits, crushed berries and grapes, purees of deciduous fruits (such as apricots, apples, pears, peaches, etc.) can be used to impart a natural, fresh and characteristic flavor and aroma to food products and confections, ice cream, etc. or reincorporated into the concentrated source material. Orange essence obtained by this process can be added to concentrated orange juice and convert the ususal flat, cooked taste of reconstituted beverages made from such concentrates into beverages which cannot be distinguished from natural fresh juice. Citrus essences obtained by the methods herein disclosed are free from the terpene-like odors and flavors which characterize citrus oils. One of the important characteristics of the essences recovered by this process is stability upon storage; this may be due, in part at least, to the fact that hydrolysis and decomposition are minimized at the low temperature and pressure conditions, and to the fact that all of the constituents (including naturally contained stabilizing agents) are present in their usual, natural proportions. Diagrams of the apparatus are included in the patent.

Distillation in Vacuum Concentration System

Prior attempts to collect the volatile flavor elements or essence from evaporator concentration of juice and particularly vacuum evaporator concentration of juice have been inefficient because of incomplete recovery of the essence even though they have employed extremely low temperatures and expensive equipment. Heretofore, attempts have been made to condense the essence under vacuum and remove it from the noncondensable gases with cold wall condensers. These operate at extremely low temperatures and are expensive both in installation and operation. Furthermore, it has not been practical to separate the essence from the noncondensable gases by means of scrubbers when they are operated under high vacuum.

The process of *J.A. Brent, C.W. DuBois and C.F. Huffman (U.S. Patent 3,248,233; April 26, 1966; assigned to The Coca-Cola Company)* obviates the aforementioned difficulties and results in the recovery of large percentages of the essence in vacuum concentration systems with little added investment in equipment and high efficiency.

In practicing the process, single strength fresh orange juice is subjected to a flash evaporation in which from 15 to 20%, or as little as 5% of the liquid is evaporated in a vacuum flash evaporator. This operation removes substantially all of the alcohols, esters, aldehydes and other volatile flavor constituents which go to make up the flavor essence of the fresh orange juice. The juice which has been stripped of the essence in this way is then passed on to conventional concentrating equipment such as vacuum concentrators. The vacuum for the flash vacuum evaporator is created by making use of a stream of water or other liquid capable of condensing and absorbing or dissolving the vaporized essence, which stream entrains the vaporized essence and becomes intimately mixed and associated therewith.

Generally, the essence which has been flashed off is freed from excessive water vapors by means of condensers adapted to condense the water vapors before the esence is entrained in the stream of liquid. The stream of liquid used to create the vacuum may be the liquid seal of a liquid ring pump or it may be the jet stream of a jet exhauster or aspirator. Both of these devices, although somewhat different in nature, pump gases by making use of a stream of liquid which comes into intimate contact with the gases, and both in their operation increase the pressure on the gases and intimately associated liquid prior to discharging the gases so that these gases insofar as they separate from and are not taken up by the liquid may be discharged from the device, for instance, into the atmosphere.

The vacuum condition for concentration of the juice is brought about by the pump or aspirator along with the condensation of the water vapors pulled from the vacuum chamber of the evaporator. The essence in gaseous phase, along with the noncondensable gases such as oxygen and nitrogen, partially freed from water vapors, is carried out of the evaporation system by the pump or aspirator. The essence and noncondensable gases come into intimate contact with the stream of liquid and tend to be entrained thereby. After removal from the low pressure area of the vacuum system, the essence, the noncondensable gases and the liquid of the stream are subjected to forces tending to increase the pressure thereon.

This results in the absorption and dissolution of a very high percentage of the essence in the water of the liquid stream where the essence is collected and thus concentrated. The noncondensable gases, which are quite insoluble in the water, are vented and, since the water is no longer under vacuum when it is withdrawn from the system, it retains the essence just as the orange juice did originally at atmospheric pressure. The operation of bringing the pressure over the water to atmospheric or higher may be accomplished in a single stage or by a plurality of stages.

When the liquid ring pump is employed, the operation of the pump with its water seal serves to separate the essence from the noncondensable gases even though the concentration of the essence in these gases is very low and even though the system is operated under a high vacuum in a vacuum system. The same effect is obtained when a liquid jet exhauster or aspirator is employed. In each case, the liquid ring pump or the liquid jet aspirator merely replaces the apparatus formerly used to bring about the creation of the vacuum thus involving little capital expenditure.

The stream of liquid is preferably refrigerated to lower the vapor pressure of the liquid and thereby allow a higher vacuum to be reached and also to assist it in condensing the vapors and dissolving and retaining them, and the pump or jet exhauster is set up either to operate on a batch principle in which, when the liquid has achieved a certain concentration of essence, it is replaced by fresh liquid; or, in a continuous operation, where portions of the liquid are bled off and replaced as the concentration of essence reaches the desired point.

The essence thus recovered may be added back to juice concentrate or may be used separately or may be employed for any other purpose. The system is simple and easy to operate and is highly efficient in recovering substantially all of the essence from the fresh juice. The patent further describes, with many illustrations, details of the apparatus used in the process.

EXTRACTION OF FLAVORS FROM FRUIT

Aqueous Essence Emulsion of Citrus Peel

Where the concentration of citrus fruit juices is effected by either high or low temperature distillation or evaporation, there is an unavoidable loss of some of the delicate aroma of the natural, freshly expressed fruit juice, and this loss is considerably greater where a higher degree of concentration of the fruit juice is effected. In those cases where the concentration is such as to impart to the citrus fruit juice concentrate a Brix value of from 33° up to as high as 72°, there is such a noticeable loss of the flavor quality, or aroma, of the product that it has become customary to add to the concentrate a sufficient quantity of unconcentrated freshly expressed fruit juice to compensate for such loss.

In some cases, it is the practice to add to the concentrate a small proportion of volatile oils drived from the peel by cold pressing, and/or other ingredients to fortify the taste and flavor of the resulting product. These additions have not been found to be entirely satisfactory as to palatability and taste from the standpoint of consumer acceptability.

A.O.T. Ostrus; U.S. Patent 3,120,442; February 4, 1964; assigned to Freshway Products Company describes a continuous method of treating citrus fruit, in accordance with which the fruit is finely subdivided in a cutting or shredding operation; the resulting subdivided mass is immediately sprayed with an aqueous liquid to entrain the volatile oils and fluids released from the fruit and to form a flowable mass thereof; such flowable mass is subjected to a continuous centrifugal filtering action to remove solid portions therefrom and to give a filtrate containing the flavor and other fluids from the fruit; and the filtrate is recovered. Either the whole citrus fruit or the hulls of the citrus fruit could be used as the starting material.

This method provides an aqueous essence emulsion of the natural constituents of the peel of citrus fruits, which contains such constituents, including recoverable volatile oils, in substantially their original natural state and in a concentration particularly adapting the emulsion for addition to frozen citrus fruit concentrates and the like.

The method provides an aqueous essence emulsion derived directly from citrus fruit peel without the use of added chemical emulsifying or treating agents and without the application of any substantial amount of heat, yet of such concentration as to be suitable to use directly, or upon dilution, in the making of food products, confections and the like.

The aqueous essence emulsion has superior flavor and keeping qualities and contains virtually all of the natural constituents of the citrus fruit peel unchanged by the use of any heat process and in relatively high concentrations in terms of the recoverable volatile oil content of the emulsion.

Example 1: 20 to 25 pounds of orange peel were subjected to the process hereinabove described while controlling the amount of water sprayed through to give 1 gallon of an aqueous essential emulsion having a recoverable volatile oil content of 1 volume percent.

Example 2: 60 to 75 pounds of orange peel were processed without the use of any spray water, or else only sufficient amount of spray water, to give 1 gallon of an aqueous emulsion having a recoverable oil content of 3 volume percent.

Since the recoverable oil content of citrus fruit peel will vary with the type of citrus fruit and also with the species selected of any particular type, whether oranges, lemons or other type, no exact quantities of peel and of spray water can be specified for giving a specific volume percent of recoverable volatile oil in the resulting aqueous essence emulsion.

Where it is desired to impart the natural taste and aroma to a citrus fruit juice reconstituted from a citrus fruit concentrate of 33 to 72°Brix that is deficient in recoverable volatile oil content, a sufficient quantity of the aqueous essence emulsion is added to the concentrate, at the time it is prepared and before freezing, to give approximately 0.02 volume percent of recoverable volatile oil in the reconstituted juice. This would mean, in the case of an orange juice concentrate of 42°Brix, adding a sufficient amount of the aqueous essence emulsion to bring the recoverable volatile oil content of the concentrate up to 0.08 volume percent. Then upon 3 to 1 dilution of the concentrate, the resulting reconstituted orange juice would contain 0.02 volume percent of volatile recoverable oil. Such a result cannot be obtained by adding fresh citrus juice, itself, to a concentrate, since such juice normally contains only about 0.02 volume percent of recoverable volatile oil.

Fortifying Prune Juice with Pit Extract

A well-known article of commerce is the so-called prune juice which is made by extracting dried prunes with water. Although this product is a tasty and wholesome beverage, it is dark in color and has a rather muddy appearance. For this reason food processors in recent years have sought to put out juice products of a more attractive color and appearance. To this end, the product designated as fresh prune juice has been placed on the market. This product is made by blanching fresh prunes, mashing the blanched fruit, removing the pits, treating the macerate (pulp) with a pectinolytic enzyme, pressing the mass in a bag press to separate the juice from the skins and other fibrous material, filtering the juice, and finally pasteurizing and bottling the juice.

Although fresh prune juice is more attractive than regular prune juice from an appearance standpoint, being a clear red liquid, it is lacking in true prune flavor. Thus although it is sweet, it lacks the fruity aroma of the product prepared from dried prunes.

In an investigation of this situation, *F.S. Nury and G.G. Watters; U.S. Patent 3,211,557; October 12, 1965; assigned to U.S. Secretary of Ariculture* conducted vapor phase chromatographic tests on conventional prune juice, fresh prune juice, and on the whole fruit and the several parts thereof. They have found that the fresh prune juice is lacking in a flavor peak which is characteristic of the prune pits. This flavor peak is, however, present in regular prune juice which accounts for the satisfactory flavor of this product. This finding of the significance of a flavor element in prune pits is utilized to fortify the flavor of prune products, typically fresh prune juice.

Basically, the process involves adding the flavor principles of prune pits to prune products which are deficient in flavor. In a preferred modification of the process, this is achieved by adding prune pit extract to prune products which are deficient in flavor. The proportion of prune pit extract to be added in any particular case will depend on such factors as the flavor of the product to be fortified, the concentration of flavoring substances in the pit extract, and the flavor desired in the final product. In any specific sitution, pilot trials are made, using different proportions of pit extract and selecting for the main batch the proportion which provides a product which has a desired level of fruity aroma.

The prune pit extract can be prepared in various ways. A convenient and preferred procedure involves grinding prune pits and extracting them with hot or cold water. After separation of the undissolved woody material, for example, by centrifuging, the aqueous liquid is ready for direct use in flavor fortification of prune products. The prune pit extract can also be prepared by conventional distillation techniques. As an example, the prune pits are ground, put in water and the mixture subjected to distillation, the overhead being condensed and cooled in a conventional manner. Another plan for preparing the pit extract involves the use of solvent extraction.

To this end, the ground pits are extracted with a low-boiling solvent such as tetrafluoromethane, trifluoromethane, trifluoromonochloromethane, hexfluoroethane, trifluoromonobromomethane, difluoromonochloromethane, pentafluoromonochloroethane, difluorodichloromethane, 1,1-difluoroethane, symmetrical tetrafluorodichloroethane, monofluorodichloromethane, octafluorocyclobutane, or the like. The resulting extract, after removal of undissolved material, is subjected to evaporation to remove the solvent and the residual material, the pit extract, containing the flavoring principles is used for flavor-fortifying prune products.

In another modification, the flavor fortification is achieved by using prune pits directly rather than in the form of an extract. One method of utilizing this principle involves contacting edible prune material such as pulp or juice with crushed prune pits. For example, in preparing fresh prune juice, the fruit material is crushed in such type of equipment, for example, a hammermill, that not only is the flesh macerated but also the pits are cracked and disintegrated. By contact of the pulpy fruit material with the disintegrated pits, flavor principles derived from the latter are transferred to the pulpy material. It is to be emphasized that in this technique, the pits are deliberately crushed with the meaty part of the fruit.

This is a complete departure from conventional practice wherein the fruit is mashed in a device such as a paddle finisher which results only in a pulping of the meaty part of the fruit, while leaving the pits whole and intact. Under such conditions there occurs no flavor fortification of the fruit material; the flavor principles in the pits are locked in the woody pits and cannot be transferred to the pulp or juice.

The pits used for flavor fortification of the prune material need not be derived from the same fruit but can be recovered, for example, from plants which de-pit dried prunes. Such recovered pits may be crushed and contacted with the prune pulp or juice for flavor fortification thereof. Where the flavor of prune products such as flesh, pulp, or juice is fortified by contact of the material with crushed prune pits, the degree of flavor fortification will depend on such factors as the proportion of pits in contact with the fruit material and the time of such contact. Such factors as increasing the proportion of crushed pits and increasing the time of contact will enhance the degree of flavor fortification. These conditions may be adjusted in correlation with the original flavor of the prune material to produce an enhanced flavor.

Example: (a) A batch of fresh prune juice was prepared in a conventional manner. To this end, fresh prunes were heated to 212°F and the blanched fruit passed through a paddle finisher to macerate the prune flesh and to separate the pits from the mashed fruit flesh. The macerate was allowed to remain for 12 hours with added pectinolytic enzyme (0.25%). Then, the mass was pressed through a filter cloth to separate the skins and other fibrous material. The resulting juice was pasteurized and bottled while still hot.

(b) A batch of prune pit extract was prepared as follows: a quantity of pits removed from dried prunes was ground. To 1 part of the ground pits was added 2 parts of cold water and the mixture allowed to stand for about 2 hours. The mixture was then centrifuged, the supernatant liquid constituting the pit extract.

(c) The fresh prune juice and pit extract, prepared as described above in parts (a) and (b), respectively, were mixed in various proportions, as indicated below to provide three samples of flavor fortified juice.

Sample	Proportion of Fresh Juice, (% Volume Basis)	Proportion of Pit Extract, (% Volume Basis)
1	90	10
2	95	5
3	97.5	2.5

(d) The flavor fortified juices prepared as above described, were submitted to a panel of skilled tasters for evaluation. In each case the flavor fortified product was compared with fresh juice which had been diluted with water to the same level. The judges were provided with unmarked samples of which they were required to select the flavor fortified and untreated juice and to rate them for flavor. The results are tabulated below:

Sample	Pit Extract Content, (% Volume Basis)	Correct Identification of Flavor Fortified Product and Fresh Juice, (% of Judges)	Preference for Flavor Fortified Product (% of Judges)
1	10	93	89
2	5	100	96
3	2.5	81	90

Centrifugal Separation of Citrus Juice Flavors

The process of *A.P. Distelkamp and O.R. McDuff; U.S. Patent 3,300,320; January 24, 1967)* consists of subjecting the fresh, finished juice prior to any intense heat treatment to the action of a centrifugal force so as to produce a light phase consisting of an emulsion enriched wtih taste and flavor components and a heavy phase consisting of juice reduced in taste and flavor components. It has been found that when proceeding in this manner, it is possible to recover an emulsion which contains a substantial portion of all the oil and/or flavoring substances present in the fruit.

High speed liquid-liquid centrifuges of the solid bowl desludger or nozzle type have proved to be especially suitable for carrying out the process. The discharge for both the lighter emulsion phase and the heavier juice phase is preferably fully enclosed. If open centrifuges are used, they should be operated under a nitrogen blanket in order to prevent oxidative changes in the juice and/or the emulsion.

After centrifuging, the partly deoiled juice is further processed in the conventional manner. The flavor carrying emulsion phase obtained on centrifuging is preferably chilled immediately after centrifuging and is stored at reduced temperatures. Cold stablization of the emulsion before further processing, for instance, by radiation pasteurization might be of advantage.

The resulting emulsion is either added immediately or after a certain storage time back to the finished juice or the concentrate subsequently to any heat treatment thereof, but ahead of the packaging operation. Thereby, substantially, the original natural flavor and taste are imparted to the juice or concentrate. Depending on flavor and quality requirements, it is possible to blend all or only part of the initially present amount of emulsion back into the juice or concentrate.

It is also possible to further refine the emulsion, by breaking the emulsion, for instance, by heating and separation of the layers so as to produce a pure oil. The emulsion or oil may further be processed by distillation, folding and/or degasifying in order to remove any off-flavors which might be present. Folding is effected by fractional distillation while degasifying may be achieved by spraying the emulsion or the essence obtained therefrom into a vacuum chamber. Subsequent homogenization of the emulsion may also be of advantage in order to produce a more uniform flavor additive. The emulsion may be freeze concentrated because, thereby, the amount of concentrated flavoring agent to be added to the fruit juice or concentrate is reduced and the stability and storability is increased. If necessary, all these methods of further processing the emulsion may be combined with each other to meet special specifications.

Example: 3,200 gallons of a finished citrus fruit, i.e., orange juice of 10.3°Brix having 2% light pulp and 12% heavy pulp (determined by standard spin test) and 0.034% oil (determined by standard quick oil method) was introduced into a centrifuge of the automatic desludger type. The juice effluent or heavy phase contained 10% pulp and 0.015% oil. The light phase or emulsion, consisting of about 50 gallons, contained 1.2% oil and only a trace of pulp. The emulsion was stored for several weeks at ordinary refrigerator temperature, 30° to 40°F, and still retained its characteristic fresh and fruity aroma.

This emulsion is added to the evaporator pump-out obtained from the centrifuged juice in an amount equivalent to the amount of peel oil ordinarily added for flavor improvement. The taste of the resulting juice after reconstitution is excellent. Even addition of an excess of the emulsion does not impart to the reconstituted juice the usual bitter taste associated with high peel oil levels. This is in contrast to the addition of excess peel oil to concentrated juice because it creates a rather bitter taste. It is also very difficult to determine the exact amount of peel oil to be added because a slight excess might produce a bitter taste, while no such difficulties arise when using this emulsion.

Citrus Essence of High Aldehyde Content by Continuous Extraction

C.D. Atkins and J.A. Attaway; U.S. Patents 3,782,972, January 1, 1974 and 3,787,593, January 22, 1974; assigned to State of Florida, Department of Citrus describe a method by which an aqueous citrus essence is prepared having an enhanced content of components which contribute to the natural flavor of the citrus juice, particulary certain aldehyde type compounds and a decreased content of components, such as easily oxidized fatty substances, which detract from the flavor of the juice.

Preparation of the enhanced citrus essence is accomplished by increasing the alcoholic content of the aqueous phase of the essence so that its capacity for desirable aldehyde type components is increased. The increase in alcoholic content is effected by recirculation under appropriate conditions of temperature and pressure of the aqueous phase of the essence in contact with fresh essence. Enhanced essence produced by this method is particulary useful for reconstituting the flavor of citrus juice concentrates such as orange juice.

Orange juice essence contains, amoung other components, peel oil, consisting largely of d-limonene, fats (including various lipids or fatty esters, e.g., triglycerides) and diacetyl. This large amount of d-limonene has been found to adversely affect flavor and aroma of the essence and to be far in excess of what is required for reconstitution of the flavor of juices. Further, the lipids present are easily oxidized during heating (as in evaporation and concentration) to components having decidedly unpleasant flavor and aroma characteristics. These undesirable features have also been found to be characteristic of the diacetyl present in the essence.

Of course, present along with these components in the essence are the various other compounds which are conveniently grouped as alcohols, esters, and aldehydes (including ketones and diacetyl). Of these compounds, the "aldehyde" type compounds in particular, contribute significantly to the natural flavor and aroma of the juice. Typical of these compounds are n-decanal, geranial, citronellal, ethanol, linalool, n-octanol, terpinolene, d-terpineol, and sabinene; although it is appreciated that not all of these compounds are, strictly spreaking, aldehydes, nor is this an exhaustive list of those components present in orange essence which can be said to enhance the natural orange flavor and aroma.

It is however, a problem in separating the desirable and undesirable flavor and aroma affecting components of citrus, and especially orange essence, that the essence readily separates into an aqueous and an oil phase, both of which phases contain desirable essence components. The oil phase in particular also, however, contains the greater part of the undesirable flavor components.

According to the process, volatile essence vapors are passed into a reflux type stripping column having heater and condenser sections where pulp, insoluble solids, fatty materials, and excess water are removed. Air and entrained volatiles (consisting largely of distilled peel oil, diacetyl, etc.) are removed from the top of the stripping column, while the condensible water and oil essence phases are collected and removed from the side of the column. In order to properly carry out this separation as well as subsequent refluxing procedures whereby the alcohol content of the aqueous essence phase is increased, the column is maintained by a heater at a temperature of about 140°F to 200°F and a pressure of 24 to 29 inches of mercury.

The combined oil and water essence which is removed from the column is separated into its respective oil and water phases, for example, by decanting, the lighter oil phase readily rising to the top of the heavier water phase. The water phase is recycled back into the stripping column and refluxed in contact with additional fresh essence vapor whereby the level of naturally occurring alcoholic components in the water phase is increased.

Enrichment of the water phase by flavor enhancing aldehyde type components also occurs during the refluxing in the stripping column. Subsequently, this water phase containing an increased level of alcoholic components is further contacted with the oil phase and scrubbed with the air and entrained volatile vapors and gases removed previously from the stripping column to further enhance removal of aldehydes into the aqueous phase.

This scrubbing procedure removes various ester and aldehyde components (except the esters of formic acid and diacetyl) into the aqueous phase containing enhanced alcohol content. Both the aqueous and oil phases are then removed from the bottom of the scrubber. Noncondensible gases, diacetyl, oxidized fatty components, air, and traces of other components from the combined water and oil phase are conveyed to a condenser where the remaining alcohol, aldehyde, and ester components are selectively trapped and combined in desired amounts with the oil and enriched aqueous phase removal earlier from the scrubber.

The two phases being mutually immiscible are readily separated and the enriched aqueous essence phase retained. The noncondensed discharge from the condenser-trip is normally for evaluation to determine the extent of removal from the system of the undesirable essence components comprising largely di-acetyl, fatty vapors, formic acid, and the esters of formic acid. The oil phase which is separated from the aqueous essence phase is largely (about 94 to 97%) d-limonene along with minor amounts of aldehydes, esters, and alcohols.

Generally, the water-soluble essence prepared has the composition shown in the following table although it is to be appreciated that it is a feature of this process that water-soluble essences having other ranges of components can also be prepared as desired.

Water-Soluble Essence

Component	Volume Percent
Alcohols	4 – 12
Aldehydes	0.27 – 0.71
Esters	0.05 – 0.15
Oils	0.020 – 0.080

(mostly d-limonene)

The following table gives the composition of the oil phase from which the water-soluble essence above is separated.

Oil Phase

Component	Volume Percent
d-Limonene	94 – 97
Aldehydes	0.93 – 1.60
Esters	0.04 – 1.50
Alcohols	1.0 – 2.0

The table below gives the composition of actual aqueous essences prepared by the process. The water-soluble essence derived from 100 gallons of orange juice of 12.8°Brix or 12.8% sugar solids is compressed to the indicated gallons of essence at a vacuum corresponding to 24.04 inches of mercury.

(a) . . . 1 gal. 100 fold essence . . . . 4.0% 40,000 p.p.m. alcohol (ethyl).
0.27% 2,700 p.p.m. aldehydes.
0.05% 500 p.p.m. esters.

(b) . . . ½ gal. 200 fold essence . . . 8.0% 80,000 p.p.m. alcohol (ethyl).
0.54% 5,400 p.p.m. aldehydes.
0.10% 1,000 p.p.m. esters.

(c) . . . ⅓ gal. 300 fold essence . . . 12.0% 120,000 p.p.m. alcohol (ethyl).
0.71% 8,100 p.p.m. aldehydes.
0.15% 1,500 p.p.m. esters.

Depending, among other things, on the degree of concentration of the juice, the water-soluble essence of this process can be preared to the desired concentration (fold) of aldehyde, ketone, alcohol, and oil content.

JUICE ENHANCERS

ADDITIVES TO ENHANCE FLAVOR

Glutaminase Hydrolysis of Glutamine to Glutamic Acid

Seasonings distinguished for flavoring effect, such as L-glutamic acid, 5'-inosic acid, or 5'-guanylic acid are added in a wide range of processed foods and beverages that are especially required to be delicious, including, for example, pickles, seasonings, canned meats and vegetables, tomato ketchups, various juices, etc. It has heretofore been known that some of these food and beverage materials contain glutamine which is readily convertible into glutamic acid. However, the glutamine is transformed into pyroglutamic acid devoid of flavoring effect during the course of conventional processing treatments such as heating, and during the storage of processed materials.

As a result of studies upon the means for an effective utilization of glutamine, *T. Yokotsuka, T. Iwaasa and M. Fujii; U.S. Patent 3,717,470; February 20, 1973; assigned to Kikkoman Shoyu Co., Ltd., Japan* have developed a process for preparing foods and beverages, excellent in flavor, which comprises adding glutaminase to the glutamine-containing materials to convert the glutamine into glutamic acid by hydrolysis.

In the process, free glutamine in the raw materials is converted into free glutamic acid by hydrolysis of the amide linkage. The hydrolysis of the amide linkage can be effected either enzymically or chemically by use of acids, etc. In the preparation of foods, the enzymic means is preferably used because chemical decompositions accompanying the formation of by-products are undesirable in most of the cases. Glutaminase for use as the enzyme capable of hydrolyzing the amide linkage of glutamine may be of any origin. Ordinarily, there is advantageously used glutaminase produced by microorganisms such as yeasts, molds, bacteria, and actinomycetes.

These microorganisms are cultured under aerobic conditions using culture media which are suitable for producing ordinary glutaminase. The cultivation may be effected either by the stationary method or by the aerating and agitating method. For the medium, ordinary substrates which are consumable by the microorganism to be cultured are used.

Examples include carbon sources such as glucose, maltose, sucrose, dextrin, starch, and the like, and nitrogen sources such as soybean cake, soybean meal, gluten, yeast extract, peptone, meat extract, cornsteep liquor, ammonium salts, nitrates, etc. These substances are used either alone or in admixtures. If necessary, other salts of magnesium, calcium, potassium sodium, phosphoric acid, a trace amount of iron, manganese, etc., are used. The microorganisms can also be cultured by use of a medium containing in addition to the abovementioned nutrient sources other substrates for glutaminase such as L-glutamine. The glutaminase thus produced may be used as contained in the microorganism cells, since glutaminase is ordinarily an intracellular enzyme.

However, for the sake of efficiency, it is used in the form of microorganism cells suspended liquor obtained by autolysis of the exhausted broth, or in the form of an aqueous suspension of triturated microorganism cells, or more preferably in view of food preparation, in the form of crude enzyme extract, powder, or purified enzyme. According to the type of foods and beverages, glutaminase in any form of the abovementioned may be properly selected for use therein.

The amount of glutaminase to be added can be properly controlled according to the content of glutamine in the raw material. In general, the addition of glutaminase in an amount of at least 0.1% by weight based on the food or beverage material is sufficient. Glutaminase is preferably used at temperatures within a range of $10°$ to $70°C$, in which temperature range glutaminase can remain active.

Example: 1 kg of fresh tomato was washed with water and crushed to obtain juice. 1 g of a glutaminase preparation (extracted enzyme obtained from fungus cells of cultured *Cryptococcus albidus* (ATCC 20294) was added to the juice and mixed thoroughly, after which the mixture was left standing at $40°C$ for 1 hr. Then, after having been kept at $100°C$ for 2 min the mixture was centrifuged to obtain tomato juice. The content of free glutamic acid in 1 ml of the juice was 1.82 mg, whereas the content was 0.73 mg in the case where tomato was treated in the same manner as abovementioned except that no glutaminase was used.

Addition of β-Hydroxybutyrates to Enhance Grape Flavor

Various methods have been used to reduce the loss of flavor and aroma components during the processing of grapes. For example, it is known to collect and condense the vapors of flavor and aroma components of grape juice and to subsequently reintroduce the condensed vapors at a later point in the process. The vapors are usually recovered in a form that is enriched in the flavor and aroma components of the fresh juice to provide a 100- to 150-fold essence, that is, a material in which the flavor and aroma components are from about 100 to 150 times more concentrated than in fresh juice. As used hereinafter, the term "essence" refers to concentrated flavor and aroma components of fresh grape juice.

The essence thus produced, when added to processed grape products such as juice concentrate, aids in enhancing its aroma and flavor to more nearly duplicate that of a fresh grape product. However, when a taste comparison is made, such as between fresh grape juice and a reconstituted grape juice prepared from a grape juice concentrate to which essence has been added, the fresh product is almost always preferred.

It is an object of the process of *J.L. Michael and H.W. Jackson; U.S. Patent 3,427,167; February 11, 1969; assigned to National Dairy Products Corporation* to improve the flavor and aroma of grape products, such as grape juice, by the addition of small amounts of particular compounds thereto. In this connection, the principal compounds present in natural grape essence have been identified and it is known that the aroma and flavor of a synthetic essence prepared from such identified compounds only slightly resembles the aroma and flavor of natural grape juice essence.

However, it has now been found that grape products having substantially improved flavor and aroma may be prepared by adding thereto ethyl β-hydroxybutyrate, methyl β-hydroxybutyrate, or mixtures thereof. Such compounds may be utilized in natural products to enhance their flavor, or they may be utilized as components of an artificial grape flavor to provide a grape-like product. The flavoring compounds are added at a total level of from about 30 to about 100 parts per million of the finished product, expressed as parts by weight. Generally, it is preferable to use mixtures of ethyl β-hydroxybutyrate and methyl β-hydroxybutyrate. A preferred ratio is 3 parts of ethyl β-hydroxybutyrate to 1 part methyl β-hydroxybutyrate.

Example: A grape juice concentrate is prepared from natural grape juice by a vacuum evaporation process. A concentrate of 46° Brix is obtained, which is combined with 100-fold natural grape essence in the ratio of 100:1. To this is added sufficient ethyl β-hydroxybutyrate and methyl β-hydroxybutyrate to provide a level of 50 ppm of each in reconstituted grape juice prepared from the concentrate.

The reconstituted grape juice produced using the flavoring compounds of this process is then compared to reconstituted concentrated grape juice to which natural grape essence alone has been added, and to natural grape juice. The natural grape juice and the reconstituted grape juice of this process are substantially similar and are substantially more flavorful than the reconstituted grape juice to which essence alone is added.

2-Ethylpyromeconic Acid

It is a matter of common knowledge and experience that the addition of maltol, also known as 2-methylpyromeconic acid, a valuable gamma-pyrone, to many foods improves the flavor and aroma thereof to such an extent that wide consumer acceptance of the practice has been obtained. This appreciation of improved flavor is reflected in increased sales volume of foods so treated. Furthermore, numerous taste panel tests demonstrate that many foods containing maltol are preferred over those from which it is omitted.

Maltol is extremely beneficial in the replacement of certain other classical flavor and aroma enhancers in that it is generally much more powerful and, for this reason, can be used in lower amounts. An advantage in this practice is immediately obvious in that such a high strength enhancer may be used at lower levels and, as a result, the natural taste of maltol itself does not overpower the desired edible flavor and aroma or perfume aroma.

For example, it is known that maltol can replace four times its weight of coumarin. Although coumarin has been used very widely in the past, it has such a powerful aroma of its own, resembling that of vanilla beans, that great care must be used to prevent so much being added as to overpower the compositions, maltol, on the other hand, is used in smaller amounts that coumarin, thus providing a margin of safety. Because of this and its lack of toxicity, maltol has replaced coumarin in many foods.

It has been found by *C.R. Stephens, Jr. and R.P. Allingham; U.S. Patent 3,446,629; May 27, 1969; assigned to Chas. Pfizer & Co., Inc.* that the compound 2-ethylpyromeconic acid is very much more effective than maltol as a flavor and aroma enhancer. In fact, 2-ethylpyromeconic acid has an aroma and flavor enhancing power of about 6 times that of maltol. Thus, on a relative basis, 1 part by weight of 2-ethylpyromeconic acid is equivalent to about 24 parts of the abovementioned coumarin in its flavor and aroma enhancing effect.

The advantage in using 2-ethylpyromeconic acid becomes immediately obvious after considering that the relative costs of the 2-ethylpyromeconic acid and of maltol are of approximately the same order of magnitude. Thus, the consumer is able to use only about one-sixth as much of the 2-ethylpyromeconic acid to achieve the same level of flavor and odor enhancement and realizes very significant savings in manufacturing cost. 2-ethylpyromeconic acid is a gamma-pyrone of the formula below.

It is an acidic substance which forms salts with bases, which salts can be used interchangeably with the free acid in the process. 2-ethylpyromeconic acid is prepared readily and economically by a combination of a fermentation technique and organic synthesis. The starting material for the synthesis in kojic acid and the process generally comprises the steps of oxidizing kojic acid to comenic acid, of decarboxylating comenic acid to pyromeconic acid, of treating pyromeconic acid with acetaldehyde to form 2-(1-hydroxyethyl)-pyromeconic acid, and reducing this to 2-ethylpyromeconic acid.

The enhancer may be added to the food directly in the dry form or, alternatively, as a solution. Care should be taken to obtain even distribution through the use of premixing if necessary, since such small quantities have such a powerful effect.

With respect to enhancing the aroma and flavor of edibles, particular mention is made of the especially desirable increase in appeal which is obtained when 2-ethylpyromeconic acid is added in an amount to provide from about 1 to 100 ppm by weight. It is observed that below about 1 ppm there is a tendency for some of the test subjects to have difficulty in discerning the beneficial effect of the addition and that above about 100 parts per million, some of the subjects begin to notice an aroma effect contributed by the 2-ethylpyromeconic acid itself.

Example: Pineapple juice flavor is pleasingly enhanced when 2-ethylpyromeconic acid is added at 4 ppm, and compared with a control. 10 ppm of 2-ethylpyromeconic acid added to grape juice greatly amplifies the natural sweet grape aroma.

2-Alkylthiazoles

Efforts have been made to identify chemical compounds and to determine the practical use of these compounds, which when added to tomato-containing foods would enhance the agreeable tomato aroma and flavor of such foods. A great deal of research was directed to isolating and identifying the complex chemical compounds naturally occurring in the common tomato, usually found in the form of volatiles, which constitute or contribute significantly to the tomato aroma and flavor. Research was also directed toward acquiring an understanding why particular varieties of tomatoes, such as Campbell variety No. 146, have a unique, highly pleasant flavor while other varieties possess this flavor to a lesser degree.

A number of problems were encountered. First, it was noted that several volatiles which appeared to affect the tomato flavor in certain foods were altered by the standard preparation treatments employed to identify the volatiles. The presence and nature of the volatiles appear to depend on the physical condition and maturity of the fruit from which they are extracted as well as the type of crushing used, the holding time of the juice or pulp after crushing, and the presence of heat and oxygen during extraction. Many of the volatiles were found to be highly labile during normal processing and frequently broke down into other compounds even after they were added to the tomato product.

In addition, synergistic action among the compounds in the fruit often causes the flavor evaluation of the pure compound in a pure medium to be quite different from the flavor contribution of the compound when added to the fruit or fruit product. Because of the complexity of the well-known tomato flavor, it was most difficult to identify any particular compound as contributing significantly to the overall flavor. This was particularly true for 2-isobutylthiazole as this compound had not previously been reported as existing in natural products and, consequently, the presence and identification of this compound in a natural product was not predictable nor common knowledge.

S.J. Kazeniac and R.M. Hall; U.S. Patent 3,660,112; May 2, 1972; assigned to Campbell Soup Company have succeeded in isolating and identifying a compound, namely, 2-isobutylthiazole, which is largely responsible for the unique flavor of certain varieties of tomatoes, for example, the Campbell 146 and VF-145.

In many varieties of tomatoes, 2-isobutylthiazole is present at levels that are too low to affect the flavor and, as a result, such varieties are bland and less desirable in flavor quality. It has also been found that 2-isobutylthiazole, as well as other 2-alkylthiazoles, has exceptionally strong flavor enhancing properties. This compound produces a more intense, fresh tomato flavor, provides a better overall blending of the flavor of the tomato or tomato food product and improves the mouthfeel properties.

The rather unpleasant odor of pure 2-isobutylthiazole, as well as other 2-alkylthiazoles, does not suggest that this compound will improve the flavor of food products. The pure compound in aqueous solution has a spoiled, vine-like, slightly horseradish-type flavor which is rather objectionable. However, when, for example, it is added to canned tomato juice, it produces a more intense fresh tomato flavor. The characteristic flavor of 2-isobutylthiazole is distinctly detectable in slices from tomatoes of the varieties high in this compound, such as Campbell 146, once its flavor qualities are known to the taster.

Many of the alkylthiazoles have been found to possess flavor enhancing effects similar to 2-isobutylthiazole. The size of the substituent has been found to be preferably any alkyl radical from C_2 to C_5. The branched 2-alkyl derivatives are generally more effective than the straight chain or linear 2-alkylthiazoles, although the latter have desirable flavor enhancing properties at the proper concentration.

Example: When the alkylthiazole compounds were added to a blended vegetable juice prior to pasteurization, canning and evaluation, the panel testing results were similar to those obtained when the compounds were added to tomato soup. It was found that 2-isobutylthiazole at approximately 50 ppb depressed the celery note, blended the flavors in a pleasant manner and provided a slight increase in fresh tomato flavor. The addition of 2-tert-butylthiazole at 50 ppb to another sample provided a fresh, viney tomato flavor and at 100 ppb this flavor became strong in intensity.

Addition of 2-sec-amylthiazole produced about the same flavor enhancing effect as that of 2-tert-butylthiazole at the same concentrations. Addition of 2-sec-butylthiazole at 200 ppb to another sample had an effect similar to that of 2-isobutylthiazole. Addition of 2-isopropylthiazole at 200 ppb or of 2-n-amylthiazole at 400 ppb increased the vegetable-like flavor. The remaining compounds, 2-n-butylthiazole and 2-n-propylthiazole, produced more limited flavor enhancing effects at about 400 ppb.

COLORING AGENTS

Carotenoids Dissolved in Abietic Acids

For imparting an orange or yellow coloration to foodstuffs, beverages, pharmaceuticals, cosmetics, etc., use has heretofore been made of coloring agents such as Orange 1, Orange SS, Yellow AB, Sunset Yellow FCF, most of which are azo-compounds. These known orange or yellow-coloring agents are not always harmless to living bodies, and therefore, the pharmacological problem entailed in the use thereof has been a long-existing and much explored problem.

In the absence of a satisfactory solution of the problem, foodstuffs, pharmaceuticals, cosmetics, etc. have in recent years been colored with carotenoid pigments which have no toxicity or are harmless to living bodies. Carotenoid pigments are, however, in most cases essentially insoluble in solvents such as water, ethanol, etc., and this is very disadvantageous in the practical use of such pigments.

The method heretofore employed is that β-carotene is dissolved in a vegetable oil at about 140°C, an aqueous colloid containing gelatin and sugar is added to the solution to disperse the β-carotene in the water and the suspension is spray dried, and then the thus obtained suspension or spray dried material is incorporated into the material to be colored. However, even when β-carotene is thus dissolved in a vegetable oil at about 140°C, it gradually separates out with lowering of the temperature of the solution, so that only 1% of β-carotene is dissolved when the solution is allowed to stand for 8 hr at room temperature (about 20° to 30°C). The solubility of the β-carotene is still further decreased with lapse of time to cause separation of a large quantity of crystals and creaming of the solution.

H. Mima, M. Terasaki and M. Kato; U.S. Patent 3,227,561; January 4, 1966; assigned to Takeda Chemical Industries, Ltd., Japan report the use of abietic acid or hydrogenated abietic acid or a lower aliphatic alcohol ester thereof as a solvent for the carotenoid pigment used as a colorant.

The carotenoid can be dissolved in abietic acids in relatively high concentration and the solution is stable and even after the solution has been kept for a long time, the relatively high concentration is retained. Further abietic acids have no substantial toxicity and no unpleasant odor or taste. The specific gravity of abietic acids being approximately equal to that of fruit juice, it is slightly heavier than water.

The basic procedure is to dissolve the carotenoid pigment in abietic acids under heating to about relatively low temperature. Preferably the pigment may be dissolved by heating within 60 min at 90° to 140°C, most preferably at about 98° to 100°C for about 30 to 60 minutes. The solubility of carotenoid in abietic acids solution thus obtained decreases very slowly when it is cooled to room temperature, but still the concentration of carotenoid remains at more than 3% even after the solution is preserved at room temperature for several months.

In order to protect the carotenoid or abietic acids or an essential oil, etc., against oxidation and degeneration, an antioxidant may optionally be added to the solution. As the antioxidant, there may be used, for example, oil soluble antioxidants such as butylated hydroxyanisole, butylated hydroxytoluene hereinafter abbreviated as BHA and BHT, etc., or water-soluble antioxidant such as ascorbic acid or the salt thereof.

The solution in abietic acids of one or more carotenoids may be directly emulsified in water, or it may be suspended or emulsified in water after adding a dispersing agent such as a surface active agent, for example, glycerin monostearate; a protective colloid such, for example, as gum arabic; or a specific gravity controlling agent such, for example, as brominated vegetable oil.

Example 1: With 50 parts by weight of dihydroabietic acid ethyl ester are mixed 1 part by weight of β-carotene, 0.1 part by weight of BHT and 0.01 part by weight of BHA, while heating at about 100°C for 30 min. After cooling, the resultant mixture is mixed with an aqueous solution containing 10 parts by weight of gum arabic and 5 parts by weight of sodium ascorbate in 2,000 parts by volume of water. The entire resultant solution is emulsified in an homogenizer to obtain a stable emulsion of β-carotene.

Example 2: A stable orange juice containing no artificial pigment is prepared by incorporating 300 parts by volume of β-carotene emulsion prepared by Example 1 into 1,000 parts by volume of ⅕ concentrated fruit juice, 160 parts by volume of the solution containing citric acid to 50%, 35,000 parts by weight of sugar, 20 parts by weight of orange essence, 3 parts by weight of ascorbic acid and 27,000 parts by volume of water.

Example 3: To a mixture containing 50 parts by weight of tetrahydroabietic acid ethyl ester and 10 parts by weight of orange oil are added 1 part by weight of β-carotene, 0.1 part by weight of BHT and 0.01 part by weight of BHA, while heating at about 100°C for about 30 min.

After cooling, the resultant mixture is admixed with an aqueous solution of 10 parts by weight of gum arabic and 10 parts by weight of sodium ascorbate in 100 parts by volume of water. The entire resultant solution is homogenized at the rate of 4,000 lb/in². To the so-obtained emulsion are added 50 parts by weight of a drying agent consisting of dextrin, lactose, powdery millet jelly. The resultant mixture is spray dried to obtain a powdered product of β-carotene.

Example 4: A stable powdery orange juice containing no artificial pigment is prepared by incorporating 3 parts by weight of powder obtained by Example 3 into 500 parts by weight of powdery orange juice (spray dried or vacuum dried), 1,000 parts by weight of crystallized glucose, 35 parts by weight of citric acid, 40 parts by weight of sodium cyclohexylsulfamate, 4 parts by weight of sodium chloride, 20 parts by weight of powdery perfume and 20 parts by weight of ascorbic acid.

Benzopyrylium Compounds

It is well-known in the field of biochemistry that the characteristic color of many flowers and fruits is due to their content of natural pigments called anthocyanins. The characteristic color of cherries, cranberries, strawberries, raspberries, and grapes, for example, is primarily due to these natural coloring principles. The basic structure of the anthocyanins is the flavylium (or 2-phenylbenzopyrylium nucleus:

(1)

with variation as to the substituents on the various available positions on the A and B rings. The oxygen atom (at position 1) is in an oxonium configuration so that ordinarily the compounds are isolated in the form of salts with strong acids such as hydrochloric acid. Most anthocyanins contain a glycoside group at position 3 with several hydroxy groups on the other positions, often at positions 5, 7, and 4'. A typical anthocyanin is oxycoccicyanin chloride which has been isolated from cranberries. Its structure is:

(2)

where G represents a β-glucosyl radical. The anthocyanins may be prepared in aglycone form and these are referred to as anthocyanidins. The aglycone form of oxycoccicyanin chloride, for example, is peonidin chloride. The structure of this compound is as represented in Formula (2) above, but wherein G is hydrogen.

It is well understood in the food processing industry that the natural anthocyanin pigments are not stable. Thus, when various food products such as berries, cherries, grapes, etc. are processed and stored their natural color diminishes or even disappears completely. A typical example in this regard is the gradual change in color from bright red to brownish-red or even brown, observed with frozen strawberries.

Another example is the faded appearance of canned cherries. Many jams, jellies, and preserves display muddy brownish colors in contrast to the vivid color of the original fruit. In preparing maraschino cherries, it is conventional to brine the fresh cherries in a solution containing sulfites or bisulfites. Contact of this brine with the fruit causes a complete loss of color so that the fruit has a straw-yellow appearance, requiring addition of a food dye when the product is put up for sale.

In accordance with the process of *L. Jurd; U.S. Patent 3,301,683; January 31, 1967; assigned to U.S. Secretary of Agriculture*, foods are colored with compounds which contain the benzopyrylium nucleus of the natural anthocyanins but which differ in two significant aspects from the natural pigments. These points of distinction are as follows. (A) In these compounds the 3-position is unsubstituted or is provided with particular substituents as designated below. In either case, such structure renders the compounds of the process stable. The instability of the natural pigments is primarily due to the substituent on the 3-position. Either a sugar residue or a hydroxy group at the 3-position makes for instability. It has been found, moreover, that if the glycoside residue or hydroxy group at position 3 is replaced by any one of several other types of radicals, the problem is obviated in that the compounds are stable and retain their original color despite long exposure to adverse conditions such as contact with ascorbic acid, enzymes, light, heat, etc. It has been found that stability is imparted to the pigments when the 3-position is occupied by a lower alkyl radical, a lower alkoxy radical, a phenyl radical, a phenoxy radical, or when the 3-position is unsubstituted.

(B) The compounds of the process contain a styrene nucleus attached to the benzopyrylium at position 2. This styryl group has the advantage that the compounds exhibit deeper hues than is possible with the flavylium-type structure wherein a phenyl nucleus is attached at position 2. In particular, the 2-styrylbenzopyrylium structure makes it possible to attain bright red and blue-red shades with as few as two hydroxy groups. The compounds of the process may be described generically as benzopyrylium salts of the formula:

(3)

wherein each R represents a radical selected from the group consisting of hydrogen, hydroxyl, and lower alkoxy, wherein R' represents a radical selected from the group consisting of hydrogen, lower alkyl, phenyl, lower alkoxy, and phenoxy, and where X is an anion. The preferred category of compounds is that wherein R' is hydrogen and X is the chloride ion.

The compounds of the process are readily prepared by a variation of the method of Buck and Heilbron [*Jour. Chem. Soc.* volume 121, pp 1198 to 1212 (1922)] which involves condensation of ortho-hydroxybenzaldehyde or its substituted derivatives with benzalacetone or the substituted derivatives thereof. By selection of the substituents on the respective reactants, any desired styrylbenzopyrylium compound may be prepared.

The particular color provided by any individual compound is largely determined by its content of hydroxyl or ether (e.g., methoxy) groups. Compounds having a paucity of such groups provide colors at the orange-red end of the spectrum (similar to strawberry red) while compounds of increasing numbers of hydroxyl and/or methoxyl groups display the more blue-red or purple or what may be termed burgundy or wine-red colors.

The application of the compounds of the process in the coloring of food products is conducted as with prior coloring agents or food dyes. In situations where the food product is a liquid, the benzopyrylium compound is simply added to such liquid in the amount required to produce the desired coloration of the product.

Since the benzopyrylium compounds have intense coloring action, only minute proportions thereof are required, on the order of 1 to 200 ppm. Typical illustrative examples of foods which may be colored with the compounds of the process are fruits, vegetables, juices, syrups, concentrates, or other liquid preparations made from fruits or vegetables.

The compounds of the process have the particular advantage that they are useful in situations where the substrate to be colored contains substances which cause decomposition of natural anthocyanin pigments or in situations where the substrate to be colored is subjected to processing or storage conditions which are conductive to decomposition of natural anthocyanin pigments. Typical of substances which adversely affect the color of natural anthocyanins are oxygen and ascorbic acid.

The compounds of the process can be successfully used with food products containing such agents without loss of color, even when stored for long periods of time.

Example 1: A mixture of 2,4-dihydroxybenzaldehyde (45 g) and p-hydroxybenzalacetone (45 g) in ethyl acetate (500 ml) and alcohol (100 ml) was saturated with a rapid stream of hydrogen chloride gas. After standing for 5 hours, ether (200 ml) was added and the deeply colored product (80 g) was collected. It was purified by digestion in alcoholic HCl and recrystallized from aqueous citric acid solution by addition of concentrated hydrochloric acid.

The compound so prepared, 7-hydroxy-2-(4-hydroxystyryl)benzopyrylium chloride, forms raspberry red solutions when dissolved in aqueous citric acid at concentrations of 5 to 100 parts per million. Visually and spectrally the compound is similar to FD&C Red No. 1 and FD&C Red No. 4 and to natural pelargonidin-3-glucoside, the chief pigment of strawberry juice. The intensity of color of the compound is about three times that of the FD&C Red No. 1 and 4.

An aqueous solution was prepared containing 7-hydroxy-2-(4-hydroxystyryl)benzopyrylium chloride (5 ppm), sodium benzoate (0.1%), citric acid (0.4%) and sugar (10%). This solution had a raspberry red color. On standing for 22 days exposed to bright sunlight its absorbance indicated that the solution had retained 43.4% of its original color. In more concentrated solutions of the benzopyrylium compound, for example, 100 ppm, the color loss on such standing is only barely perceptible to the eye.

Example 2: HCl gas was passed into a solution of 2,4-dihydroxybenzaldehyde (57 g) and vanillalacetone (57 g) in ethyl acetate (500 ml) and alcohol (100 ml) until the solution was saturated. The solution was allowed to stand for 6 hours and the deep red-black crystals were separated, then purified by recrystallization from aqueous alcoholic HCl.

The compound so prepared, 7-hydroxy-2-(3-methoxy-4-hydroxystyryl)benzopyrylium chloride, forms red-blue solutions when dissolved in aqueous citric acid at concentrations of 5 to 100 parts per million. Spectrally, the compound is similar to FD&C Red No. 2. The intensity of color of the compound is about three times that of FD&C Red No. 2. Because of the bluish-red hue of the compound, it closely resembles that of natural grape pigments.

Pink Pineapple-Grapefruit Juice Blend

In recent years blends of fruit juices, as for example, pineapple and grapefruit juices, have been extensively marketed. This type of product has grown in consumer popularity due, among other things, to its unique, palatable flavor.

R.L. Handwerk and L. Allen; U.S. Patent 3,425,841; February 4, 1969; assigned to Castle & Cooke, Inc. have found that a particularly desirable blend of this type possessing enhanced flavor may be produced by suitably proportioning and mixing fruit juices, such as pineapple juice and the juice of pink or the conventional white grapefruit, and this blend may be characterized by a color which, in the case of the pineapple-grapefruit juice blend, may be similar to the color of the flesh of pink grapefruit.

The successful attainment of this process involves overcoming certain major difficulties which heretofore precluded imparting a characteristic color to the product. First, it will be understood that the natural color of many fruit juice blends is not a color which might be the most desirable from a marketing standpoint.

For example, it may be desirable to market a pink grapefruit juice blend, but the juice of pink grapefruit is not pink, but practically white. The pink color for which this species of grapefruit is distinguished is derived from a water-insoluble pigment within the flesh of the fruit, which is not removed with the expressed juice but which remains in the pulp. To attain the desirable pink color for a pink grapefruit juice blend, it is necessary to utilize a color addition agent or dye, and the choice of such color additive is restricted by U.S.

Government regulations. Marketing considerations and consumer acceptance require that the fruit juice blend have a pleasing flavor and the packaged or canned juice blend must also retain a characteristic color over the normal shelf storage periods. As will be seen subsequently, this necessity of improving color stability of the packaged product imposes serious limitations on the choice of the coloring agent used.

It is well recognized in the art that in order to maintain the original desirable flavor of the blend it is necessary to package the product in a tin lined can and not in an enameled tin lined can. It has been found through experience in this field that the enameled tin lined can undesirably affects the flavor of the packaged product during storage.

The requirement for packaging such acidic fruit juice blends in tin lined containers presents problems with respect to coloring which are difficult to overcome. It is well-known that certain colors or dyes added to fruit juice products are unstable and tend to fade during storage of the product. This color instability in such canned products appears to be due either to the action of ascorbic or other acid normally present in such juice products or to the action of metallic ions present, or to a combination of these factors.

For example, in the course of research in devising the process it was ascertained that when the certified color, FD&C Red No. 2 (amaranth) was added to a blend of pineapple juice and grapefruit juice, the dye bleached out in a relative short period and the blend ultimately became colorless. It was found that this dye could be used effectively in such pineapple-grapefruit juice blends only when the product was packaged in enameled tin lined cans. As pointed out above, this type of packaging is undesirable because it is well established that such type of container has an adverse effect on the flavor of the canned product.

The certified color FD&C Red No. 3 (erythrosine) is known to possess a greater stability with respect to ascorbic acid than does FD&C Red No. 2 and presumably might function effectively as a coloring agent in an acidic fruit juice blend. However, it has long been recognized by color chemists that this dye is insoluble in aqueous acid solutions at a pH below 4.2.

As ascorbic and other acids are often added to fruit juice blends to achieve the most desirable flavor, it has heretofore been considered impractical to sacrifice flavor in order to achieve a workable pH, and FD&C Red No. 3 has been discounted as a usable coloring agent.

In the past it has been suggested that the certified colors used in fruit drinks containing ascorbic acid and possible metallic ions might be protected or stabilized by utilizing agents such as different forms of EDTA. Another suggestion advanced for coloration of fruit juices has been the incorporation of stable plant pigments such as the red varieties of the carotenoids. Each of these expedients is unsatisfactory in that it involves additional manipulation and expense in producing the commercial canned juice blend.

In the course of extensive experimentation and research with blends of pineapple and grapefruit juice, it has been found that blends of pineapple and grapefruit juice could be developed having a pH well below pH 4.2 and that yet a characteristic color could be imparted to these blends effectively by incorporating a selected amount of erythrosine in the blend. Products thus produced have been packaged in tin lined cans and have been found to satisfactorily retain their flavor and color over storage periods of many months under ambient temperature conditions.

The following formula is representative of the fruit juice blend. This blend, which has a pH of 3.25, has been tested for prolonged periods in tin lined cans with the desirable results noted previously, namely retention of its original flavor and color. It will be understood that the proportions of the respective ingredients such as the ratio of pineapple to grapefruit juice is not critical but may be varied within the desired balance of flavor intensity and sweetness in the ultimate marketed blend. Similarly the degree of concentration of the respective juices may be varied within substantial limits.

It will also be understood that certain other dyes may be employed in selected amounts in the blend to enhance or modify the tinctorial effect of the erythrosine without effecting the flavor of the blend. Such additive dyes, for example, may be carotene yellow, yellow No. 5, cochineal, and carmine.

Pineapple concentrate	61° Brix, 330 grams
Grapefruit concentrate	58° Brix, 71 grams
Sugar	Approx. 225 grams
Citric acid	Approx. 10 grams
Sodium citrate	Variable to adjust pH to 3.25
Color: U.S. Certified Red #3 (3% sol)	Approx. color sufficient to 0.035 gm.
Vitamin C (to maintain minimum daily adult requirement)	30 mg. per 6 oz.
Grapefruit oil and/or orange oil	0.3 ml.
Naringin	1.7 gram
Water to make 1 gallon	

Enrichment of Orange Juice with Chromoplasts

Color has been found to be one of the most influential factors affecting the preference of consumers for particular citrus juices. Based on U.S. Department of Agriculture visual scored for color it has, for example, been determined that consumers tested definitely preferred orange juice having a color score of 39 to less colored orange juice having a visual color score of only 36.

One of the problems, however, associated with the processing of citrus juices is that the color of the juice tends to vary considerably depending upon variety, condition of the fruit, and most significantly the month in which that orange crop was harvested. For example, it was determined that for oranges harvested during the months of December through June, 43% had a color score of under 36, 51% had a color score of 37, and only 6% had a color score of 39, which was the value found to produce the highest consumer acceptance.

In accordance with the process of *R.W. Barron, P.J. Fellers and R.L. Huggart; U.S. Patent 3,725,083; April 3, 1973; assigned to State of Florida, Department of Citrus* it has been found that the color of juices such as full strength and reconstituted citrus juice concentrates as well as synthetic base drinks can be substantially enhanced by the incorporation into these beverages of pigment granules which can be isolated from selected highly colored citrus fruit.

It is yet a further feature of the method that these naturally occurring pigments or chromoplasts can be sufficiently concentrated and added in sufficient quantity to beverages to produce desirably significant enhancement of coloration in the juice.

The juice of relatively highly colored citrus fruits, such as for example, Dancy tangerines or Murcott oranges, is extracted and then filtered to remove entrained solid particles such as seeds and pulp to give a juice containing chromoplasts responsible for the color of the juice. This filtered juice is then processed, for example, by centrifuging, to remove substantially all of the chromoplasts from the fluid.

The pellet of solid matter which is thereby obtained consists essentially of the solid pigment particles from the juice and is divided into fairly specific color layers, the bottom most layer obtained in solid being brown in color and the remaining layers red, orange, and in some cases yellow (although the yellow chromoplasts have been found in some instances to remain in the solution).

The brown layer is discarded and the remaining colored layers are then suspended in fresh water and rewashed with water and recentrifuged. The pigmented particles or chromoplasts which are finally obtained can then be dried to produce a colored powder which can be added, for example, to citrus juices (either single strength or concentrated) in sufficient quantity to bring that juice up to a desired color level, e.g., having a color score of about 39. Generally the amount of dried chromoplasts which is added to beverages to enhance the color will vary somewhat depending upon, for example, the color of the beverage to which the chromoplasts are added as well as the intensity and amount of specific colors present in the chromoplasts themselves.

It has, however, been found that ordinarily the color of citrus juice, for example, can often be increased by about 2 points in the U.S. Department of Agriculture color score by the addition of dried chromoplast material equivalent to the amount of chromoplast material obtained from highly colored citrus juice equal in volume to 50 to 100% of the amount of juice to which the pigment is being added.

By the addition of chromoplast obtained from a volume of juice equivalent to 100 to 150% or more of the amount of juice to which the material is being added, the color score can be raised by as much as 5 points, e.g., from 34 to 39.

Example: Isolation of Chromoplasts — About 150 milliliters of juice was extracted from each of two 300 gram samples (whole fresh weight) of Dancy tangerine and Murcott orange fruits and filtered through coarse mesh cloth. The filtered juice was then centrifuged at 4000*g* for 10 minutes.

With the tangerine juice this force was sufficient to centrifuge all of the chromoplasts out of suspension, giving a clear, opalescent supernatant fluid and a pellet containing the chromoplasts. The supernatant fluid after centrifugation of Murcott juice, however, was yellow. The pellets were found in each case to consist of several layers of particulate material of different color.

A layer of brown material was found at the bottom of the pellet with the red and orange chromoplasts above that, topped with a layer of yellow chromoplasts in the case of the tangerine juice. The yellow chromoplasts were absent from tangerine juice.

The supernatant fluid was removed by decantation, and the chromoplasts were resuspended in tap water without disturbing the brown material which adhered to the walls of the centrifuge tube. This brown substance was discarded. The chromoplasts were then washed twice by recentrifugation in tap water to remove acids and other juice components.

Prior to the final centrifugation, the chromoplasts suspension was distributed equally in 6 centrifuge tubes. Thus, each tube contained the equivalent of 50 grams of whole fruit. Water was decanted from the final pellet and the tube was allowed to drain.

Addition of Chromoplasts to Orange Juice — A 6 ounce can of commercial concentrated orange juice was reconstituted with tap water and divided into four equal portions. Appropriate amounts of the packed chromoplasts were then resuspended in the juice. A mortar and pestle were used to thoroughly disperse the particles in a small volume of juice before adding them to the remainder.

The addition of the chromoplasts in one centrifuge tube to the reconstituted juice from one-fourth of a 6 ounce can of concentrate is equivalent to adding the chromoplast material from the juice of 200 grams of whole fresh fruit to 24 ounces of juice reconstituted from one, 6 ounce can of concentrate.

Measurement of Color — The reconstituted orange juices with added chromoplasts were analyzed for lightness R_d, redness a, and yellowness b with a color difference meter. Color scores were then determined relating the R_d and a values to the U.S. Department of Agriculture visual scores for orange juice.

The addition of chromoplasts isolated from the highly colored juice of Dancy tangerines or Murcott oranges to a reconstituted commercial juice having a low color score increased the color meter a value, indicating an increase in the redness of the juice.

The treated juice was judged much more appealing in color than the untreated and no change in flavor was detected. As shown in Tables 1 and 2, a substantial decrease in the color meter R_d value, which is consistent with results observed in commercial juices, was also found when chromoplasts were added to the reconstituted juice.

TABLE 1: EFFECT OF ADDED DANCY TANGERINE CHROMOPLASTS

Amount Color Added	- - - -Color Meter Values*- - - -			Visual Color Score
	R_d	a	b	
Control	36.1	-5.4	36.8	34
200**	35.2	-1.9	36.6	36
400**	34.2	1.0	36.5	37
600**	32.7	3.5	35.9	39

*Values obtained using 0.6 cm viewing depth with Carrara plate.
**Grams of whole fruit needed to obtain chromoplasts to enhance the
  color of 24 ounces of reconstituted concentrated orange juice.

TABLE 2: EFFECT OF ADDED MURCOTT ORANGE CHROMOPLASTS

Amount Color Added	- - - -Color Meter Values*			Visual Color Score
	R_d	a	b	
Control	34.8	-5.5	38.9	34
200**	32.5	-0.1	38.9	37
400**	30.7	4.1	38.8	39
600**	29.5	7.3	38.5	40

*Values obtained using 0.6 cm viewing depth with Carrara plate.
**Grams of whole fruit needed to obtain chromoplasts to enhance the
  color of 24 ounces of reconstituted concentrated orange juice.

MISCELLANEOUS PROCESSES

FRUIT JUICE AND MILK BEVERAGES

Pear Beverage

W.S. Johnston, I. Johnston, J.F. Gebhardt and M.S. Gebhardt; U.S. Patent 3,174,865; March 23, 1965; assigned to Tom Tom Beverage Co. provide a method of combining fruit and dairy products to make a palatable beverage which may be preserved indefinitely by conventional canning or bottling processes.

Example: To 58 gal of pear concentrate, 24% solids, and 29 gal of peach concentrate, 24% solids, add 50 gal of sugar syrup and ascorbic acid or citric acid as necessary to obtain a pH of about 5. Mix the following: 110⅔ lb sugar, 58.8 lb milk powder, 33⅓ lb corn syrup, 1.83 lb stabilizer such as gelatin, 4 oz egg yolk color and 30 oz pure vanilla extract.

The above milk mix will be recognized as that conventionally employed for making ice cream and which is usually homogenized prior to freezing. The ice cream mix is homogenized and about 97.5 gal of the same is then added to the above noted 137 gal of sweetened fruit nectar. The combined materials are then aerated for about 30 sec by blending in a high speed mixer and the beverage is ready for canning. The canning step preferably is carried out by preheating the mixture and then flash pasteurizing at from 200° to 295°F for about 50 sec. The mixture is then cooled and canned. When the beverage is subsequently removed from the container, it is preferably aerated again and served chilled.

As will be readily understood, the danger in combining the fruit nectar with the milk is that the milk is likely to curdle. This danger is obviated in the process by adjusting the pH ratio to between 3.5 and 5.0 and, more important, aerating the mixture prior to canning. If the aerating step is omitted, curdling of the milk results regardless of the care taken in adjusting the pH ratio.

The fact that the above described beverage may be stored for a long period of time without settling or curdling is attributable in part to the presence of finely comminuted fibers of pear dispersed throughout the mixture as a result of the aerating or blending step. The lightweight pear fibers have little tendency to settle and therefore contribute to the suspension of the other particles of the mixture to prevent settling or curdling. It will be noted that the amount of pear in the above formula is twice the amount of peach. However, surprisingly enough, the pear taste is masked and is scarcely discernable whereas the peach taste is dominant. This same result, that is the masking of the pear taste without removal of the beneficial food values of the pear, may be achieved with other fruits such as, for example, grape, pineapple and orange.

Orange Juice Beverage

The process of *H.E. Swisher; U.S. Patent 3,647,476; March 7, 1972; assigned to Sunkist Growers, Inc.* involves the method and the product from removing bittering constituents from navel orange juice by commingling such juice with a normally liquid edible vegetable oil absorbing the bitter constituents. The process includes also recovering bitter constituents from the oil. Further included is a highly nutritious drink of the debittered juice and cow's milk.

Example: 500 g of very bitter 65° Brix concentrated navel orange juice was placed in a 2,000 ml round bottom flask. With a gentle swirling action, 75 ml soybean oil was added. After attaching the flask to a Rotovac and immersing in a 30°C water bath, the flask and contents were allowed to rotate for ¾ hr under 28" vacuum. To effectively remove the soybean oil from the concentrate, the mixture was diluted back to 30° Brix, temperature adjusted to 40°C, and centrifuged. The resulting navel orange juice was of pleasing flavor and the separated soybean oil very bitter.

Referring to the previously mentioned use of the debittered navel orange juice with milk to produce an attractive and flavorful nonbitter drink, it is often desired to use 3 parts of single strength debittered juice to 1 part of milk. Where the debittered juice is concentrated, it will usually be reconstituted by addition of water to yield single strength juice. The proportion of juice to milk in the drink combination may be whatever is desired, such as 1 part juice to 1 part milk or 2 parts juice to 1 part milk. The larger proportions of juice to milk are entirely acceptable because with the debittered juice the drink is not bitter. The milk employed may be whole milk or skim milk (low fat). Especially where skim milk is used, it is not necessary to eliminate all the oil because the residual oil acts as a replacement for butterfat from the flavor and calorie standpoint.

A normal range of residual oil in the product from the example is around 0.5 to 1.5%. To control the formation of undesirable large curds, a quantity of pectin is desirably added, such as about 0.2 to 0.5% depending somewhat upon the pH of the juice, the higher acidity requiring the more pectin. The pectin should be a high methoxyl rapid set grade, as understood in the pectin art, to obtain adequate control. Various flavor additives in minor proportions may be added if desired. For example, 50 to 60 g of sugar per liter of juice-milk blend may be used, or a trace of saccharin. Further, one-tenth of a gram of vanillin might be used as desired. As an example of a product, the following is given:

Natural strength debittered navel orange juice	1,500 ml
Whole milk	500 ml
Sugar	125 g
Pectin, rapid set	3 g

Low Viscosity Milk-Orange Juice Product

The process of *D.R. Shenkenberg, J.C. Chang and L.F. Edmondson; U.S. Patent 3,692,532; September 19, 1972; assigned to U.S. Secretary of Agriculture* relates to a milk-orange juice product of low viscosity that is stable through a wide range of temperatures and pH values.

The product is obtained by a process in which a sugar stabilizer mixture is added to milk at a temperature below 90°F, and the mixture is allowed to stand for at least 10 min, after which orange juice is added to the milk mixture, and the resulting milk-orange juice mixture is aged, pasteurized and homogenized. The milk and orange juice are present in the product of this process in a ratio of about 2 parts of milk to 1 part of juice. Sweeteners and flavoring substances can be added as desired. A typical product formulation is shown on the following page.

Ingredients	Percent by Weight
Milk	60.0
Orange juice	35.0
Sugar	4.8
Stabilizer (CMC*)	0.2

*Sodium carboxymethycellulose

The process for making the product as shown above is relatively simple and conventional milk processing equipment can be used. The preferred methods of making the product of this process are set forth below.

Method 1: Dry mix sugar and stabilizer. Add sugar-stabilizer mixture to milk at not above 90°F. Allow the milk, sugar-stabilizer mixture to stand for not less than 10 min after mixing at not above 90°F. Add orange juice to the milk mixture, allowing it to age not less than 10 min at not above 90°F. Pasteurize and homogenize at normal milk condition, e.g., 3,000 + 500 psi two stage or 1,000 psi single stage. Cool and package for distribution and consumption as a fresh dairy product.

Method 2: Dry mix sugar and stabilizer. Add the sugar-stabilizer mixture to milk at not over 90°F. Allow milk, sugar-stabilizer mixture to stand for not less than 10 min at not above 90°F. Pasteurize and homogenize at normal milk conditions, e.g., 1,500 + 500 psi two stage or 1,000 psi single stage. Cool to 40°F. Pasteurize and cool orange juice and add to the milk mixture. Package for distribution and consumption as fresh dairy product.

The stability of the product is the result of a complex formed by the casein of the milk and the carboxyl groups of the CMC which prevents casein precipitation below pH 5.0. In order to stabilize effectively, the stabilizer should have acidic groups. Such common stabilizers as gelatin and vegetable gums fail to stabilize below pH 5.0; in fact, many exhibit a tendency to promote casein destabilization.

The quantity of ingredients is not critical except for the amount of stabilizer. In order to obtain maximum palatability, low levels of stabilizer must be used. Stabilizers such as gelatin and vegetable gums can stabilize at pH 5.0 and but this is not the most desired product. High levels of gelatin or vegetable gums prevent precipitation and separation but the resulting heavy bodied product lacks consumer appeal.

CMC is added at a ratio of approximately 1 part CMC to 250 to 2,500 parts of milk, depending on the protein content of the milk ingredient, type of CMC being used and desired viscosity. The particular ratio used is that which provides optimum consumer preference and maximum storage stability. An important feature of this method not found in the prior art is that sufficient time be allowed for the carboxyl groups of the CMC to react with the casein molecules. When sufficient time is not allowed, the product has an undesirable high viscosity and is not heat stable. In addition, incipient coagulation, casein precipitation and separation of ingredients occurs.

Drink from Citrus Juice Concentrate and Fermented or Acidified Milk

It is customary that the citrus fruit juices used for the production of drinks containing fermented milk or milk with added organic acid and citrus fruit juices are concentrated in advance to a weight of from ¼ to ⅙ of the original weight for the purpose of improving their stability during storage of facilitating their handling. Such concentrated fruit juices, however, upon being mixed with fermented milk or milk with added organic acid cause the coagulation and rapid precipitation of colloidal particles suspended in the fermented milk.

K. Inagami, I. Mitsui and H. Kando; U.S. Patent 3,764,710; October 2, 1973; assigned to Calpis Shokuhin Kogyo KK, Japan have established a method of producing a drink with a rich flavor in spite of containing fermented milk or milk with added organic acid and citrus fruit juices, the juices having been concentrated by entirely different methods from that of the conventional methods of producing concentrated citrus fruit juices.

Care is taken concerning the denaturation of the pectin materials which exert a large influence on the coagulation and separation of the product, and after concentrated juices and fermented milk are mixed, the mixture continues to be stable for a long time without the addition of any special stabilizer. The production of the concentrated citrus fruit juices used in this process and the addition of fermented milk are described as follows.

(1) Citrus fruits, after being peeled, are squeezed by the chopper-pulper method or the in-line extractor method, and the content of the pulp materials of the squeezed juices is adjusted to from 10 to 25% by volume of the pulp materials composed mainly of vesicle membrane of good quality. Then the juice is brought to the preparation step for concentration, without removing the pulp materials by a finisher or the like. The citrus fruits mentioned above are citrus Unshiu orange, tangerine orange, mandarin orange, Valencia orange, navel orange, summer orange, grapefruits, citron and lemon.

(2) In the preparation step, the following procedures are carried out: the deaeration treatment for preventing the loss of flavor and the decomposition of vitamin C, the heat treatment for inactivating pectinase, and the homogenizing treatment for finely crushing the pulp materials.

(3) In the subsequent concentration step in which the vacuum concentration or the freeze-concentration is applied, the concentration ratio must not fall below one-third by weight. Thus, concentrated citrus fruit juices with a rich flavor deriving from good quality pulp materials are obtained.

(4) To the concentrated citrus juices obtained in step (3), the fermented milk or other milk with organic acids is added in an amount of from 5 to 40% by weight calculated on the basis of the original fruit juice weight, and sucrose, organic acids such as lactic acid, citric acid, malic acid and fumaric acid, food colorings, food flavorings, antioxidants, antiseptics, condiments, reinforcing additives (for example, vitamin C), carbon dioxide, purified water and so forth are added as required. Thus, a citrus fruit juice drink which contains fermented milk is obtained. Then a high pressure homogenizing treatment, for example, 150 kg/cm^2, may be sometimes applied to the above process.

Example: Peeled Unshiu oranges were crushed by a chopper, fed to a pulper having the screen of 1.5 mm meshes and squeezed so that the pulp materials content of the juice might be 15% by volume. The fruit juice was deaerated under a reduced pressure of 17 mm Hg and at 20°C. The juice was then subjected to the heat treatment of 93°C for 15 sec. After cooling, it was subjected to the high pressure homogenizing treatment at 150 kg/cm^2. The resulting fruit juice was concentrated at 20°C and 20 mm Hg to obtain the Unshiu orange juice concentrated to 1/2.5 by weight.

Skim milk was sterilized by heating it at 90°C for 15 sec. After cooling down to 37°C, a 3% *L. bulgaricus* starter was added thereto. The milk was then subjected to lactic acid fermentation at 37°C for 16 hr. After the acidity as lactic acid was brought to 1.8 w/v percent, the milk was homogenized at 150 kg/cm^2.

To 4 parts of the above Unshiu orange juice concentrated to 1/2.5 by weight, 1 part of this fermented milk, 4 parts of sucrose, and 1 part of purified water, as well as a small amount of organic acids, food flavorings, and food colorings, were added. The resulting mixture was sterilized at 93°C for 15 sec to produce the fruit juice drink containing fermented milk.

FORTIFIED CITRUS JUICE

Citrus Juice with Energy Supplement

The process of *C.D. Aktins and J.A. Attaway; U.S. Patent 3,657,424; April 18, 1972; assigned to State of Florida, Department of Citrus* relates to fortified citrus juice or other acid fruit juice having a flavor closely similar to that of natural citrus juice and suitable for replenishing salts whose natural level in the body has been diminished, for example, due to strenuous physical activity. More specifically, this process relates to fortified citrus juices which contain additional amounts only of those salts naturally present in the citrus juice in sufficient quantity to meet the physiological needs of individuals whose natural level of those salts is lower than normal without adversely affecting, to a significant degree, either palatability, flavor or factors associated with flavor such as acidity.

Vigorous physical activity, whether athletic or vocational, particularly when performed in a relatively high temperature environment, can lead to a loss of body fluids which results primarily in decreased volume of interstitial fluid in the body. If this is severe and progressive, the plasma volume also decreases. Whether or not the blood undergoes contraction depends upon the extent and nature of the electrolyte loss and the consequent changes in the electrolyte concentrations in the extracellular fluids. Those individuals working in very hot and humid environments may, for example, lose 10 to 14 liters daily as perspiration.

In extreme cases of dehydration, over 900 meq of sodium, 820 meq chlorine, and 150 meq of potassium may be lost from the human body in 24 hr. This hypotonic fluid loss is accompanied by a decrease in sodium chloride content of the perspiration from a normal 40 to 80 meq/l to as low as 2.5 meq/l. Obviously, losses even remotely approaching these magnitudes cannot be tolerated by individuals for longer than brief periods of time. Further, these losses of electrolytes are in excess of those furnished in the normal diet and are not supplied by water alone when no provision is made for simultaneous replacement of the sodium, chlorine, potassium and calcium which have been lost.

It is known that citrus juices contain certain amounts of these calcium, sodium and potassium ions that are lost from the body as a result of heavy physical activity and that these ions are naturally present in amounts more than sufficient for buffering of the juices to taste, when the juices are not extended by appreciable dilution. For example, reconstituted frozen orange concentrate contains 9 mg of calcium, 1 mg of sodium and 186 mg of potassium per 100 g of reconstituted juice.

Single strength freshly extracted orange juice contains similar amounts of these ions with 10 mg of calcium, 1 mg of sodium and 199 mg of potassium available per 100 g of juice. Further, in extended clinical tests the natural electrolytes present in orange juices have been noted to supply in general the minimum requirements of a large part of the electrolytic profile and in addition many of the vitamins necessary for the actual tone or energy of the human body under normal circumstances.

U.S. Patent 3,114,641 to Sperti, et al, describes extended or diluted citrus juices wherein sodium and potassium phosphate, sodium citrate, and sodium succinate are used as buffers to control pH. Other salts such as calcium chloride, magnesium chloride and sodium and potassium citrate, and tartaric and maleic acids and their salts are used to enhance the flavor of the citrus juice.

The quantity of those salts present in the extended citrus juice of the Sperti, et al, patent and in natural citrus juices, while sufficient for buffering the flavor of the juice and providing many of the vitamins and electrolytic salts normally required by the human body is, however, not sufficient to meet the physiological needs of people whose bodies have been dehydrated, for example, as a result of strenuous physical activity with an associated loss of body salts.

Attempts to prepare entirely synthetic solutions to supplement the depleted level of these salts in individuals have not been altogether successful and in some cases highly detrimental to the well being of individuals with certain physical disorders which may be undetected. Neither has the addition of vitamins and minerals present in the peel of citrus fruits proved a satisfactory solution to the problem. According to the process, citrus juices which can be in a variety of forms and strengths, are fortified by the addition of sodium and calcium salts and chloride ions in amounts sufficient to replace those elements depleted below the natural level from the individual's body fluids. Relatively small amounts of potassium can also be added to fortify the citrus juice of this process, although, generally the amount of this element naturally present in the juice is sufficient to replace depletions in the human body and added amounts of potassium salts in excess of about 0.003 weight percent, based on the weight of the natural juice should be avoided as excessive amounts of potassium can prove harmful to some individuals.

The sodium and calcium salts employed can be, for example, chlorides, citrates or phosphates, although, advantageously, the chlorides are used since this will provide the chloride ion supplement in addition to supplying the sodium and calcium ions. Where small amounts of potassium ions are desired to be added to the citrus juice of this process, potassium chloride may advantageously be used.

The amount of supplementary salts which are added to citrus juice according to the process may vary somewhat, however, no excess of these ions beyond that possible or that will significantly effect the palatability or acidity of the juice should be included in the fortified citrus juices. Thus, the combined amount of the salts of this process which are added to citrus juice does not exceed about 0.2 weight percent.

Juices which can be employed according to the process can be any of the juices of various citrus type fruits, for example, orange, grapefruit, lemon or lime, or other acid fruit juice. The juices of these fruits can be employed in their fresh full strength form, diluted or as frozen concentrates intended for reconstitution into full strength juice.

Although it is possible to maintain substantially the natural flavor and palatability of citrus juices by supplementing the amounts of certain salts present in the juice, it may nevertheless be desired to add sweeteners to the juice. Suitable sweeteners can be any of the various natural or synthetic types employed in the art. In addition, natural citrus oils can also be added to the various compositions of this process, for example, in amounts of about 0.012 to 0.016% by volume. A typical citrus oil which can be employed in this manner is, for example, cold pressed orange oil.

Example: Preparation of Full Strength, 12°Brix Orange Juice Energy Supplement — A sufficient quantity of high Brix Valencia orange or pineapple orange concentrate was reconstituted to obtain about 120 gal of 12°Brix juice. Sinking pulp content above 10% by volume was removed by passing part of the juice through a high speed centrifuge. This centrifuged juice, containing about 2% pulp was then added back to adjust the overall pulp level to 10% by volume. In the event that a 2% pulp is desired, all of the juice would be passed through the centrifuge. To 100 gal of this juice, Valencia orange peel oil was added to adjust the total oil content to about 0.014% by volume. Chloride salts were then added as follows.

	grams/gallon
Sodium chloride	1.5142
Potassium chloride	0.5677
Calcium chloride	0.6433
Total	2.7252

Ingredients	Weight in grams	Weight percent
1 gallon 12° Brix juice	3,972.0000	99.9250
Sodium chloride	1.5142	.0381
Potassium chloride	0.5677	.0143
Calcium chloride	0.6433	.0162
Orange peel oil (0.3 ml.)	0.2520	.0063

Weight of 1 gal of 12°Brix juice equals 3,972 g. The total weight percent of chloride salts added to the 12°Brix product is 0.0686%. The juice was then heat treated by passing it through a suitable heat exchange unit. It was then filled hot into cans or glass bottles, capped, and then cooled under a water spray. An alternate method to heat treatment and hot filling was the method of aseptically cold filling followed by refrigerated storage. In this method about 0.1% by weight sodium benzoate was added as a preservative. The juice was then cold filled into sterilized cans or glass bottles and kept in refrigerated storage.

OTHER JUICES

Licorice-Containing Citrus Juice Mixture

D.H. Koski and J.B. Koski; U.S. Patent 3,585,044; June 15, 1971 describe a method for the production of a licorice-containing citrus fruit beverage, which method comprises forming an admixture of licorice and water, heating the admixture to its boiling point, adding a relatively small amount of sugar (sucrose) to the admixture at the first indication of ebullition, boiling the admixture for a period of time sufficient to result in a palatable product, e.g., between about 1 and 3 min in a substantially closed system, discontinuing the addition of heat while the system is still substantially closed, and after steeping the mixture for a relatively short period of time, e.g., between about 1 and 3 min admixing the licorice-containing admixture with citrus juice. The process provides a highly palatable licorice-containing fruit juice beverage. Furthermore, the method results in a frothy fruit juice beverage that has a fresh, natural appearance.

Example: 2½ oz of pelleted licorice root are added to ¾ cup of water and the mixture is heated to its boiling point. At the first sign of ebullition or boiling, 2 level teaspoons of granulated sugar are added to the vessel containing the boiling admixture of licorice and water. A suitable closure means, i.e., a lid is placed on the vessel and the contents of the vessel are maintained under boiling conditions for a period of 2 min.

Next, the vessel is removed from the heat and the contents are allowed to steep for a period of 2 min. The contents of the vessel are then filtered through a fine screen and admixed with 1½ cups of orange juice and ½ cup of lemon juice. This admixture of the citrus juices with the licorice containing admixture is conducted at ordinary room temperature, i.e., 75° to 78°F. The resulting beverage is cooled to below room temperature. It has a very pleasant taste and is honey beige in color with a creamy froth appearing on top.

Juice from Green Leaves of Wheat and Barley

It has been proposed that a green juice obtained by mechanical treatment, such as by home mixers or juicers of green edible vegetables and field grasses, for instance, spinach or confree leaves is good for health. It was also proposed that the powders obtained by drying the leaves of confree or bamboo grass and then pulverizing them are useful for health.

Y. Hagiwara; U.S. Patent 3,787,591; January 22, 1974; assigned to Japan Natural Food Co., Ltd., Japan describes a process whereby green juice is obtained by mechanically pulverizing the green leaves of barley or wheat in the preripe stage. Course solid materials are removed from the juice and the pH is adjusted to 6.5 to 7.5. The treated juice is then spray dried or lyophilized to a powder. The powder can be incorporated into various foods and beverages and is a source of various proteins, vitamins, and minerals.

JUICE DISPENSERS

Aeration with Inert Gas

R.T. Cornelius; U.S. Patents 3,535,124; October 20, 1970; and 3,478,929; November 18, 1969; both assigned to The Cornelius Company describes a method for preserving fresh fruit juice in a dispenser including continually recirculating a previously carbonated quantity of the juice so as to decarbonate the same within the dispenser, the quantity of juice being decarbonated, prior to being dispensed, being subject to an atmosphere of carbon dioxide or nitrogen obtained independently of the carbonated juice, such atmosphere effecting transfer of the stored fruit juice to the decarbonating chamber automatically. It has been the practice heretofore to provide a dispenser having a transparent juice storage chamber within which the juice is agitated in a suitable manner to prevent the settling of pulp, by which the juice has been subjected to aeration, which aeration has accelerated the deterioration or spoilage of the beverage in the dispenser.

According to this process a method is provided by which an inert gas such as carbon dioxide gas or nitrogen gas is employed in an effective manner to minimize or eliminate such deterioration, the beverage being dispensed in a substantially decarbonated or noncarbonated condition. Previously carbonated fruit juice is transferred from a supply of such fruit juice to a decarbonating chamber in a dispenser. In such chamber, the carbonated fruit juice is continually recirculated to cause the portion transferred thereto to give off substantially all its carbon dioxide gas while in the dispenser to prepare it for imminent consumption. Preferably the juice is sprayed through an inert atmosphere having a partial pressure of carbon dioxide gas which is less than that of the carbon dioxide gas in solution.

A fruit juice dispensing system is illustrated in Figure 8.1, generally indicated by **10**. The dispensing system includes a storing means **11** for the fruit juice, pressurizing means generally indicated at **12** for applying pressurized inert gas such as carbon dioxide gas or nitrogen gas to such fruit juice, a dispenser generally indicated at **13** and having a chamber **14** in which the juice is agitated, and a dispensing valve **15** communicating with the chamber.

The storing means **11** comprises a tank in which there is disposed a supply of fruit juice **16** in which there has been previously dissolved a substantial quantity of carbon dioxide gas. The juice in such bulk storage therefore constitutes previously carbonated fruit juice. The pressurizing means **12** includes a gas cylinder **17** in which there is a quantity of highly pressurized inert gas such as carbon dioxide gas or nitrogen gas.

FIGURE 8.1: PROCESS FOR PRESERVING FRESH FRUIT JUICE IN A DISPENSER

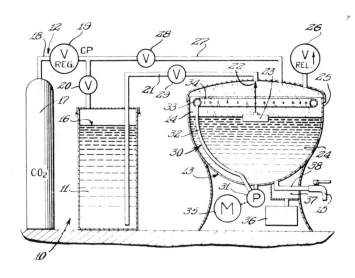

Source: R.T. Cornelius; U.S. Patent 3,535,124; October 20, 1970

The cylinder 17 communicates by means of a line 18 with a pressure regulator valve 19 which is set to provide a pressure suitable for propelling carbonated fruit juice 16, and for maintaining the carbonation of the supply of carbonated fruit juice 16 where the inert gas is carbon dioxide. Preferably, a manually operable valve 20 is provided between the regulator valve 19 and the tank 11 for facilitating replacement of the tank with a similar full tank. The gas pressure in the storing means or tank is substantially constant, for example, between 40 and 60 psi, and thus the gas serves both to preserve and to propel or expel the fruit juice.

The dispenser chamber 14 receives a portion of the supply of carbonated fruit juice through a line 21 which extends to the lower portion of the tank 11 and which opens into or discharges into the upper portion of the chamber. Suitable means are provided to regulate the admission of additional carbonated fruit juice to the chamber. In the figure, there is schematically shown a normally closed valve 22, the position of which is under the control of a float 23, the height of which is controlled by the level of fruit juice 24 disposed in the chamber. Thus, the normally closed means 22 controls the flow of fruit juice automatically from the supply 16 to the chamber 14 through the fluid connection 21, in accordance with demand.

The normally closed means 22 is operative to reduce the pressure on the juice flowing through the line 21 as it flows past such means. Preferably, the means is so constructed as to create a high degree of agitation or turbulence in the juice as it enters the chamber 14, thereby agitating or spraying it into the chamber. The reduction in pressure on that portion of the supply of fruit juice which is transferred, which reduction in pressure is effected by the means 22, aids in rendering carbonated juice unstable in that it serves to cause dissolved carbon dioxide gas to be released or to leave or to be given off from such transferred portion.

Thus, the decarbonation begins with the reduction of pressure and with the ensuing agitation or spray which further serves to cause the release of carbon dioxide gas from such portion. This transfer of juice into the chamber continues until the chamber is partially filled so as to cause the means 22, 23 to close the fluid connection line 21 automatically.

The chamber 14 is defined by means 25 so constructed as to be pressurizable, there being a relief valve 26 communicating with the chamber 14, the relief valve 26 being set to open or crack at a pressure within the chamber which is above atmospheric pressure. The relief valve thus retains inert gas including any released carbon dioxide gas in the space or portion of the chamber lying above the juice 24 therein. This retained gas is thus maintained therein at a pressure above atmospheric, and any excess in such gas is vented to the atmosphere by the relief valve 26. Since the relief valve is disposed so as to vent the upper portion of the chamber, there is separation within the chamber of any released gas, which rises, and the liquid, which settles.

The structure further includes a pressurizing and purging line 27 having a manually operated control or purging valve 28 communicating with the downstream side of a pressure regulator valve 40 upstream of the valve 20 and with the chamber defining means 25 for selectively admitting gas from the cylinder 17 into the chamber 14. The valve 40 is connected to the downstream side of the regulator valve 19. The air within the chamber 14 may be initially purged out of such chamber by such inert purging gas which is thus vented to the atmosphere by the relief valve 26, a portion of such purging gas being retained therein so that the entire internal atmosphere is an inert gas.

Alternatively, carbonated fruit juice may be first transferred into the chamber by opening of a normally open manually controllable valve 29. Although some purging will thus take place automatically, the valve 28 may thereafter be opened to ensure a reasonably pure atmosphere of carbon dioxide gas, nitrogen gas, or a mixture thereof in the space above the fruit juice. The system 10 further includes means for substantially totally decarbonating the carbonated fruit juice for imminent consumption. In this form, such decarbonating means comprises further means for physically agitating the portion 24 of fruit juice which has been admitted into the chamber. Such agitation is provided by circulating means generally indicated at **30** which includes a pump **31** which continually withdraws juice from the chamber and propels it through a line **32** to a suitable spray member **33** which is suitably apertured or nozzled to discharge the juice as a spray **34**. Such handling or circulation thus further acts to decarbonate the fruit juice in the chamber in a continual manner.

Since there is virtually no oxygen present in the upper portion of the chamber, such aeration in an oxygen-free or inert atmosphere precludes deterioration due to conventional aeration, and the aerating circulating means that has been a prime factor in causing previous deterioration is thus employed in a preferred form of this process to obtain an opposite or new result, namely to release a protective quantity of carbon dioxide gas into the chamber to preclude such deterioration, while retaining the visual enhancement of the beverage in the dispenser **13**.

The pump **31** is driven by a motor **35** disposed in the base of the dispenser. If desired, a temperature control system **36** may be employed with a heat exchange jacket **37** associated with a line **38** leading to the dispensing valve **15**, for lowering or raising the temperature of the juice **24** in the dispenser.

Aeration with Volatile Additive

The process of *R.G. Sargeant; U.S. Patent 3,728,129; April 17, 1973* is based on method steps which accomplish not only more effective mixing of the major constituents of a drink, such as a juice concentrate and water, but also a more thorough aeration, with the air advantageously carrying vapors of a volatile additive, than has heretofore been possible in the short mixing times allowable when dispensing drinks on a per drink basis.

Considering a drink to be prepared from a concentrate and a diluent, the method is carried out by establishing a high velocity stream of one of the constituents, typically the diluent, in a first zone in a fashion that establishes a partial vacuum in that zone and employing the partial vacuum to effect a regulated flow of the other constituent, typically the concentrate, into the first zone.

The energy of the high velocity stream is employed to project a preliminary mixture of the constituents into a final mixing zone where the stream is impinged on a traverse baffle surface, the stream being disrupted and caused to flow transversely and in recirculating fashion in the final mixing zone upstream of the baffle surface. Air, or air carrying entrained vapors of an additive, is introduced either to the first zone, in which case the air is drawn in under influence of the partial vacuum, or at a point just downstream from the baffle surface, in which case the air is supplied under a pressure greater than atmospheric pressure.

In either case, the volatile additive is entrained in the air by causing the air to pass through a chamber in which a quantity of the additive is confined. Advantageously, the first zone and the final mixing zone are coaxial and inclined upwardly in the direction of travel of the high velocity stream in such manner that, when each mixing operation is complete and the high velocity stream terminated, a quantity of the drink mixture drains back into the first zone in recycle fashion so that, when the high velocity stream is reestablished, for mixing of the next drink, the stream is projected through a quantity of the mixture prepared during mixing of the previous drink.

The method can be carried out with orange juice concentrates having densities in the range of 40° to 72° Brix and viscosities at 75°F of 3,000 to 7,000 cp, and is particularly advantageous when orange juice concentrates of high density, e.g., in excess of 50° Brix, are employed.

Dispensing of Semifrozen Comestible

In the process of *R.T. Cornelius; U.S. Patent 3,642,174; February 15, 1972; assigned to The*

Cornelius Company, a concentrated comestible such as orange juice is stored at atmospheric pressure under refrigeration and is thereafter reconstituted by the addition of water. Such reconstituting is done by admixing the desired proportion of ingredients in an atmosphere of food-grade gas such as nitrous oxide that is soluble in the liquid. The amount of concentrate used in such admixing is carefully metered and the amount of water used is governed by a flow-rate control valve whereby the admixing is carried out under pressure. The mixture is thereafter further refrigerated in a separate freezing chamber to form nitrous ice and on dispensing, the nitrous oxide breaks out of the semifrozen comestible and in doing so renders the semifrozen comestible fluffy, without having imparted any significant flavor thereto and without constituting any adulterant therein.

The principles of the process are particularly useful when embodied in a juice-dispensing system such as shown in Figure 8.2, generally indicated by **10**. The system **10** includes a storage source **11** of the product to be partially frozen and a freezing and dispensing cylinder **12**. The storage source includes a blending and storage device **13** to which is connected a source of water **14** and a source of concentrated comestible or concentrated juice **15** and a source of food-grade gas **16** such as nitrous oxide.

The source of water is connected to a conventional supply of water which is normally treated by a filter **17** and then delivered at a controlled pressure by a constant delivery pump **18** that is driven by a motor **19**, the output of the delivery pump being under the further control of a solenoid valve **20**, and an adjustable flow-rate control valve **21**. A double check valve **22** leads from the flow control valve through a line **23** to a refrigerated precool plate **24** and through an insulated line **25** to the inlet of the blending and storage device **13**.

The source of gas **16** comprises a conventional cylinder that has a shutoff valve **26** which leads to an adjustable pressure regulator valve **27** and then through a line **28** and through a check valve **29** of the snifter valve type to discharge into the interior of the blending and storage device.

FIGURE 8.2: DISPENSER FOR SEMIFROZEN COMESTIBLE

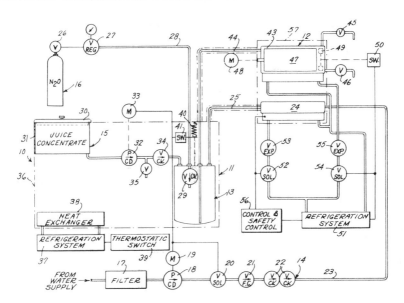

Source: R.T. Cornelius; U.S. Patent 3,642,174; February 15, 1972

The source of concentrated comestible or juice concentrate is a container that is disposed for ready access, the interior of which is at atmospheric pressure. It has an opening in the top thereof closed by a manually removable cover 30, and at one end it has a sight glass 31 or equivalent means enabling the operator to know the amount of concentrate contained therein. The source of concentrated comestible is connected by a proportioning pump 32 of the metering type which is driven by a motor 33, the pump leading through a check valve 34 to another inlet of the blending and storage device 13.

A sampling valve 35 is provided downstream of the pump 32 to enable it to be used for drawing off samples of concentrate for verifying the rate of delivery of the pump 32. It is also used in connection with priming such pump and may be used in connection with draining the source 15. The source of concentrated comestible and the blending and storage device are disposed within a refrigerated housing 36 to which is connected a refrigeration system 37 that includes a heat exchanger 38 in the chamber 36. The refrigeration system is under the control of a thermostatic switch 39 which senses the temperature inside the chamber.

The blending and storage device is vertically movable and is in part supported by a spring 40. When the amount of mixture in the blending and storage device has reached a lower limit, the blending and storage device rises sufficiently to actuate a switch 41 which is connected to turn on the concentrate pump motor 33, the water pump motor 19 and the water solenoid 20. When sufficient concentrate and water have entered the blending and storage device, the switch terminates the filling operation.

The freezing cylinder 12 has an internal chamber 43 which is connected by an insulated line 44 to the outlet of the blending and storage device. A combined automatic relief valve and manual vent valve 45 is connected to the upper part of the chamber 43 to enable complete filling of the chamber. A somewhat larger dispensing valve 46 is connected to the lower part of the chamber. This valve is of a known type which agitates the product as much as possible during dispensing.

The product is agitated by a combined scraper and stirrer 47 driven by a continuously operating motor 48. The proportion of ice that has been frozen out of the mixture is determined by a pivotally supported drag-sensing element 49 that is connected to operate a switch 50. A second refrigeration system 51 has an outlet that is divided, one branch being under the control of a solenoid valve 52 and an expansion valve 53 while the other branch is under the control of a solenoid valve 54 and an expansion valve 55. The expansion valve 53 brings refrigerant to the precool plate 24 and the expansion valve 55 brings refrigeration to the freezing cylinder 12.

The switch 50 is connected to control the solenoid valve 54 and the refrigeration system 51, while a control switch 56 is connected to sense the temperature of the precool plate for controlling the solenoid valve 52 and the refrigeration system 51. The control 56 includes a secondary control as a safety to shut the system down in the event that freezing of water in the precool plate becomes imminent. If desired, various other controls and interlocks can be provided as is known in the refrigeration and dispensing art. The chain line 57 denotes insulation for the freezing chamber 12 and the precool plate.

The control 56 is normally set so that water discharging from the precool plate through the line 25 will have a temperature on the order of 34°F. The thermostatic switch 39 is set to about this same value so that the temperature in the chamber 36 should be between 33° and 35°F.

An adjustment on the switch 50 (not shown, but conventional) is set so that when the product in the chamber 43 has about 60% ice, it will provide sufficient drag to enable the switch to close the solenoid valve 54. Such a percentage of ice will be obtained when a temperature of about 25°F is reached in the chamber. The motor 48 has an output on the order of 125 rpm which is the rotational speed of the combined scraper-stirrer 47. The example given as to percentage ice and temperature in the chamber 43 is based on the adjustable flow control valve's **21** being set to deliver a flow rate which is exactly four times that of the metered rate provided by the pump **32**, and is further based on the use of a concentrate such as orange juice in the source **15** which has a Brix of 51.2°, which therefore provides a Brix of about 12.8° in the line **44**. This is a normal degree of sweetness for reconstituted orange juice. However, as ice is formed in the chamber, the sugar that was in solution with the portion becoming frozen separates therefrom so that pure ice is formed and such sugar goes into solution with the remaining liquid portion, thereby rendering it sweeter.

Nitrous oxide gas provides the pressure in the blender and storage device and transfers that pressure hydrostatically to the chamber. Some such gas dissolves in the liquid in the blending and storage device, and the dissolved gas leaves the portion of the liquid being frozen in the chamber to become absorbed by the remaining liquid portion which can now take on additional gas since it has a lower temperature than the blending and storage device. The solution of the nitrous oxide gas with the liquid portion in the chamber is highly unstable so that upon discharge to atmospheric pressure, as aided by an agitating type of dispensing, the gas immediately breaks out of the product, thereby fluffing it up or whipping it to make the semifrozen comestible light and fluffy.

OTHER APPARATUS

Apparatus for Thawing Frozen Juices

High frequency electromagnetic heating apparatus for cooking food has been the subject of substantial development in recent years, and such equipment is commercially available as electronic ovens, radar ranges, and the like. Also considerable interest has developed in thawing of frozen juices which are to be served cold. The direction application of high frequency heating apparatus to the thawing of frozen juices has not proven wholly satisfactory. A quantity of frozen juice placed in a high frequency cooker tends to result in a mixture of overly warm liquid and residual frozen juice.

If heating is terminated before the frozen juice is completely melted, a satisfactory equilibrium temperature can be reached by allowing the continued melting to cool the overheated liquid. The time required for this to be accomplished, however, is substantial and is totally incompatible, for example, with equipment for promptly supplying a quantity of cold juice from a supply of frozen juice.

In accordance with the process of *J.L. Lawson; U.S. Patent 3,336,142; August 15, 1967; assigned to General Electric Co.* the frozen liquid is subjected to a high frequency electromagnetic field and the liquid removed from the region of the field as fast as it is produced by melting. This eliminates the preferential heating of the liquid and permits the efficient continued melting of the frozen juice, while retaining the melted liquid outside the electromagnetic field and at a cool temperature suitable for consumption.

Since only the frozen juice remains within the electromagnetic field, it presents a much more constant electrical impedance than would a mixture of liquid and frozen juice and, accordingly, simplifies the problem of coupling electromagnetic energy from the high frequency source to the frozen juice.

Referring to Figures 8.3a and 8.3b there is shown a high frequency electromagnetic oven **10** in the form of a generally rectangular enclosure of conducting material closed on the front by a door **11**. Electromagnetic wave energy is supplied to the interior of the oven by means of an oscillator **12** energized from a suitable supply line **13** under the control of a switch **14**, and the output of which is coupled to the interior of the oven by a concentric transmission line **15** having the internal conductor terminating in a loop **16** conductively connected to one wall of the oven and forming an inductive coupling with the oven. As shown in Figure 8.3b, the juice to be stored in a frozen condition and then melted for consumption is preferably contained in one part **17** of a two part container **18**, the second

FIGURE 8.3: APPARATUS FOR THAWING FROZEN JUICES

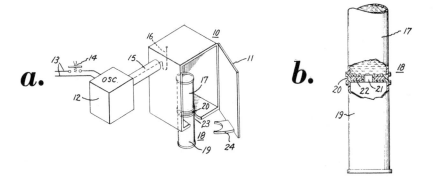

Source: J.L. Lawson; U.S. Patent 3,336,142; August 15, 1967

part **19** of which provides a receptacle for the liquid when it is melted. The material of
the container is nonconducting so as not to provide an electromagnetic shield and may be
of paper suitably treated, or one of the many plastics used for packaging foodstuffs. In
accordance with the preferred construction of the container, it is provided with a restriction
or surrounding groove **20** at its midsection, i.e., at the boundary between the two parts of
the container.

Also, this boundary preferably provides a restricted passage **21** for the melted liquid to flow
into the empty half of the container when it is melted. It will be understood that several
passages may be provided if desired. If the transverse dimension of the package is too large
at the restricted region so that high frequency energy may tend to escape from the enclosure
providing the oven, an electromagnetic shielding member in the form of a conducting washer
22 may be molded into the package.

In Figure 8.3a, it will be noted that the floor of the oven is provided with a slot **23** for
the reception of the restricted portion of the container so that the container is supported
with the frozen liquid within the oven and the liquid receiving portion outside of the oven.
A sheet metal closure member **24**, attached to the door, moves into the slot in the oven
floor to complete the oven enclosure after insertion of the container. It will be apparent
that, in the operation of the apparatus described above, the container with the frozen juice
at one end is inserted in the oven and the shield **24** moved into position as the door is
closed.

The switch **14** is then closed and electromagnetic energy which, in accordance with known
practice, would be in the frequency range 900 to 3,000 megacycles, is generated and coupled
to the oven. In the particular form shown, the oven is designed to have a transverse dimension of one-half wavelength, so that the maximum electric field exists at the central region
of the oven in the vicinity of the frozen juice.

As the frozen juice starts to melt, the liquid is immediately drained into the lower portion
of the container and the overheating of the liquid which tends to result from the preferential absorption of energy by the liquid when it is all maintained within the oven is prevented.
It should be pointed out that heating of the frozen portion of the juice is essentially dielectric heating and the heating of the melted juice is essentially conductive heating, giving
a preferential heating for the liquid about a hundred times that of the frozen or solid juice.
Also, this method minimizes the variation in load impedance presented by the juice as it
melts, since the liquid is removed and the impedance is determined by the frozen material.
This facilitates proper coupling of the energy from the oscillator to the frozen juice.

COMPANY INDEX

The company names listed below are given exactly as they appear in the patents, despite name changes, mergers and acquisitions which have, at times, resulted in the revision of a company name.

INVENTOR INDEX

U.S. PATENT NUMBER INDEX

NOTICE